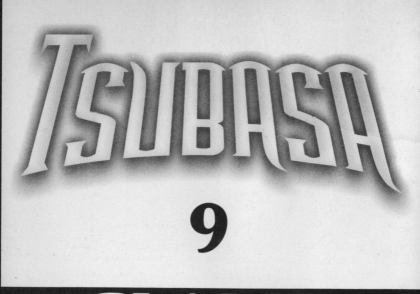

TSUBASA

9

CLAMP

TRANSLATED AND ADAPTED BY
William Flanagan

LETTERED BY
Dana Hayward

Chase Branch Library
17731 W. Seven Mile Rd.
Detroit, MI 4823

DEL REY

BALLANTINE BOOKS · NEW YORK

Tsubasa, Volume 9 is a work of fiction. Names, characters, places, and incidents are the products of the author's imagination or are used fictitiously. Any resemblance to actual events, locales, or persons, living or dead, is entirely coincidental.

A Del Rey Trade Paperback Original

Tsubasa copyright © 2004 by CLAMP
English translation copyright © 2006 by CLAMP

All rights reserved.

Published in the United States by Del Rey Books, an imprint of The Random House Publishing Group, a division of Random House, Inc., New York.

DEL REY is a registered trademark and the Del Rey colophon is a trademark of Random House, Inc.

First published in Japan in 2004 by Kodansha Ltd., Tokyo

Library of Congress Control Number: 2004101711

ISBN 0-345-48429-0

Printed in the United States of America

www.delreymanga.com

9 8 7 6 5 4

Lettered by Dana Hayward

Translation and adaptation by William Flanagan

Contents

Honorifics Explained

Throughout the Del Rey Manga books, you will find Japanese honorifics left intact in the translations. For those not familiar with how the Japanese use honorifics and, more important, how they differ from American honorifics, we present this brief overview.

Politeness has always been a critical facet of Japanese culture. Ever since the feudal era, when Japan was a highly stratified society, use of honorifics — which can be defined as polite speech that indicates relationship or status — has played an essential role in the Japanese language. When addressing someone in Japanese, an honorific usually takes the form of a suffix attached to one's name (example: "Asuna-san"), or as a title at the end of one's name or in place of the name itself (example: "Negi-sensei," or simply "Sensei!").

Honorifics can be expressions of respect or endearment. In the context of manga and anime, honorifics give insight into the nature of the relationship between characters. Many translations into English leave out these important honorifics, and therefore distort the "feel" of the original Japanese. Because Japanese honorifics contain nuances that English honorifics lack, it is our policy at Del Rey not to translate them. Here, instead, is a guide to some of the honorifics you may encounter in Del Rey Manga.

-san: This is the most common honorific, and is equivalent to Mr., Miss, Ms., Mrs., etc. It is the all-purpose honorific and can be used in any situation where politeness is required.

-sama: This is one level higher than "-san." It is used to confer great respect.

-dono: This comes from the word "tono," which means "lord." It is an even higher level than "-sama" and confers utmost respect.

-kun: This suffix is used at the end of boys' names to express familiarity or endearment. It is also sometimes used by men among friends, or when addressing someone younger or of a lower station.

-chan: This is used to express endearment, mostly toward girls. It is also used for little boys, pets, and even among lovers. It gives a sense of childish cuteness.

Bozu: This is an informal way to refer to a boy, similar to the English term "kid" or "squirt."

Sempai/senpai: This title suggests that the addressee is one's senior in a group or organization. It is most often used in a school setting, where underclassmen refer to their upperclassmen as "sempai." It can also be used in the workplace, such as when a newer employee addresses an employee who has seniority in the company.

Kohai: This is the opposite of "sempai," and is used toward underclassmen in school or newcomers in the workplace. It connotes that the addressee is of lower station.

Sensei: Literally meaning "one who has come before," this title is used for teachers, doctors, or masters of any profession or art.

-[blank]: Usually forgotten in these lists, but perhaps the most significant difference between Japanese and English. The lack of honorific means that the speaker has permission to address the person in a very intimate way. Usually, only family, spouses, or very close friends have this kind of permission. Known as *yobisute*, it can be gratifying when someone who has earned the intimacy starts to call one by one's name without an honorific. But when that intimacy hasn't been earned, it can also be very insulting.

Tsubasa crosses over with *xxxHOLiC*. Although it isn't necessary to read *xxxHOLiC* to understand the events in *Tsubasa*, you'll get to see the same events from different perspectives if you read both!

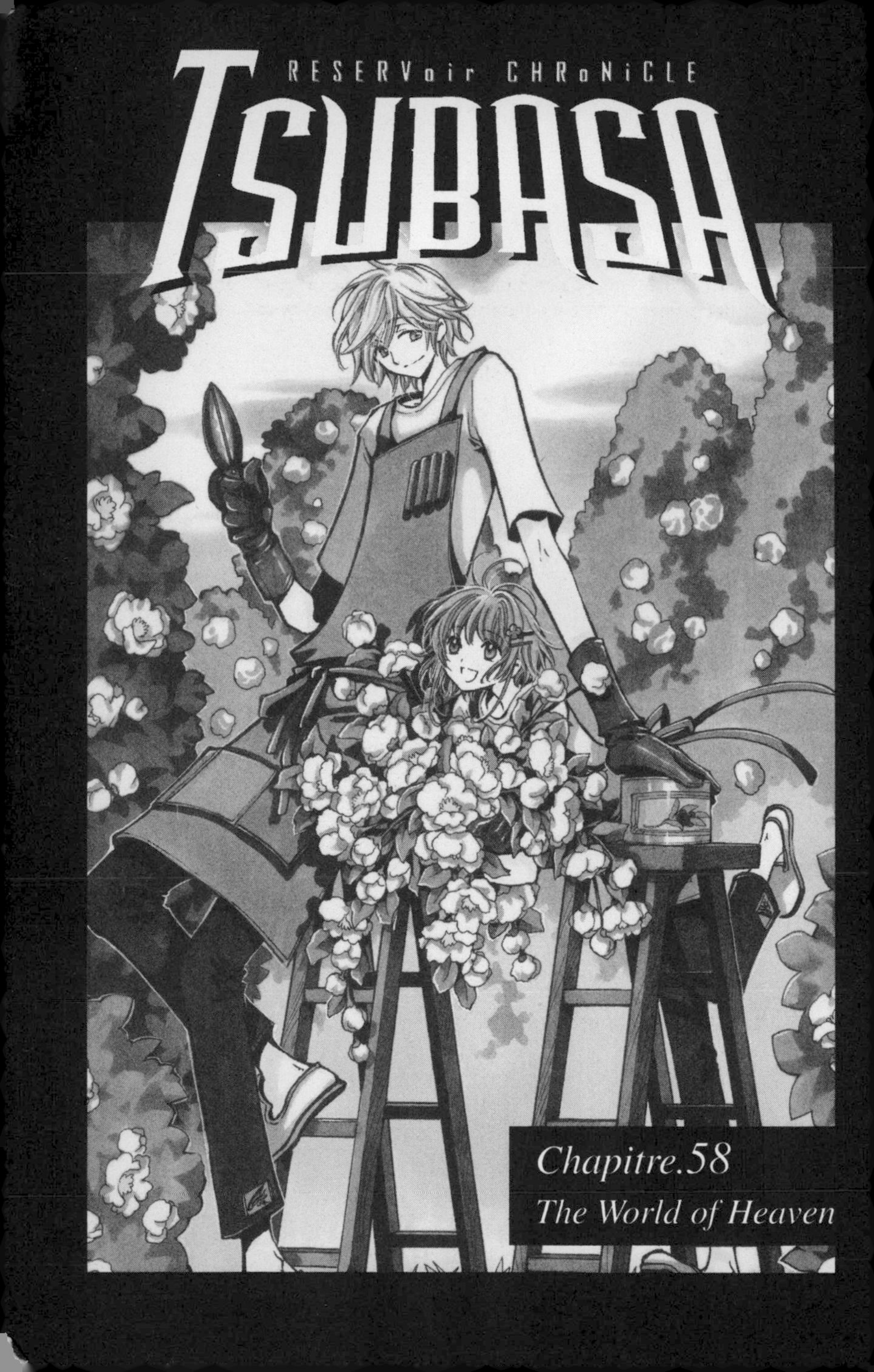
RESERVoir CHRoNiCLE
TSUBASA
Chapitre.58
The World of Heaven

ツバサ

RESERVoir CHRoNiCLE

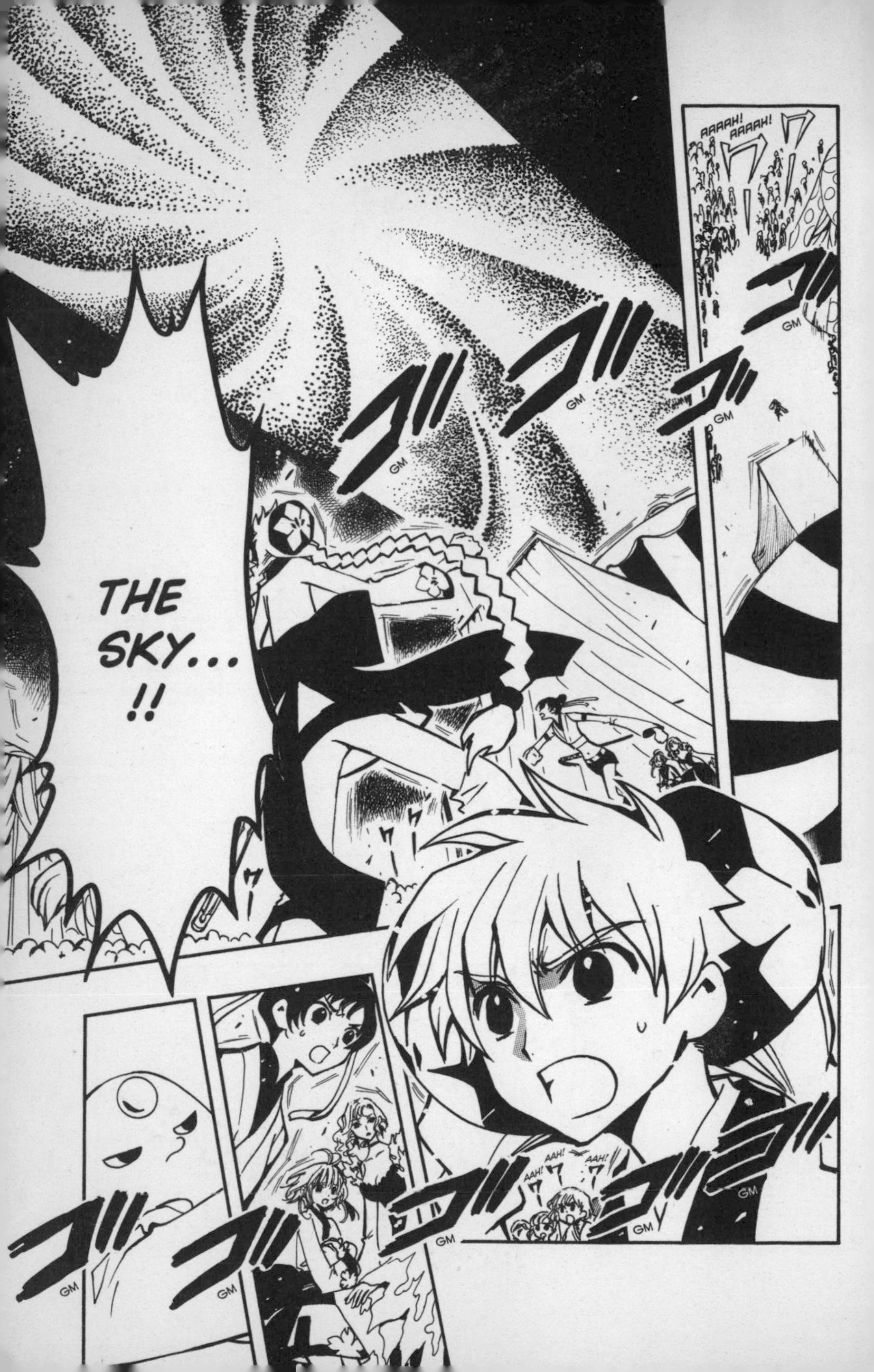
AAAAH! AAAAH!
GM
GM
GM
GM
THE SKY... !!
AAH! AAH! AAH!
GM
GM
GM
GM
GM

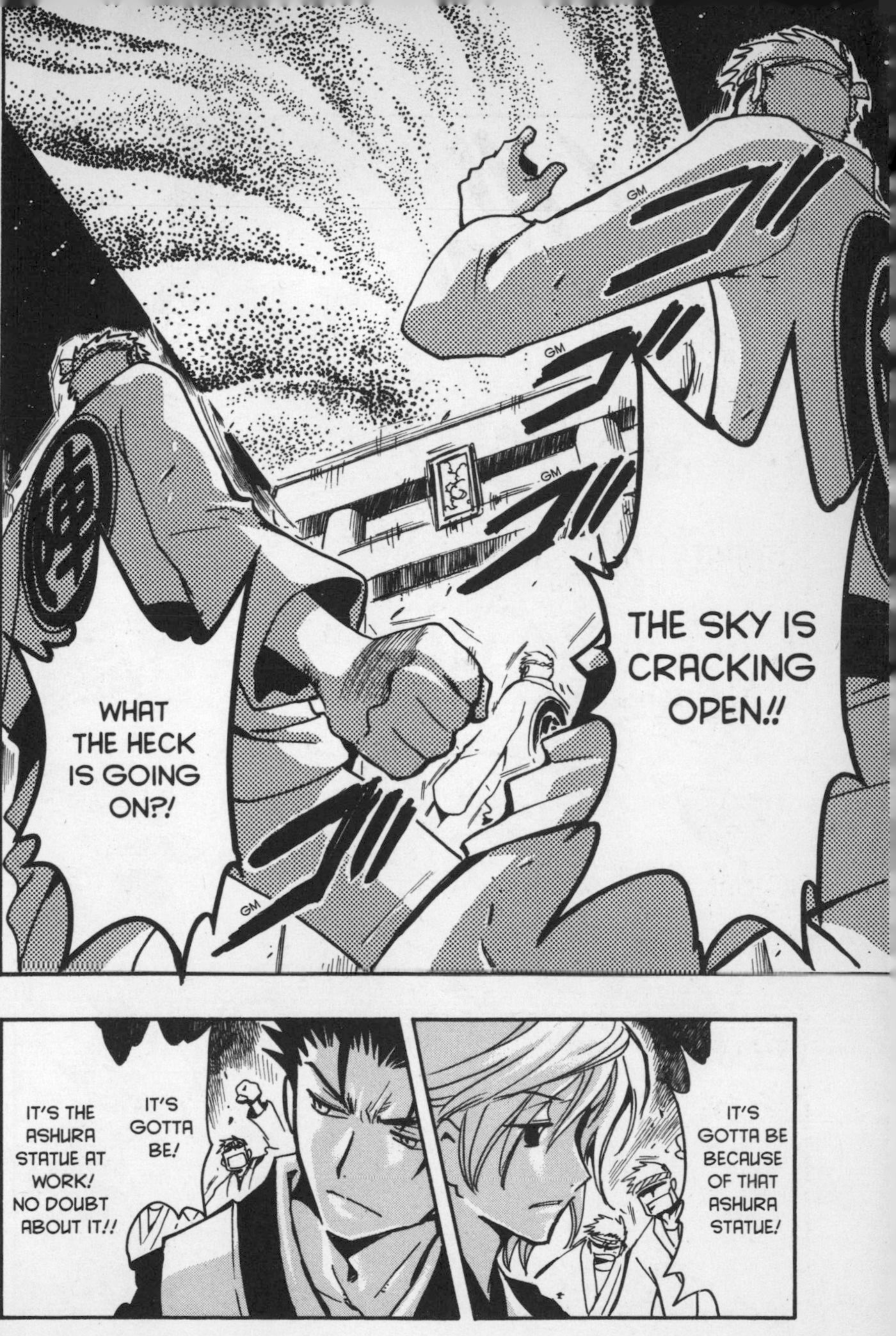
GM
GM
GM
THE SKY IS CRACKING OPEN!!
WHAT THE HECK IS GOING ON?!
GM
IT'S GOTTA BE BECAUSE OF THAT ASHURA STATUE!
IT'S GOTTA BE!
IT'S THE ASHURA STATUE AT WORK! NO DOUBT ABOUT IT!!

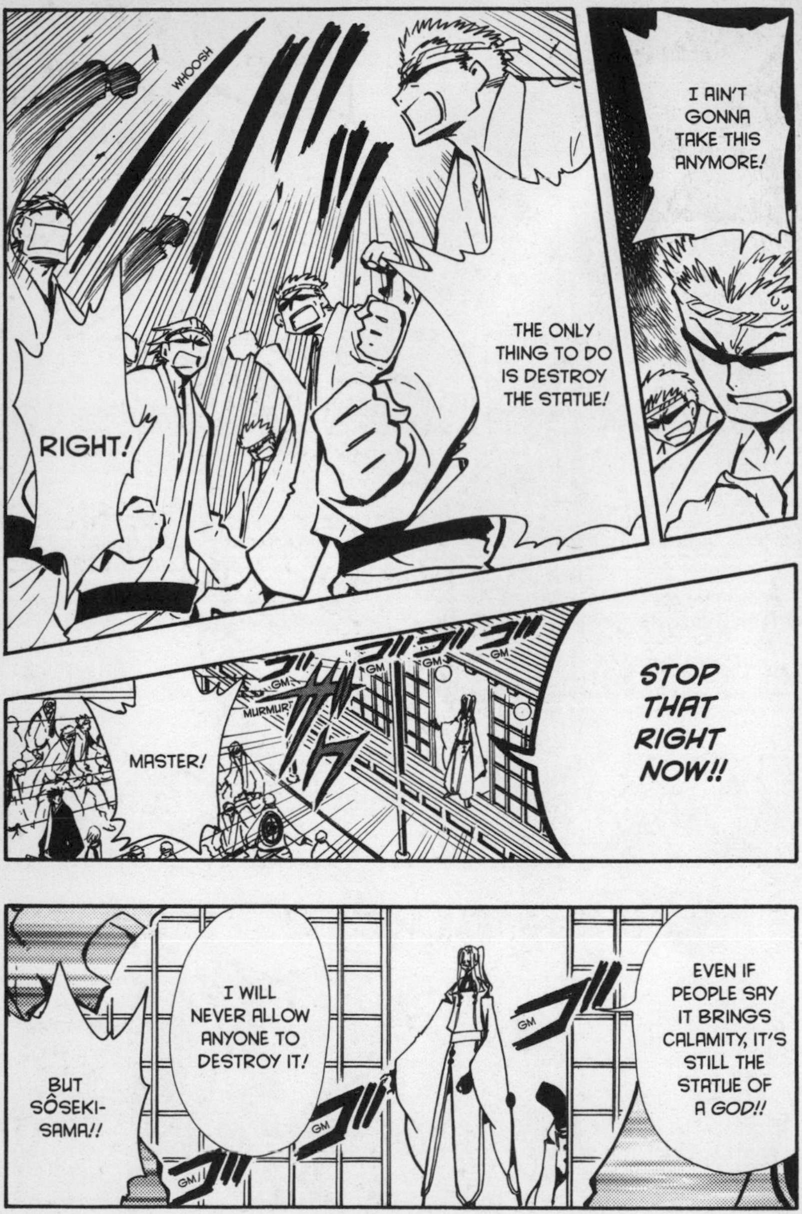
I AIN'T GONNA TAKE THIS ANYMORE!
THE ONLY THING TO DO IS DESTROY THE STATUE!
WHOOSH
RIGHT!
STOP THAT RIGHT NOW!!
GM
GM
GM
GM
MURMUR
MASTER!
EVEN IF PEOPLE SAY IT BRINGS CALAMITY, IT'S STILL THE STATUE OF A *GOD*!!
GM
I WILL NEVER ALLOW ANYONE TO DESTROY IT!
GM
GM!!
BUT SÔSEKI-SAMA!!

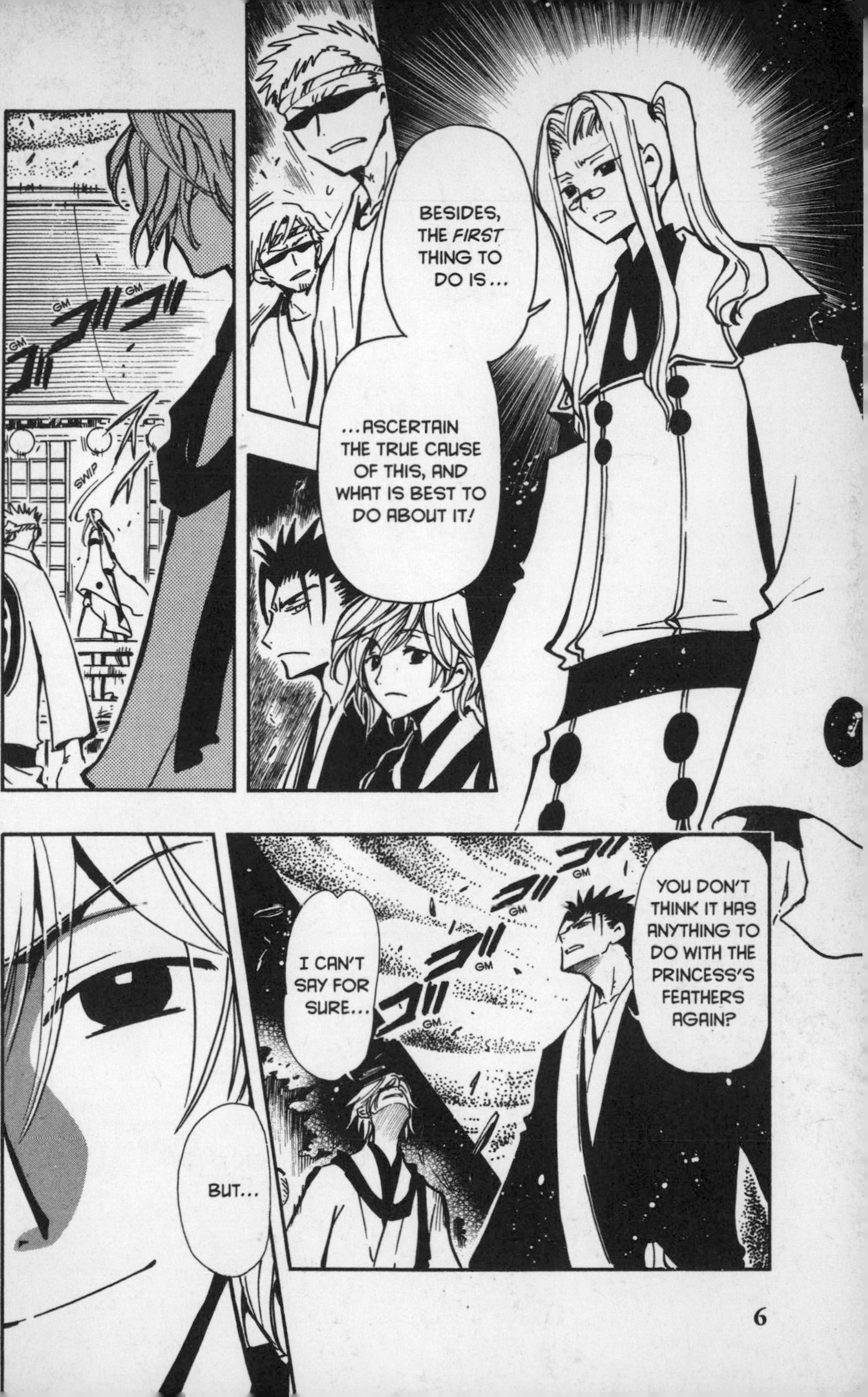
BESIDES, THE *FIRST* THING TO DO IS...
...ASCERTAIN THE TRUE CAUSE OF THIS, AND WHAT IS BEST TO DO ABOUT IT!
GM
GM
GM
SWIP
GM
GM
YOU DON'T THINK IT HAS ANYTHING TO DO WITH THE PRINCESS'S FEATHERS AGAIN?
I CAN'T SAY FOR SURE...
GM
GM
BUT...

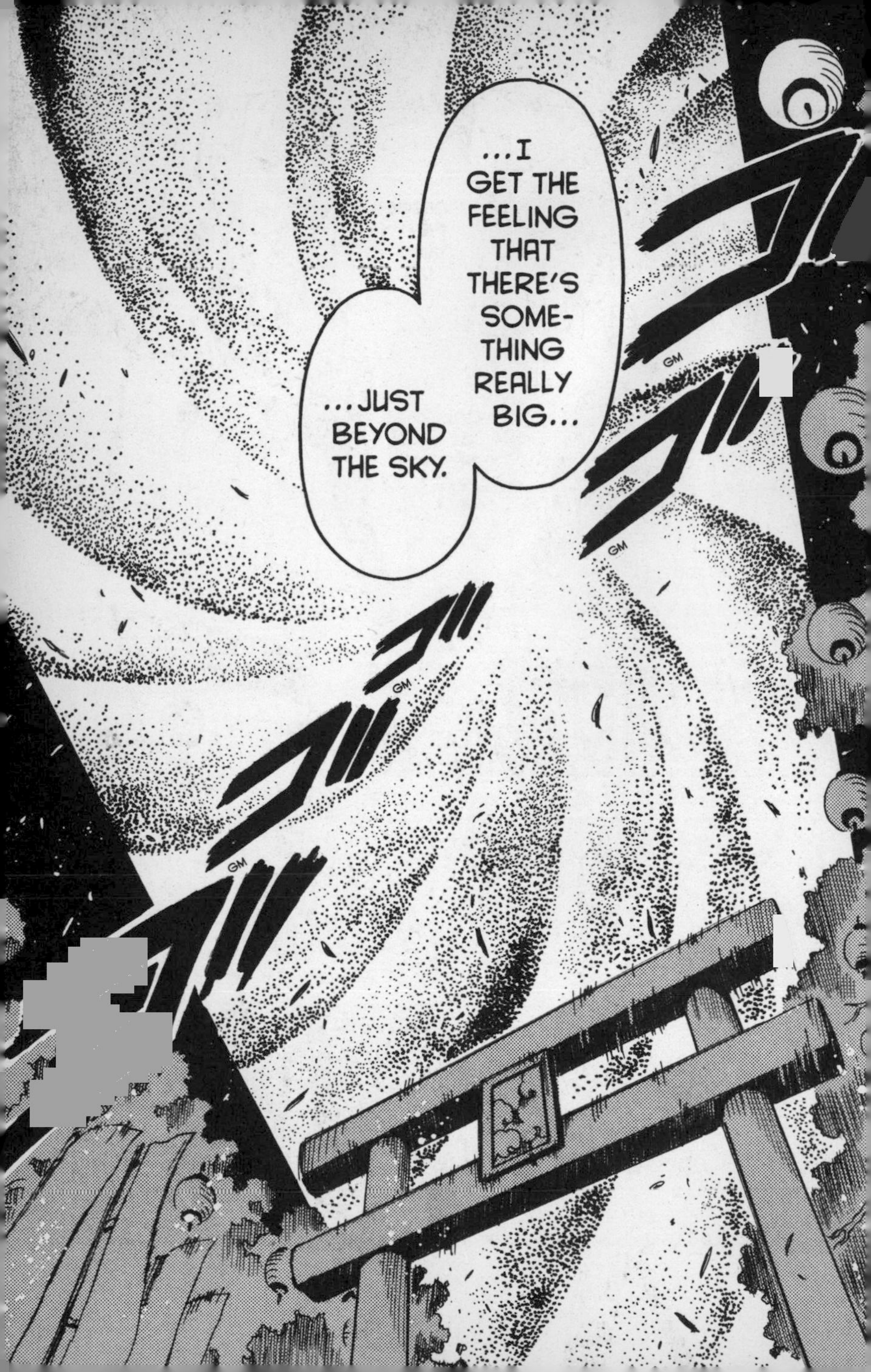
...I GET THE FEELING THAT THERE'S SOME-THING REALLY BIG...
...JUST BEYOND THE SKY.
GM
GM
GM
GM

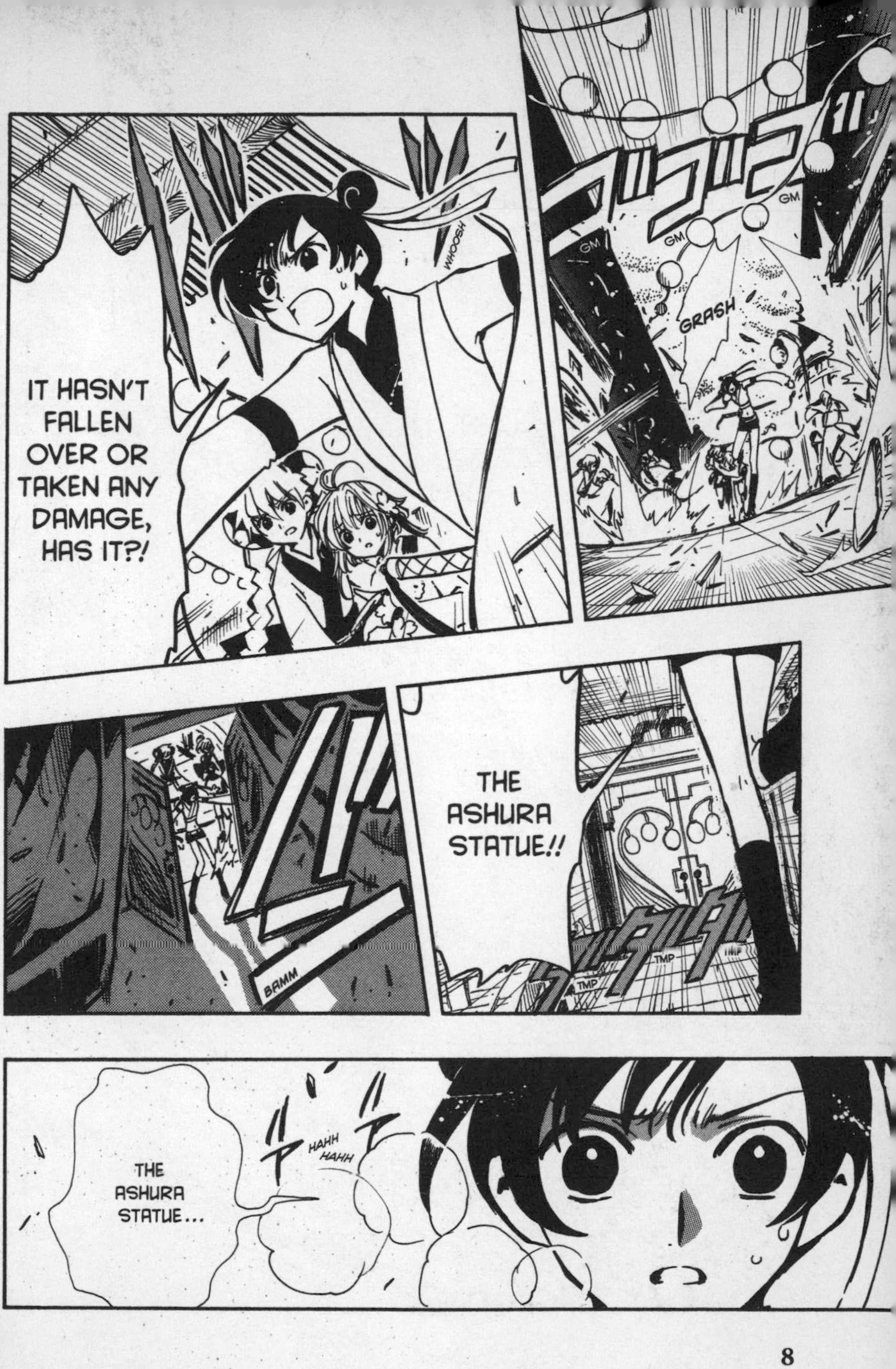
GM
GM
GM
GRASH
WHOOSH
IT HASN'T FALLEN OVER OR TAKEN ANY DAMAGE, HAS IT?!
THE ASHURA STATUE!!
TMP
TMP
BAMM
HAHH HAHH
THE ASHURA STATUE...

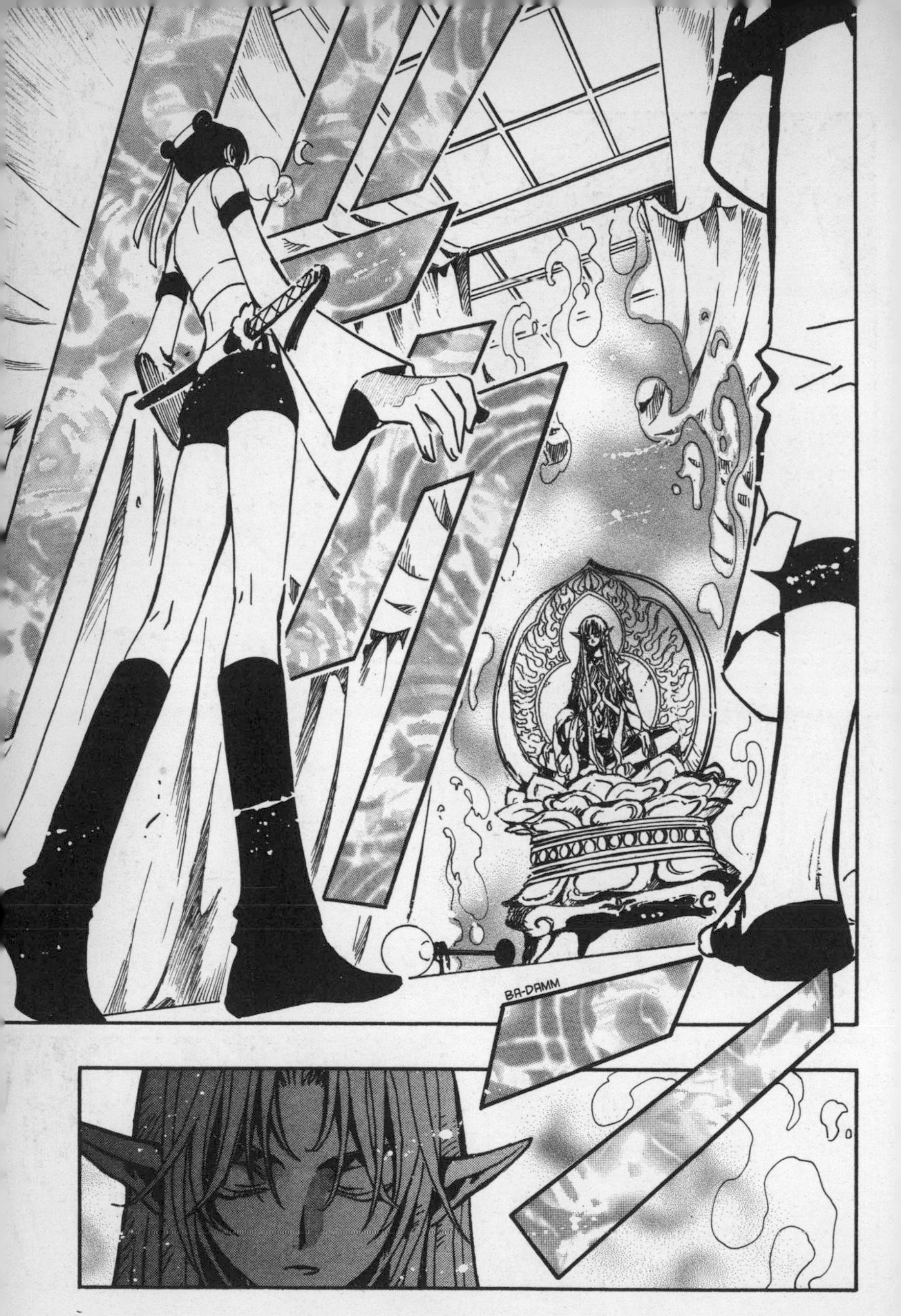
BA-DAMM

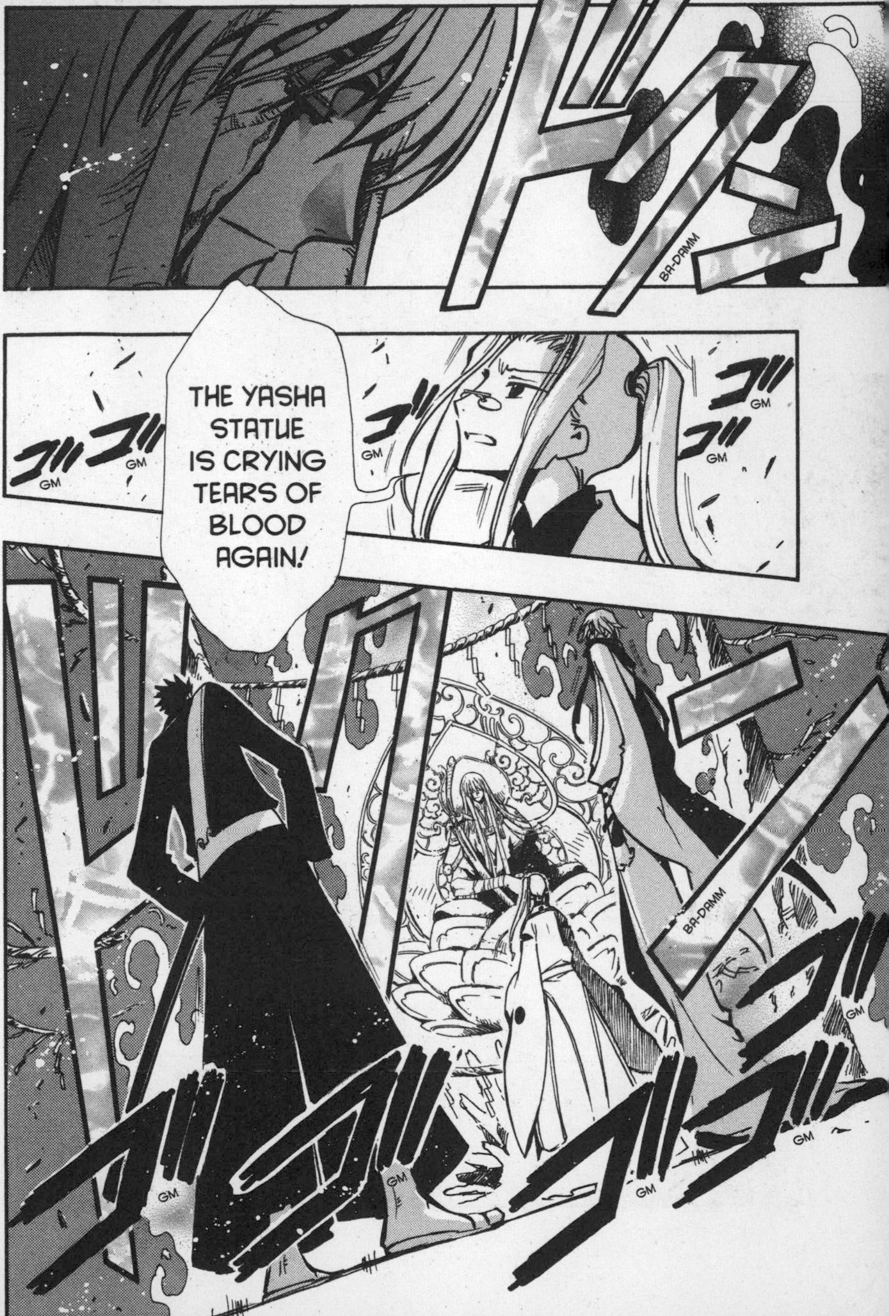
BA-DAMM
GM
GM
THE YASHA STATUE IS CRYING TEARS OF BLOOD AGAIN!
GM
GM
GM
BA-DAMM
GM
GM
GM
GM
GM

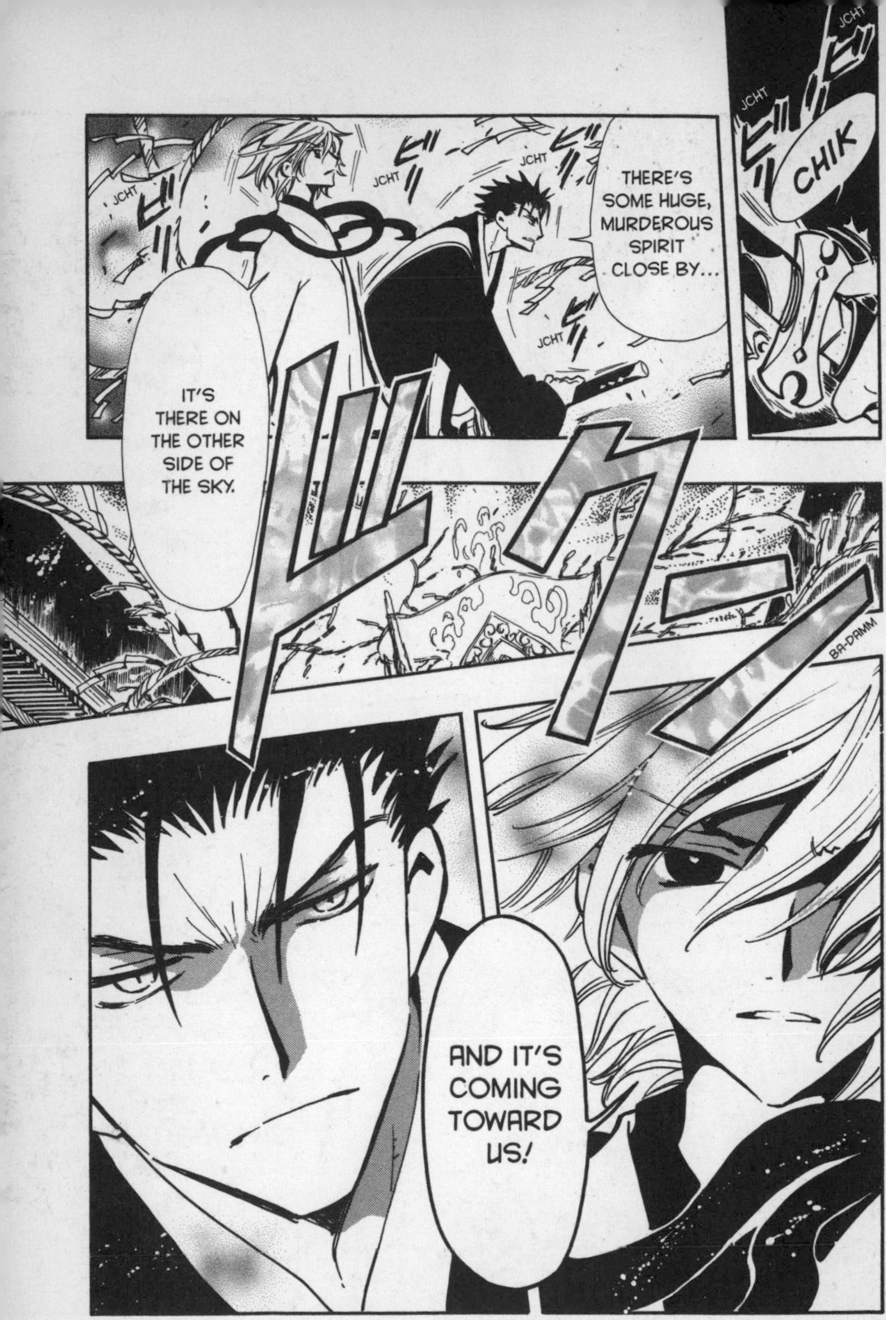
JCHT
JCHT
CHIK
JCHT
JCHT
JCHT
JCHT
THERE'S SOME HUGE, MURDEROUS SPIRIT CLOSE BY...
IT'S THERE ON THE OTHER SIDE OF THE SKY.
BA-DAMM
AND IT'S COMING TOWARD US!

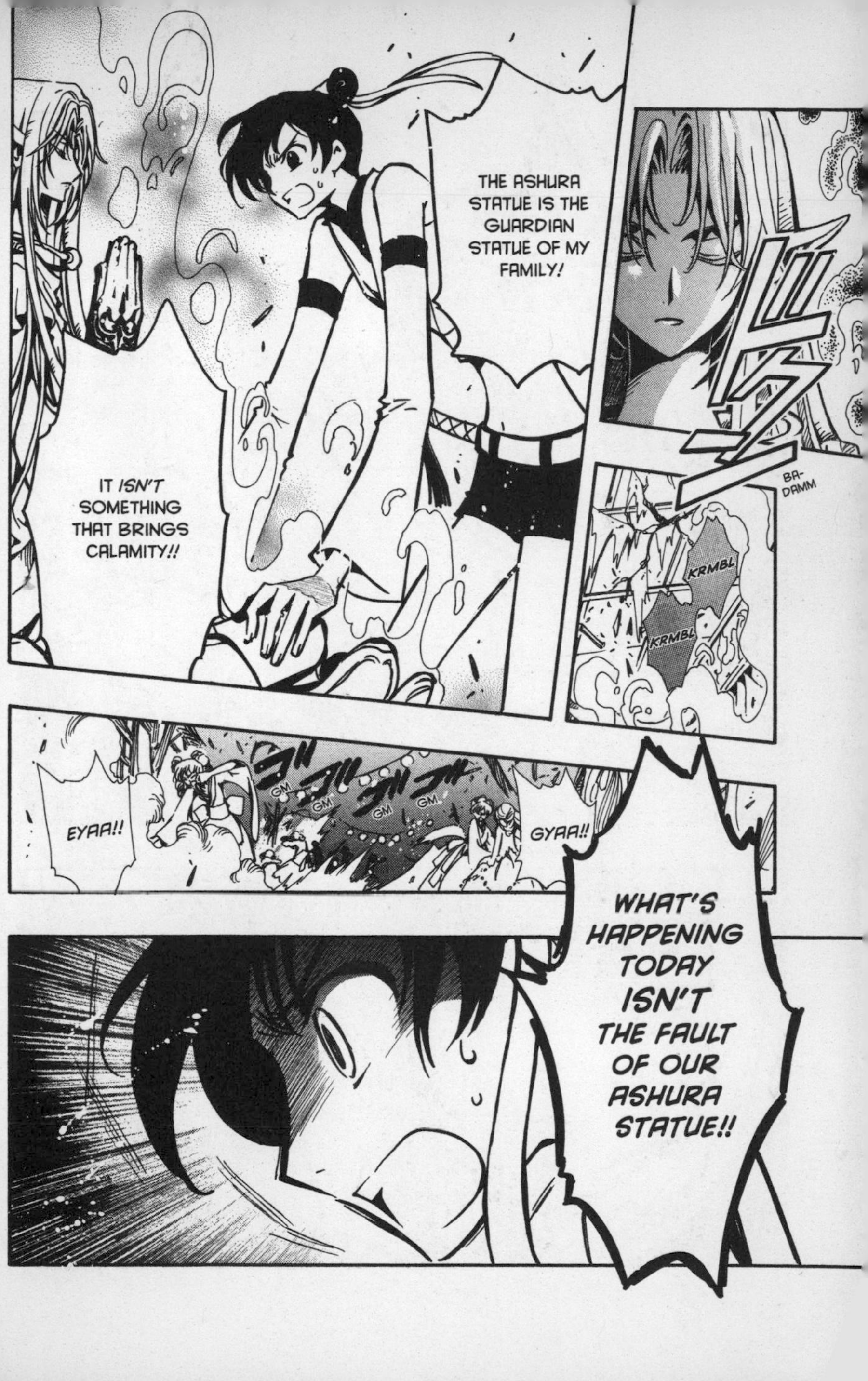
BA-DAMM
KRMBL
KRMBL
THE ASHURA STATUE IS THE GUARDIAN STATUE OF MY FAMILY!
IT ISN'T SOMETHING THAT BRINGS CALAMITY!!
GYAA!!
GM
GM
GM
GM
EYAA!!
WHAT'S HAPPENING TODAY ISN'T THE FAULT OF OUR ASHURA STATUE!!

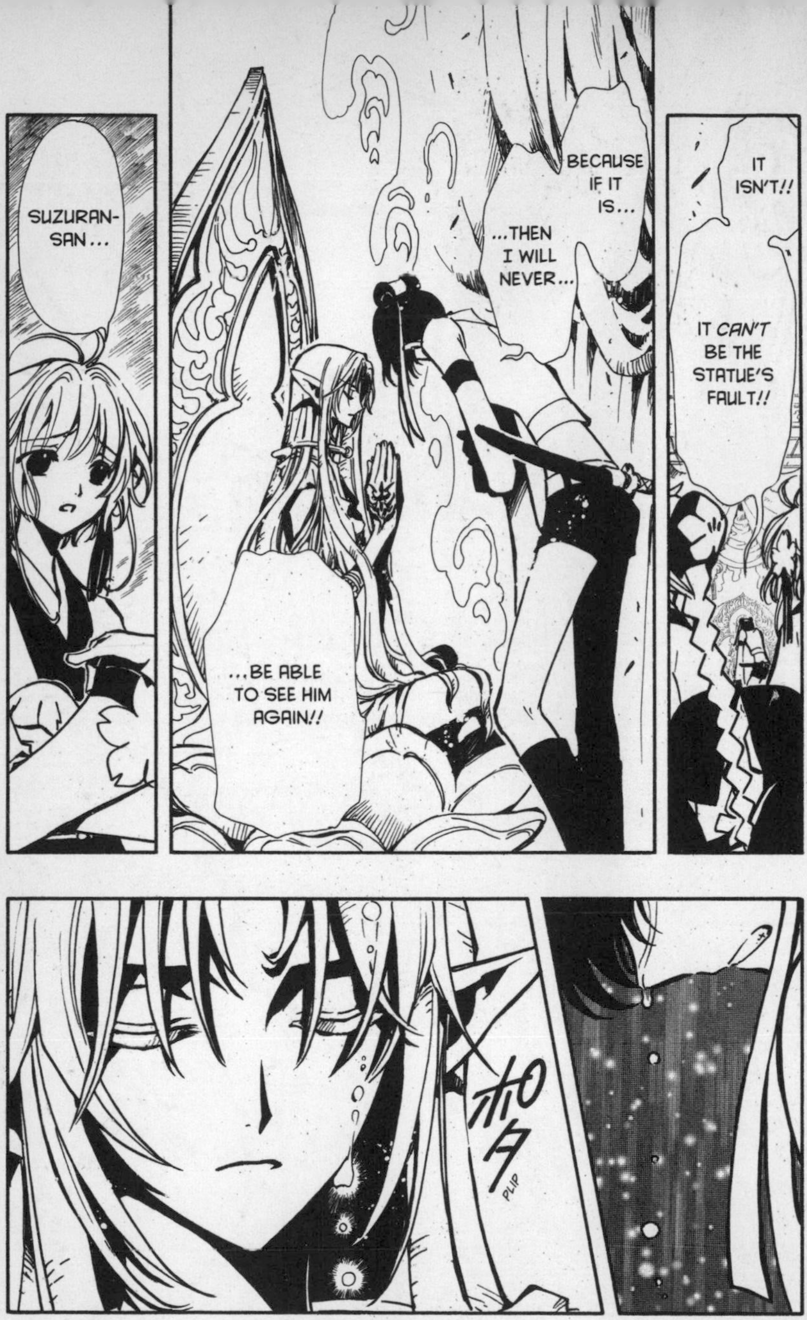
IT ISN'T!!
IT *CAN'T* BE THE STATUE'S FAULT!!
BECAUSE IF IT IS...
...THEN I WILL NEVER...
...BE ABLE TO SEE HIM AGAIN!!
SUZURAN-SAN...
ポタ
PLIP

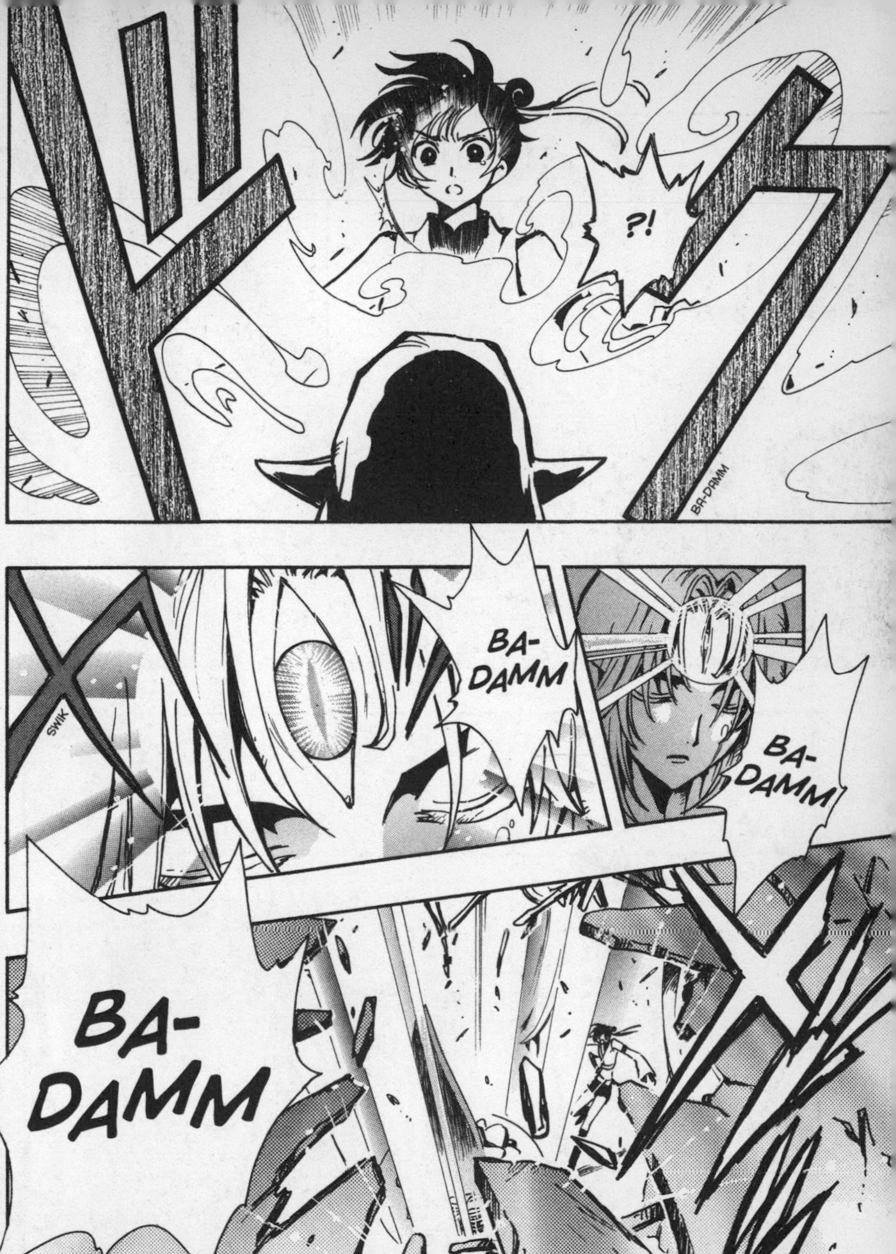
?!
BA-DAMM
BA-DAMM
BA-DAMM
SWIK
GRATCH
BA-DAMM

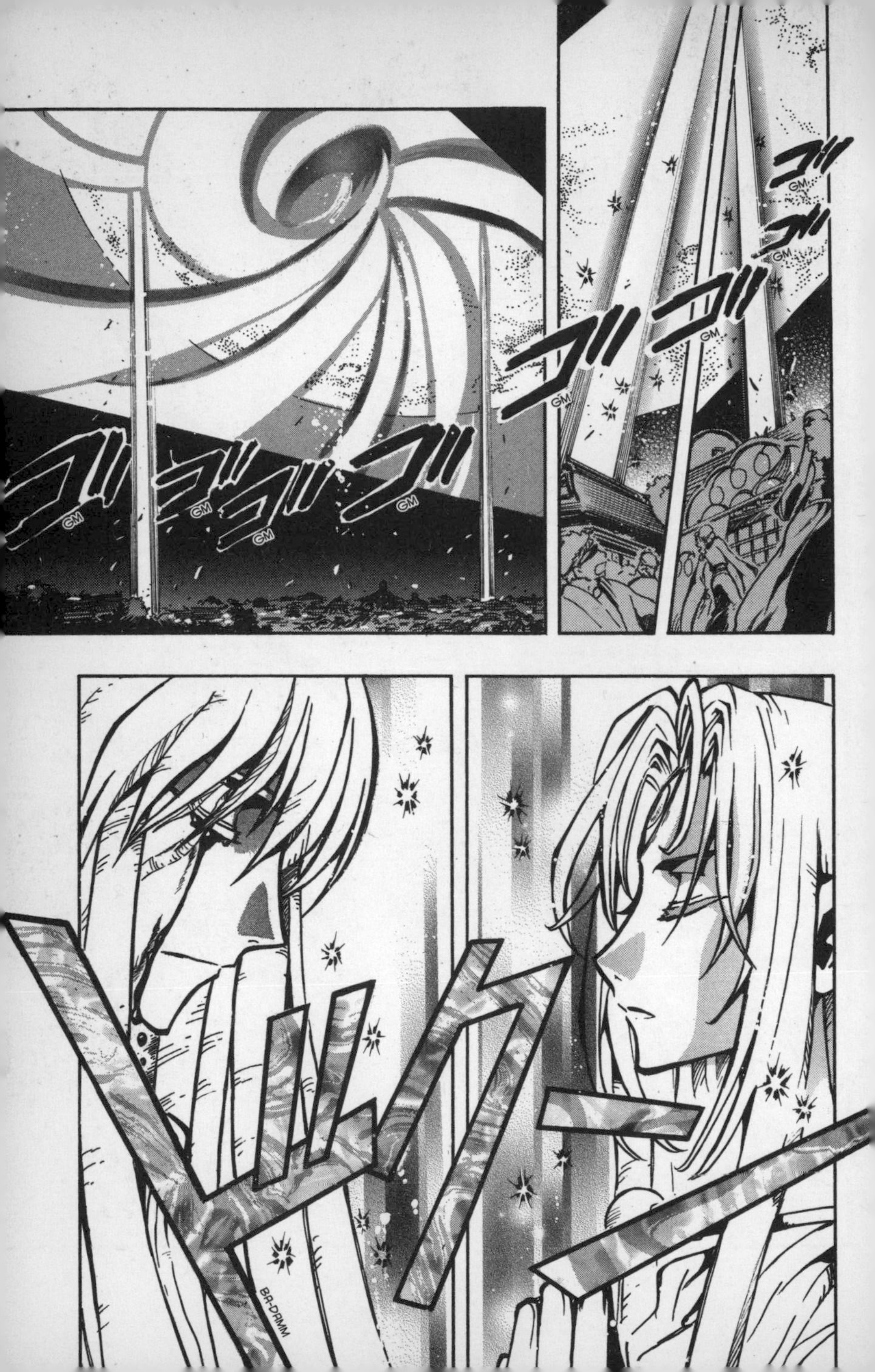
ゴゴゴゴゴゴゴゴ
GM GM GM GM GM GM GM GM
ドクン
BA-DAMM

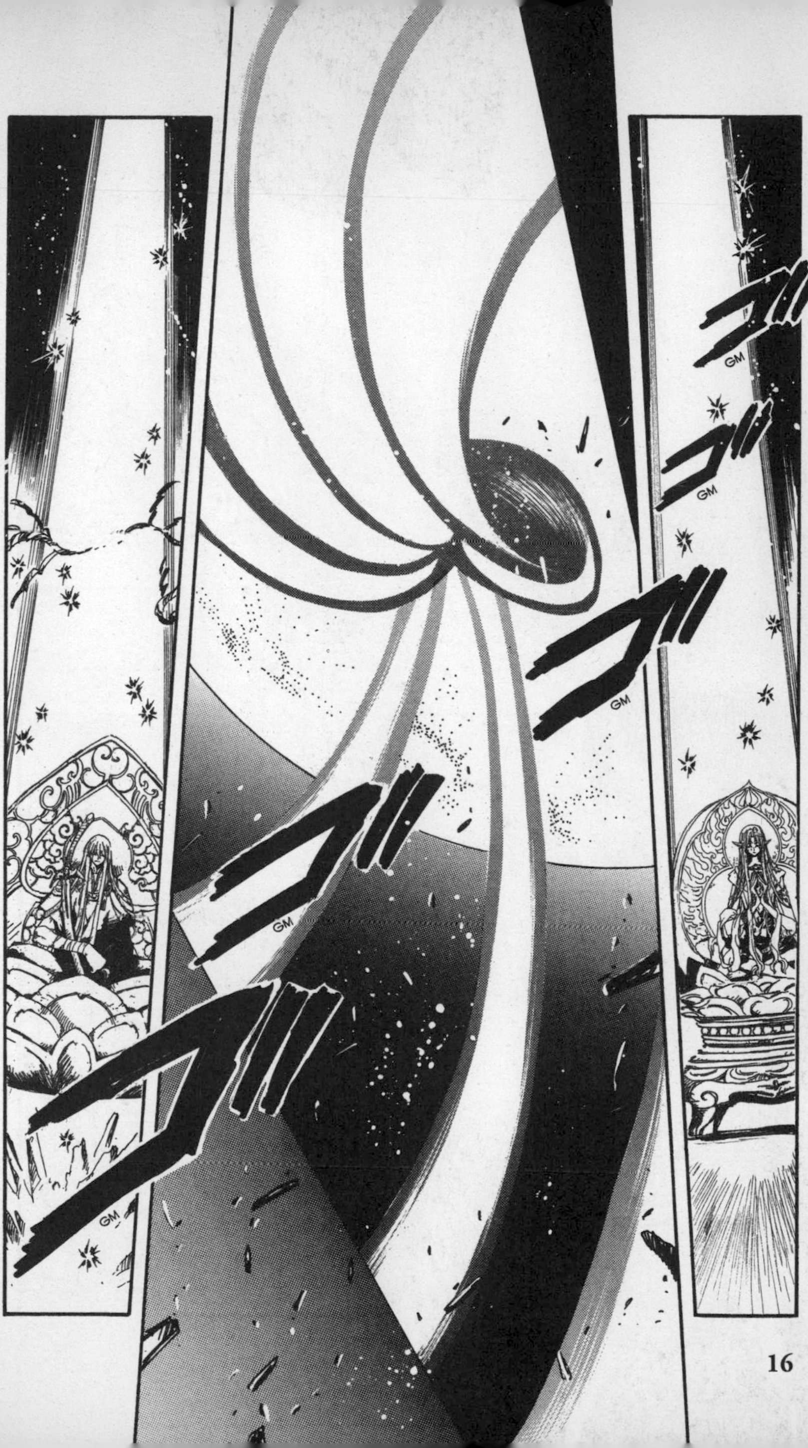
ゴ
GM
ゴ
GM
ゴ
GM
ゴ
GM
ゴ
GM

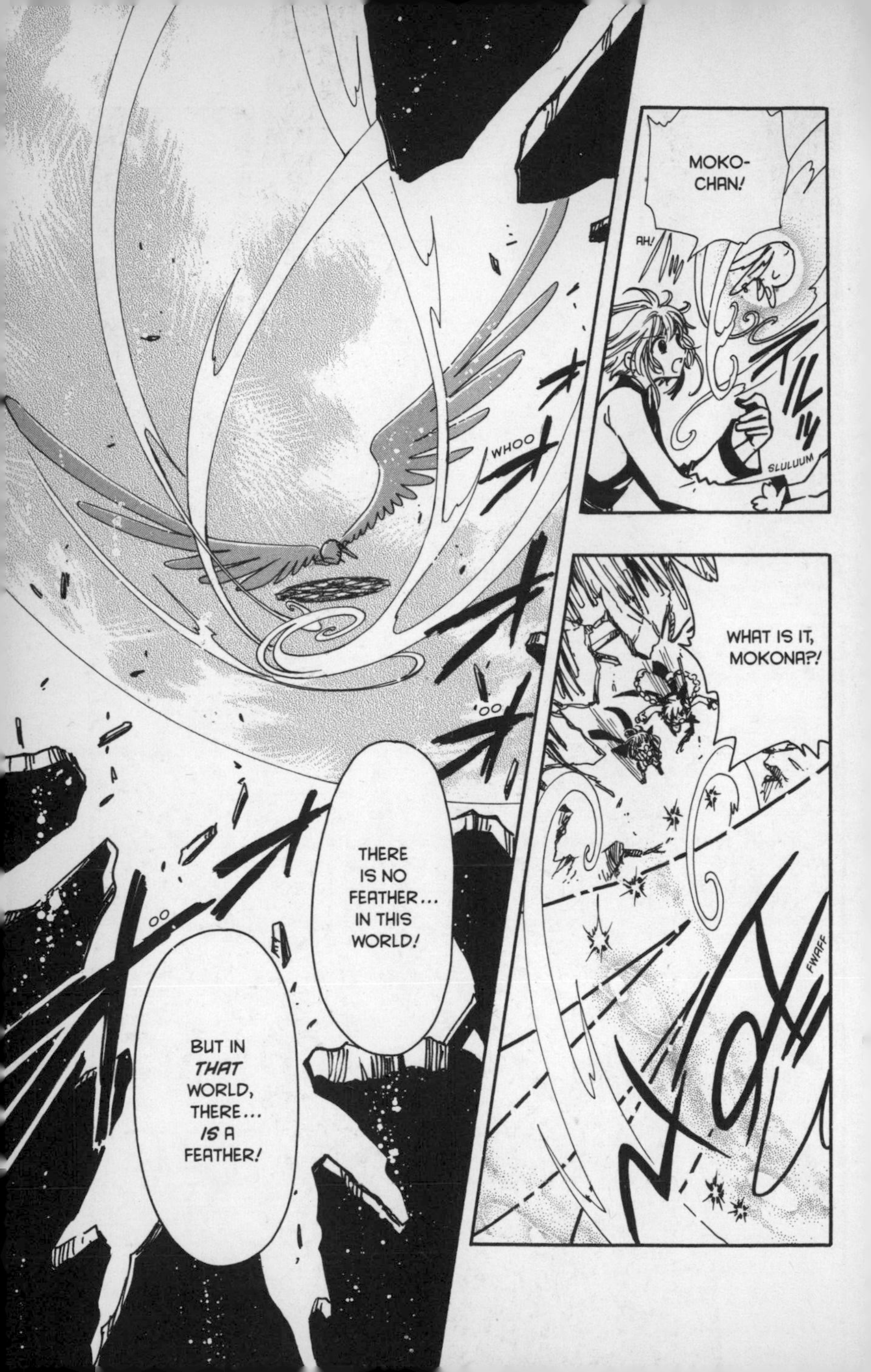
MOKO-CHAN!
AH!
SLULUUM
WHAT IS IT, MOKONA?!
FWAFF
WHOO
THERE IS NO FEATHER... IN THIS WORLD!
BUT IN *THAT* WORLD, THERE... *IS* A FEATHER!

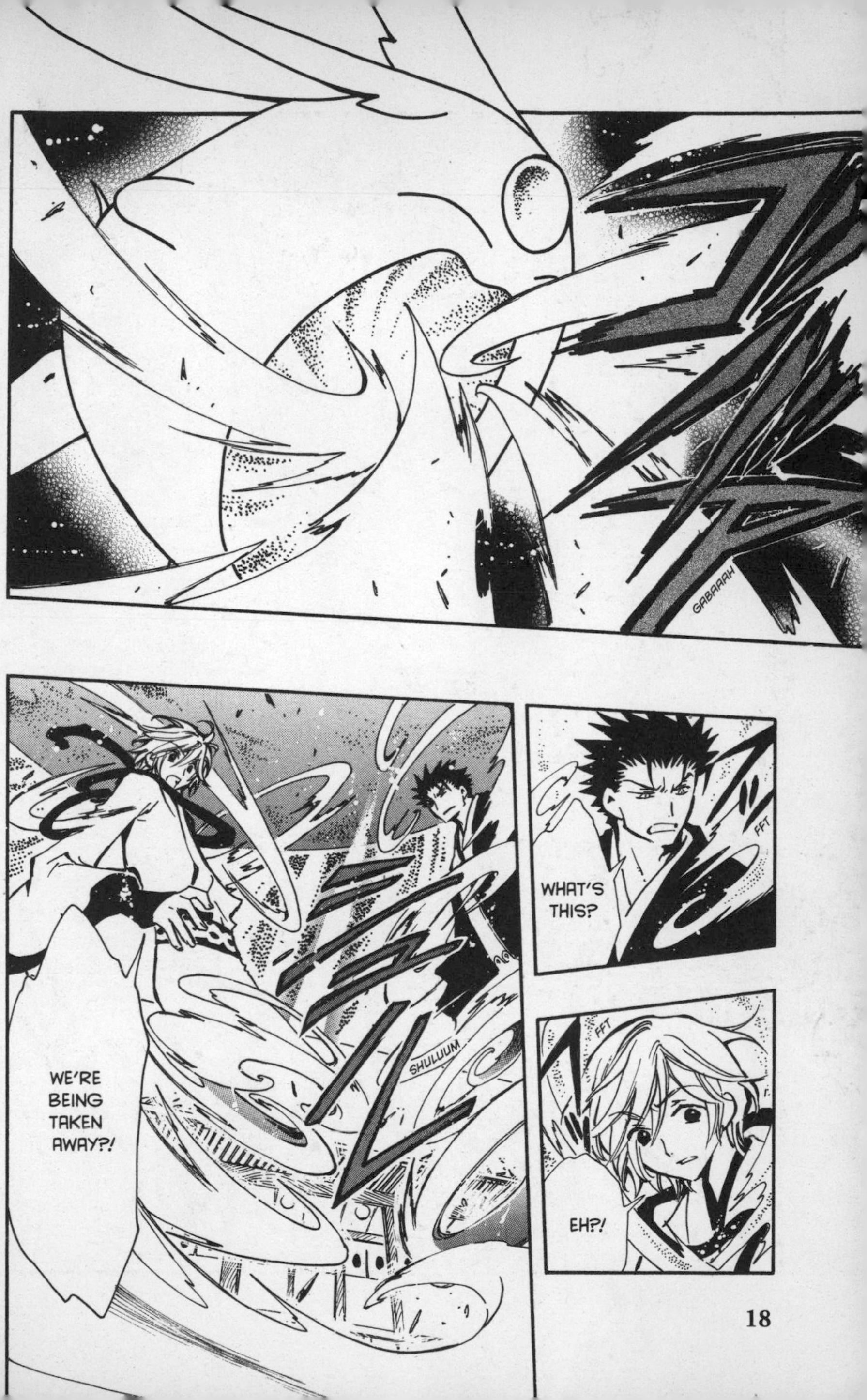
GABAAAH
FFT
WHAT'S THIS?
FFT
EH?!
SHULUUM
WE'RE BEING TAKEN AWAY?!

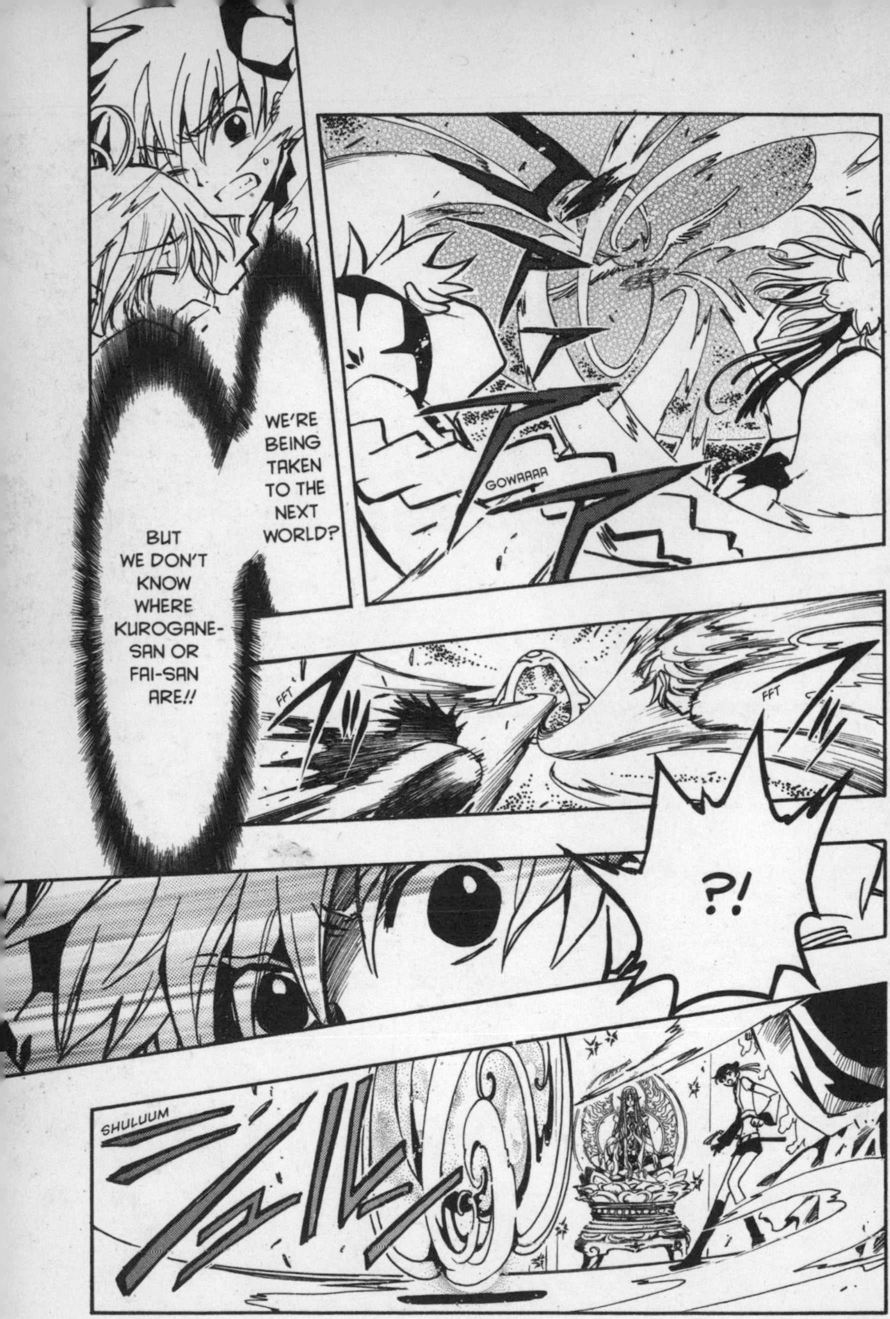
GOWAAAA
WE'RE BEING TAKEN TO THE NEXT WORLD?
BUT WE DON'T KNOW WHERE KUROGANE-SAN OR FAI-SAN ARE!!
FFT
FFT
?!
SHULUUM

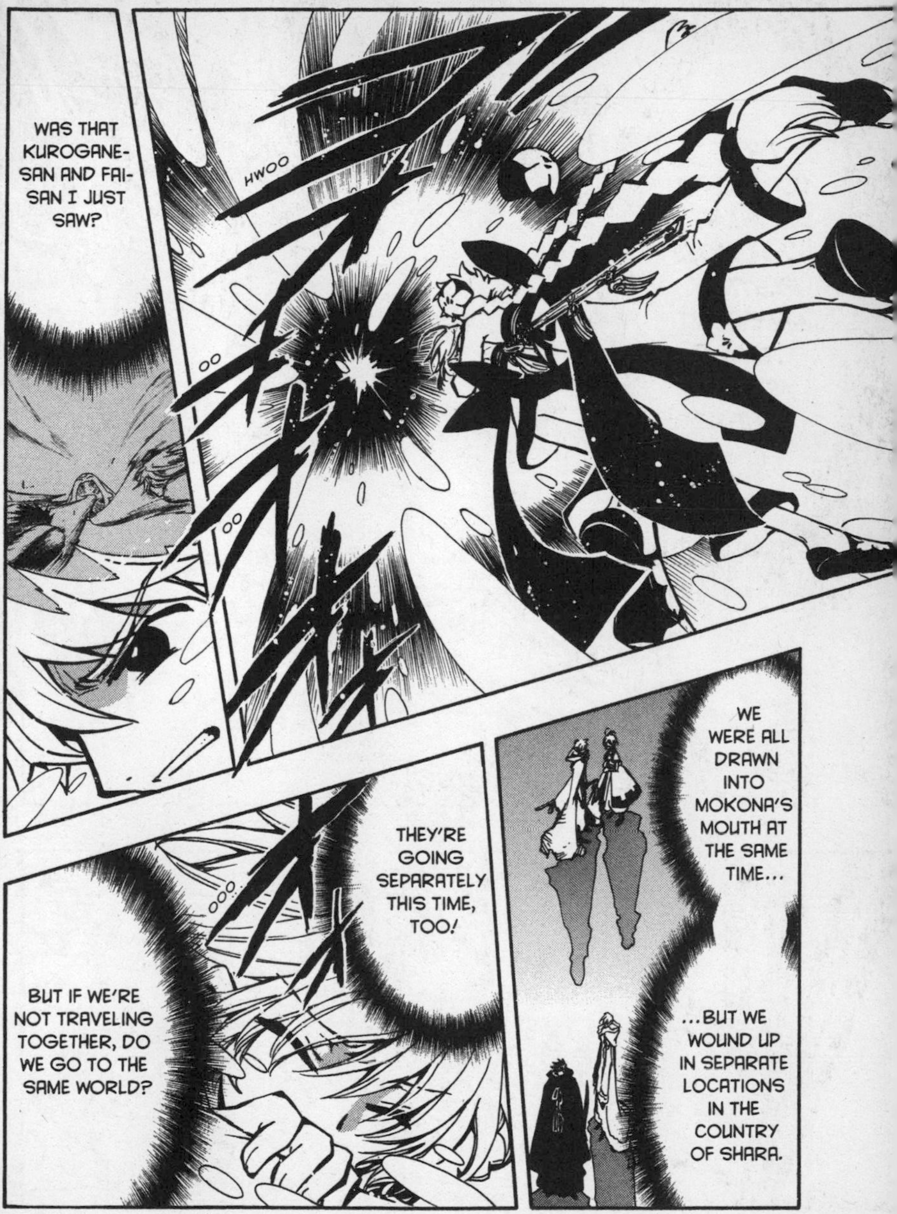
HWOO
WAS THAT KUROGANE-SAN AND FAI-SAN I JUST SAW?
WE WERE ALL DRAWN INTO MOKONA'S MOUTH AT THE SAME TIME...
...BUT WE WOUND UP IN SEPARATE LOCATIONS IN THE COUNTRY OF SHARA.
THEY'RE GOING SEPARATELY THIS TIME, TOO!
BUT IF WE'RE NOT TRAVELING TOGETHER, DO WE GO TO THE SAME WORLD?

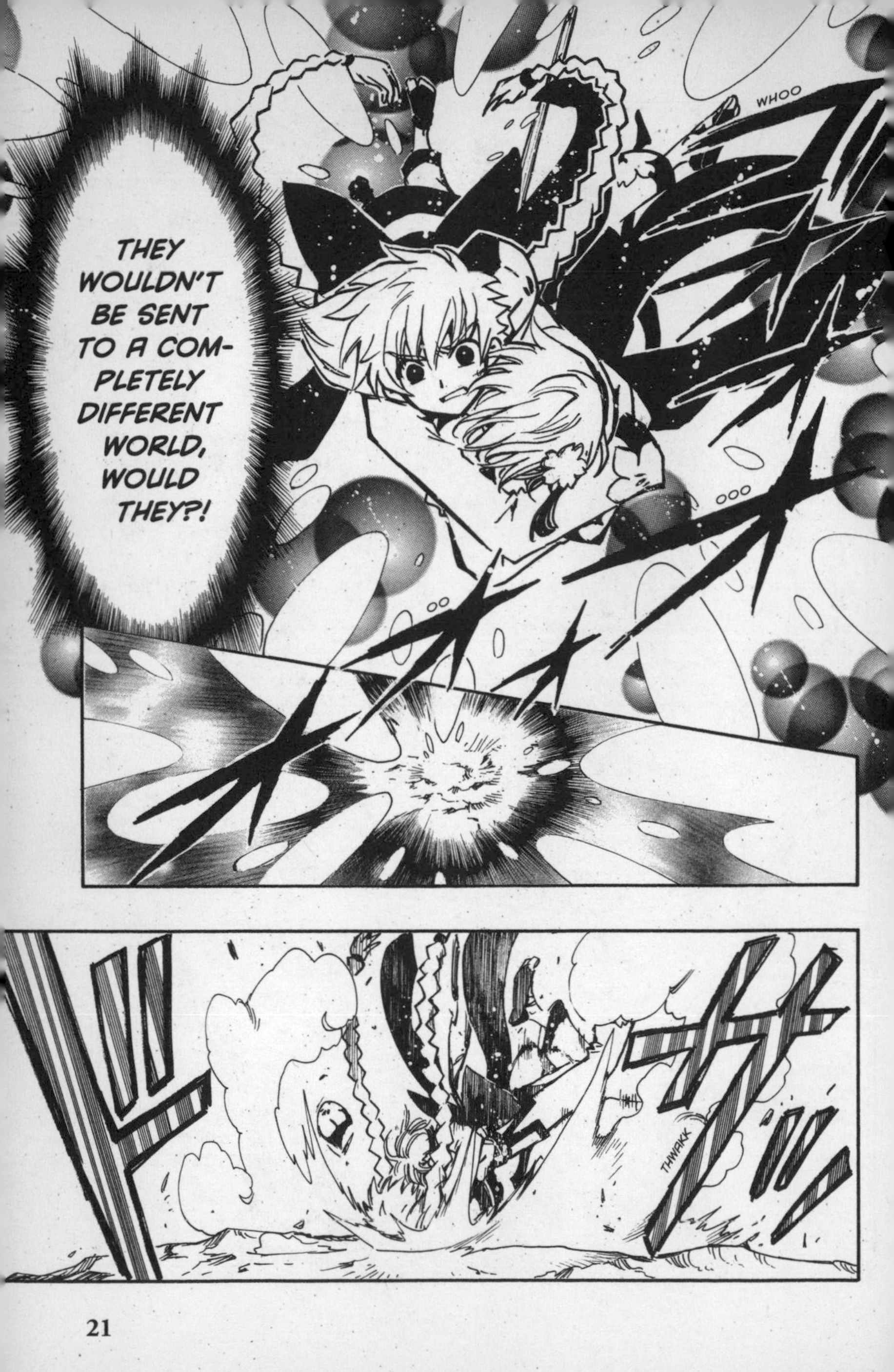
THEY WOULDN'T BE SENT TO A COMPLETELY DIFFERENT WORLD, WOULD THEY?!
WHOO
THWAKK

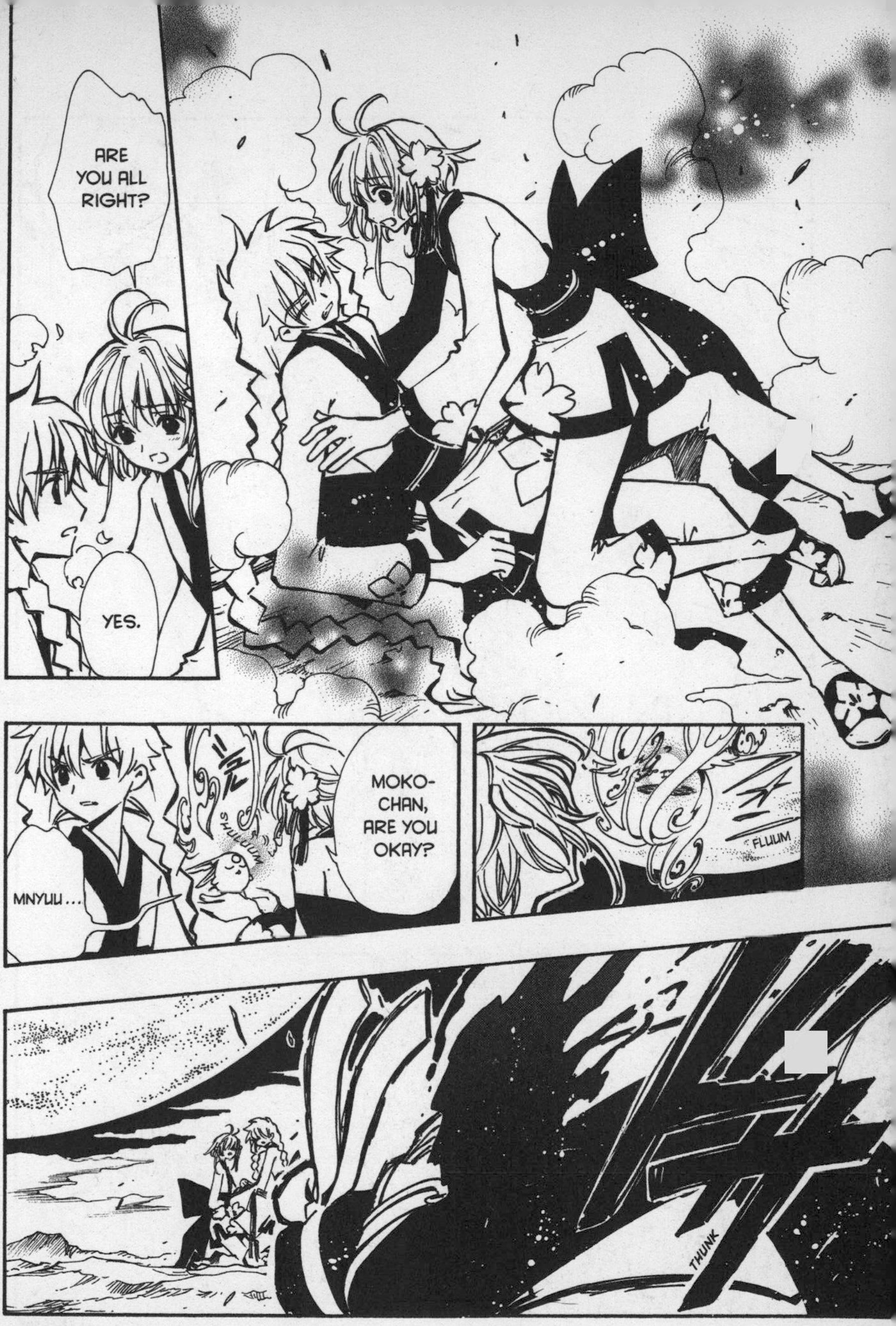
ARE YOU ALL RIGHT?
YES.
FLUUM
MOKO-CHAN, ARE YOU OKAY?
SHULUUM
MNYUU...
THUNK

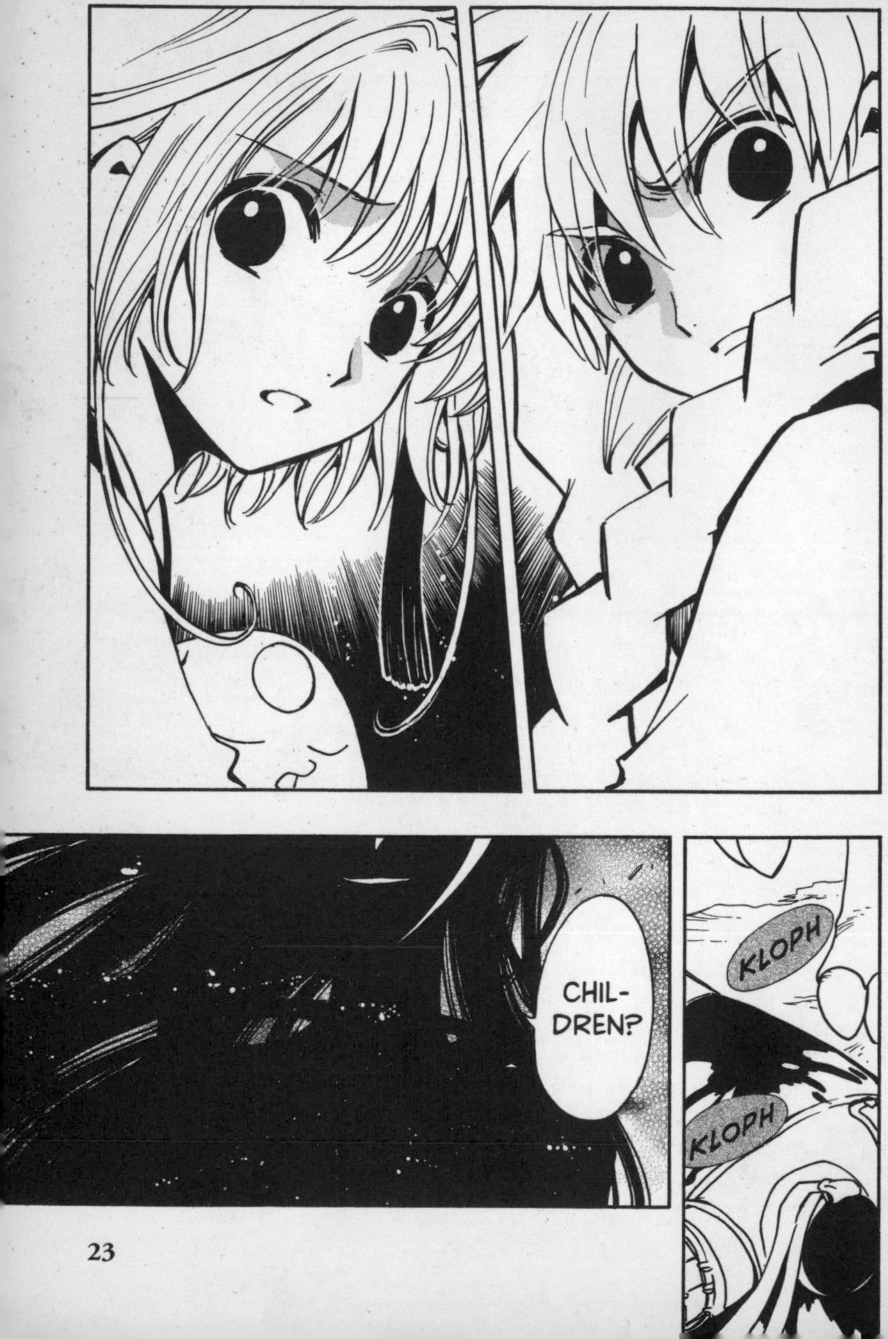
KLOPH
KLOPH
CHIL-
DREN?

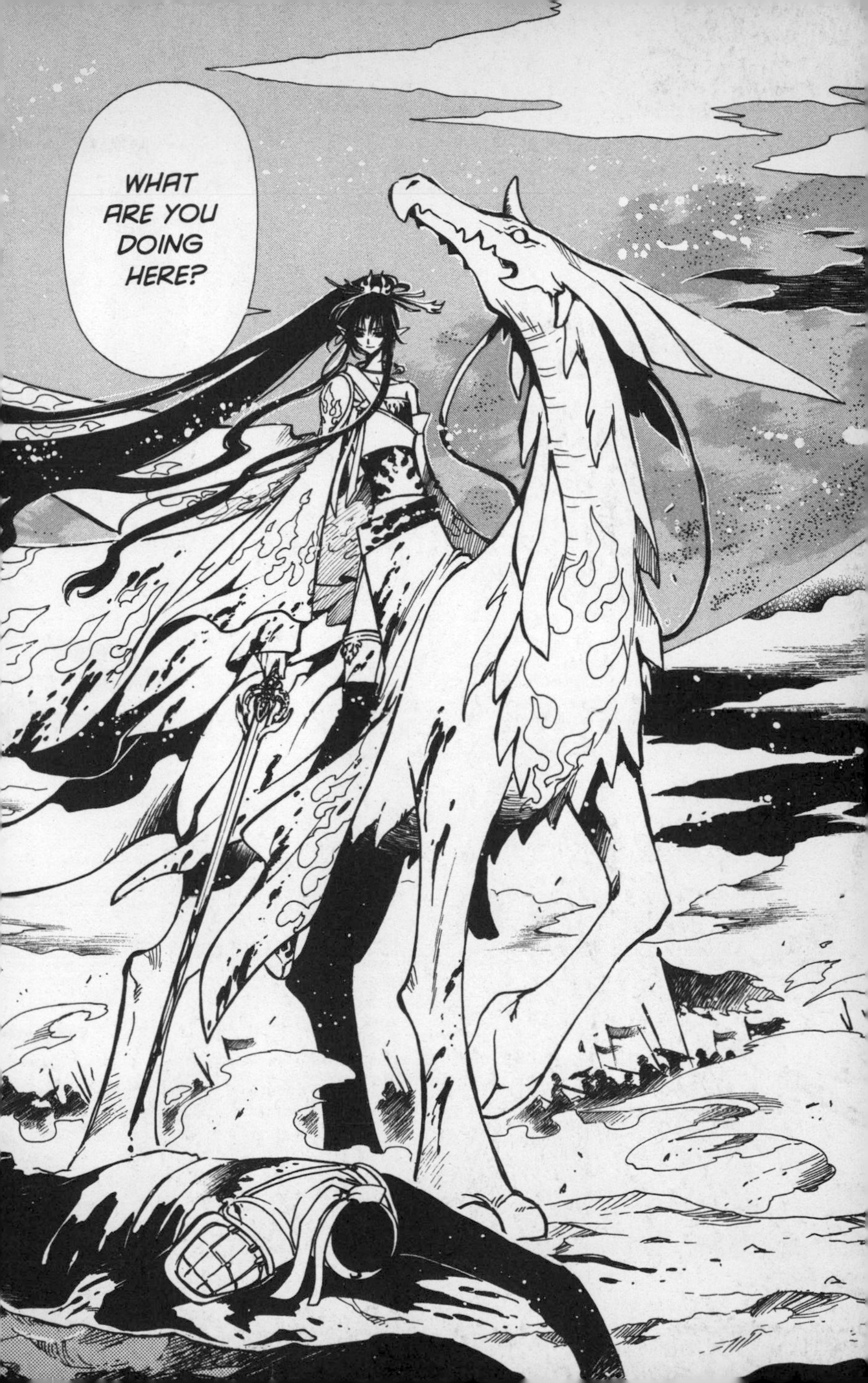
WHAT ARE YOU DOING HERE?

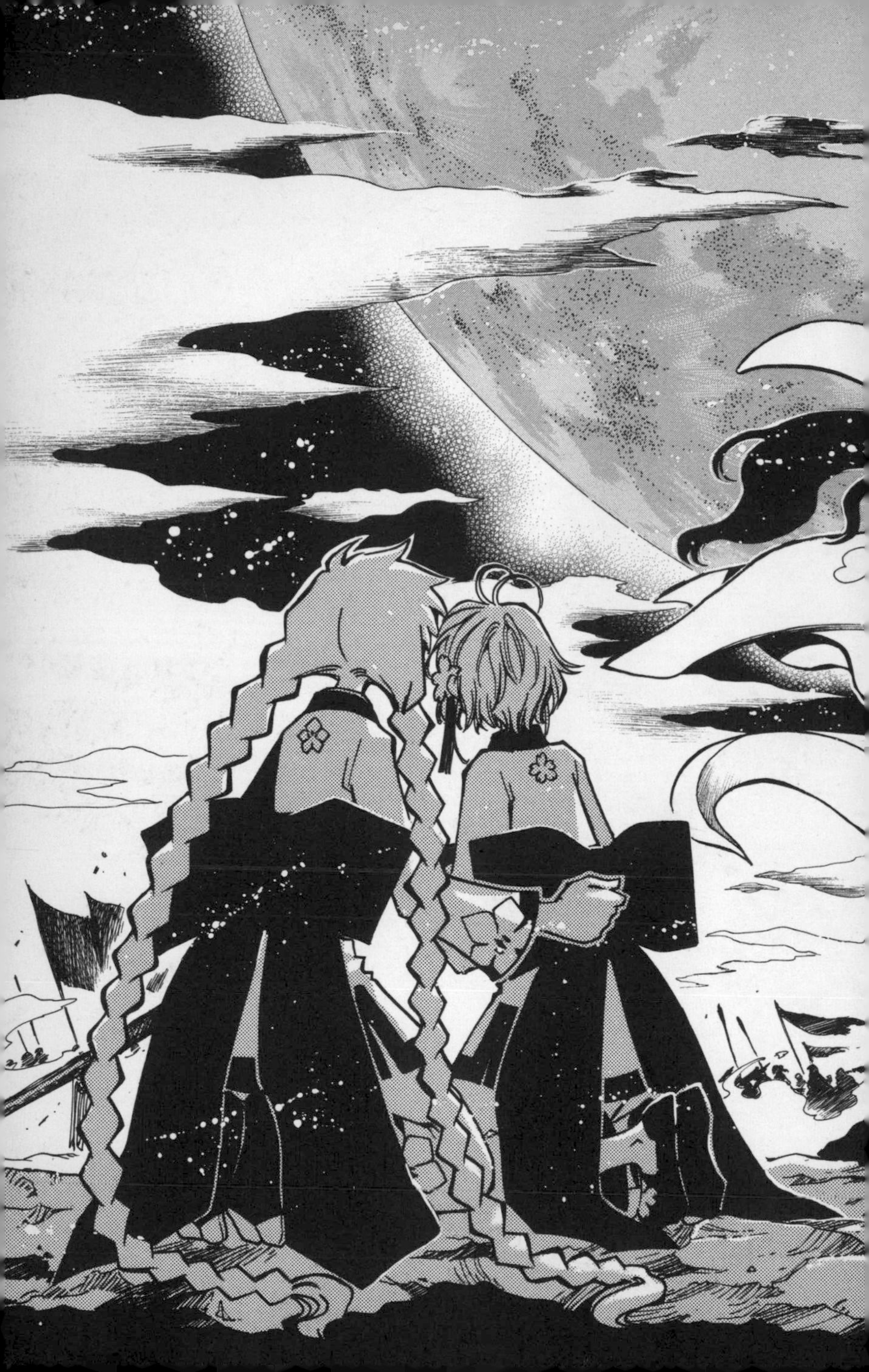

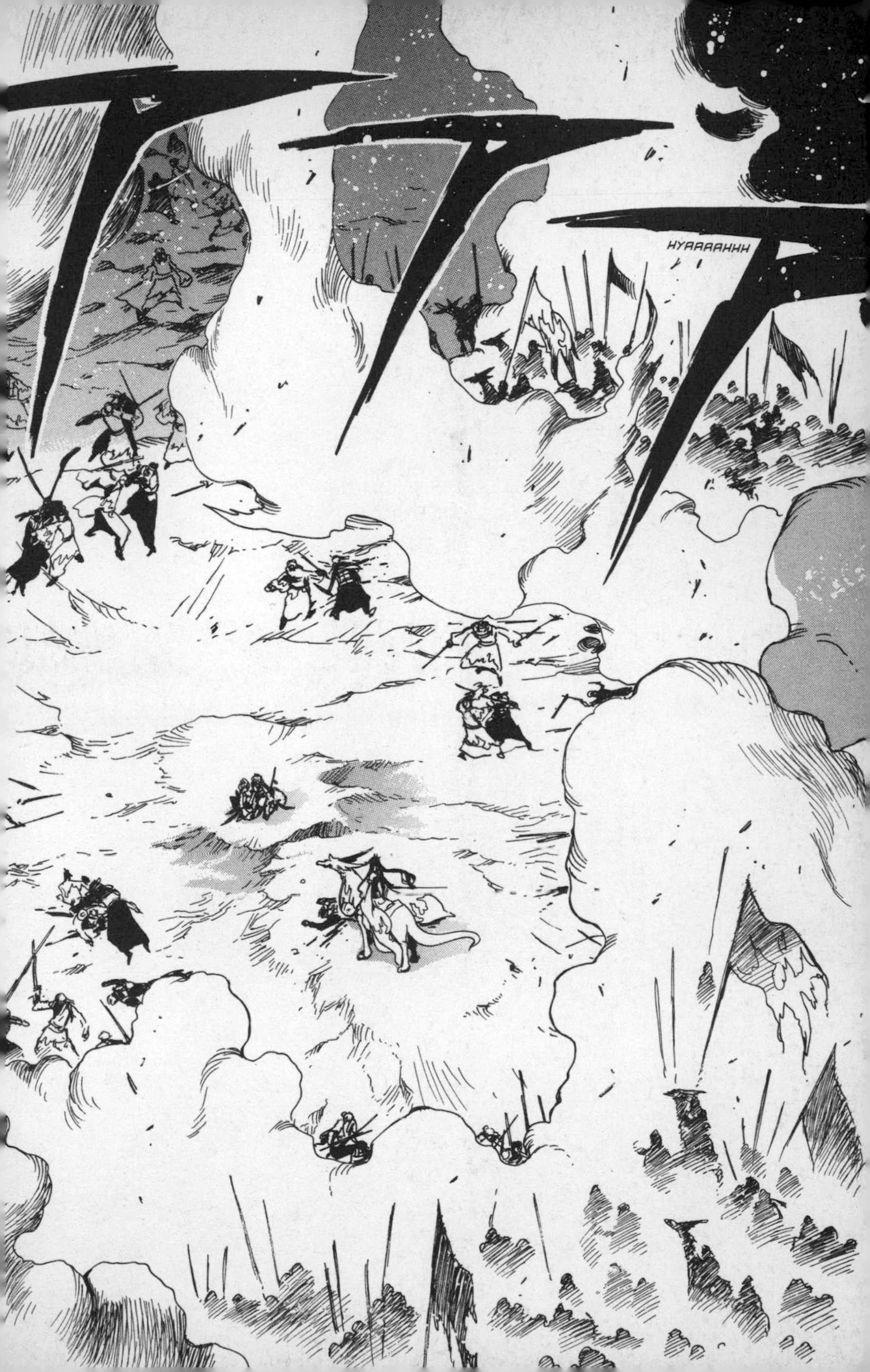
HYAAAAHHH

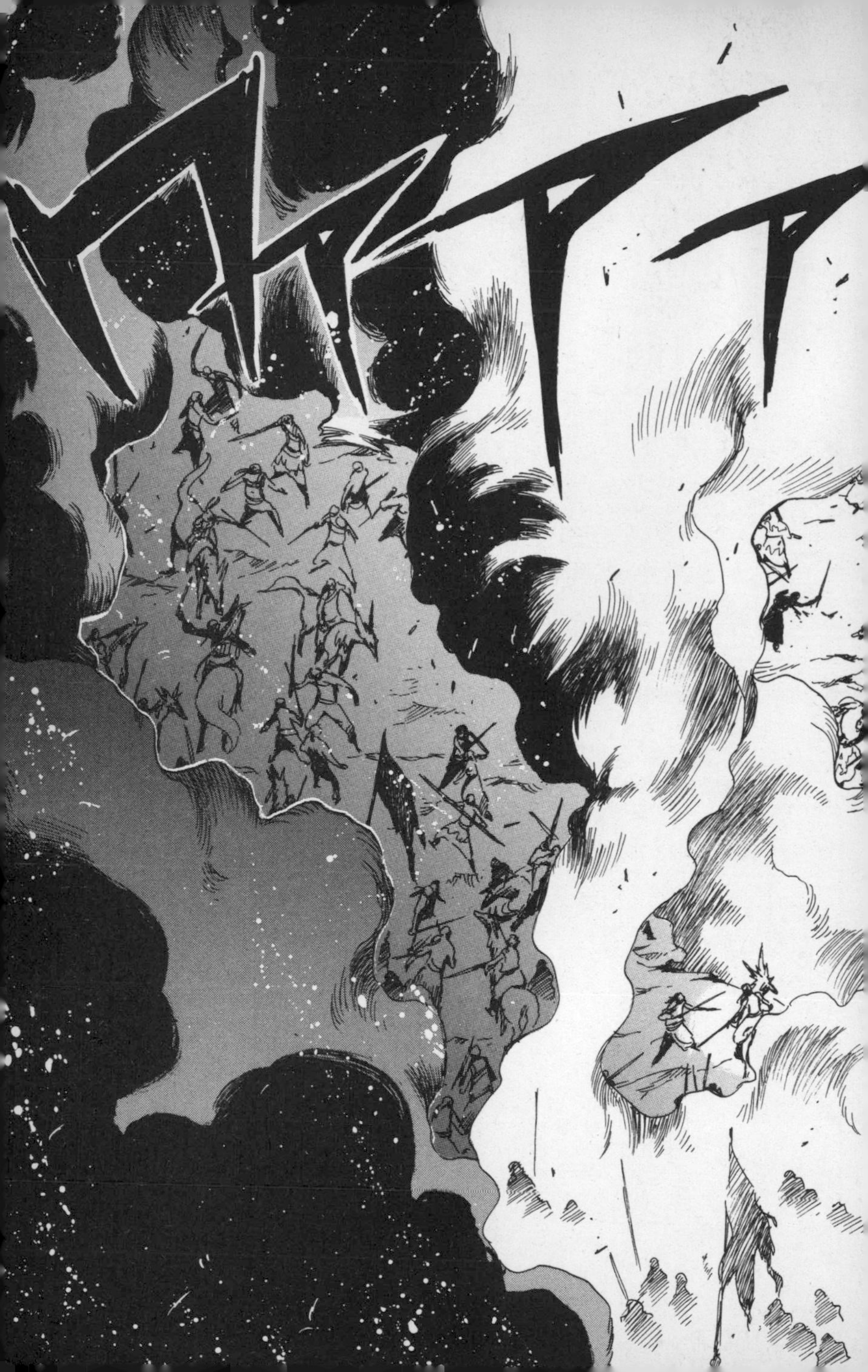

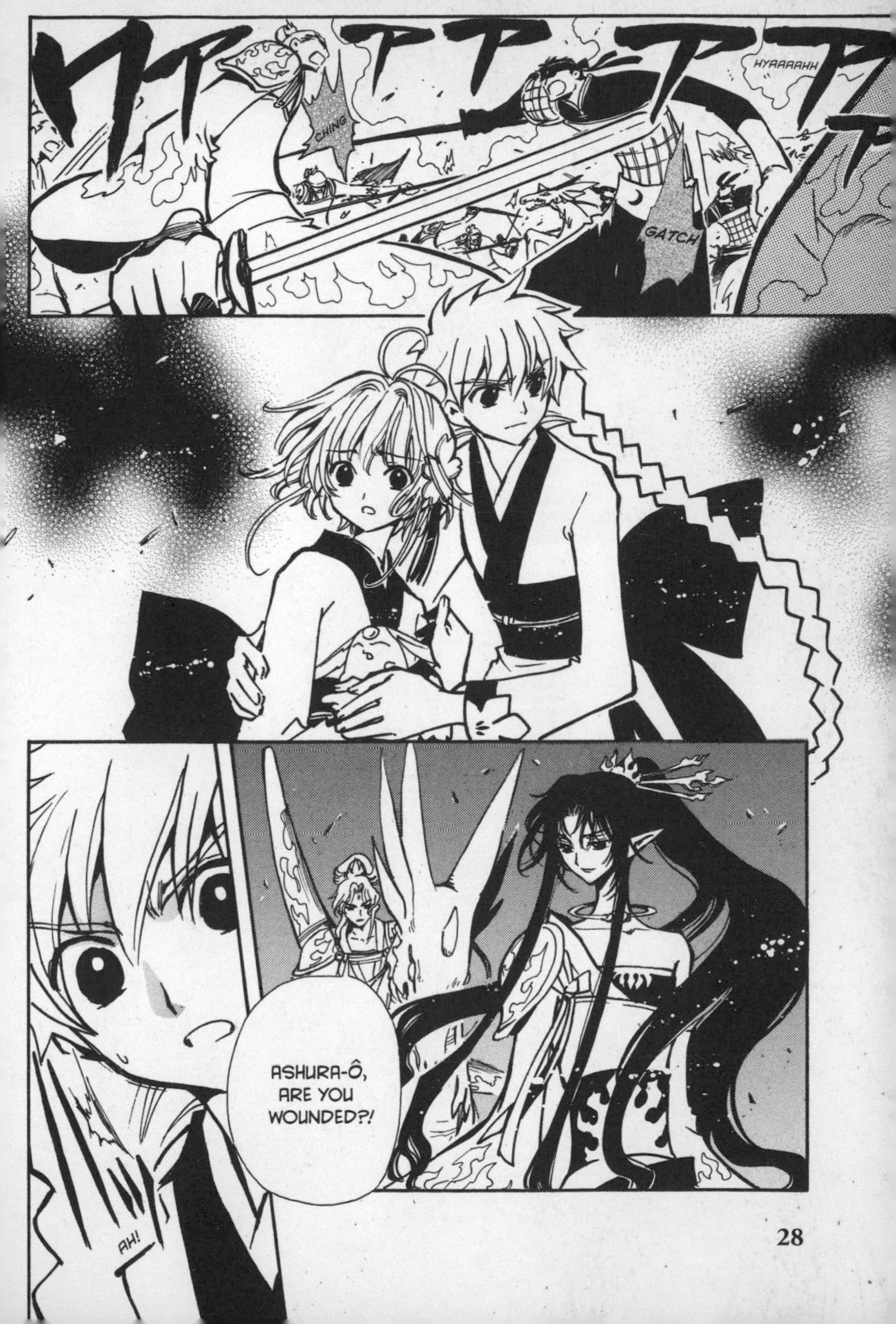
HYAAAAAHH
GATCH
CHING
ASHURA-Ô, ARE YOU WOUNDED?!
AH!

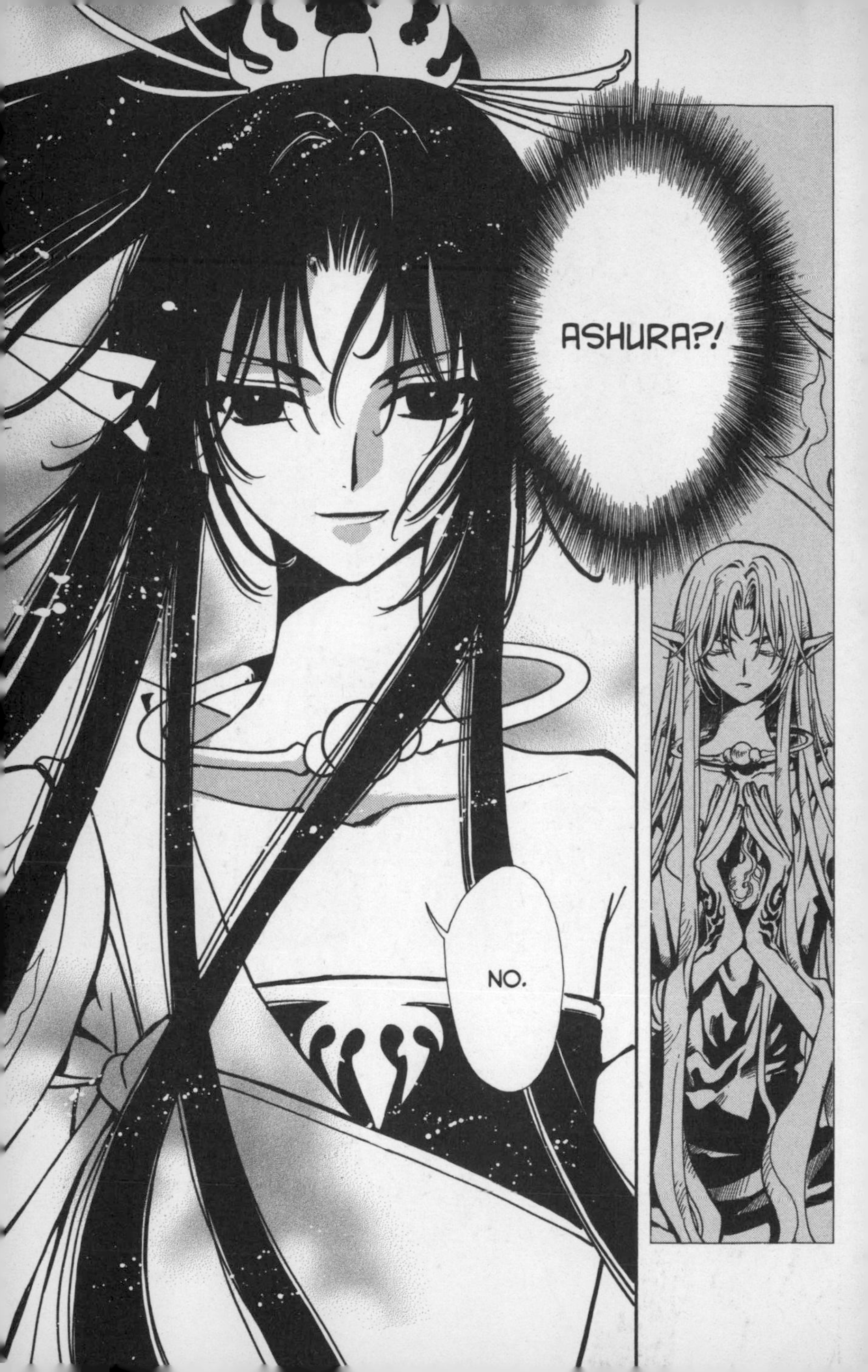
ASHURA?!
NO.

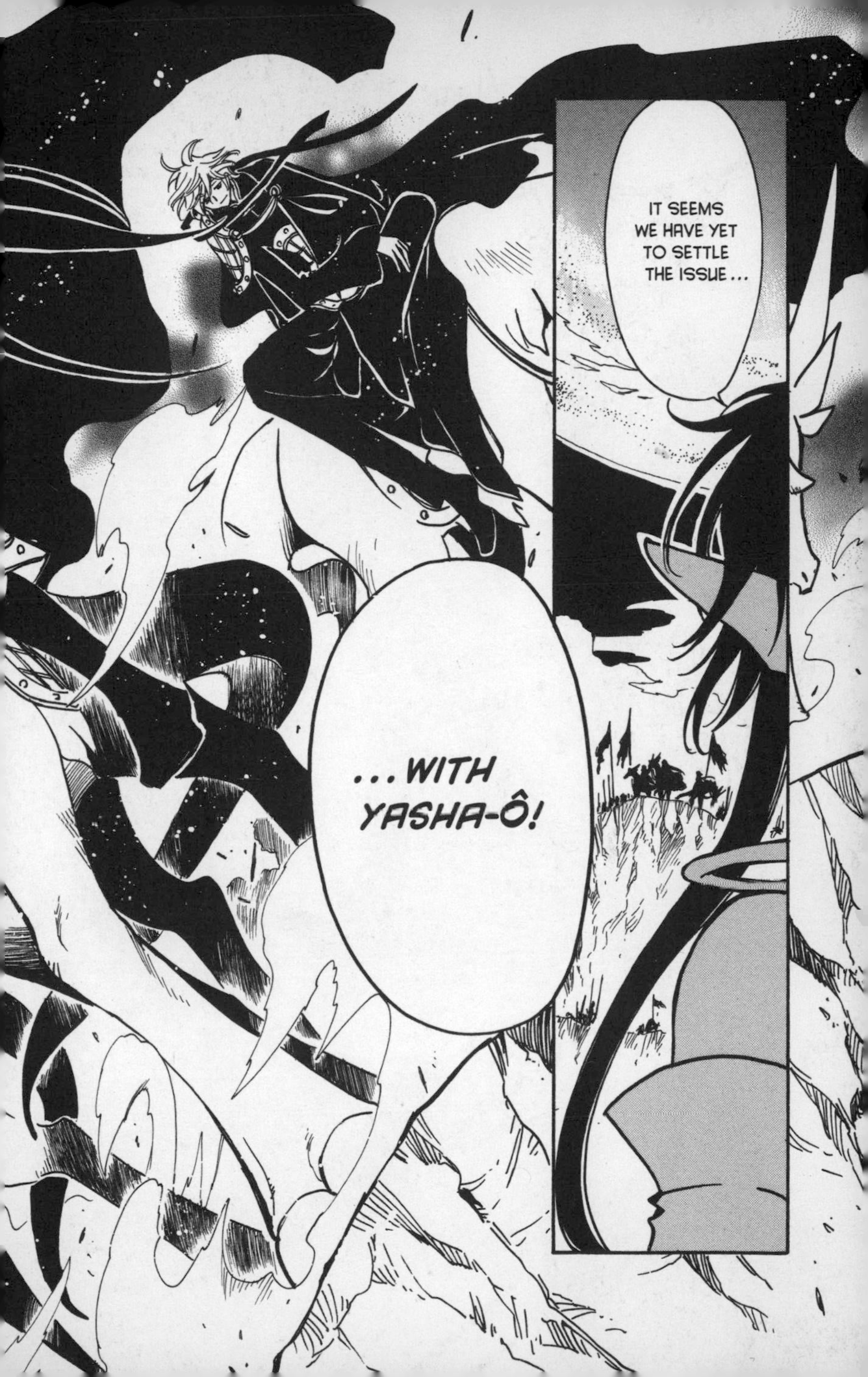
IT SEEMS WE HAVE YET TO SETTLE THE ISSUE...
...WITH YASHA-Ô!

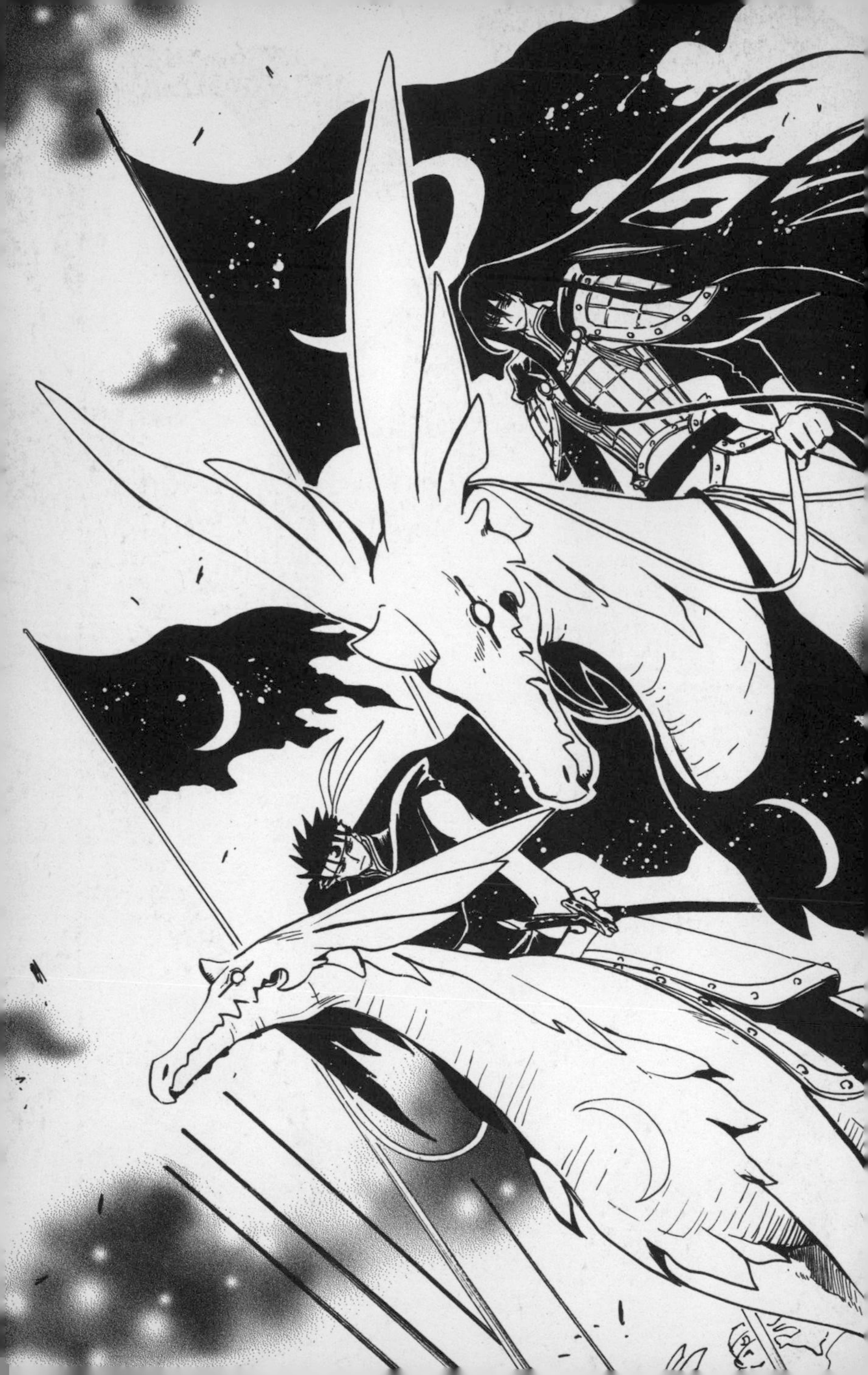

ツバサ
RESERVoir CHRoNiCLE

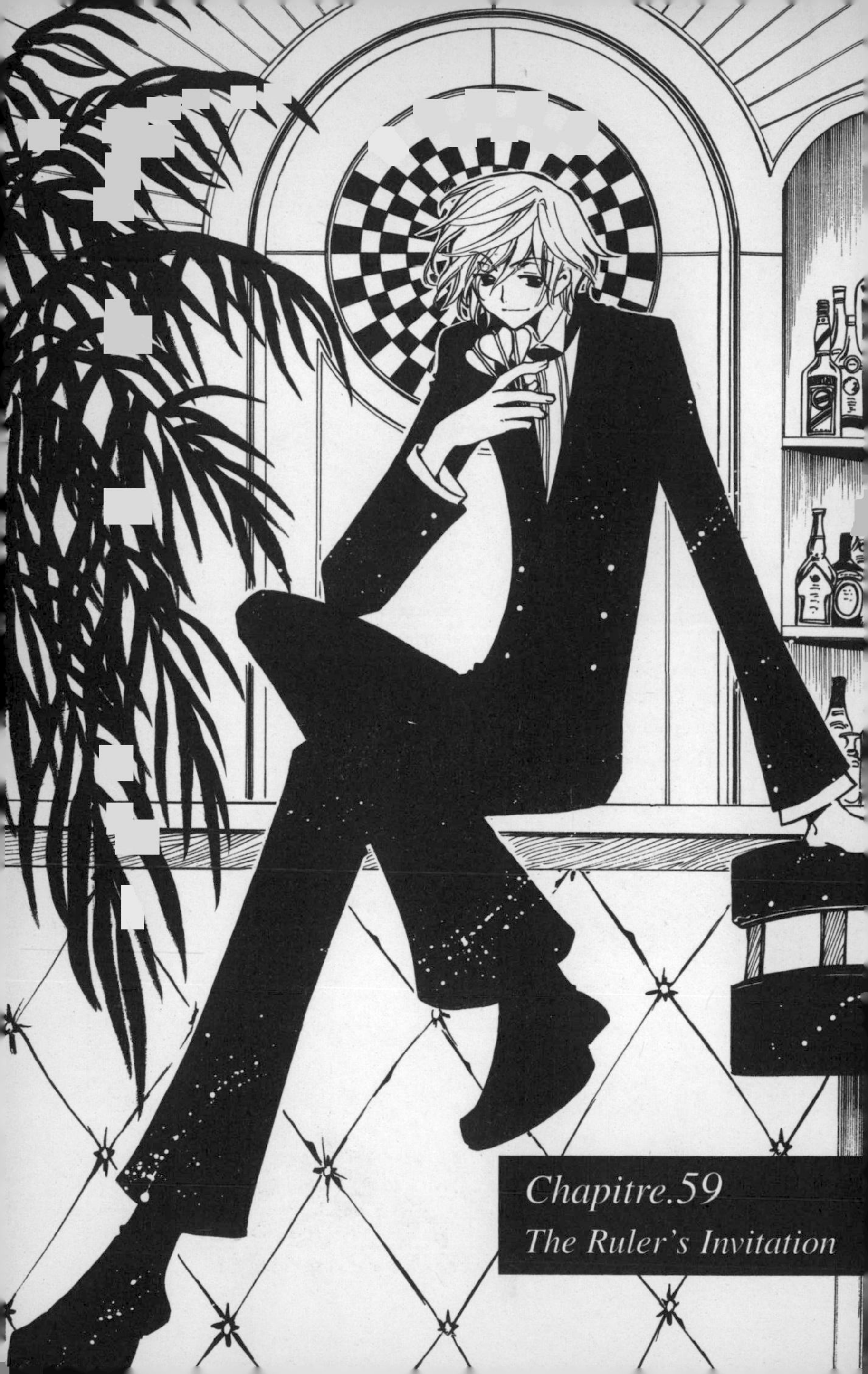
Chapitre.59
The Ruler's Invitation

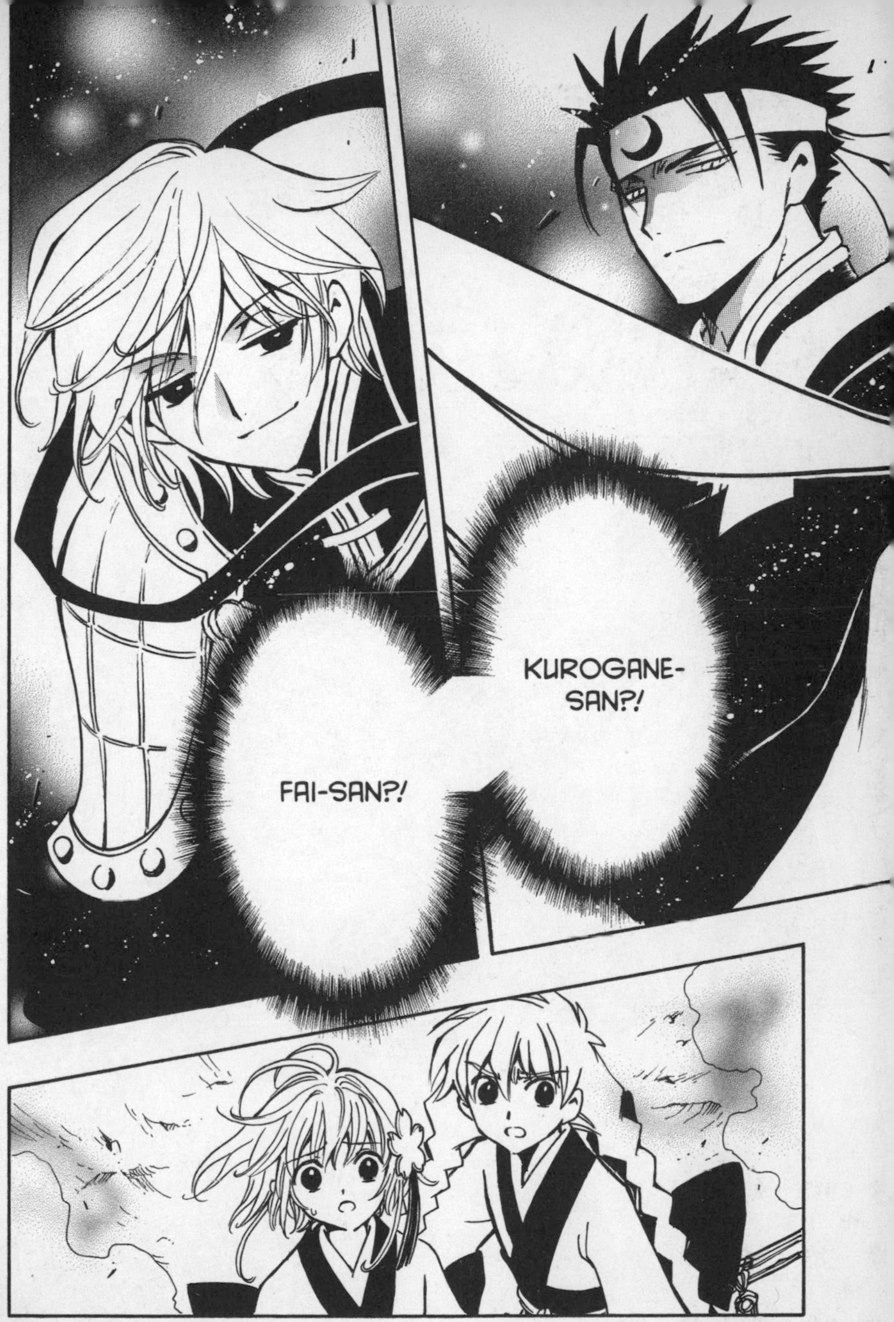
KUROGANE-SAN?!
FAI-SAN?!

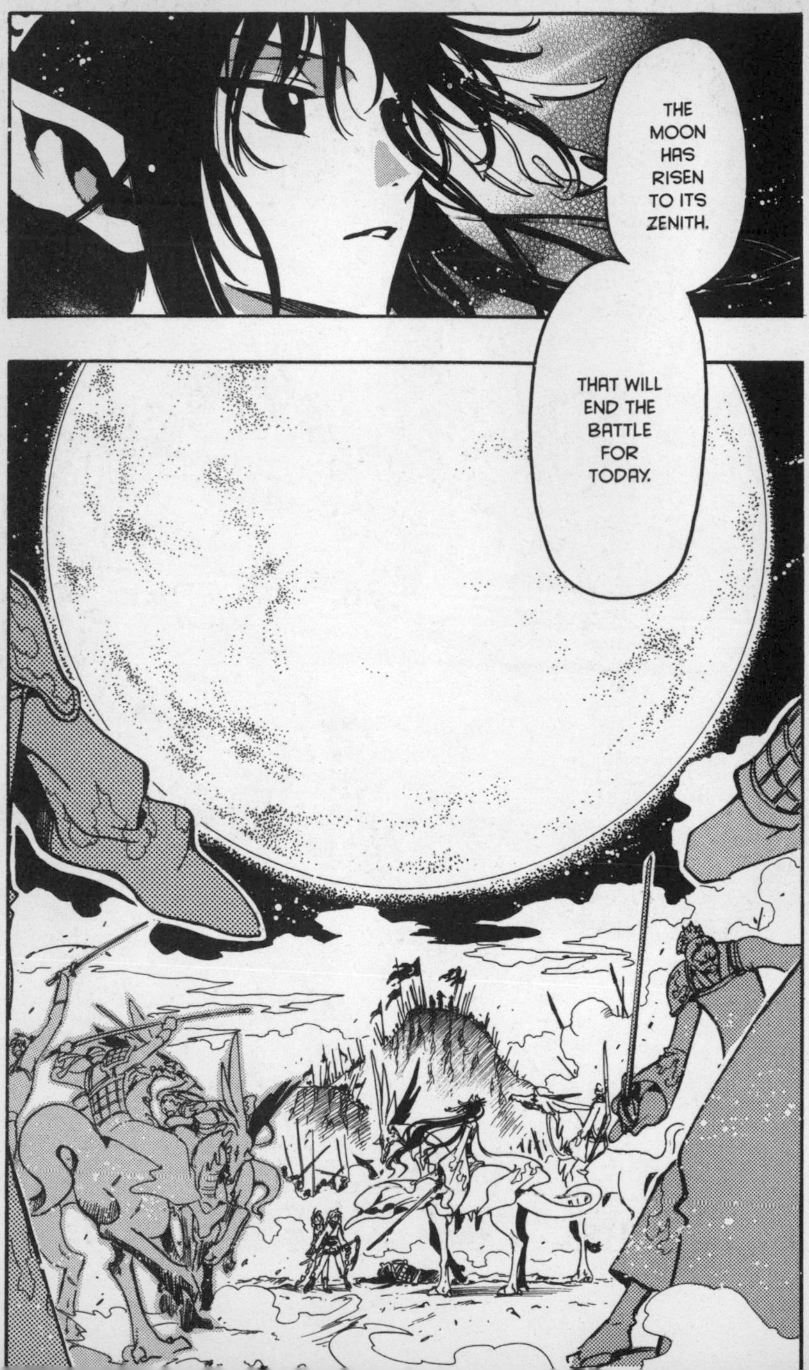
THE MOON HAS RISEN TO ITS ZENITH.
THAT WILL END THE BATTLE FOR TODAY.

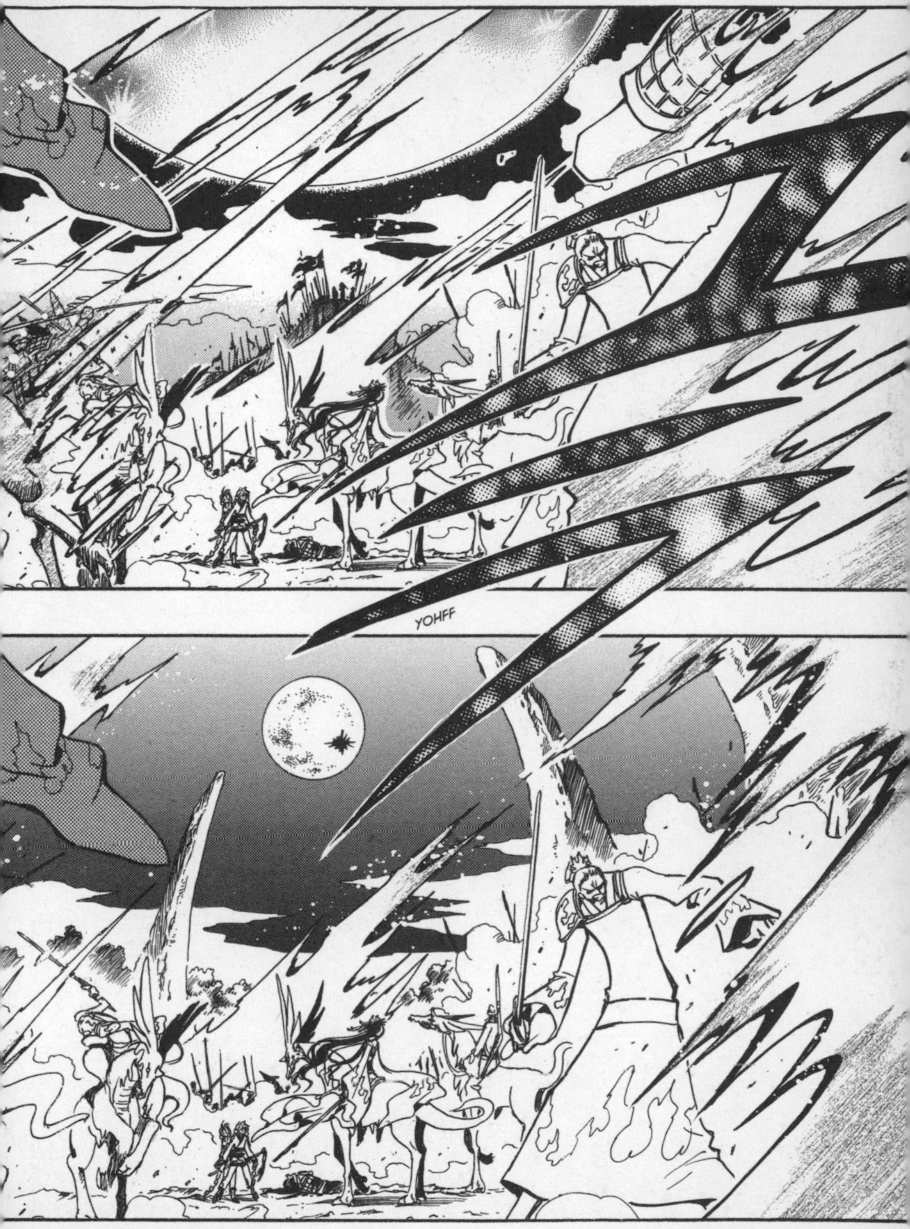
YOHFF

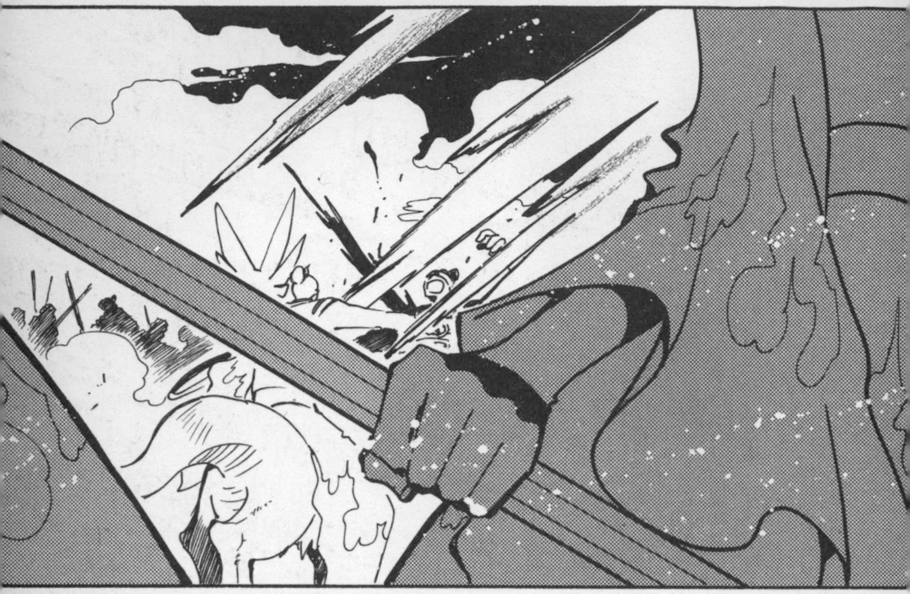

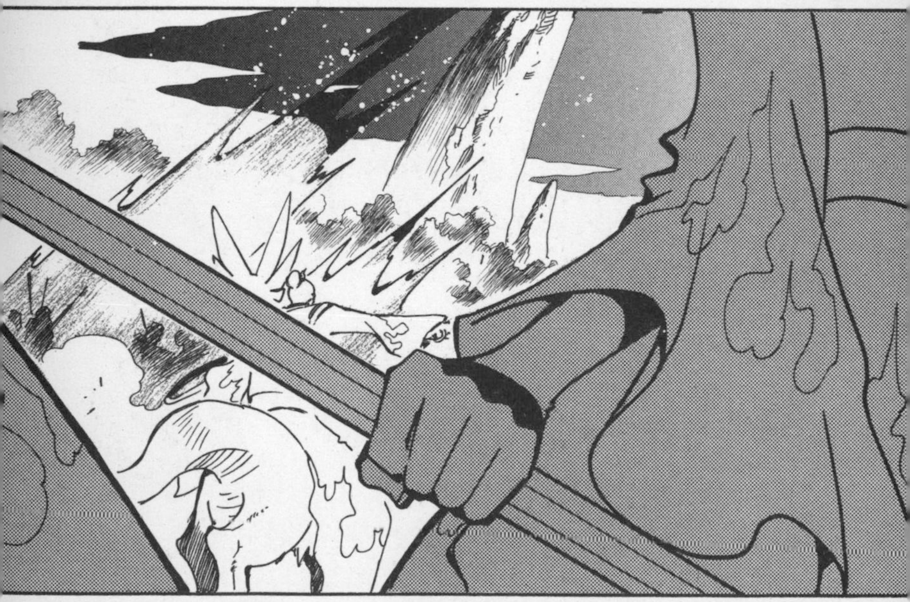

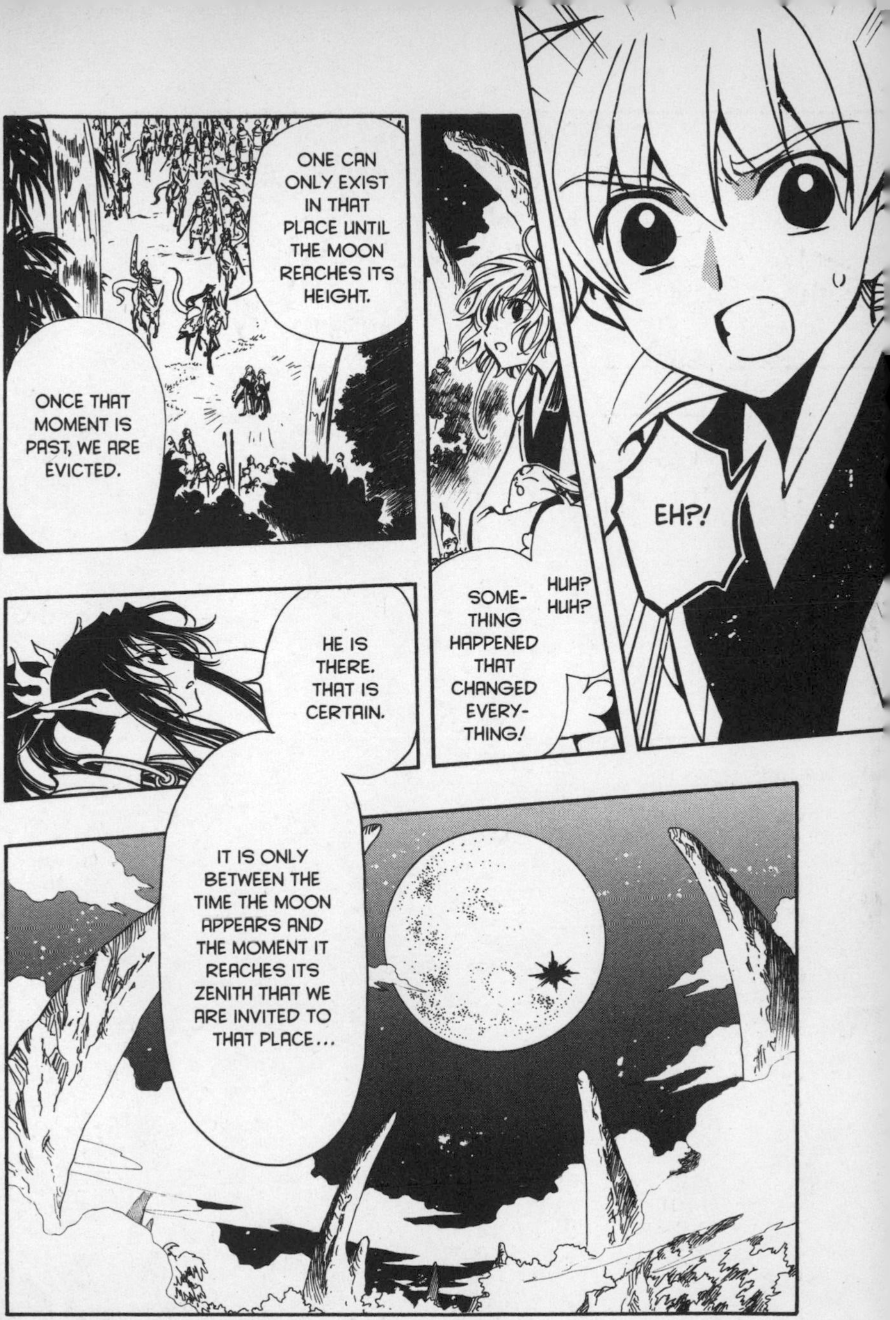
EH?!
HUH? HUH?
SOME-THING HAPPENED THAT CHANGED EVERY-THING!
ONE CAN ONLY EXIST IN THAT PLACE UNTIL THE MOON REACHES ITS HEIGHT.
ONCE THAT MOMENT IS PAST, WE ARE EVICTED.
HE IS THERE. THAT IS CERTAIN.
IT IS ONLY BETWEEN THE TIME THE MOON APPEARS AND THE MOMENT IT REACHES ITS ZENITH THAT WE ARE INVITED TO THAT PLACE...

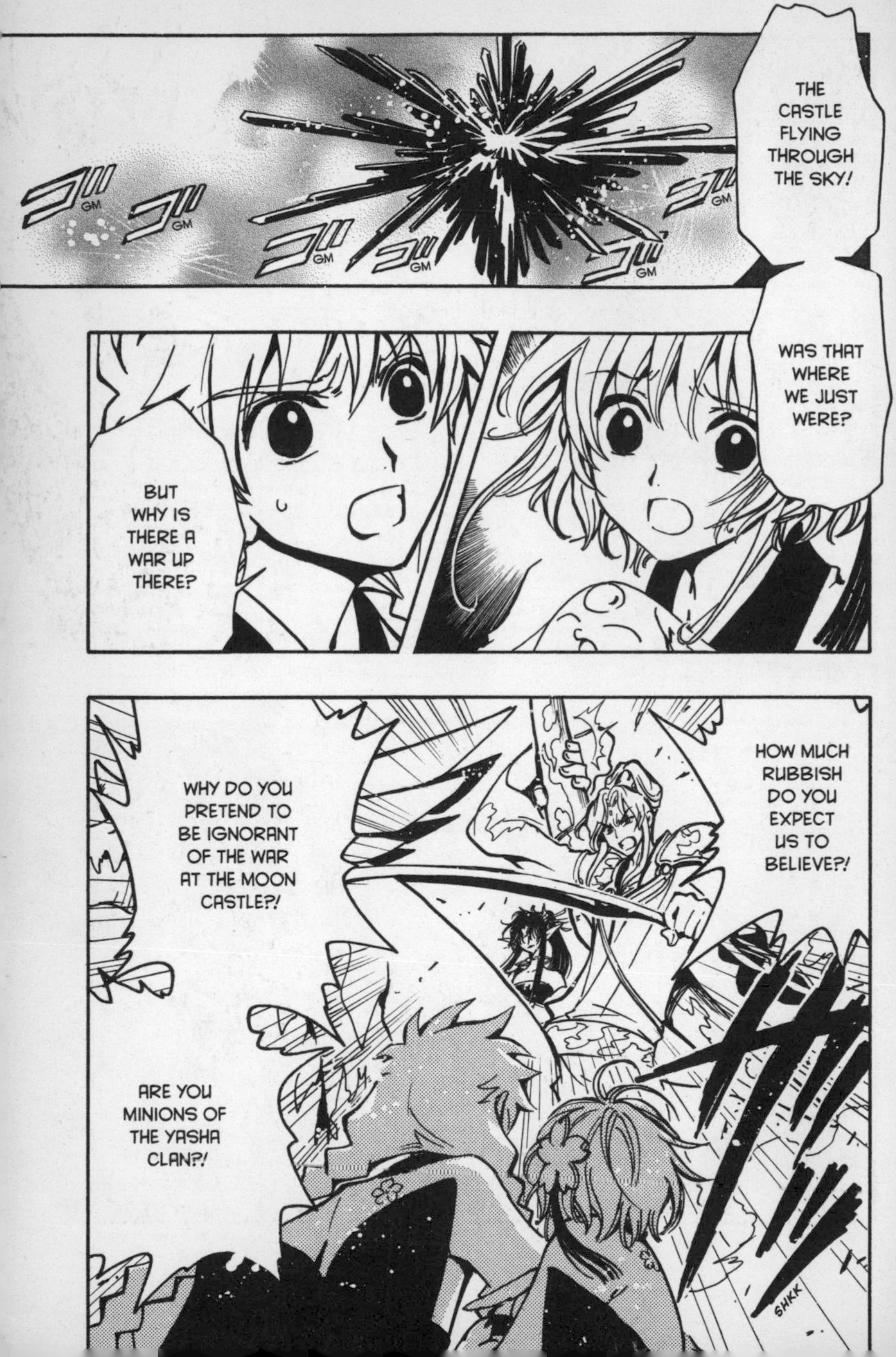
THE CASTLE FLYING THROUGH THE SKY!
GM GM GM GM GM GM GM
WAS THAT WHERE WE JUST WERE?
BUT WHY IS THERE A WAR UP THERE?
HOW MUCH RUBBISH DO YOU EXPECT US TO BELIEVE?!
WHY DO YOU PRETEND TO BE IGNORANT OF THE WAR AT THE MOON CASTLE?!
ARE YOU MINIONS OF THE YASHA CLAN?!
SHKK

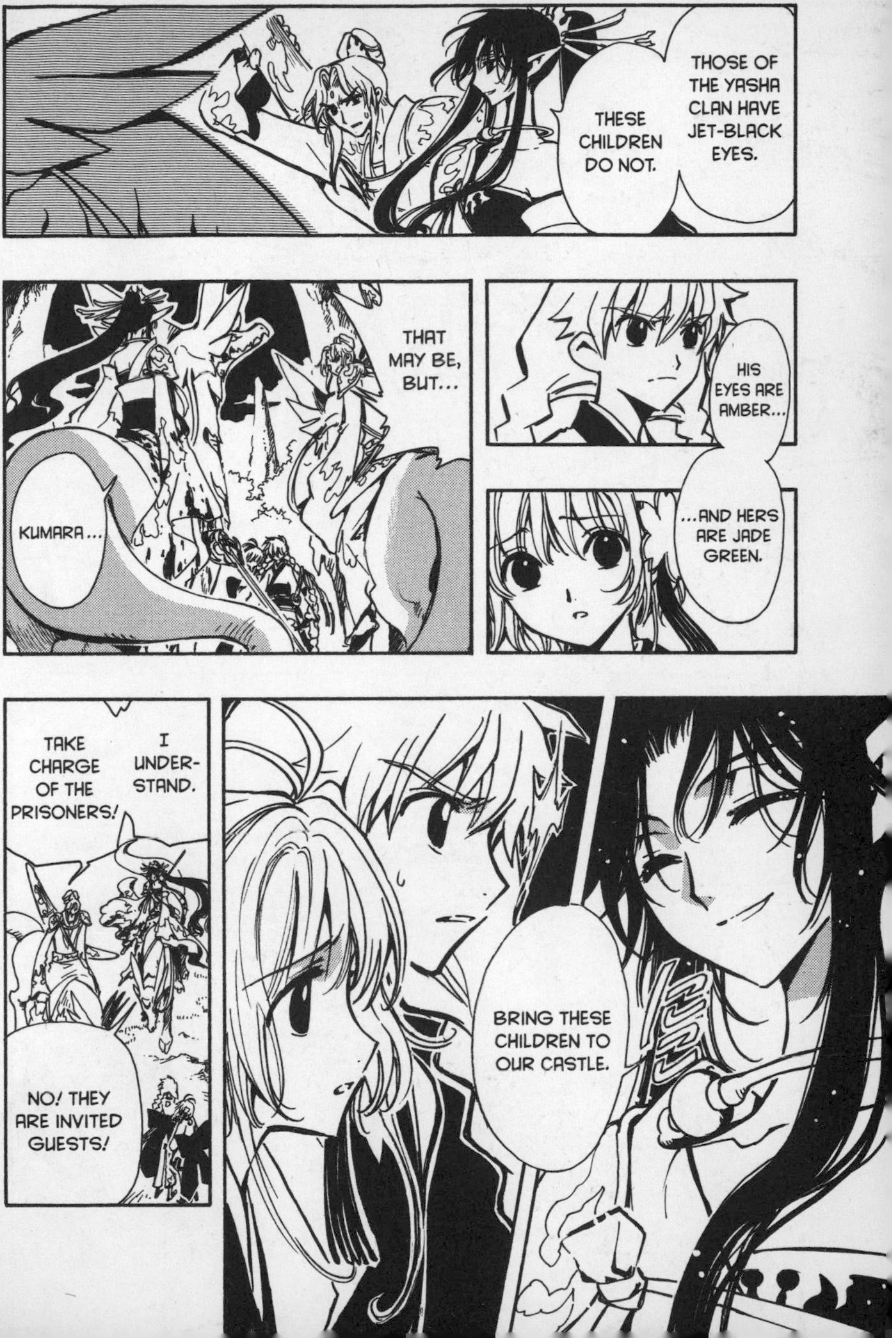
THOSE OF THE YASHA CLAN HAVE JET-BLACK EYES.
THESE CHILDREN DO NOT.
HIS EYES ARE AMBER...
...AND HERS ARE JADE GREEN.
THAT MAY BE, BUT...
KUMARA...
BRING THESE CHILDREN TO OUR CASTLE.
I UNDER-STAND.
TAKE CHARGE OF THE PRISONERS!
NO! THEY ARE INVITED GUESTS!

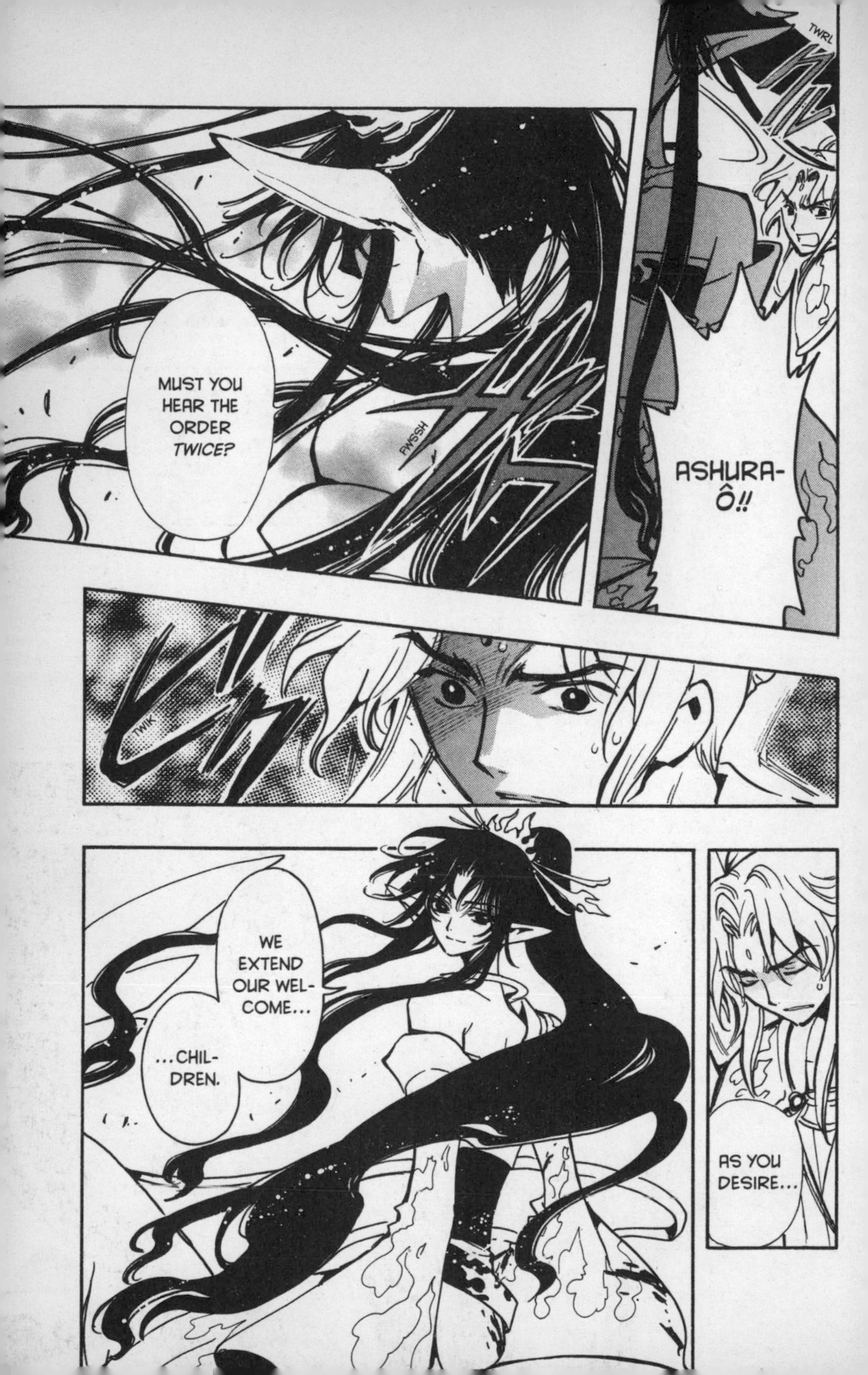
TWRL
ASHURA-Ô!!
MUST YOU HEAR THE ORDER *TWICE?*
FWSSH
TWIK
AS YOU DESIRE...
WE EXTEND OUR WELCOME...
...CHILDREN.

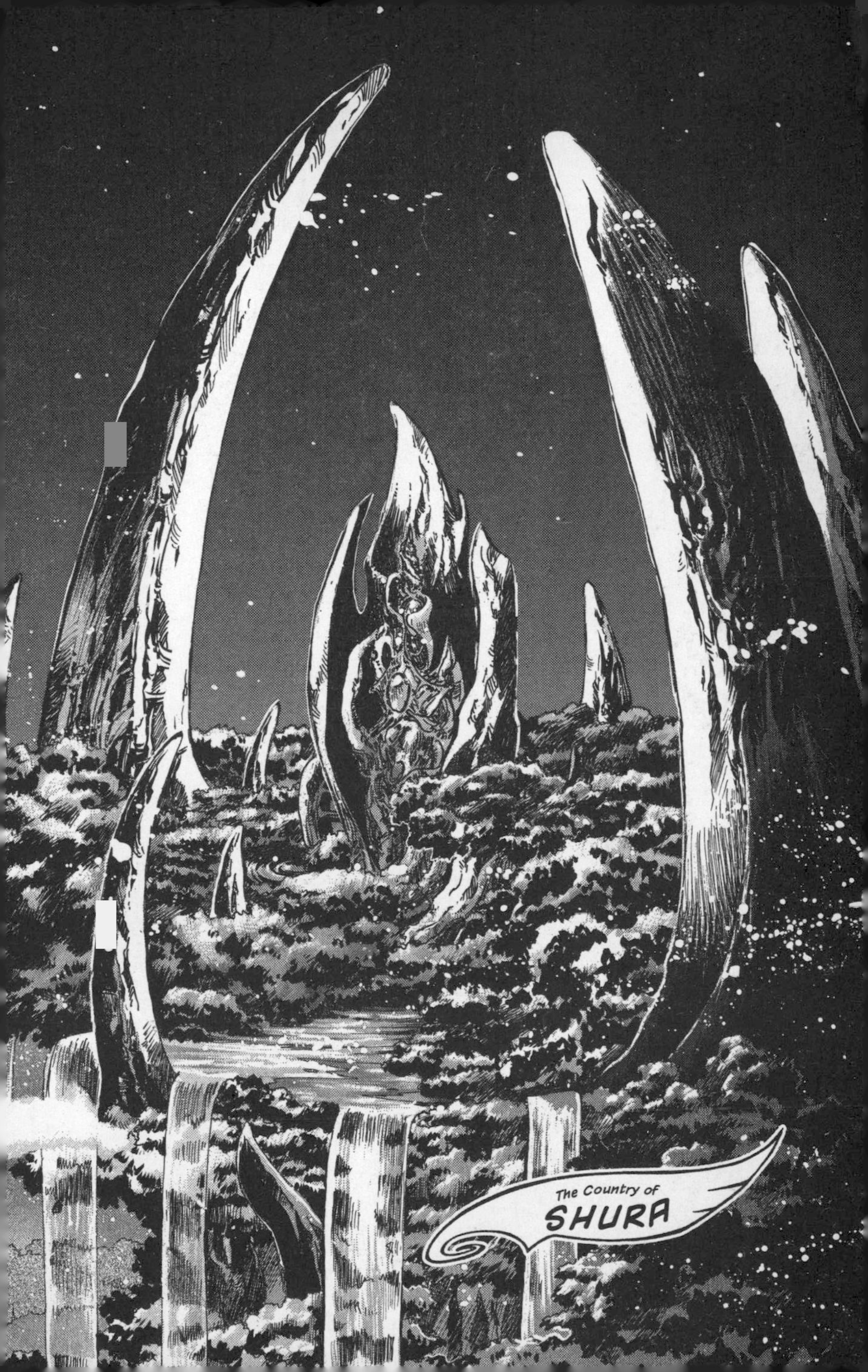
The Country of
SHURA

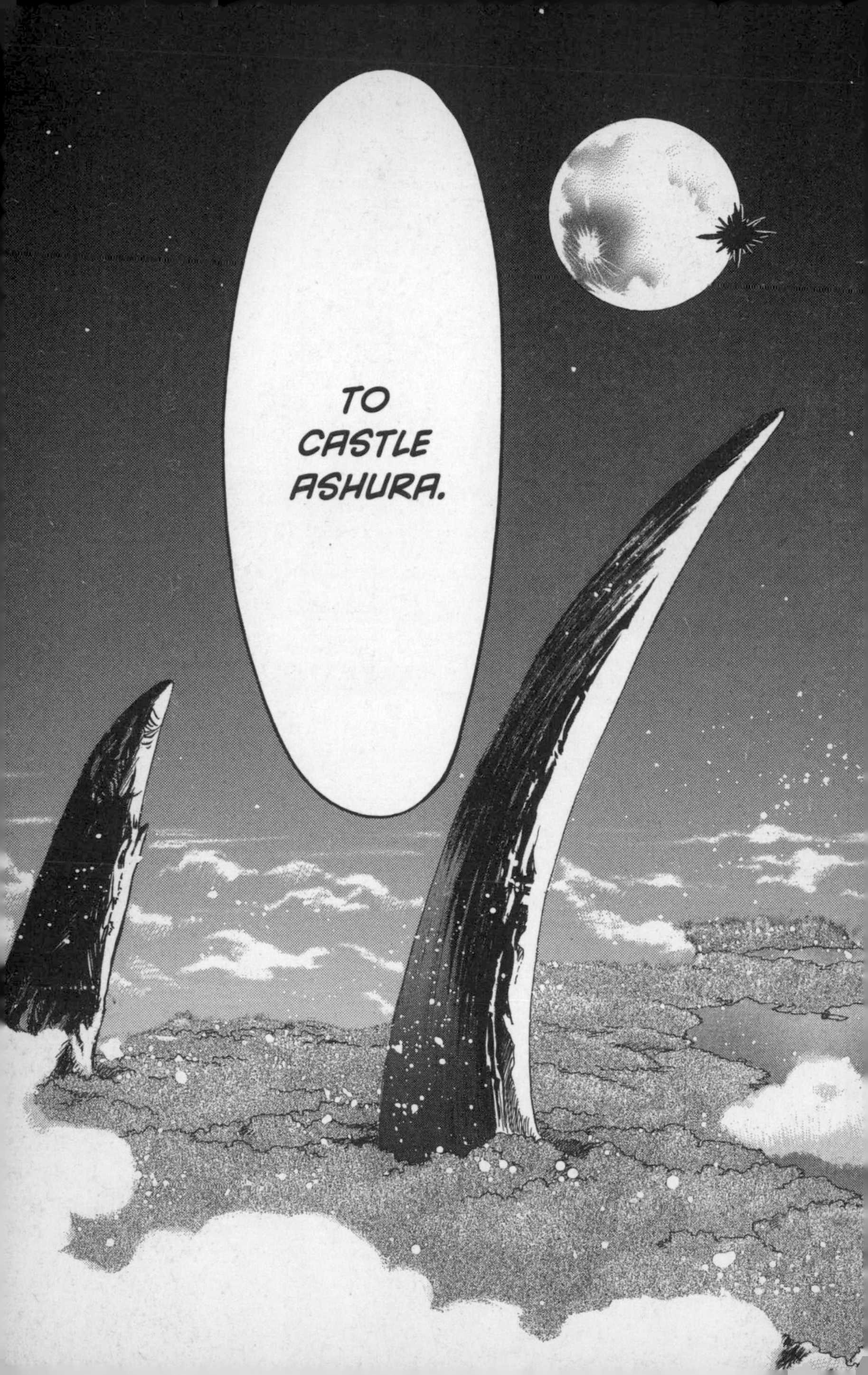
TO CASTLE ASHURA.

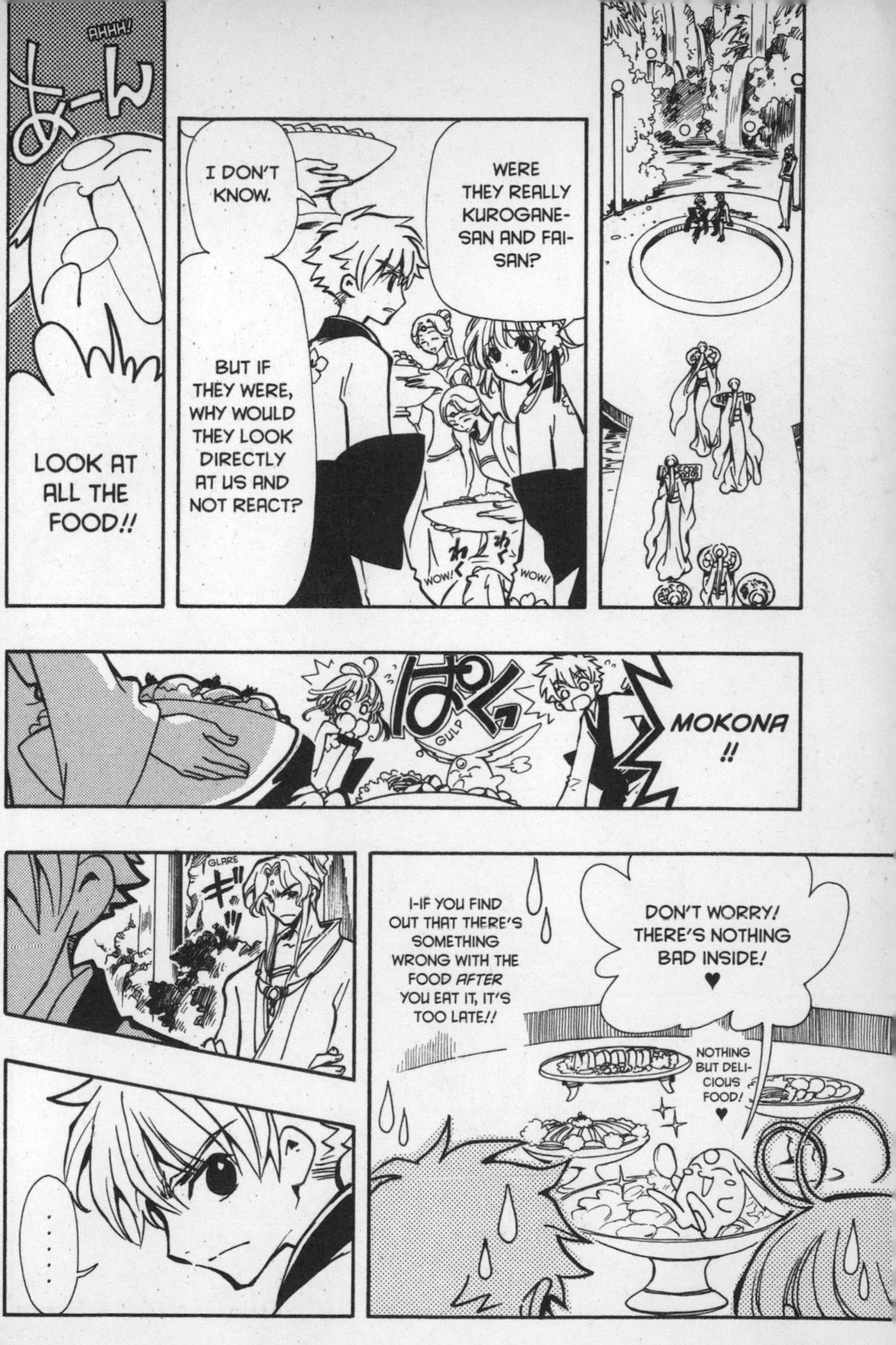
WERE THEY REALLY KUROGANE-SAN AND FAI-SAN?
I DON'T KNOW.
BUT IF THEY WERE, WHY WOULD THEY LOOK DIRECTLY AT US AND NOT REACT?
WOW!
WOW!
AHHH!
あーん
LOOK AT ALL THE FOOD!!
MOKONA!!
ぱく
GULP
DON'T WORRY! THERE'S NOTHING BAD INSIDE! ♥
I-IF YOU FIND OUT THAT THERE'S SOMETHING WRONG WITH THE FOOD AFTER YOU EAT IT, IT'S TOO LATE!!
NOTHING BUT DELICIOUS FOOD! ♥
GLARE
......

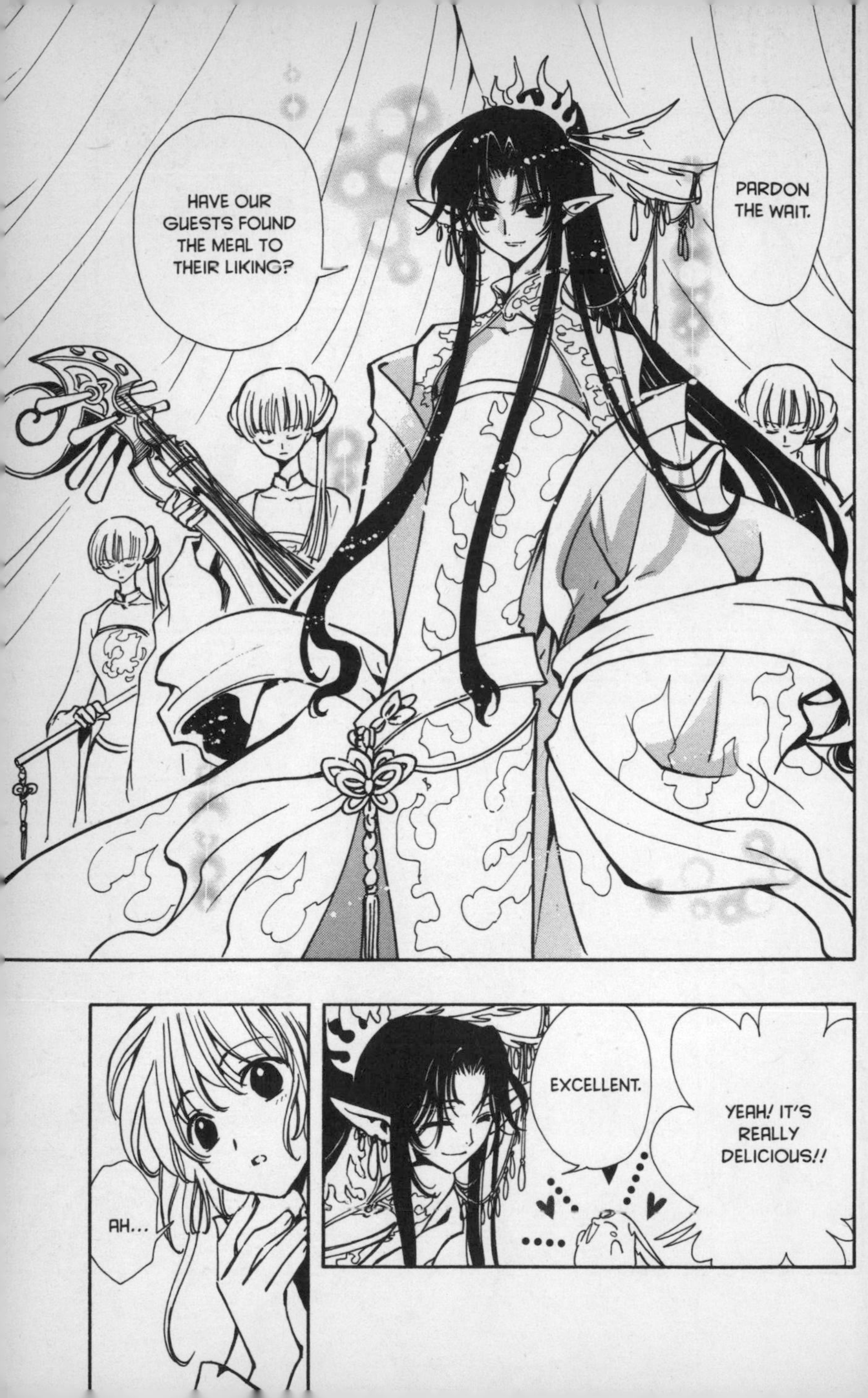
PARDON THE WAIT.
HAVE OUR GUESTS FOUND THE MEAL TO THEIR LIKING?
YEAH! IT'S REALLY DELICIOUS!!
EXCELLENT.
....
AH...

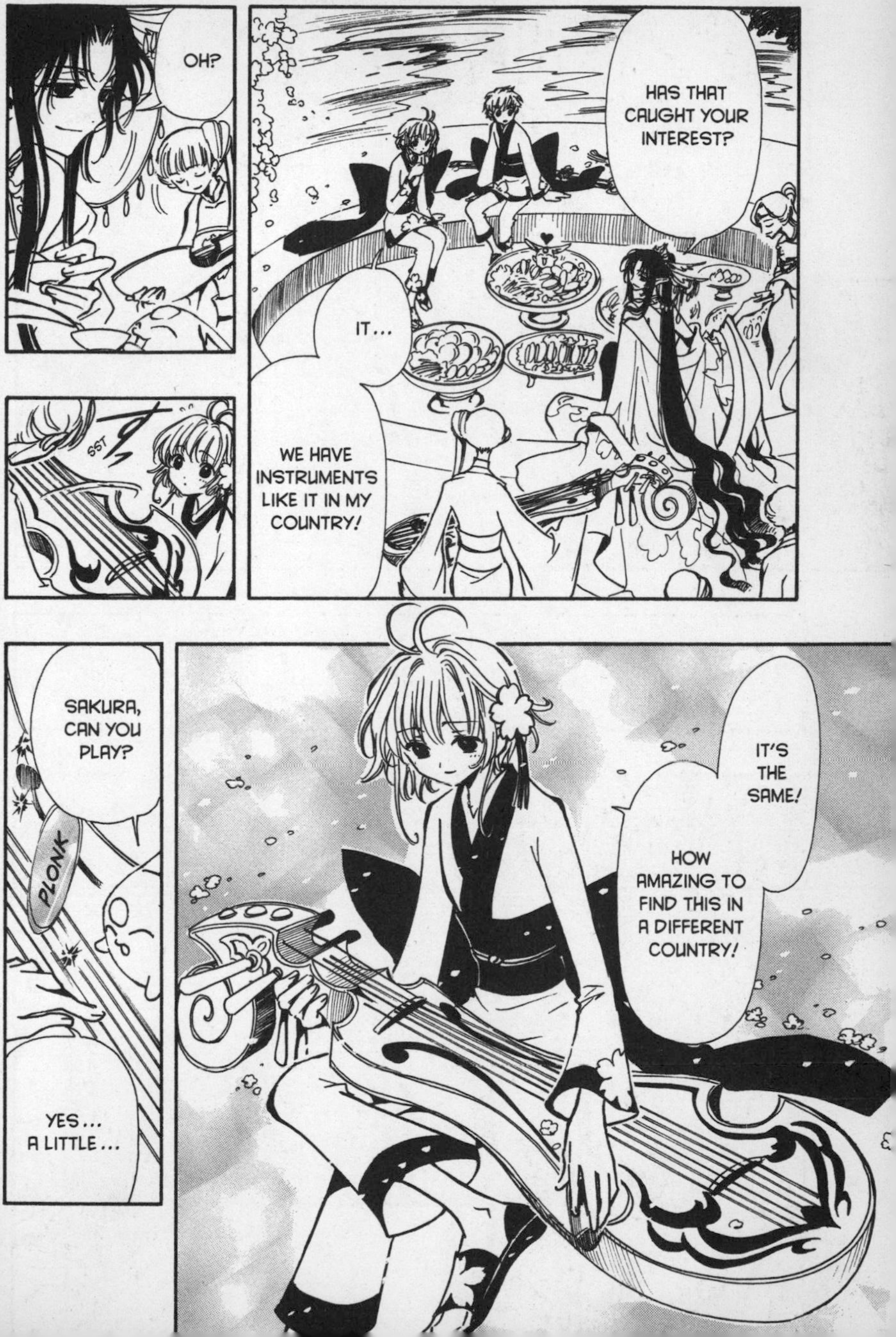
HAS THAT CAUGHT YOUR INTEREST?
IT...
WE HAVE INSTRUMENTS LIKE IT IN MY COUNTRY!
OH?
SST
IT'S THE SAME!
HOW AMAZING TO FIND THIS IN A DIFFERENT COUNTRY!
SAKURA, CAN YOU PLAY?
PLONK
YES... A LITTLE...

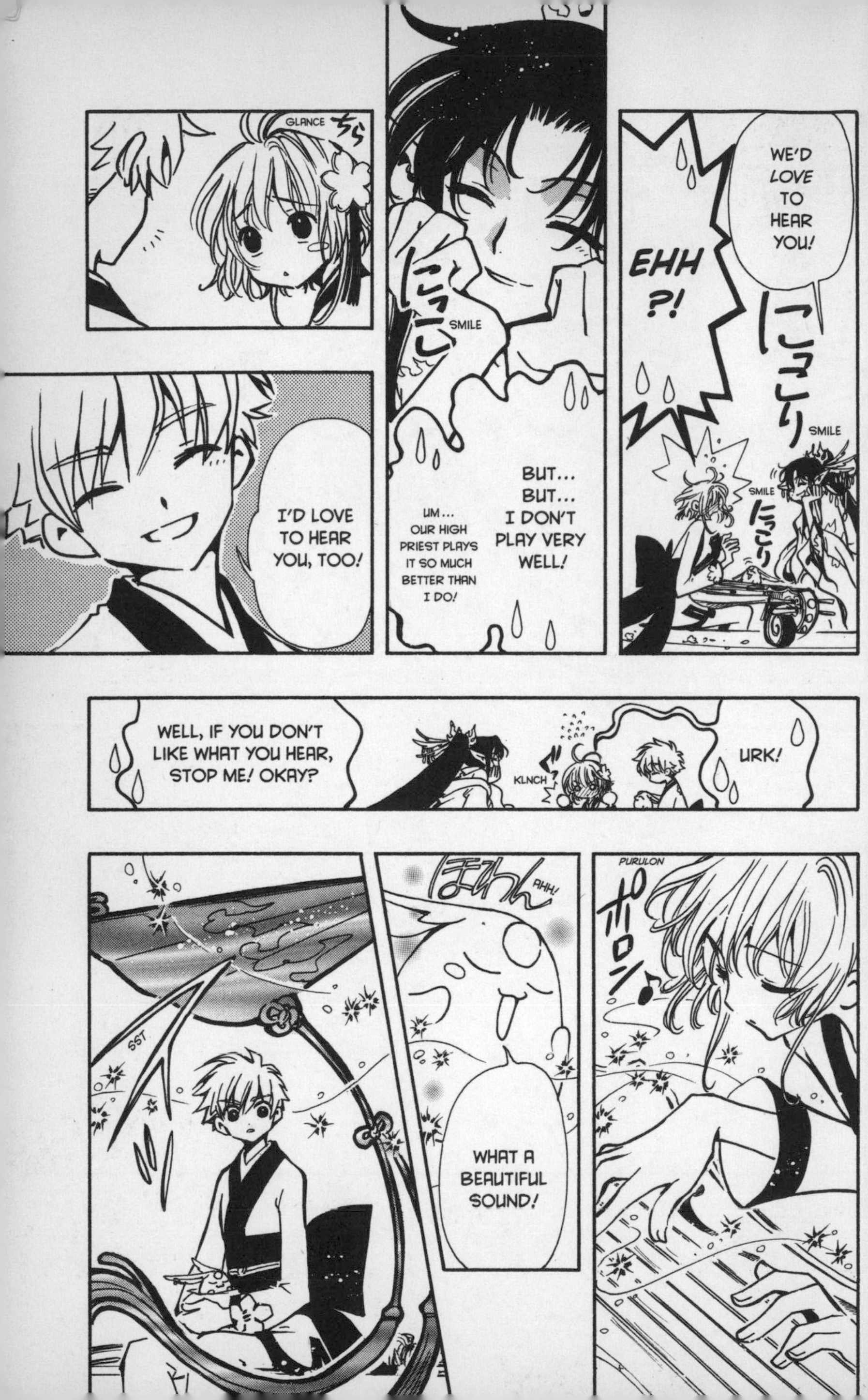
WE'D LOVE TO HEAR YOU!
EHH?!
SMILE
SMILE
SMILE
BUT... BUT... I DON'T PLAY VERY WELL!
UM... OUR HIGH PRIEST PLAYS IT SO MUCH BETTER THAN I DO!
GLANCE
I'D LOVE TO HEAR YOU, TOO!
URK!
KLNCH
WELL, IF YOU DON'T LIKE WHAT YOU HEAR, STOP ME! OKAY?
PURULON
AHH!
WHAT A BEAUTIFUL SOUND!
SST.

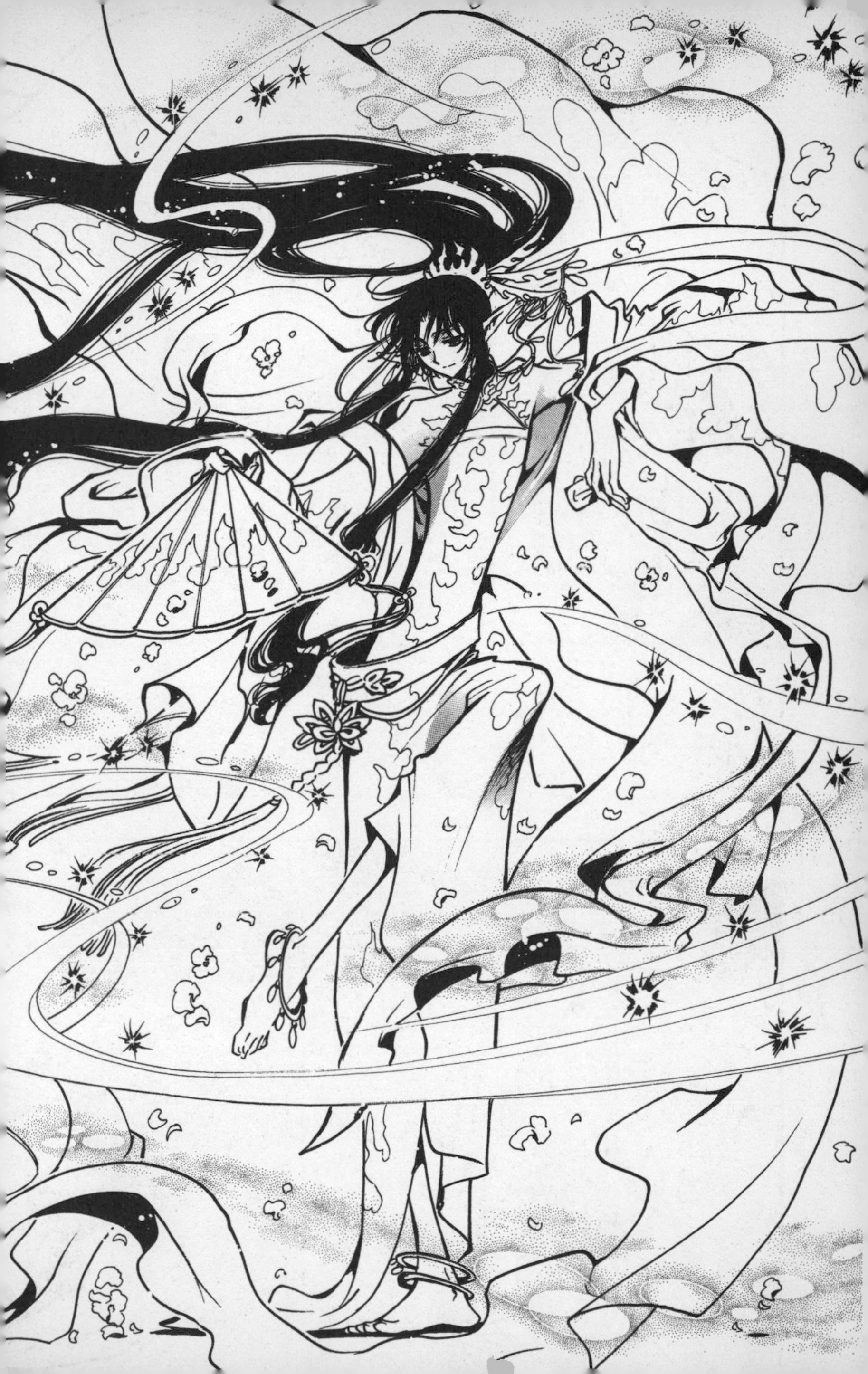

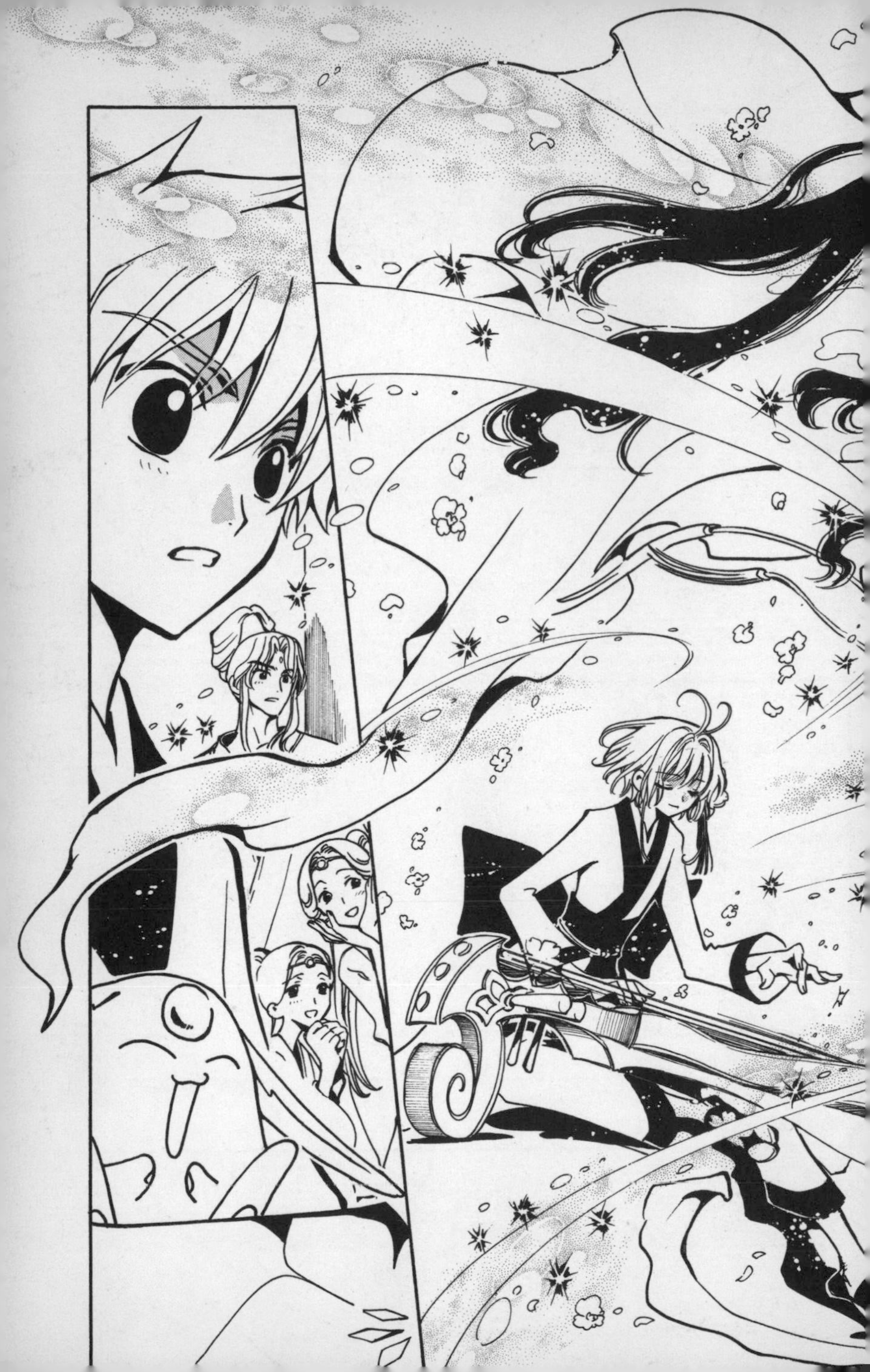

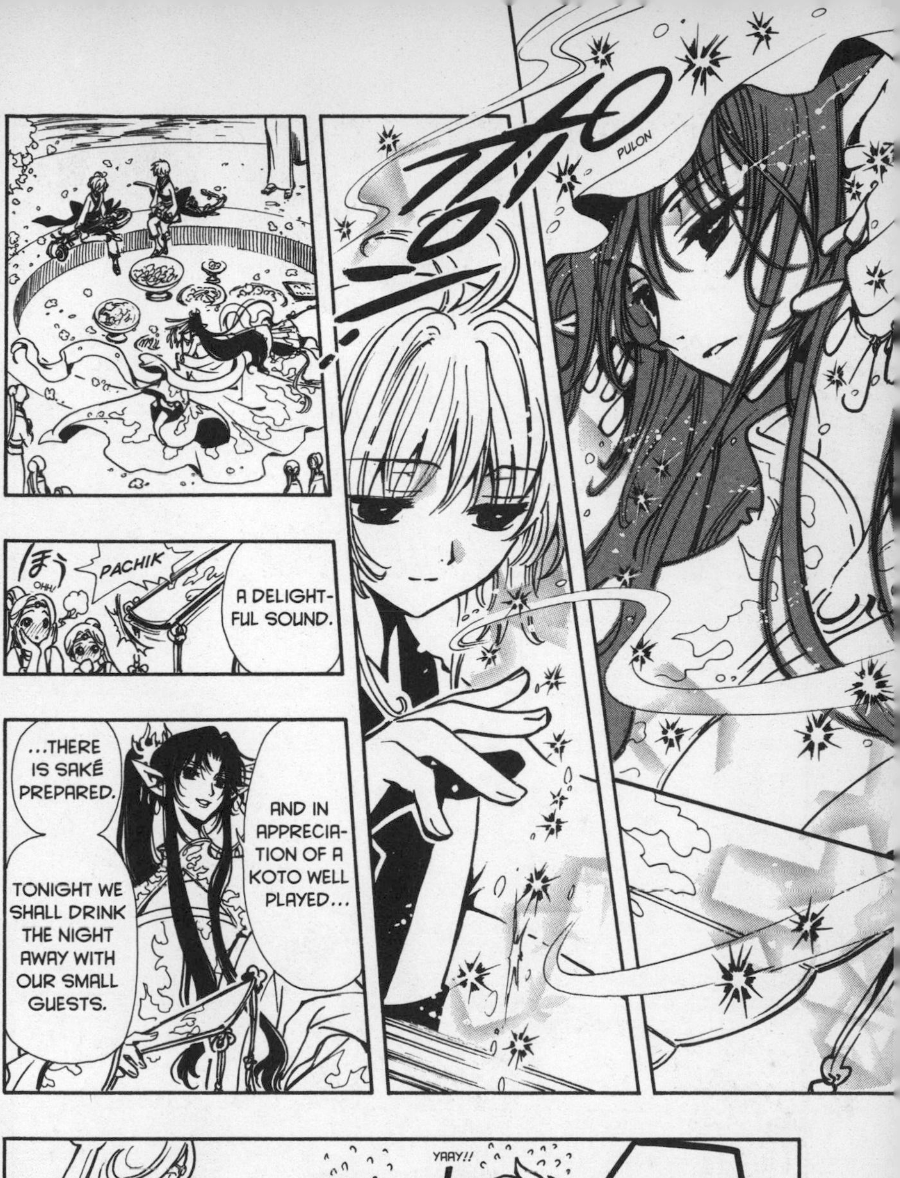
PULON
ほう
OHH!
PACHIK
A DELIGHTFUL SOUND.
AND IN APPRECIATION OF A KOTO WELL PLAYED...
...THERE IS SAKÉ PREPARED.
TONIGHT WE SHALL DRINK THE NIGHT AWAY WITH OUR SMALL GUESTS.
EHH?!
わーい
YAAY!!

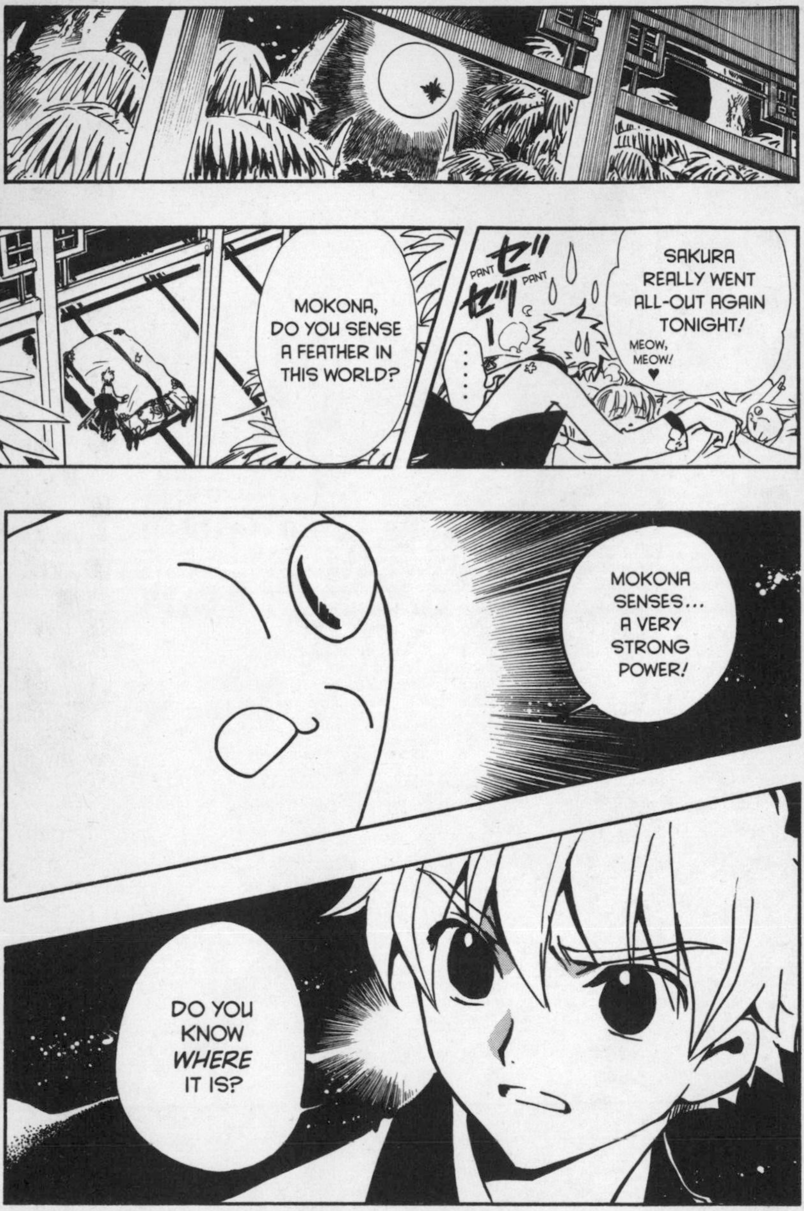
SAKURA REALLY WENT ALL-OUT AGAIN TONIGHT!
MEOW, MEOW! ♥
PANT ゼ PANT
ゼ
......
MOKONA, DO YOU SENSE A FEATHER IN THIS WORLD?
MOKONA SENSES... A VERY STRONG POWER!
DO YOU KNOW *WHERE* IT IS?

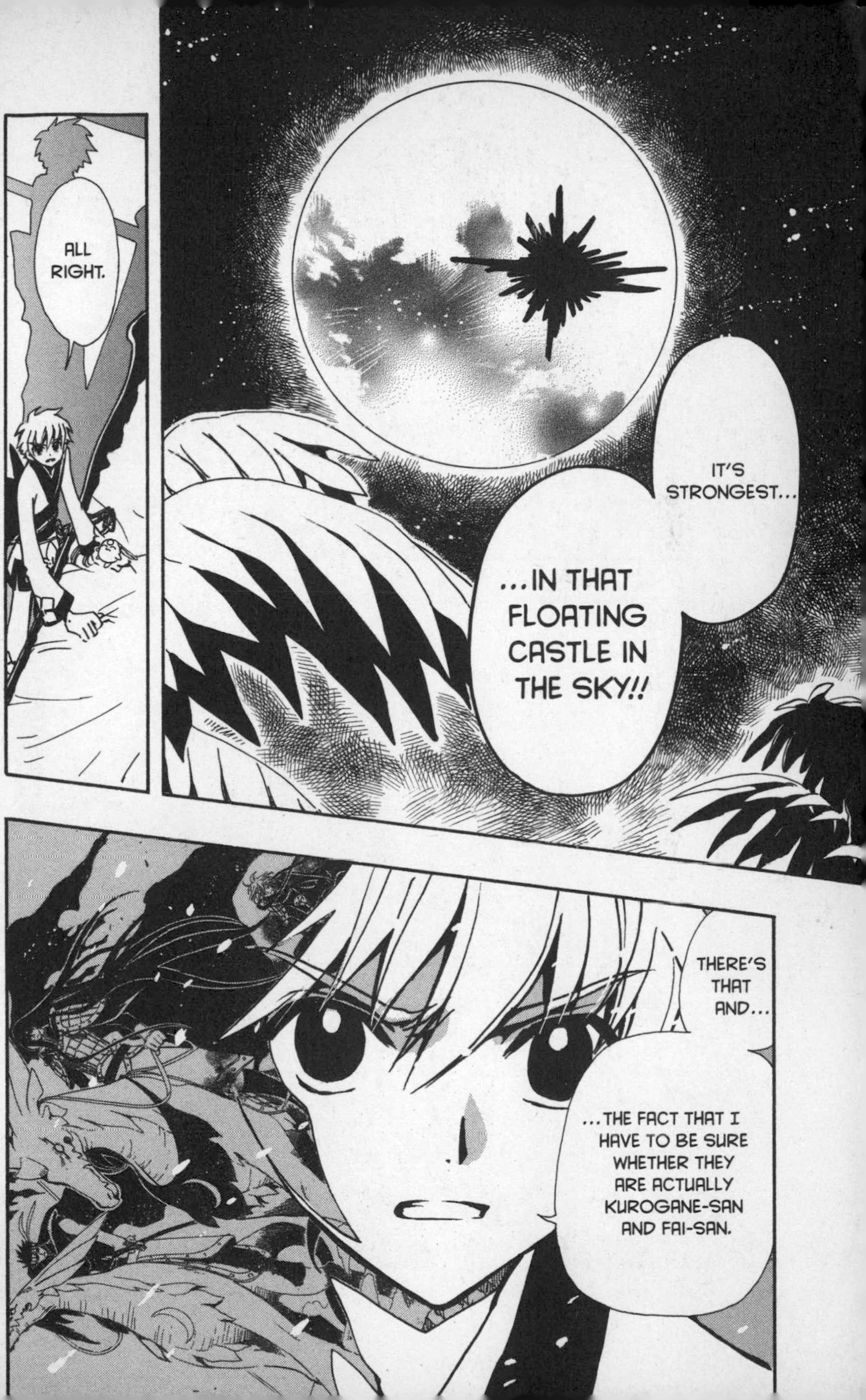
IT'S STRONGEST...
...IN THAT FLOATING CASTLE IN THE SKY!!
ALL RIGHT.
THERE'S THAT AND...
...THE FACT THAT I HAVE TO BE SURE WHETHER THEY ARE ACTUALLY KUROGANE-SAN AND FAI-SAN.

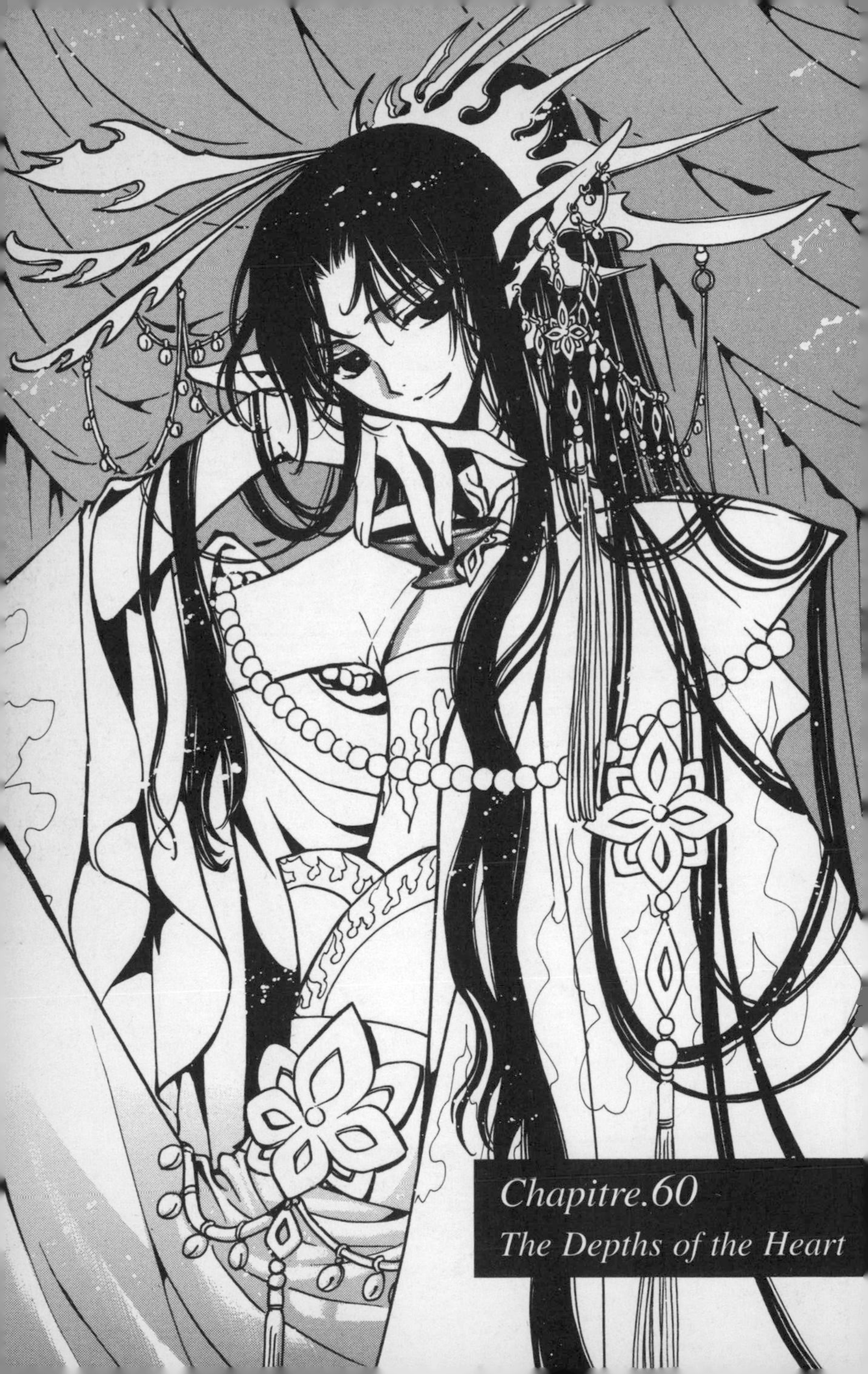
Chapitre.60
The Depths of the Heart

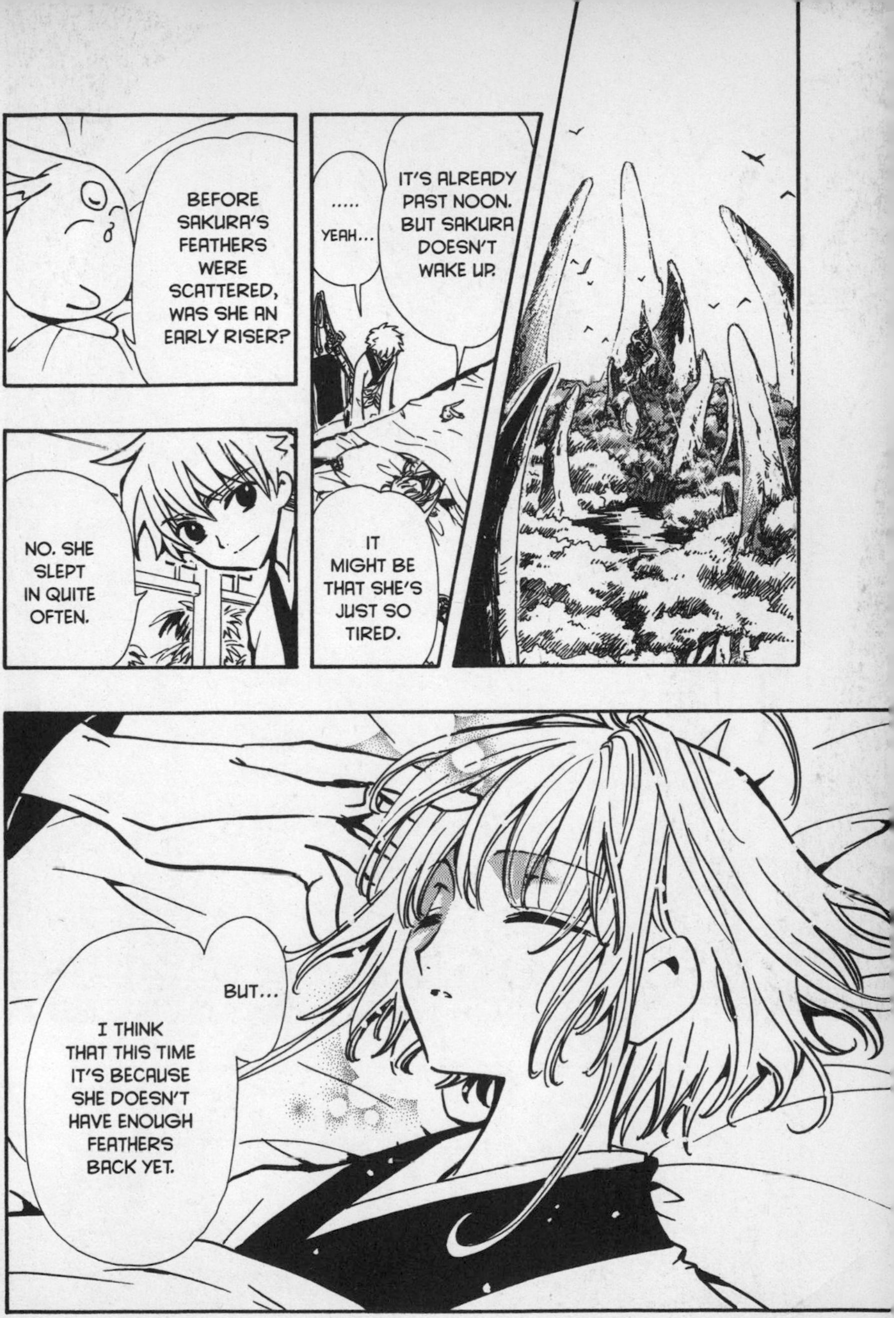
IT'S ALREADY PAST NOON. BUT SAKURA DOESN'T WAKE UP.
..... YEAH...
IT MIGHT BE THAT SHE'S JUST SO TIRED.
BEFORE SAKURA'S FEATHERS WERE SCATTERED, WAS SHE AN EARLY RISER?
NO. SHE SLEPT IN QUITE OFTEN.
BUT...
I THINK THAT THIS TIME IT'S BECAUSE SHE DOESN'T HAVE ENOUGH FEATHERS BACK YET.

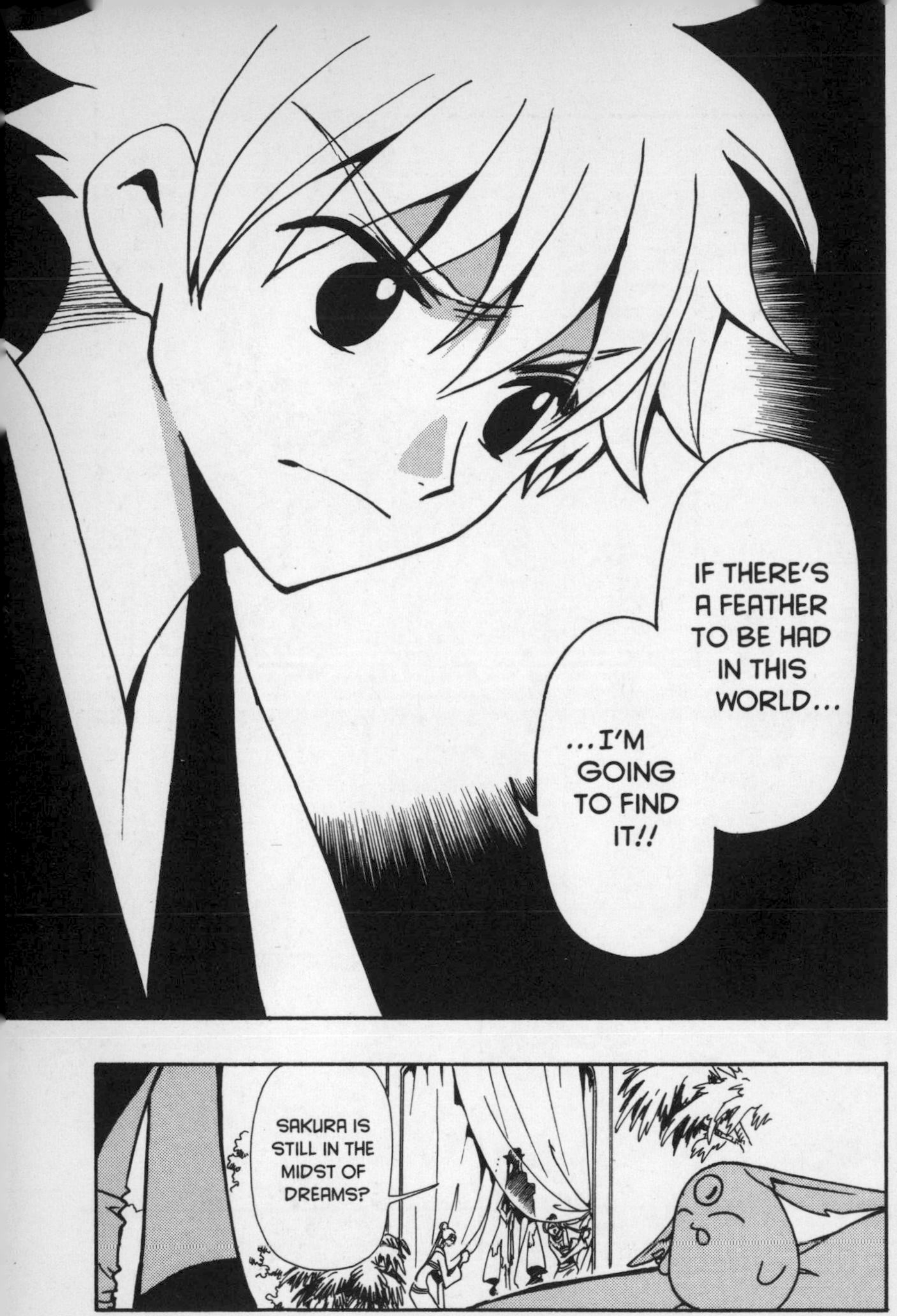
IF THERE'S A FEATHER TO BE HAD IN THIS WORLD...
...I'M GOING TO FIND IT!!
SAKURA IS STILL IN THE MIDST OF DREAMS?

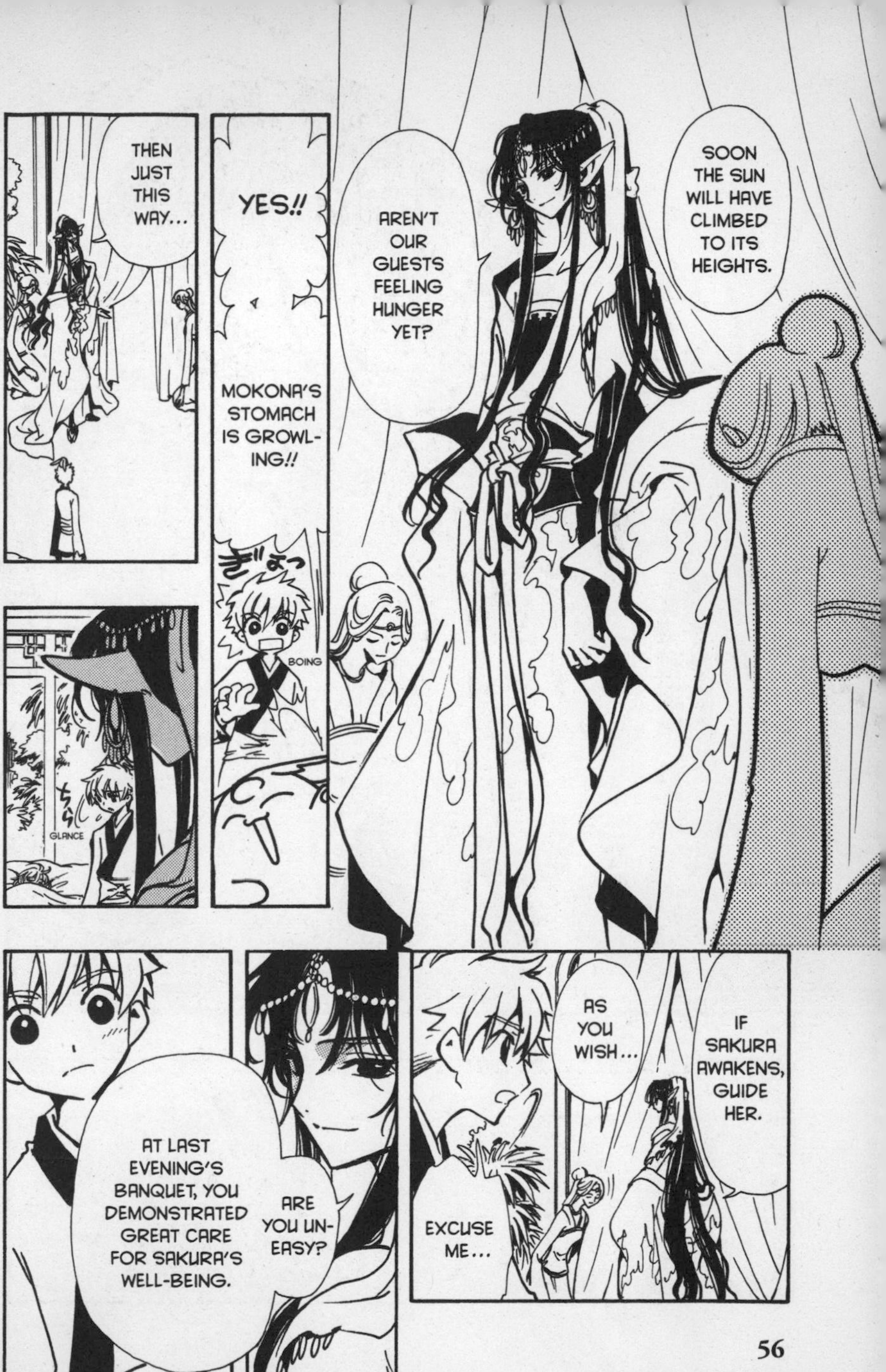
SOON THE SUN WILL HAVE CLIMBED TO ITS HEIGHTS.
AREN'T OUR GUESTS FEELING HUNGER YET?
YES!!
MOKONA'S STOMACH IS GROWL-ING!!
ぎょっ
BOING
THEN JUST THIS WAY...
ちら
GLANCE
IF SAKURA AWAKENS, GUIDE HER.
AS YOU WISH...
EXCUSE ME...
AT LAST EVENING'S BANQUET, YOU DEMONSTRATED GREAT CARE FOR SAKURA'S WELL-BEING.
ARE YOU UN-EASY?

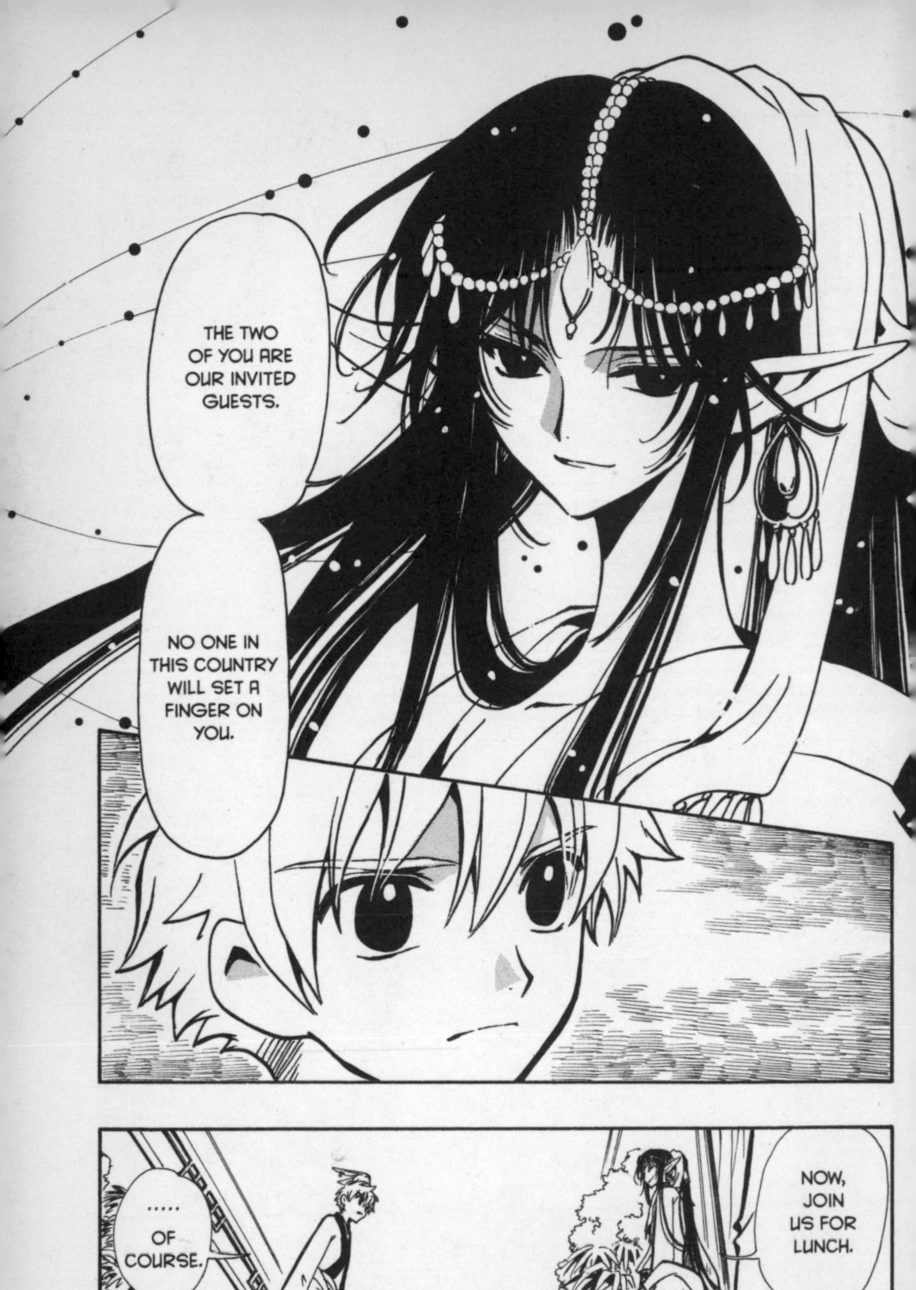
THE TWO OF YOU ARE OUR INVITED GUESTS.
NO ONE IN THIS COUNTRY WILL SET A FINGER ON YOU.
NOW, JOIN US FOR LUNCH.
..... OF COURSE.

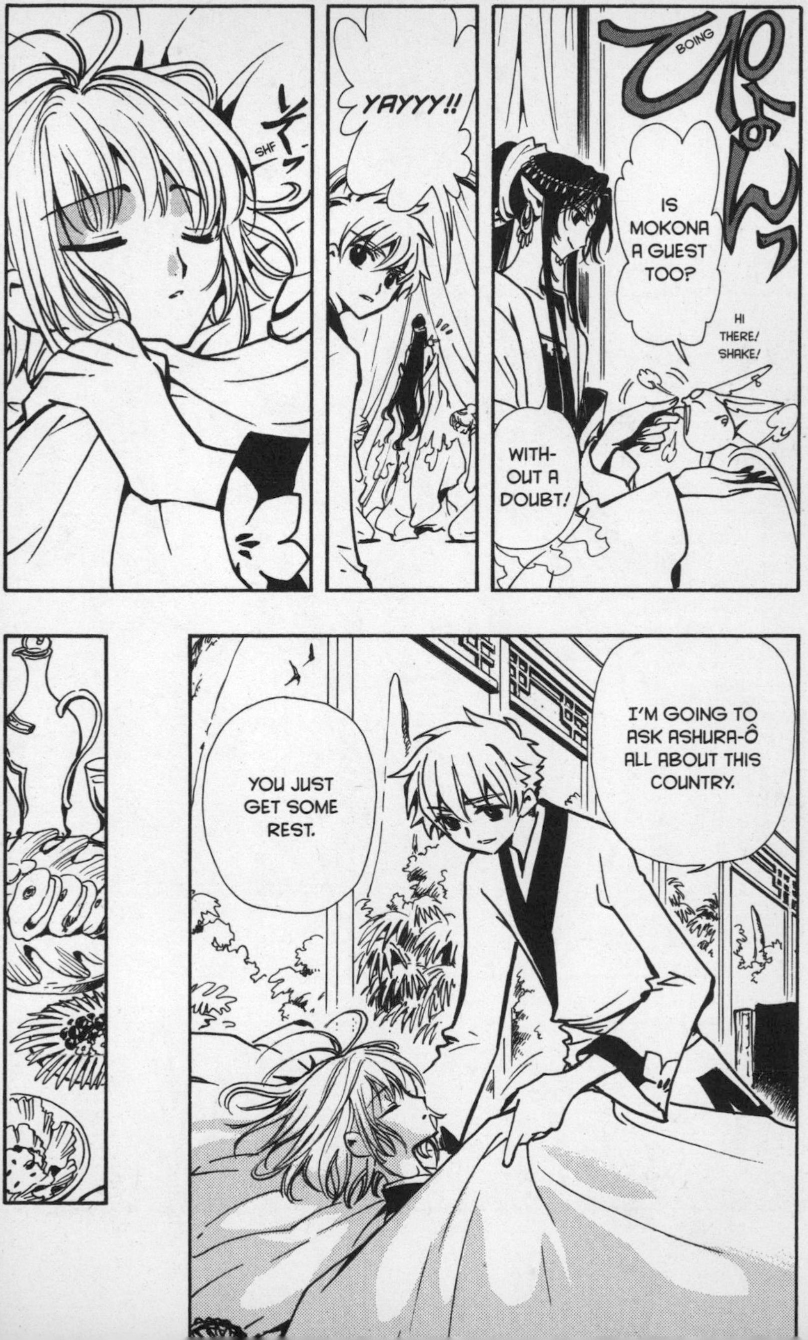
BOING
IS MOKONA A GUEST TOO?
HI THERE! SHAKE!
WITH-OUT A DOUBT!
YAYYY!!
SHF
I'M GOING TO ASK ASHURA-Ô ALL ABOUT THIS COUNTRY.
YOU JUST GET SOME REST.

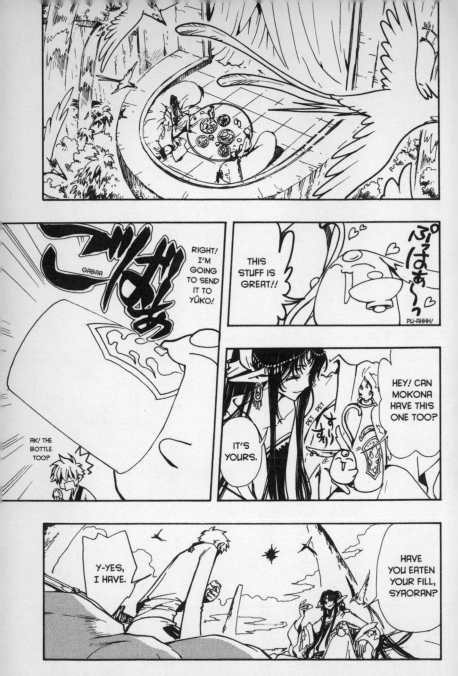

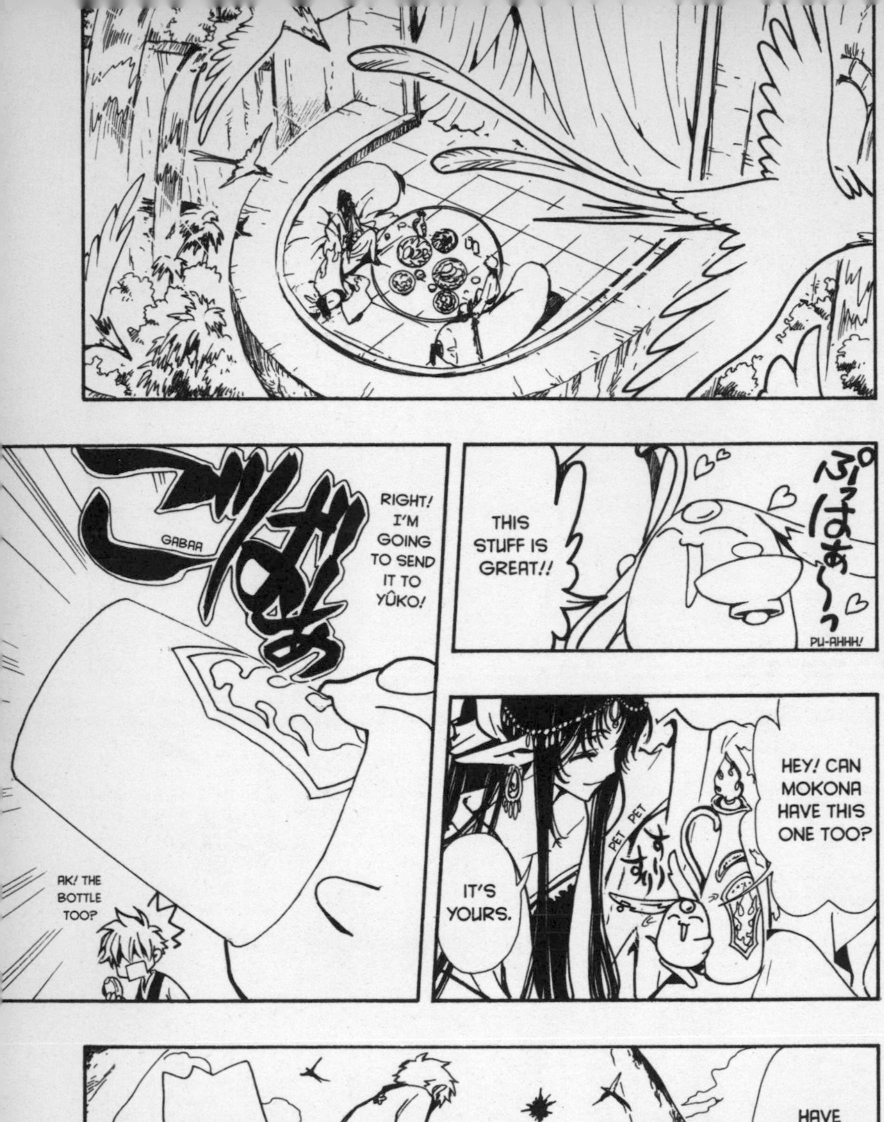
ぷはぁ~っ
PU-AHHH!
THIS STUFF IS GREAT!!
HEY! CAN MOKONA HAVE THIS ONE TOO?
PET PET
IT'S YOURS.
RIGHT! I'M GOING TO SEND IT TO YÛKO!
GABAA
AK! THE BOTTLE TOO?
HAVE YOU EATEN YOUR FILL, SYAORAN?
Y-YES, I HAVE.

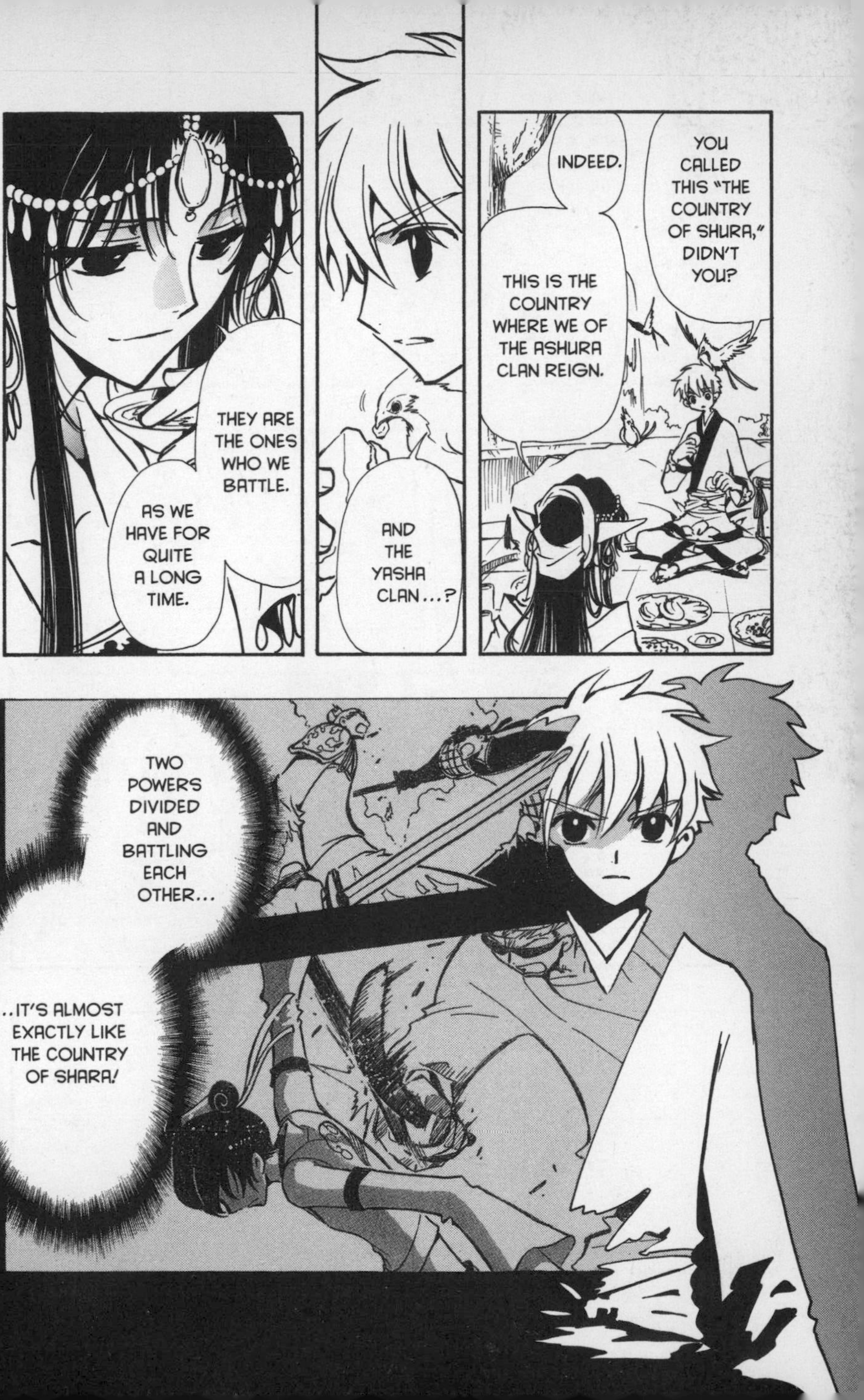
YOU CALLED THIS "THE COUNTRY OF SHURA," DIDN'T YOU?
INDEED.
THIS IS THE COUNTRY WHERE WE OF THE ASHURA CLAN REIGN.
AND THE YASHA CLAN...?
THEY ARE THE ONES WHO WE BATTLE.
AS WE HAVE FOR QUITE A LONG TIME.
TWO POWERS DIVIDED AND BATTLING EACH OTHER...
...IT'S ALMOST EXACTLY LIKE THE COUNTRY OF SHARA!

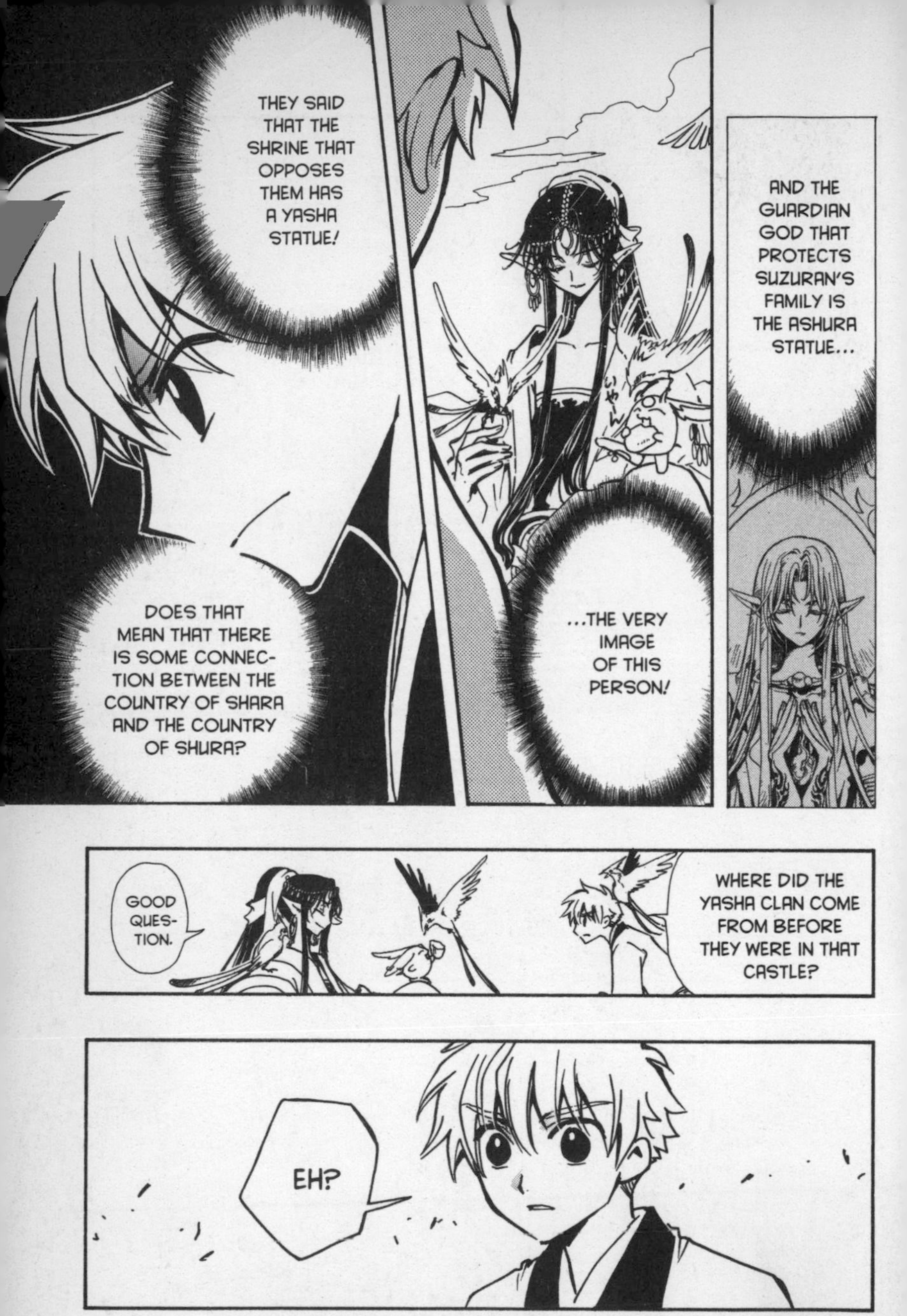
AND THE GUARDIAN GOD THAT PROTECTS SUZURAN'S FAMILY IS THE ASHURA STATUE...
...THE VERY IMAGE OF THIS PERSON!
THEY SAID THAT THE SHRINE THAT OPPOSES THEM HAS A YASHA STATUE!
DOES THAT MEAN THAT THERE IS SOME CONNECTION BETWEEN THE COUNTRY OF SHARA AND THE COUNTRY OF SHURA?
WHERE DID THE YASHA CLAN COME FROM BEFORE THEY WERE IN THAT CASTLE?
GOOD QUESTION.
EH?

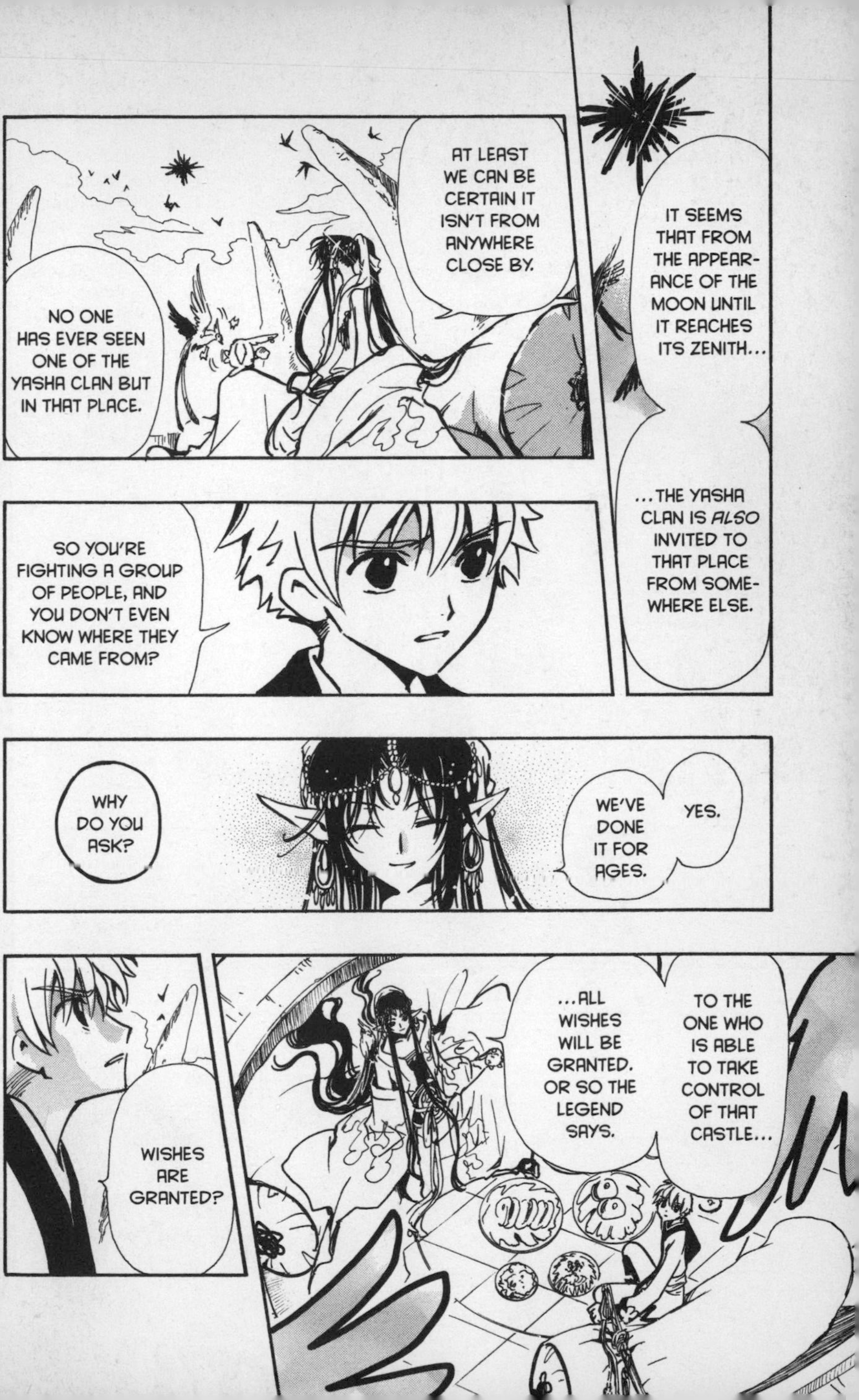
IT SEEMS THAT FROM THE APPEARANCE OF THE MOON UNTIL IT REACHES ITS ZENITH...
...THE YASHA CLAN IS *ALSO* INVITED TO THAT PLACE FROM SOMEWHERE ELSE.
AT LEAST WE CAN BE CERTAIN IT ISN'T FROM ANYWHERE CLOSE BY.
NO ONE HAS EVER SEEN ONE OF THE YASHA CLAN BUT IN THAT PLACE.
SO YOU'RE FIGHTING A GROUP OF PEOPLE, AND YOU DON'T EVEN KNOW WHERE THEY CAME FROM?
YES.
WE'VE DONE IT FOR AGES.
WHY DO YOU ASK?
TO THE ONE WHO IS ABLE TO TAKE CONTROL OF THAT CASTLE...
...ALL WISHES WILL BE GRANTED. OR SO THE LEGEND SAYS.
WISHES ARE GRANTED?

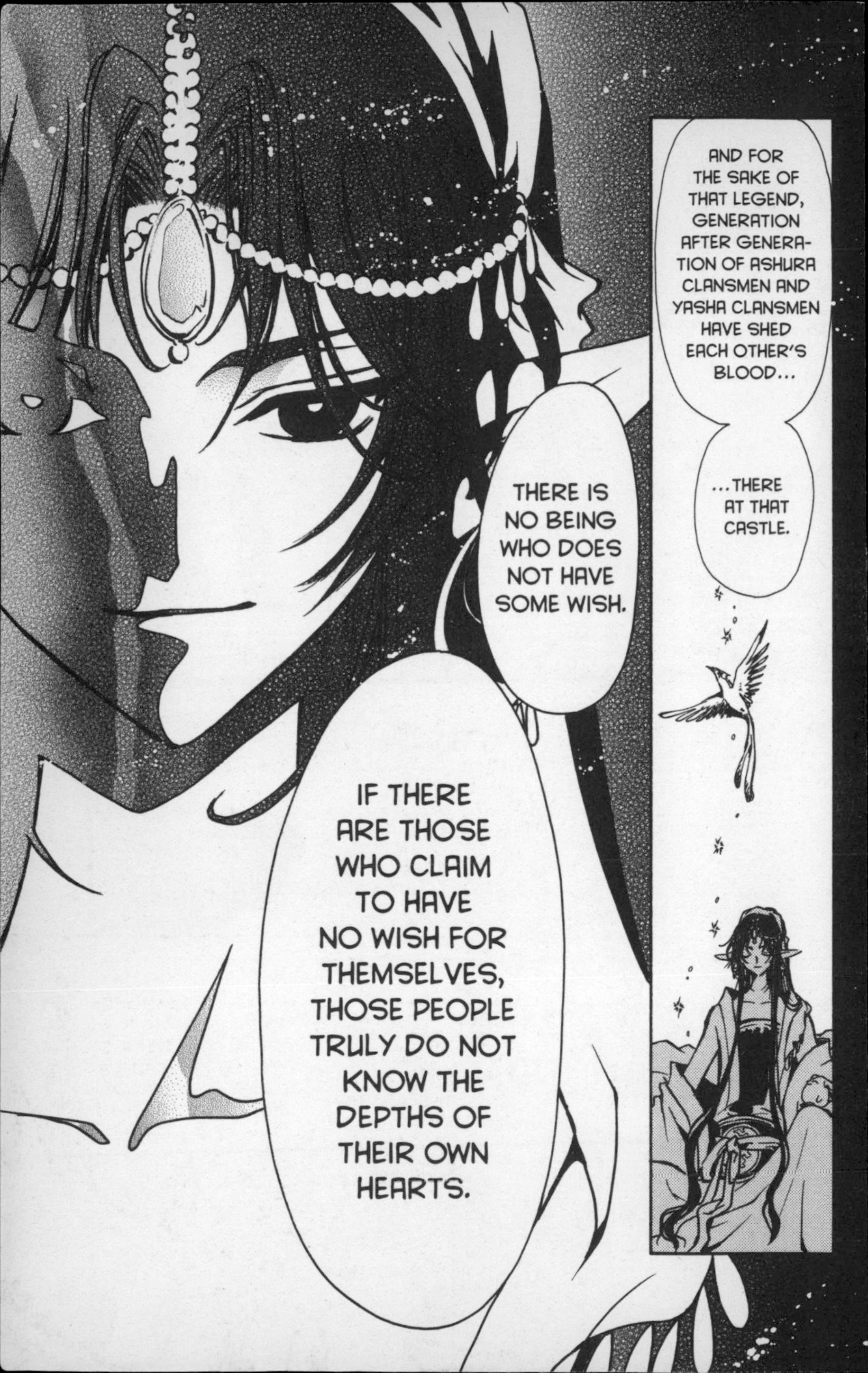
AND FOR THE SAKE OF THAT LEGEND, GENERATION AFTER GENERATION OF ASHURA CLANSMEN AND YASHA CLANSMEN HAVE SHED EACH OTHER'S BLOOD...
...THERE AT THAT CASTLE.
THERE IS NO BEING WHO DOES NOT HAVE SOME WISH.
IF THERE ARE THOSE WHO CLAIM TO HAVE NO WISH FOR THEMSELVES, THOSE PEOPLE TRULY DO NOT KNOW THE DEPTHS OF THEIR OWN HEARTS.

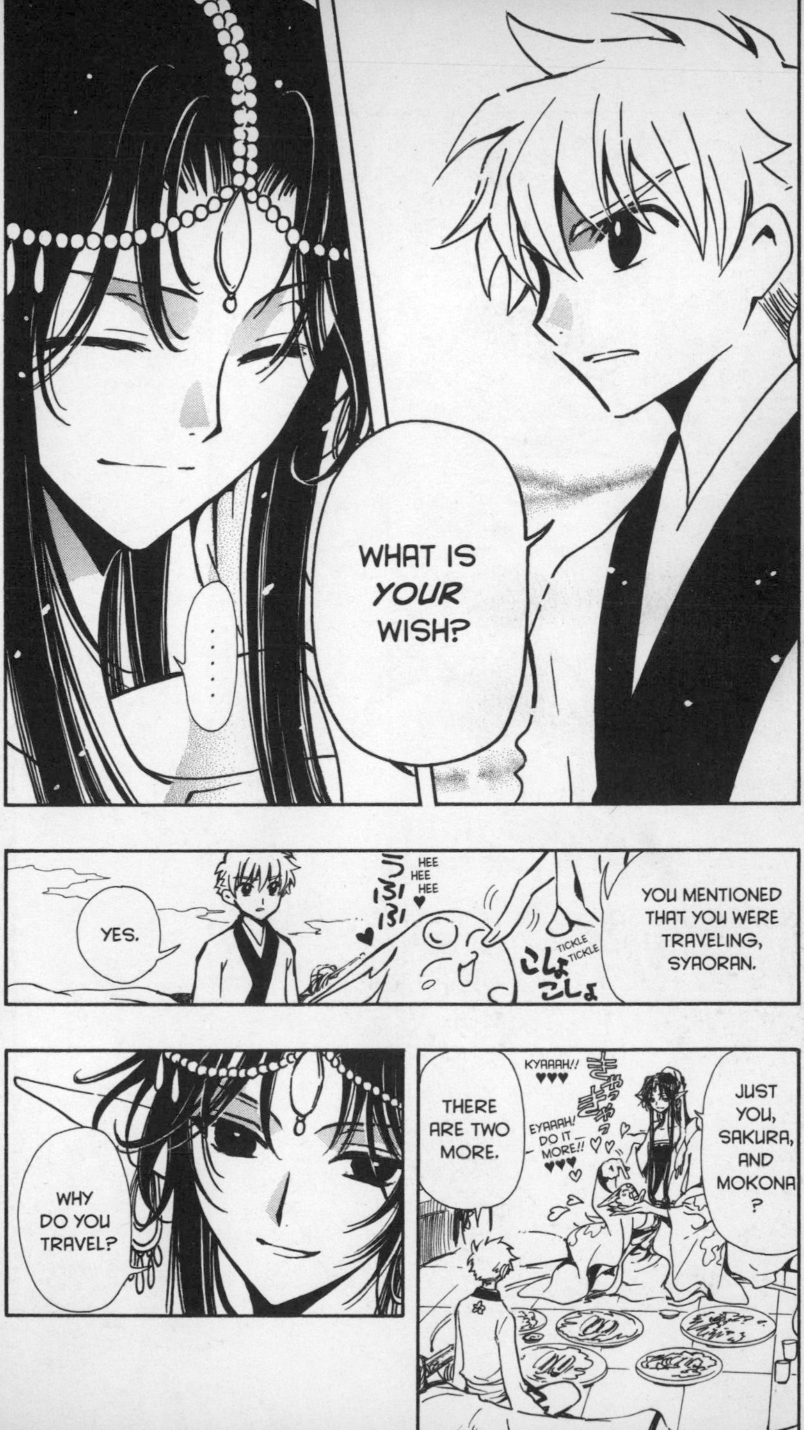
WHAT IS *YOUR* WISH?
......
YOU MENTIONED THAT YOU WERE TRAVELING, SYAORAN.
TICKLE TICKLE
こしょこしょ
HEE HEE HEE ♥
うふふ
YES.
JUST YOU, SAKURA, AND MOKONA?
KYAAAH!! ♥♥♥
EYAAAH! DO IT MORE!! ♥♥♥
THERE ARE TWO MORE.
WHY DO YOU TRAVEL?

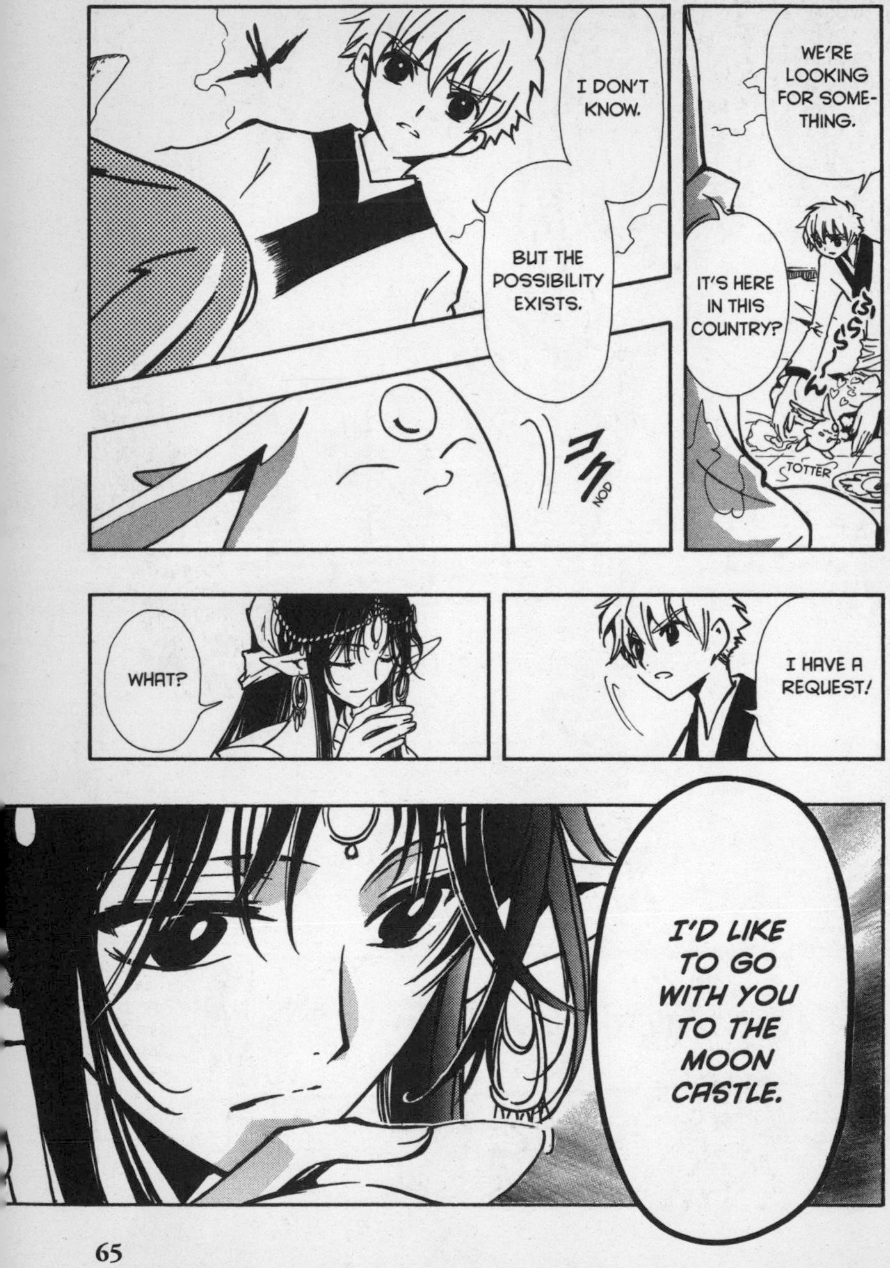
WE'RE LOOKING FOR SOME-THING.
IT'S HERE IN THIS COUNTRY?
TOTTER
I DON'T KNOW.
BUT THE POSSIBILITY EXISTS.
NOD
I HAVE A REQUEST!
WHAT?
I'D LIKE TO GO WITH YOU TO THE MOON CASTLE.

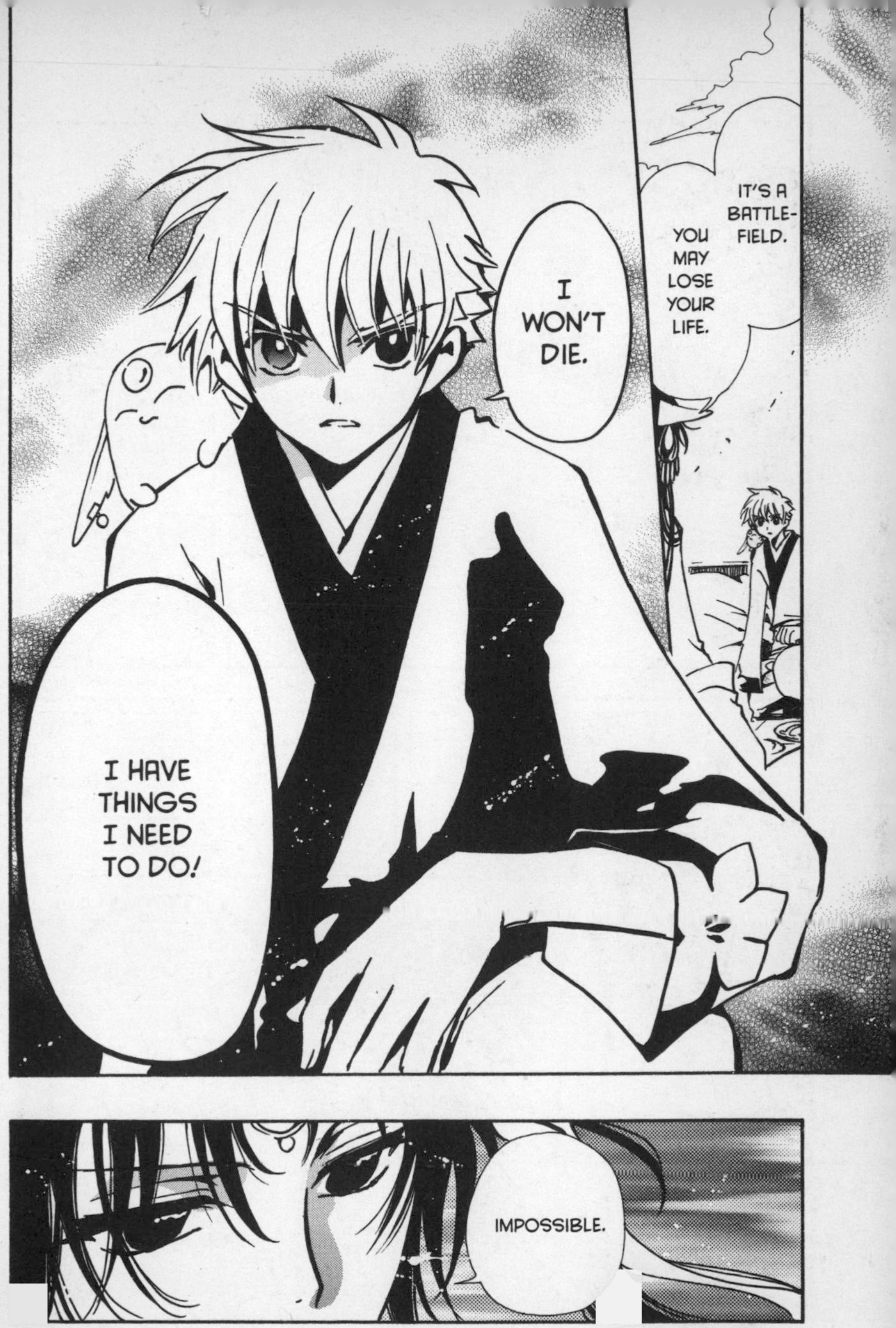
IT'S A BATTLE-FIELD.
YOU MAY LOSE YOUR LIFE.
I WON'T DIE.
I HAVE THINGS I NEED TO DO!
IMPOSSIBLE.

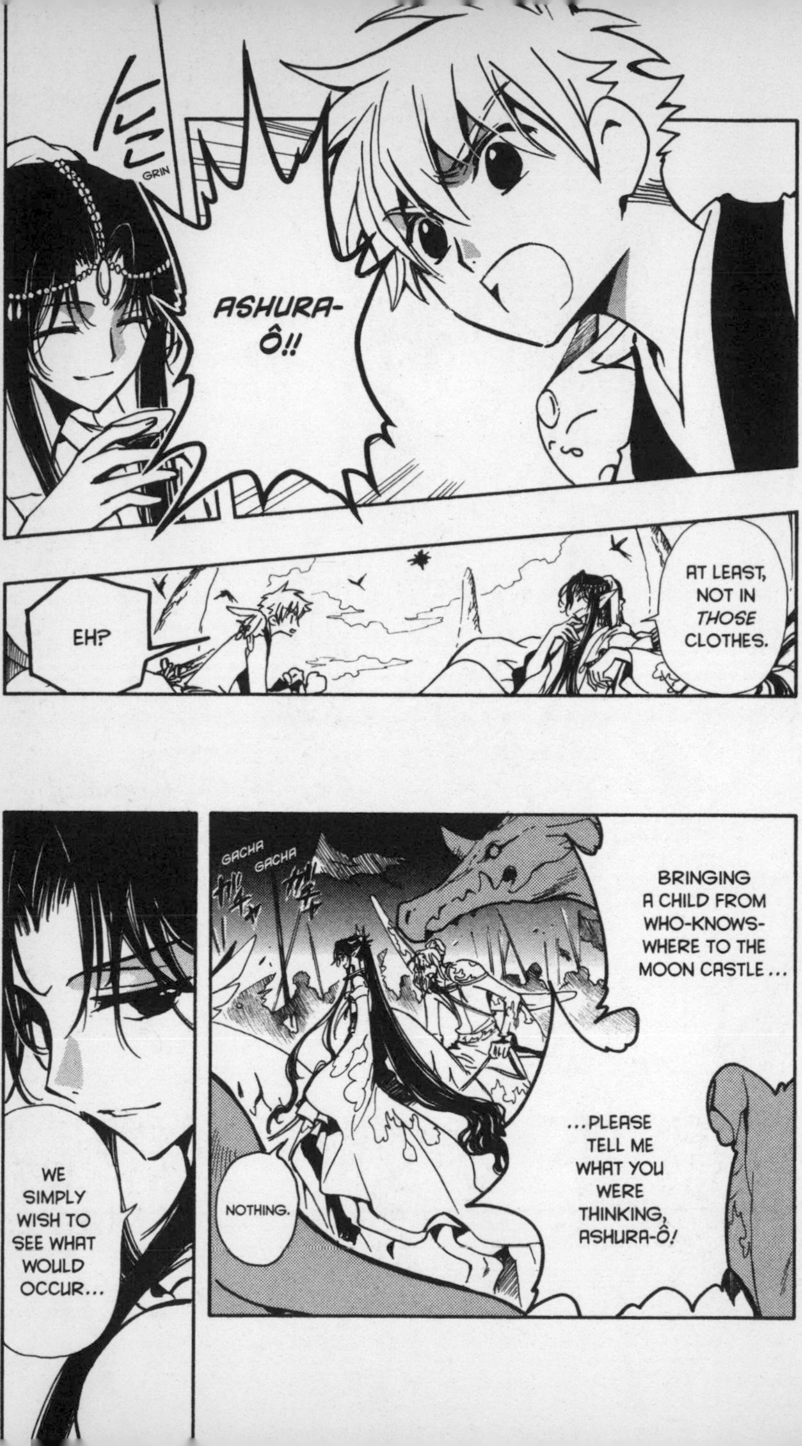
GRIN
ASHURA-Ô!!
AT LEAST, NOT IN *THOSE* CLOTHES.
EH?
GACHA GACHA
BRINGING A CHILD FROM WHO-KNOWS-WHERE TO THE MOON CASTLE...
...PLEASE TELL ME WHAT YOU WERE THINKING, ASHURA-Ô!
NOTHING.
WE SIMPLY WISH TO SEE WHAT WOULD OCCUR...

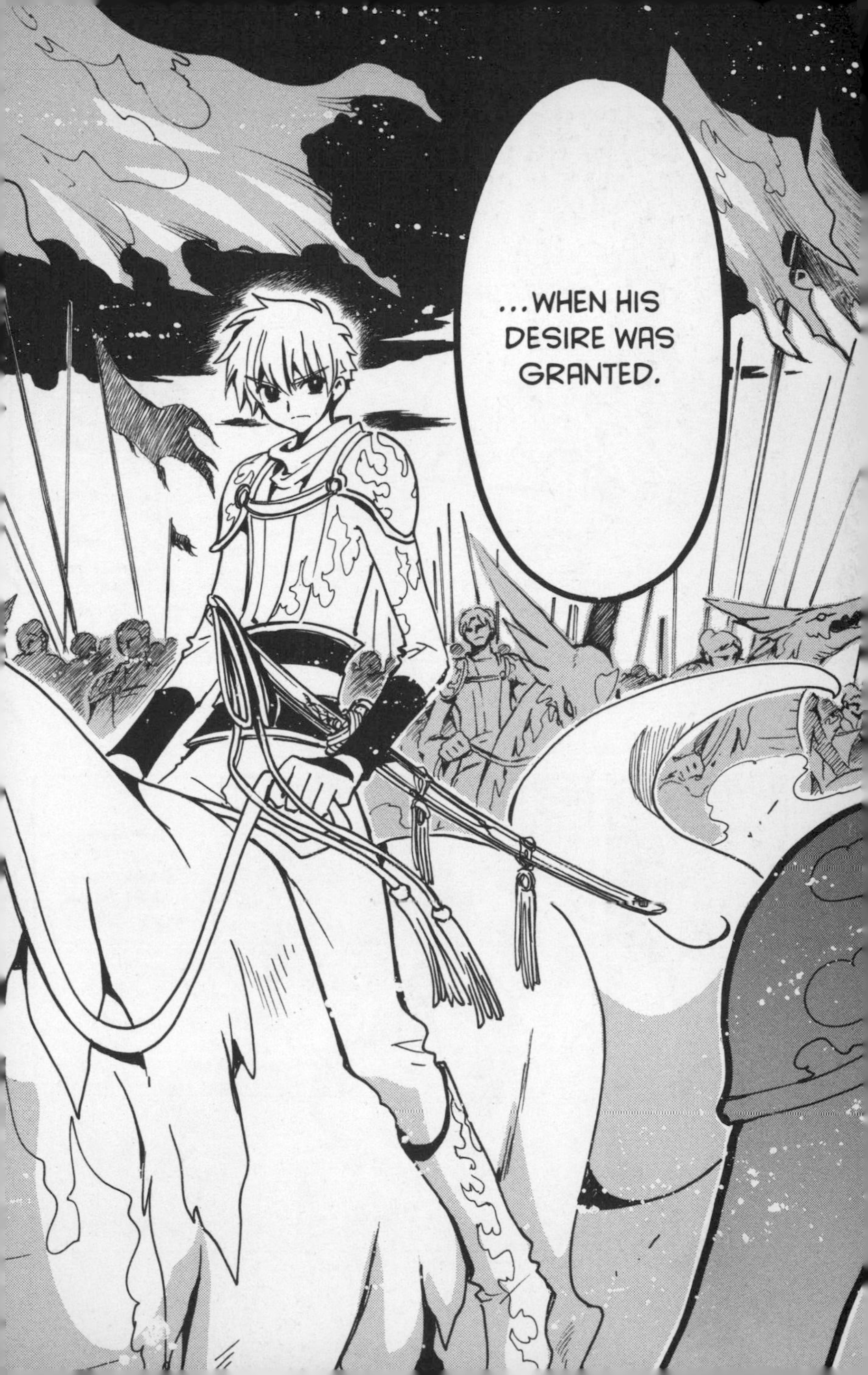
...WHEN HIS DESIRE WAS GRANTED.

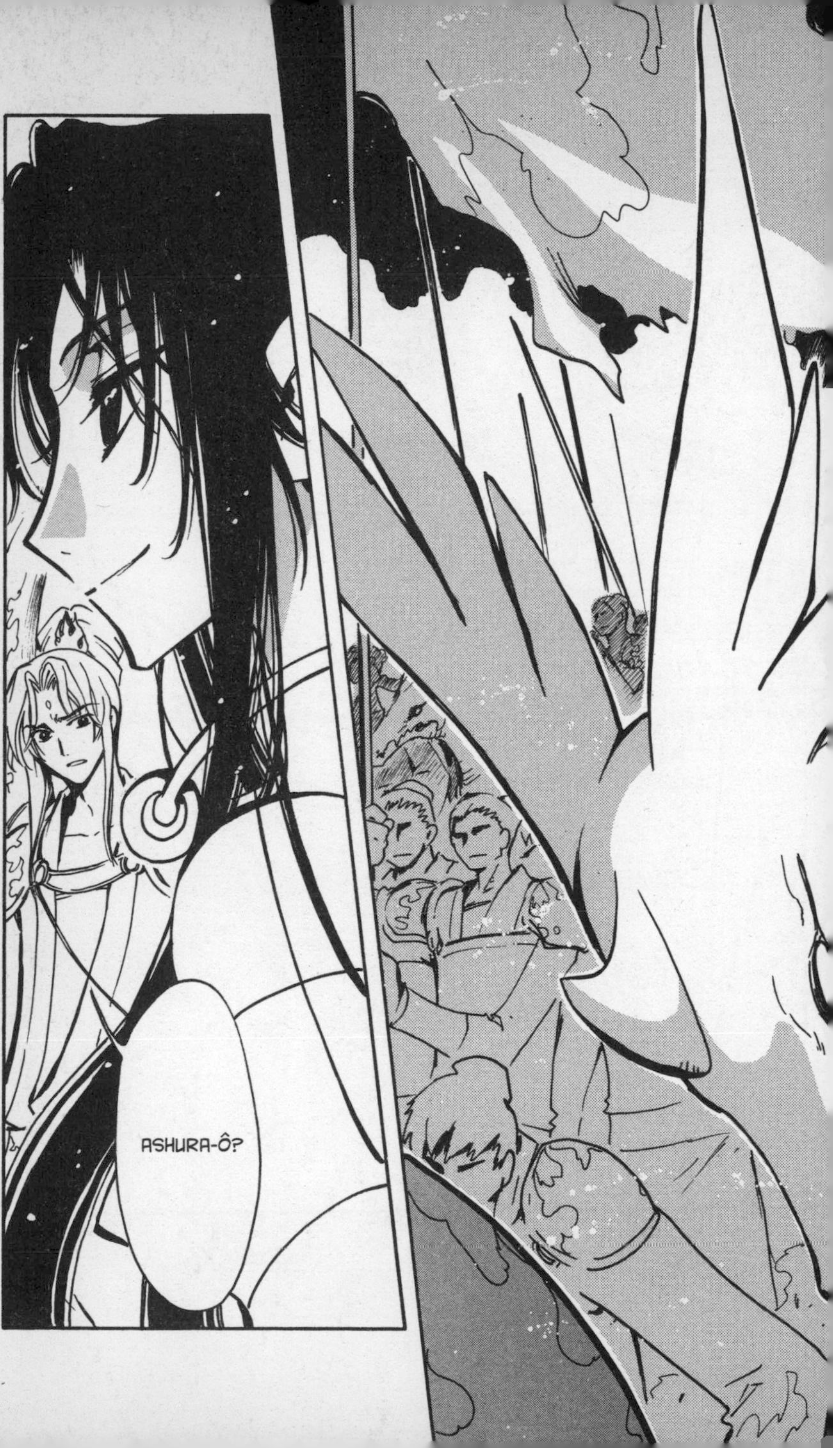
ASHURA-Ô?

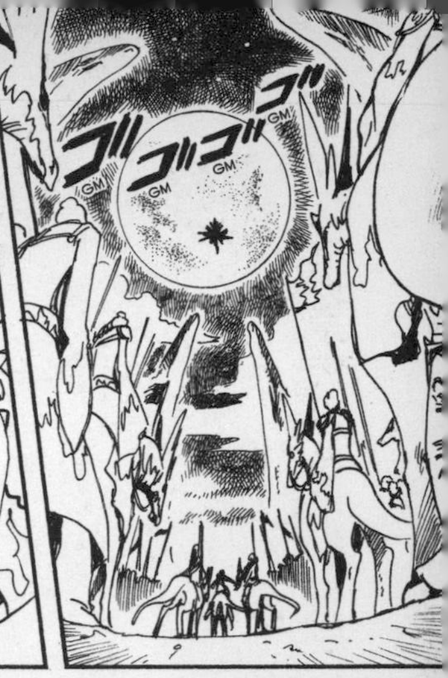
ゴゴゴ
GM GM GM

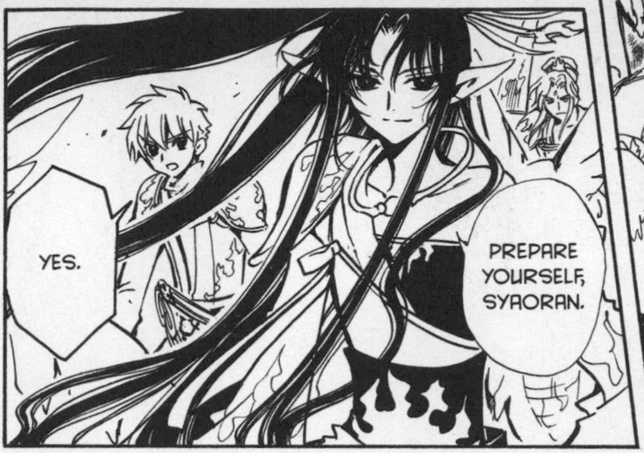
PREPARE YOURSELF, SYAORAN.
YES.

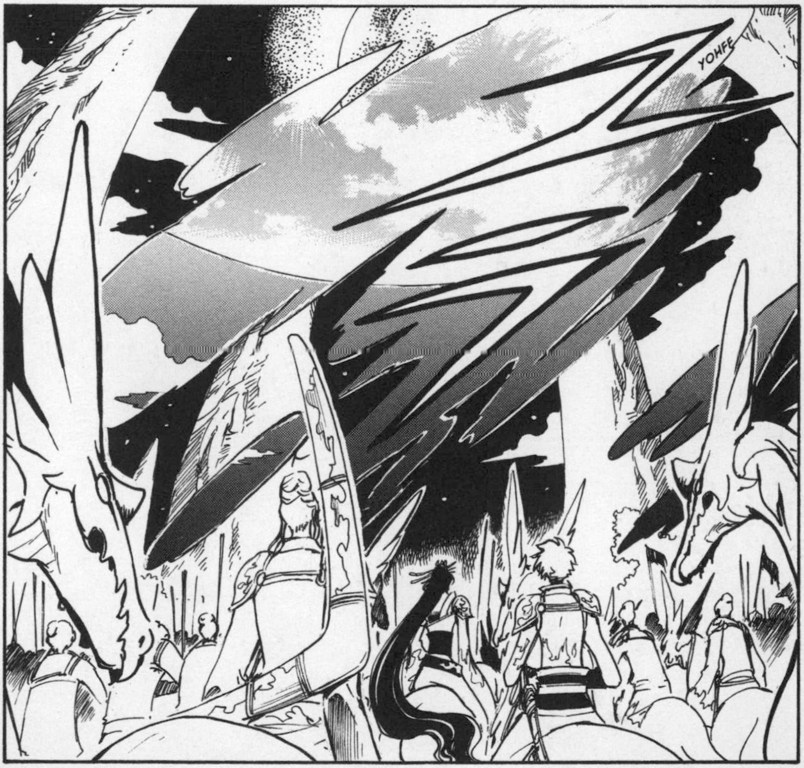
YOHFE

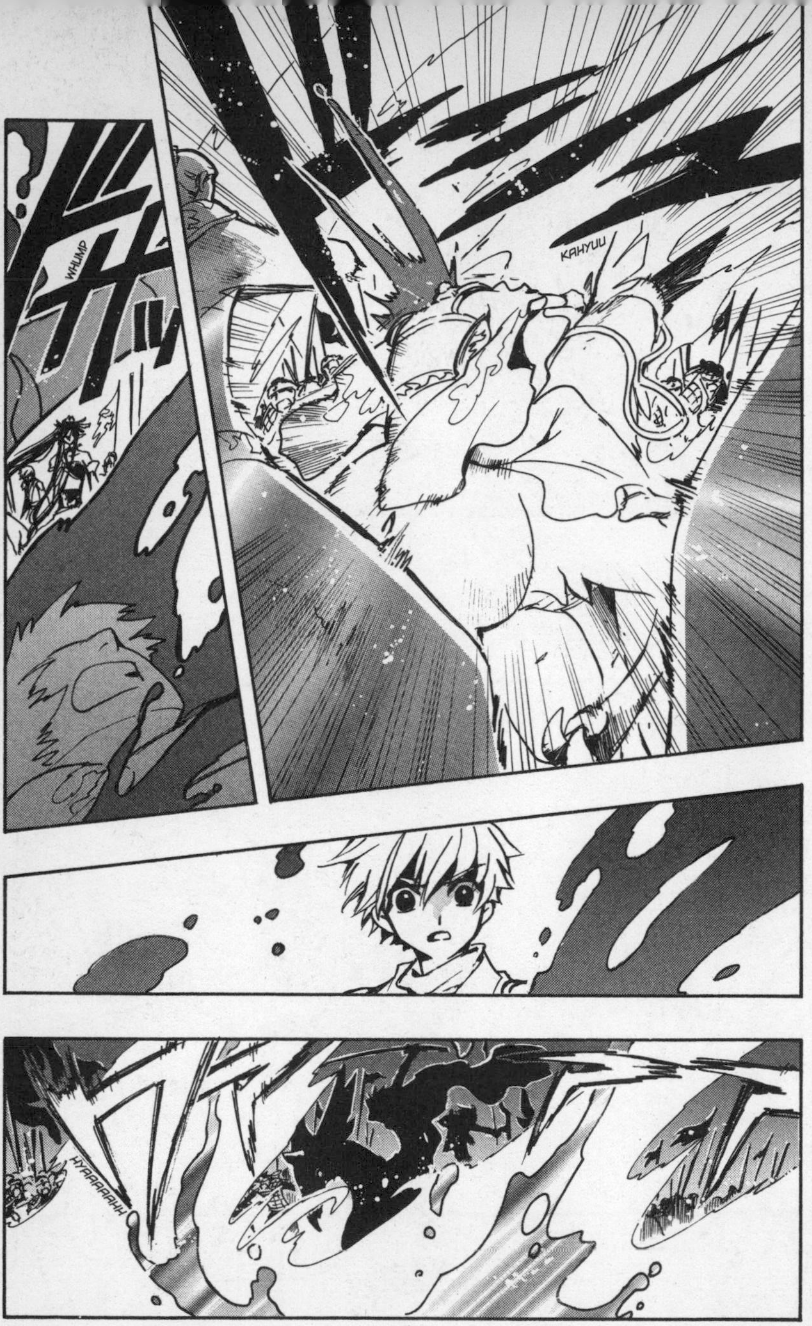
KAHYUU
WHUMP
HYAAAAAHH

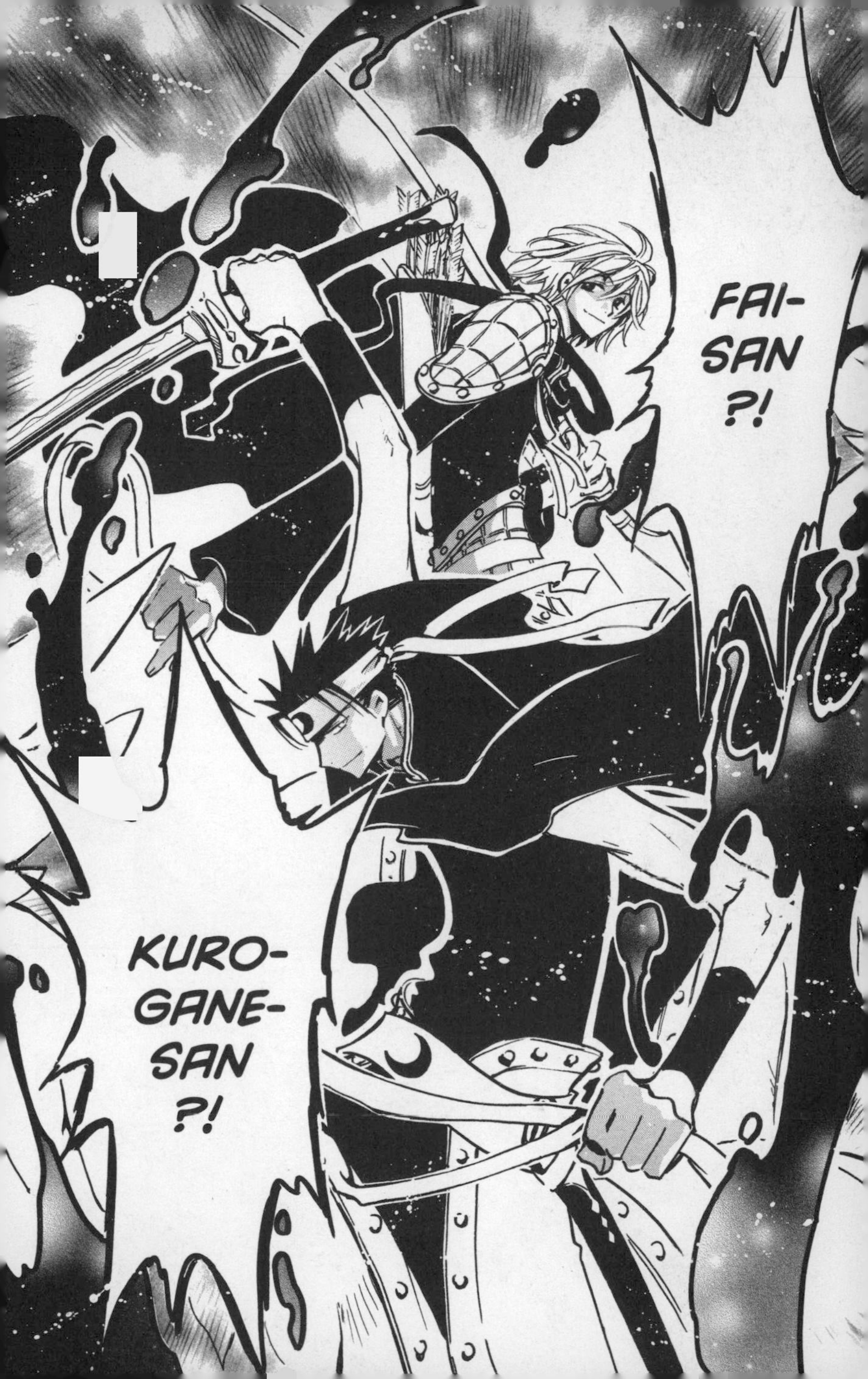
FAI-SAN ?!
KURO-GANE-SAN ?!

Chapitre.61
The Strongest Two

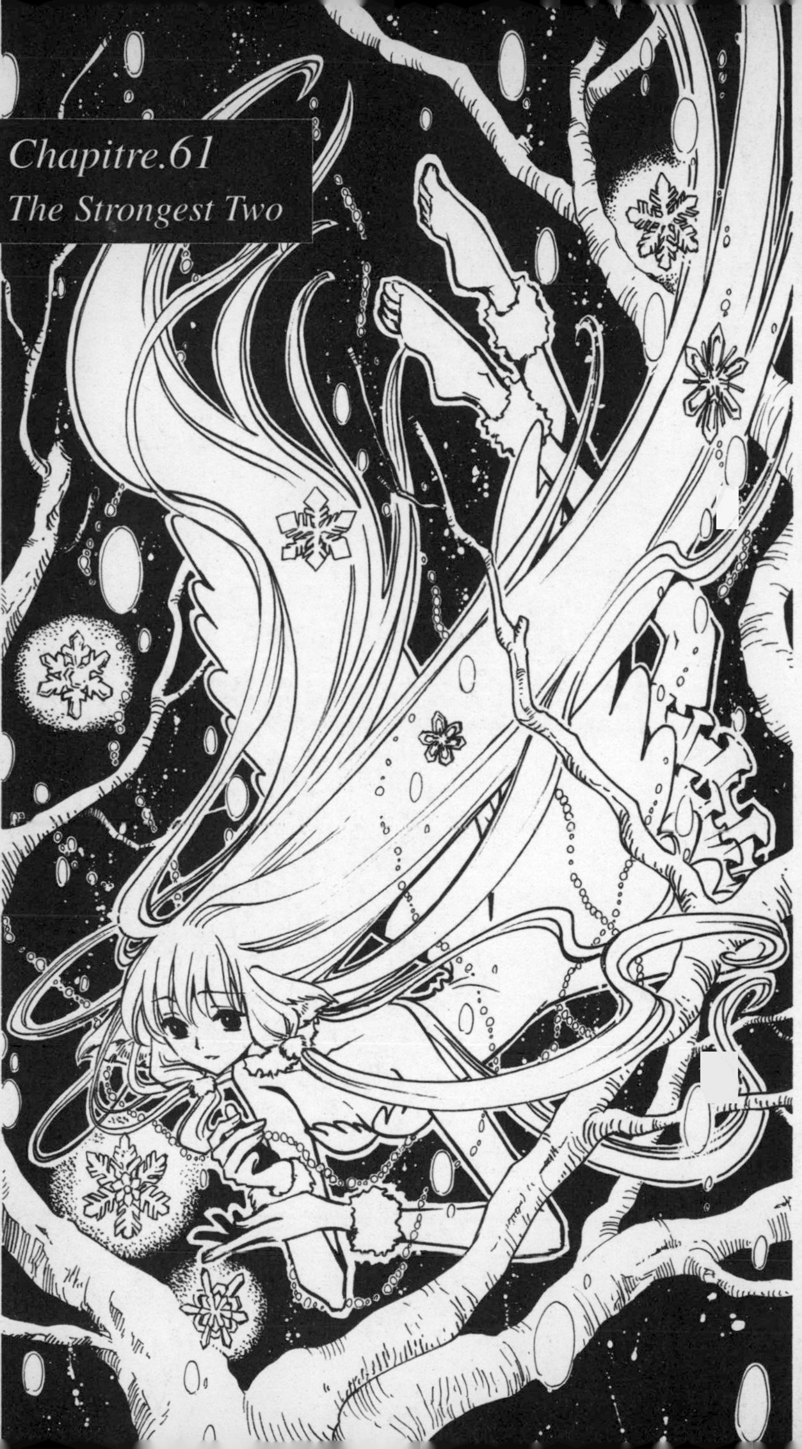

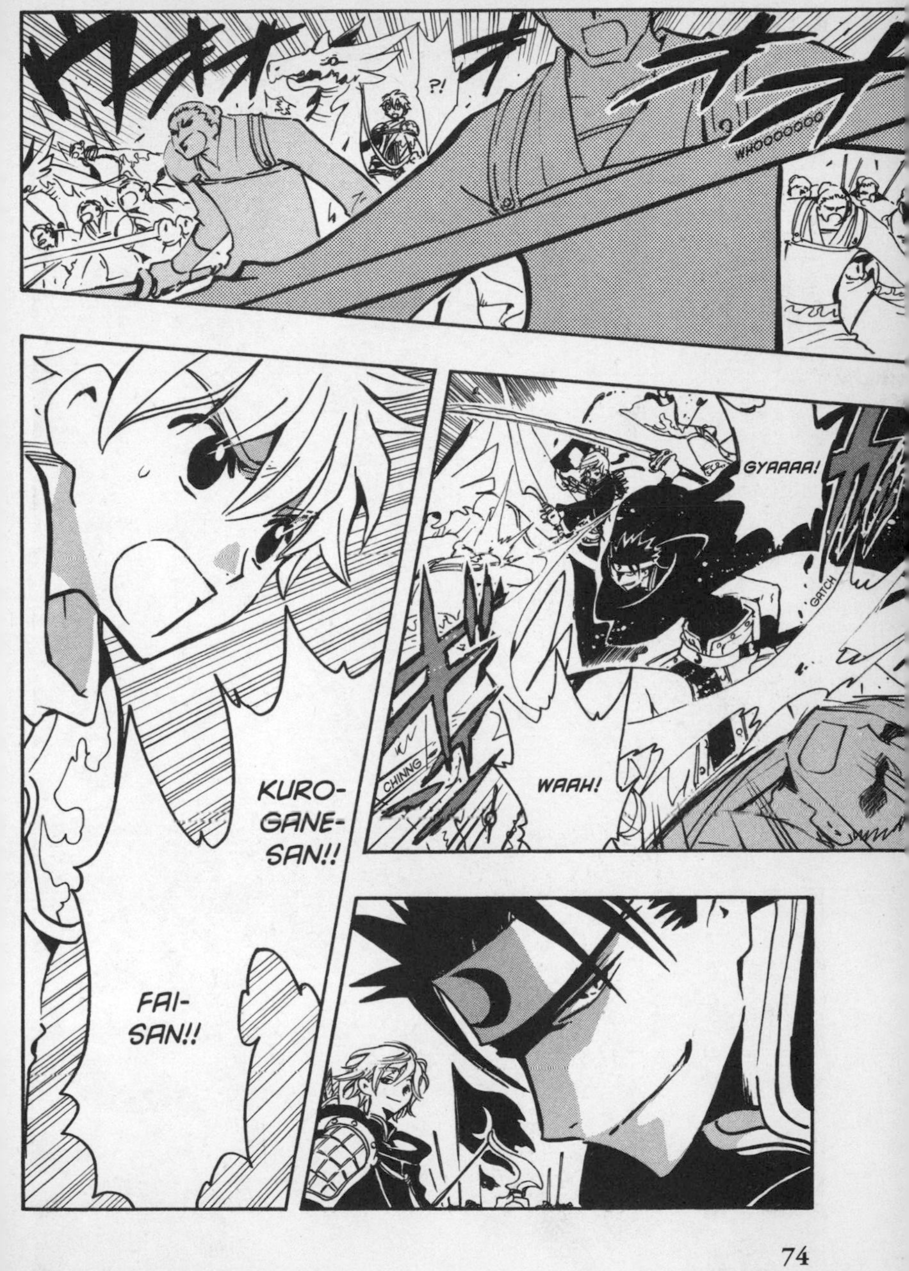
?!
WHOOOOOOOO
GYAAAA!
GATCH
WAAH!
CHINNG
KURO-GANE-SAN!!
FAI-SAN!!

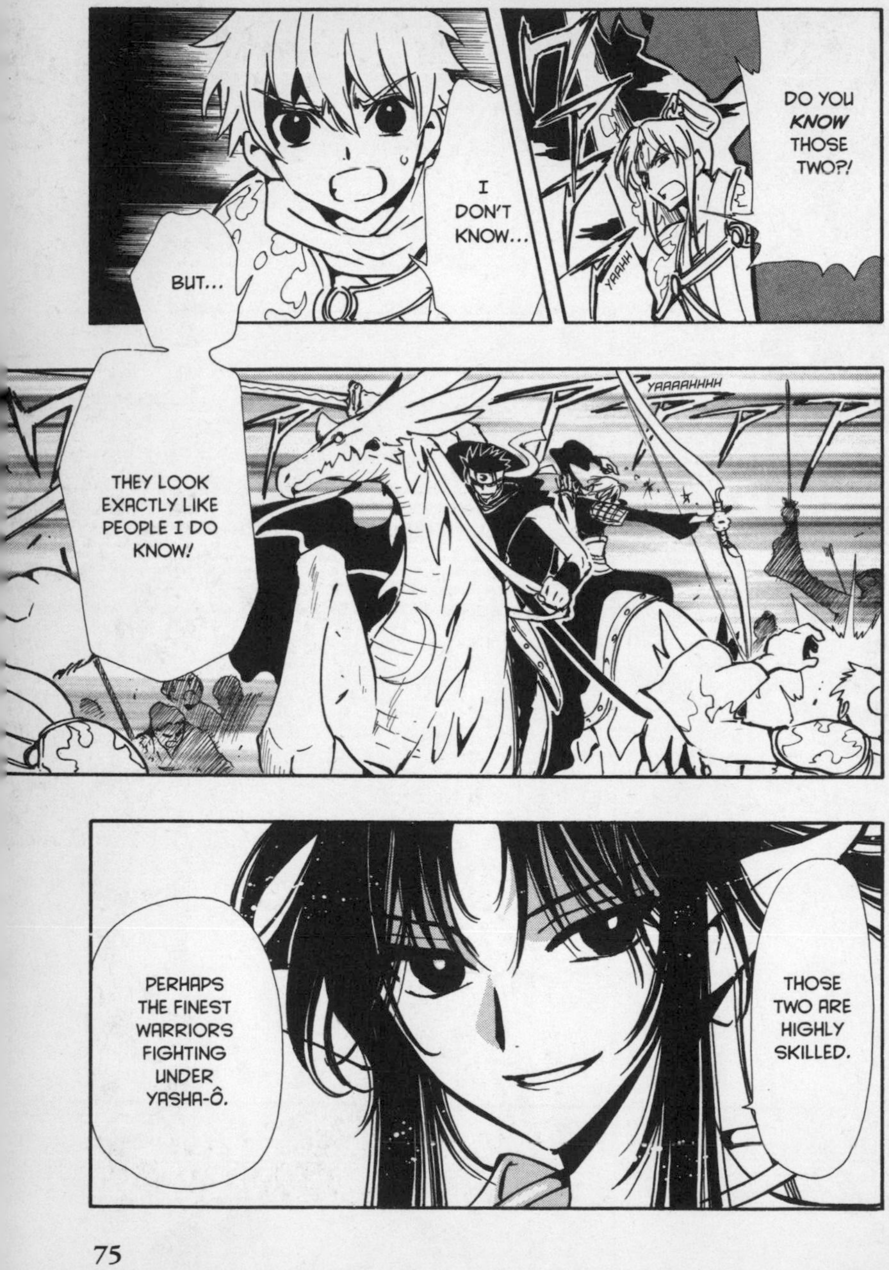
DO YOU KNOW THOSE TWO?!
YAAHH
I DON'T KNOW...
BUT...
YAAAAHHHH
THEY LOOK EXACTLY LIKE PEOPLE I DO KNOW!
THOSE TWO ARE HIGHLY SKILLED.
PERHAPS THE FINEST WARRIORS FIGHTING UNDER YASHA-Ô.

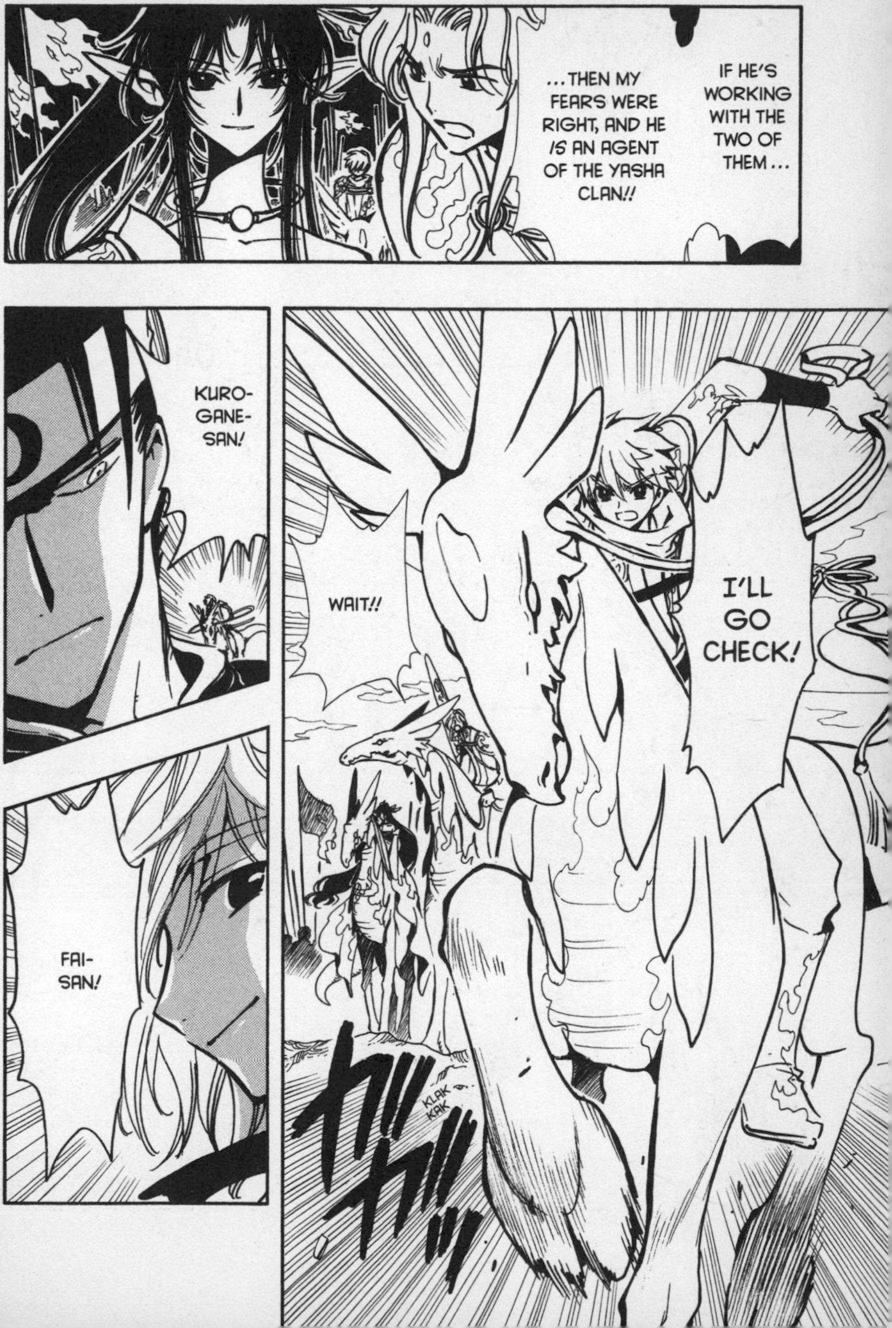
IF HE'S WORKING WITH THE TWO OF THEM...
...THEN MY FEARS WERE RIGHT, AND HE *IS* AN AGENT OF THE YASHA CLAN!!
I'LL GO CHECK!
WAIT!!
KLAK KAK
KURO-GANE-SAN!
FAI-SAN!

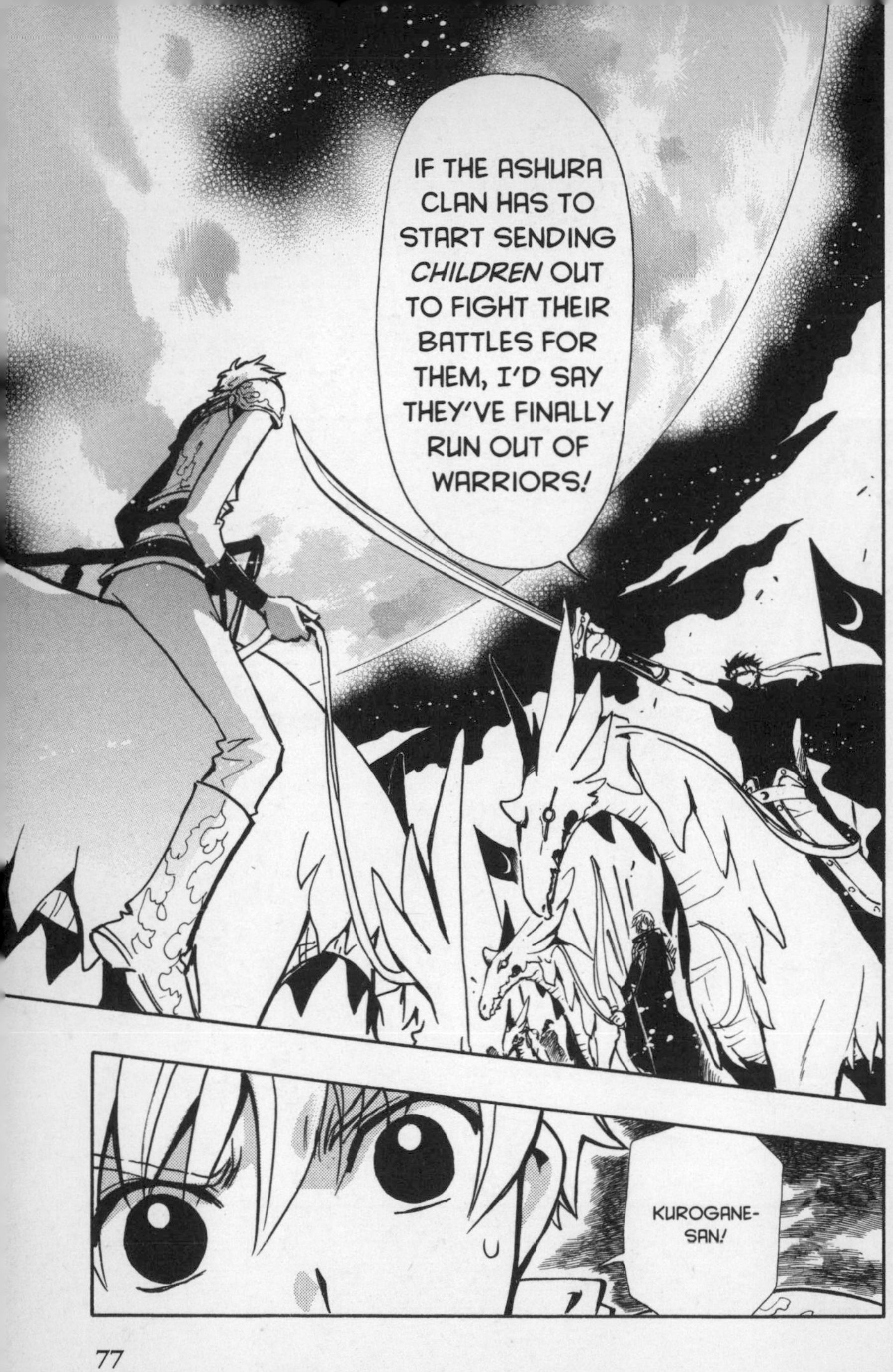
IF THE ASHURA CLAN HAS TO START SENDING *CHILDREN* OUT TO FIGHT THEIR BATTLES FOR THEM, I'D SAY THEY'VE FINALLY RUN OUT OF WARRIORS!
KUROGANE-SAN!

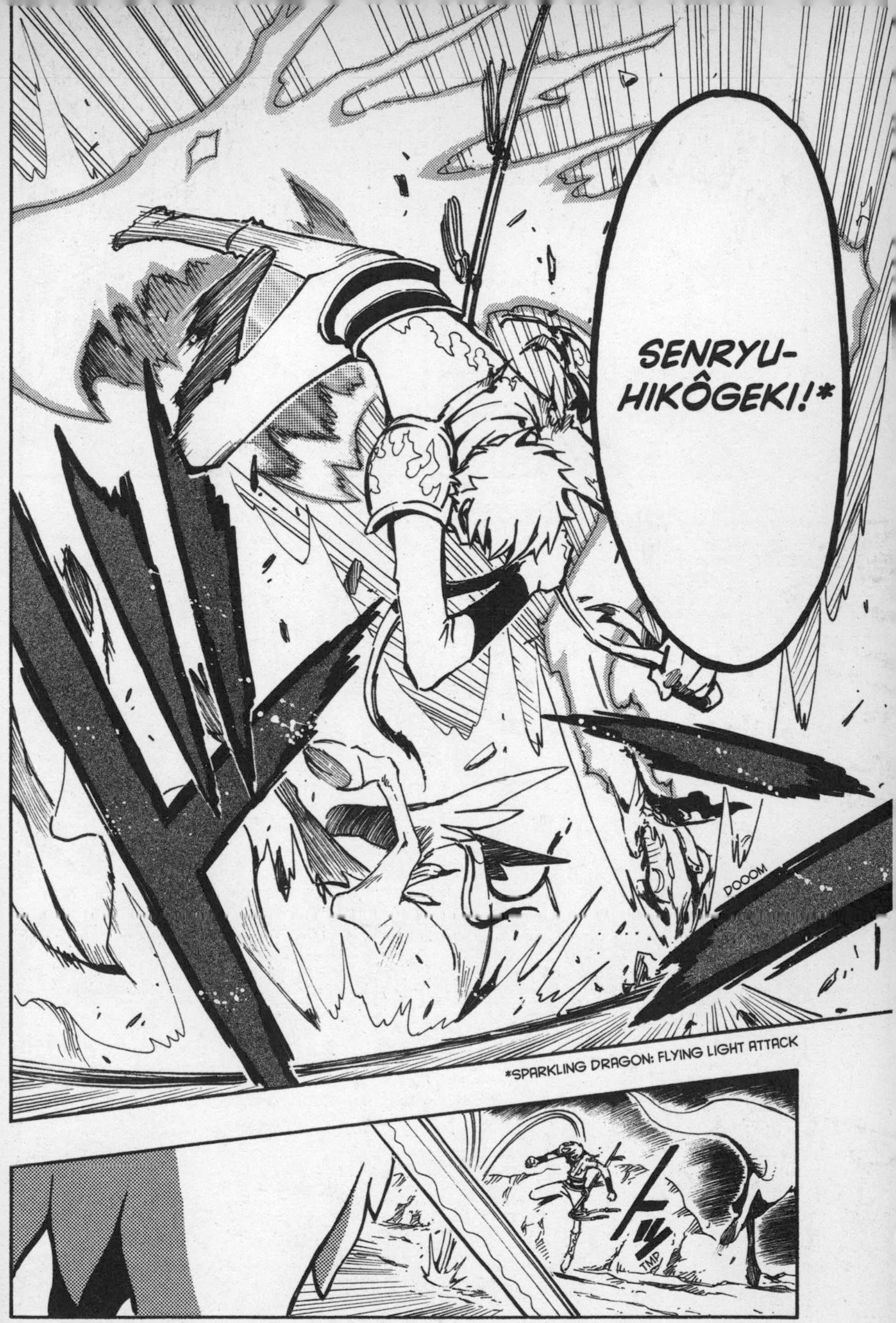
SENRYU-
HIKÔGEKI!*
DOOOM
TMP

*SPARKLING DRAGON: FLYING LIGHT ATTACK

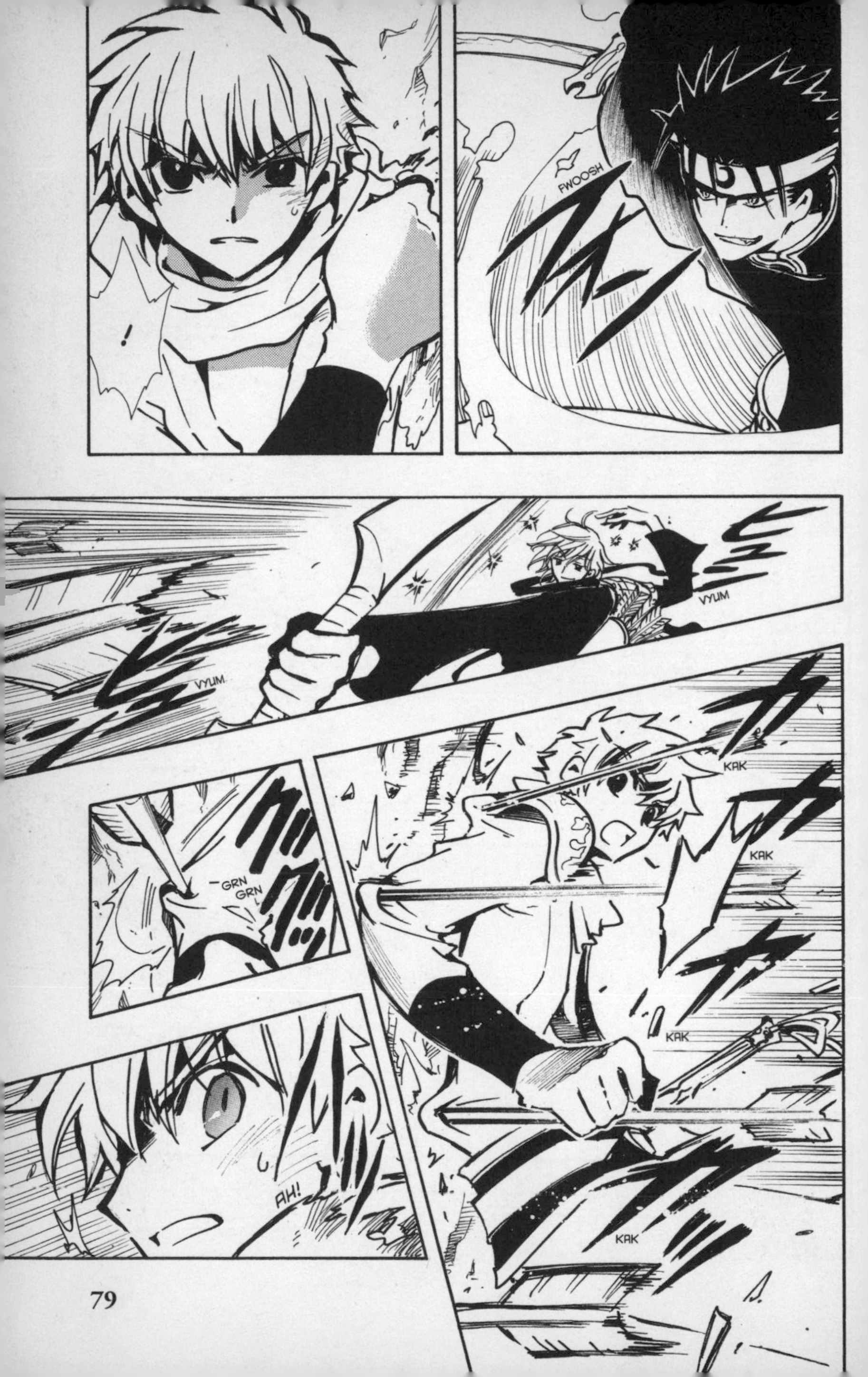
FWOOSH
!
VYUM
VYUM
KAK
KAK
KAK
KAK
GRN
GRN
AH!

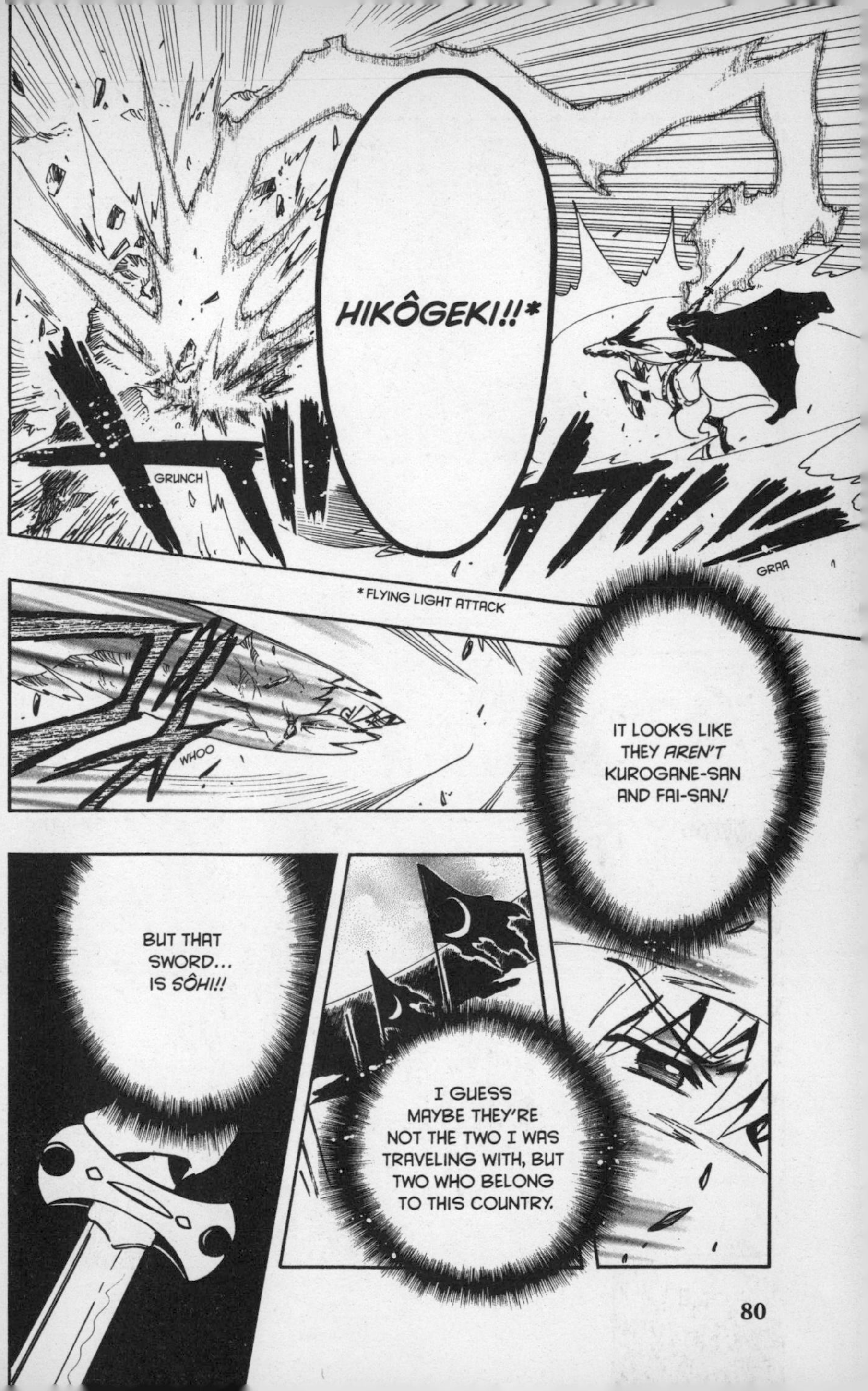
GRAA
HIKÔGEKI!!*
GRUNCH
* FLYING LIGHT ATTACK
IT LOOKS LIKE THEY AREN'T KUROGANE-SAN AND FAI-SAN!
WHOO
I GUESS MAYBE THEY'RE NOT THE TWO I WAS TRAVELING WITH, BUT TWO WHO BELONG TO THIS COUNTRY.
BUT THAT SWORD... IS SÔHI!!

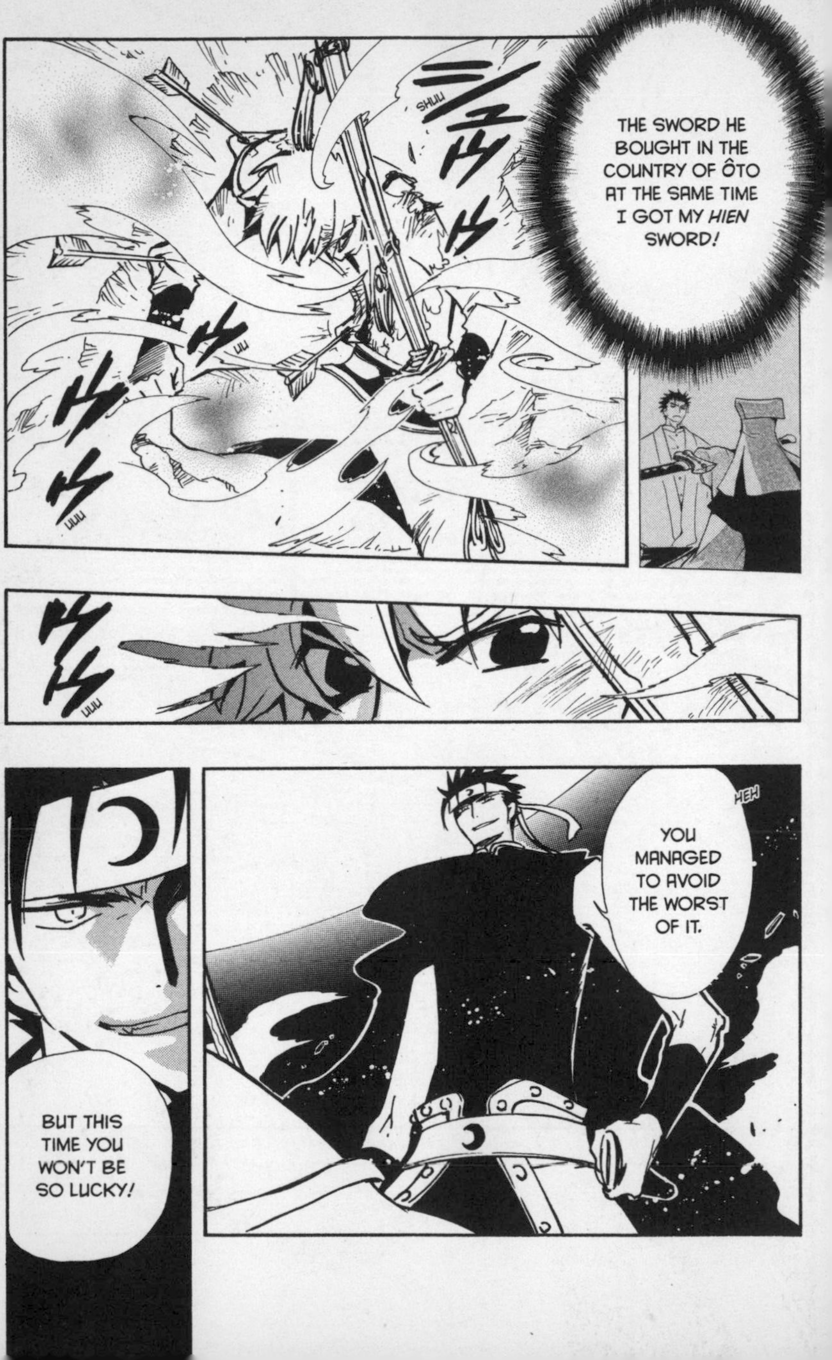
THE SWORD HE BOUGHT IN THE COUNTRY OF ÔTO AT THE SAME TIME I GOT MY *HIEN* SWORD!
SHUU
HEH
YOU MANAGED TO AVOID THE WORST OF IT.
BUT THIS TIME YOU WON'T BE SO LUCKY!

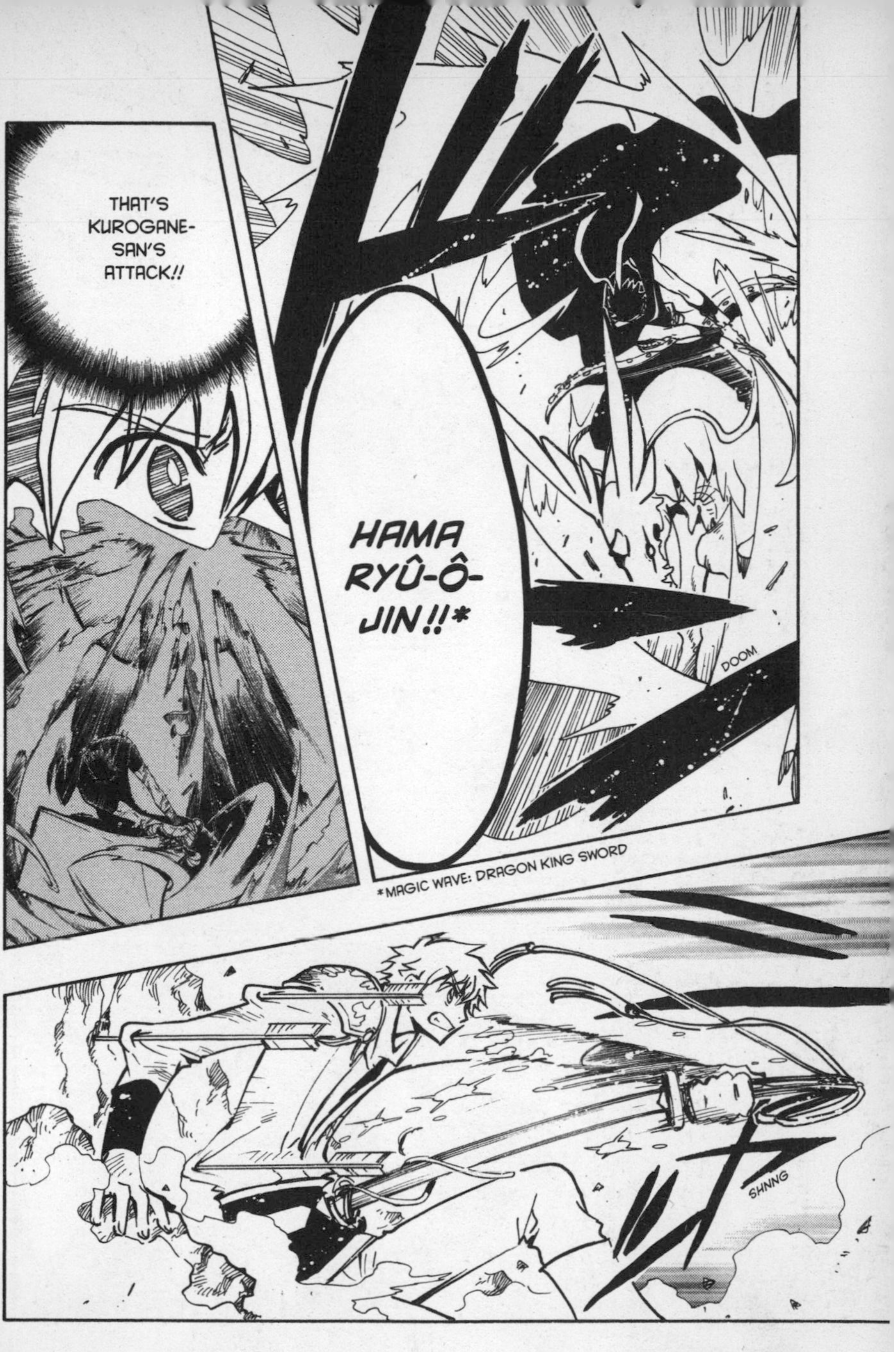
HAMA RYÛ-Ô-JIN!!*
DOOM
THAT'S KUROGANE-SAN'S ATTACK!!
*MAGIC WAVE: DRAGON KING SWORD
SHNNG

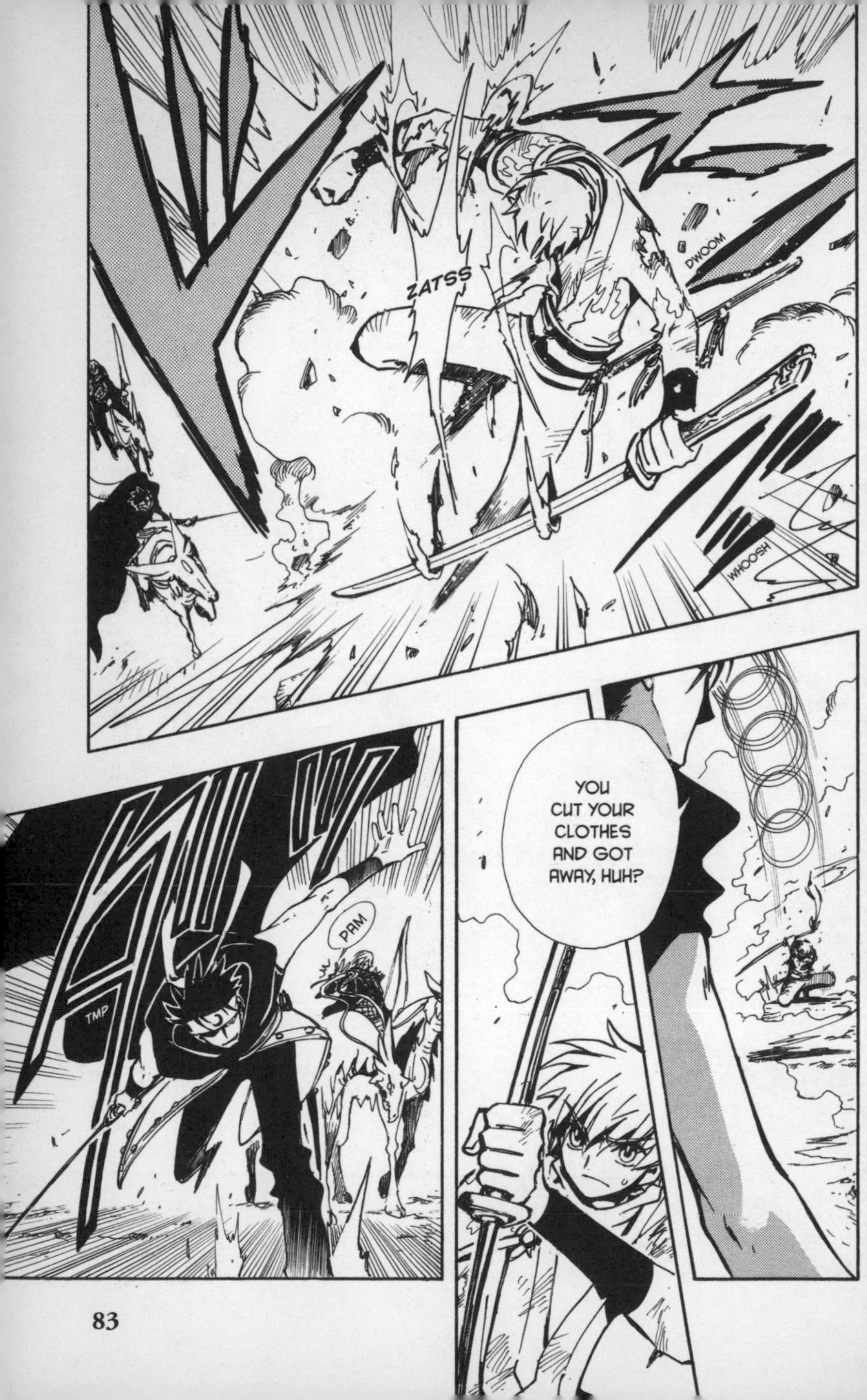
DWOOM
ZATSS
WHOOSH
YOU CUT YOUR CLOTHES AND GOT AWAY, HUH?
PAM
TMP

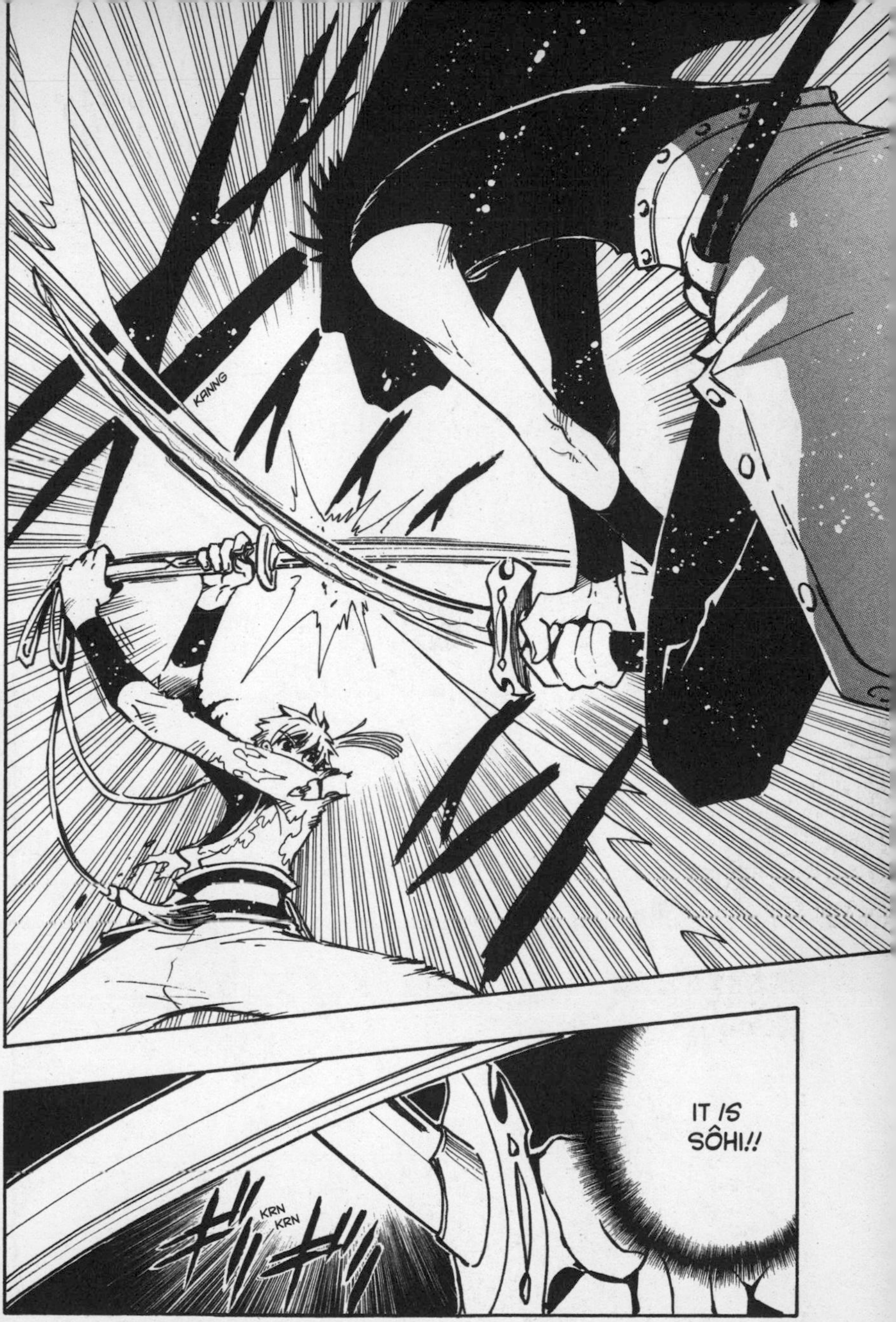
KANNG
IT IS SÔHI!!
KRN KRN

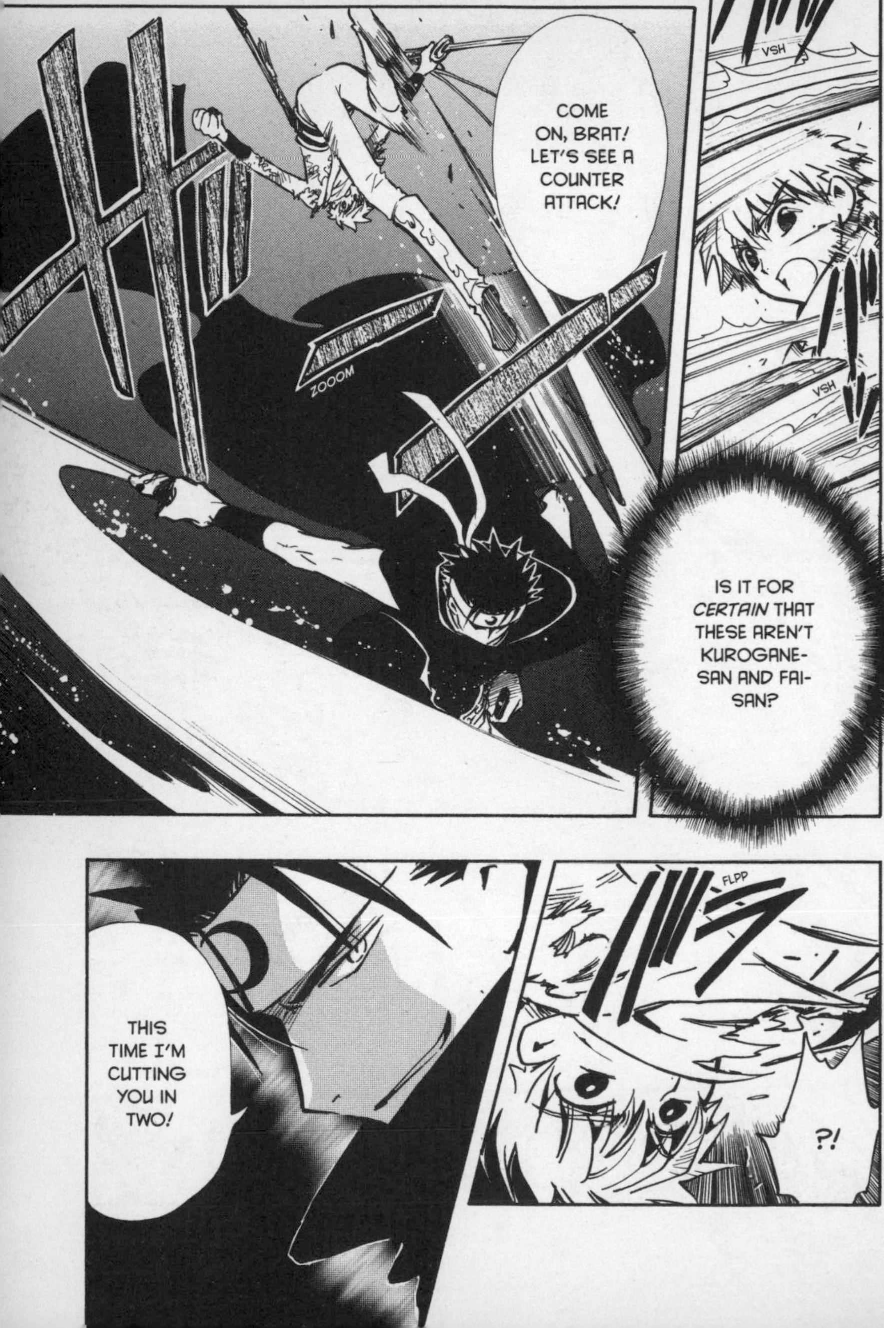
VSH
VSH
IS IT FOR *CERTAIN* THAT THESE AREN'T KUROGANE-SAN AND FAI-SAN?
COME ON, BRAT! LET'S SEE A COUNTER ATTACK!
ZOOOM
FLPP
?!
THIS TIME I'M CUTTING YOU IN TWO!

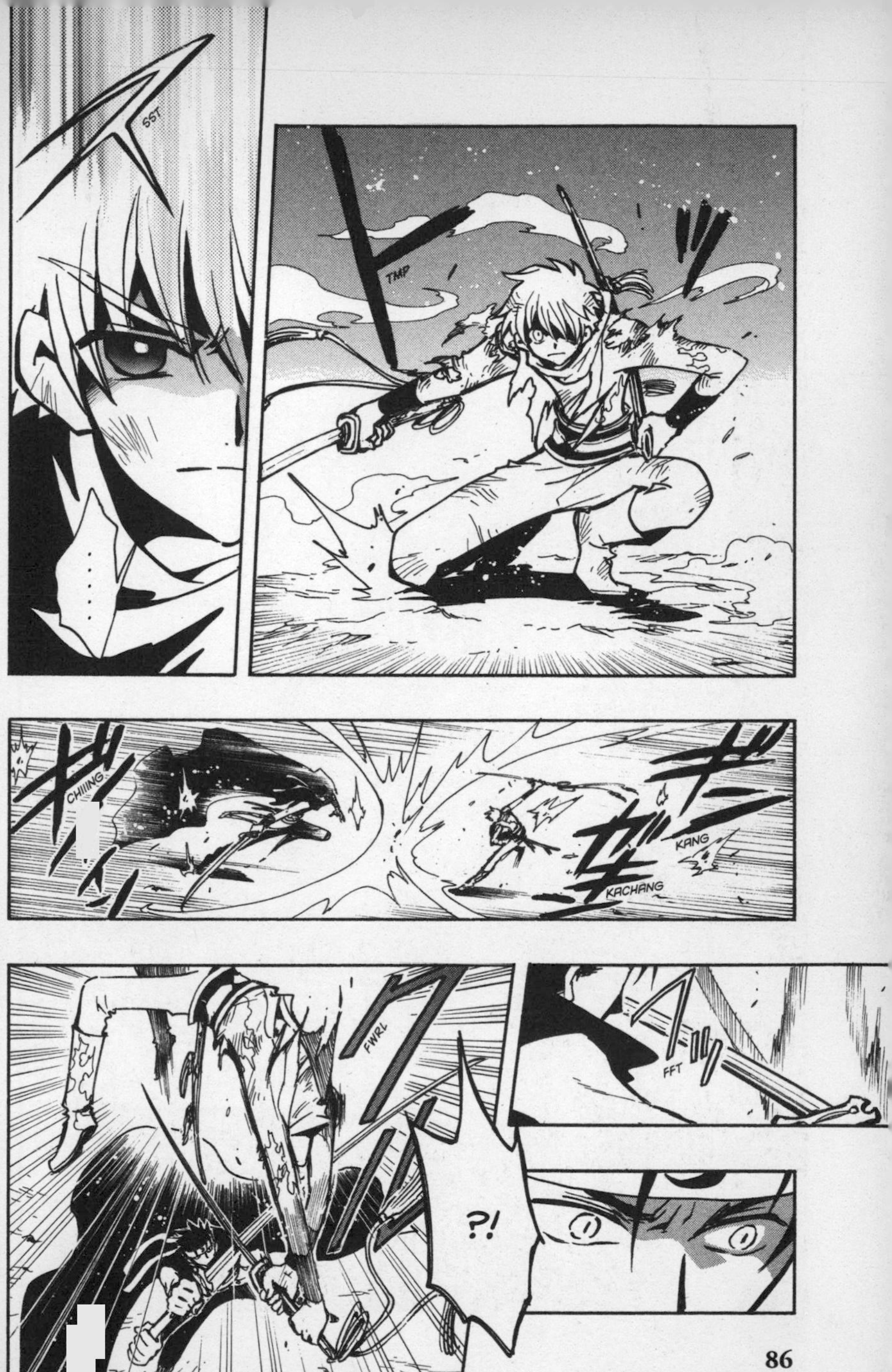
TMP
SST
KANG
KACHANG
CHIIING
FFT
?!
FWRL

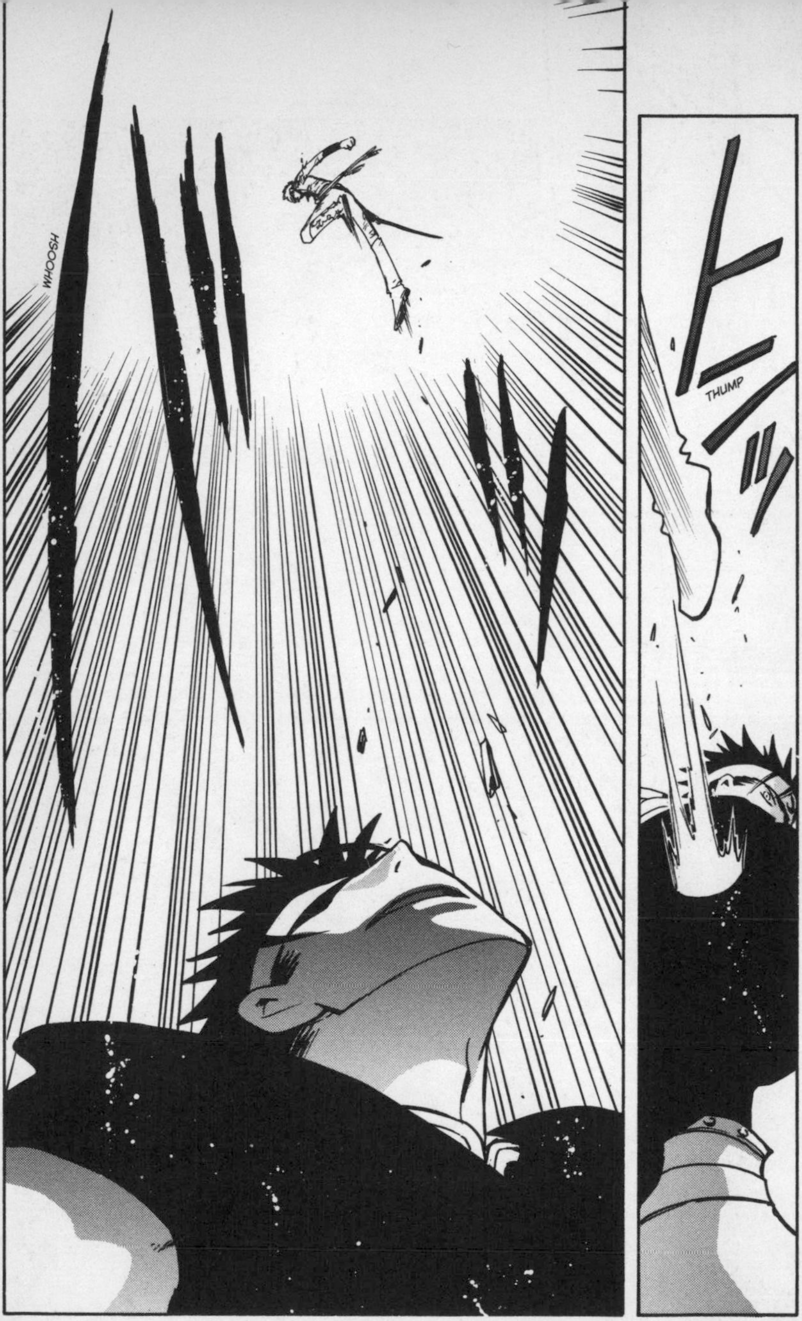
THUMP
WHOOSH

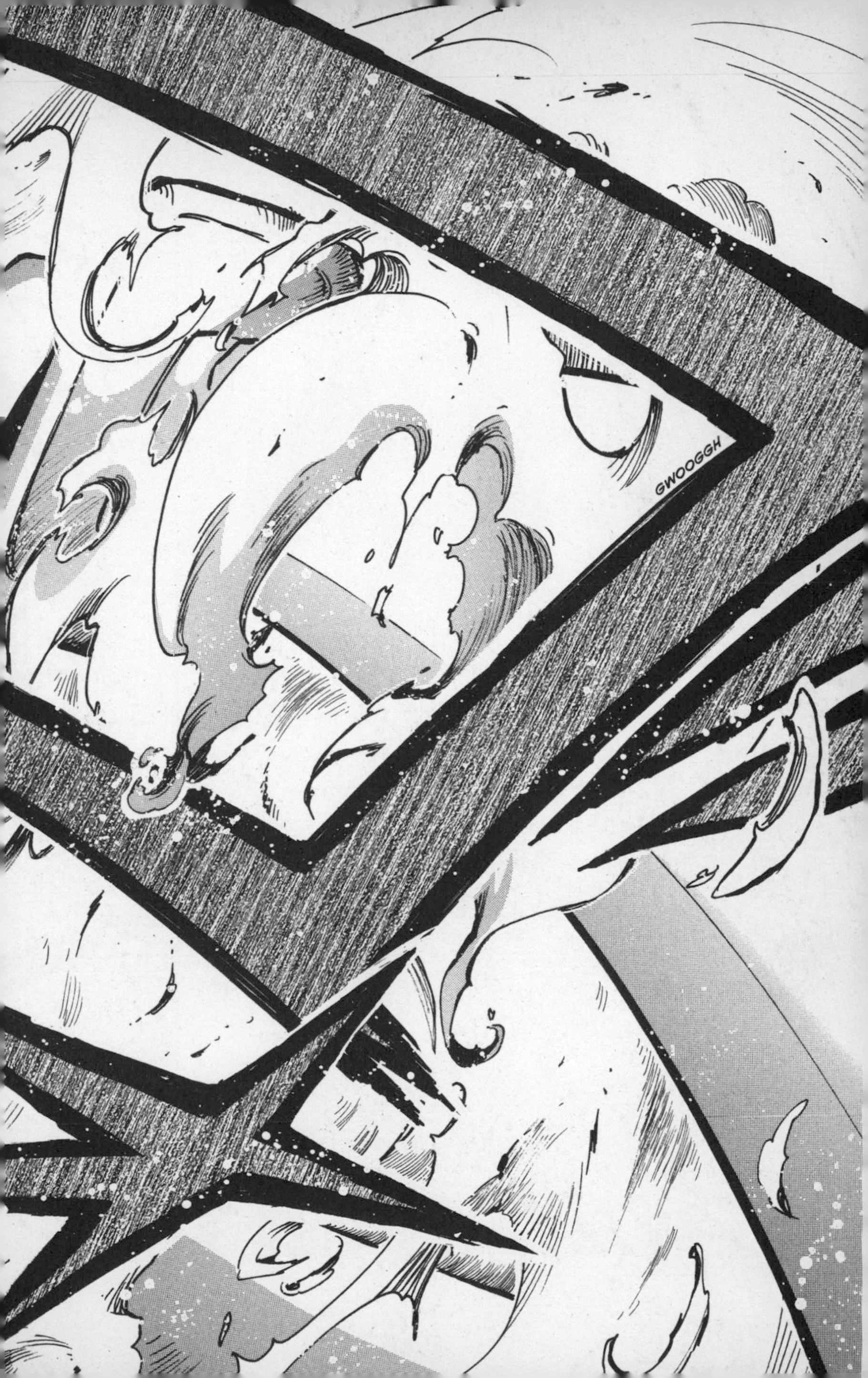
GWOOGGH

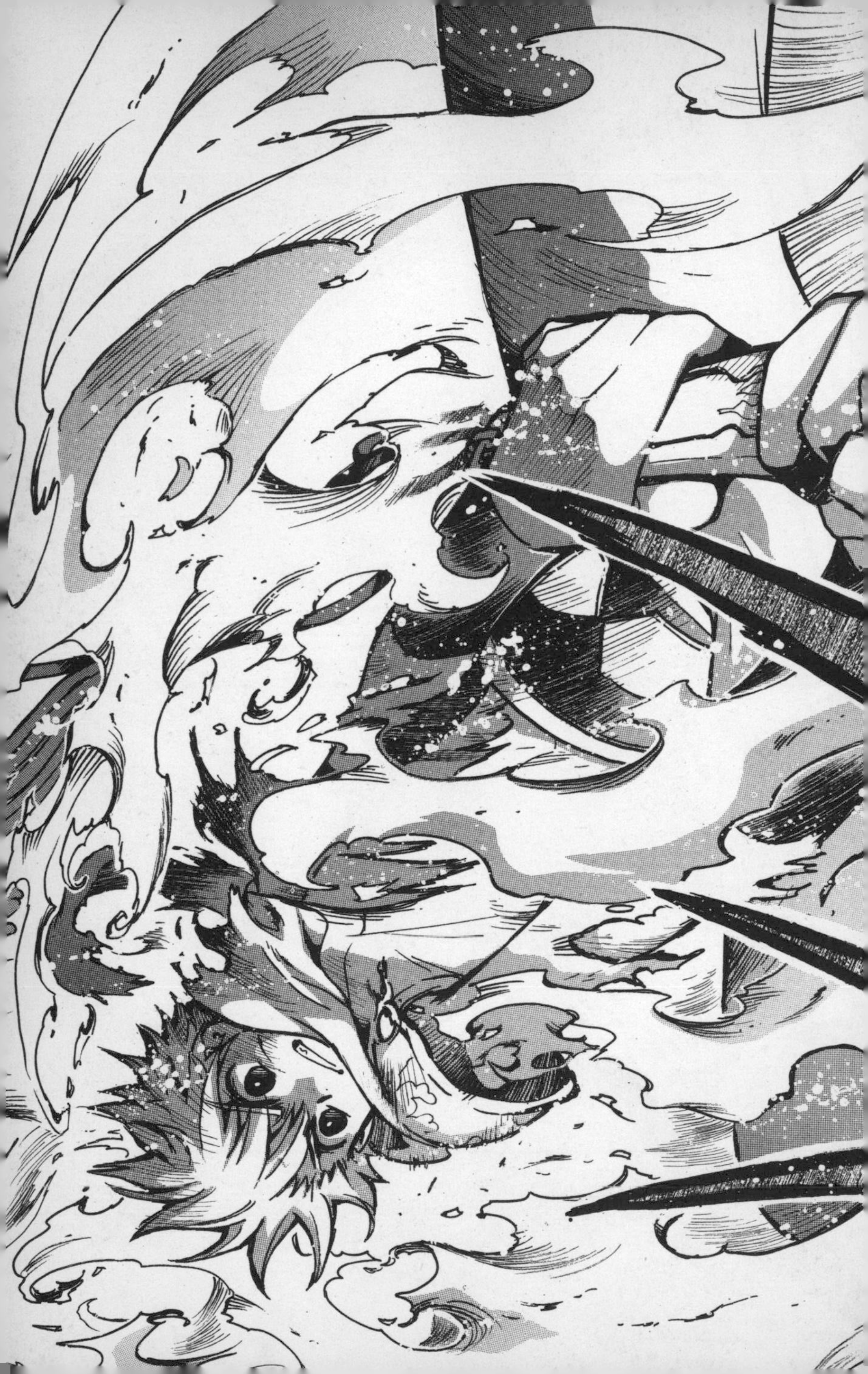

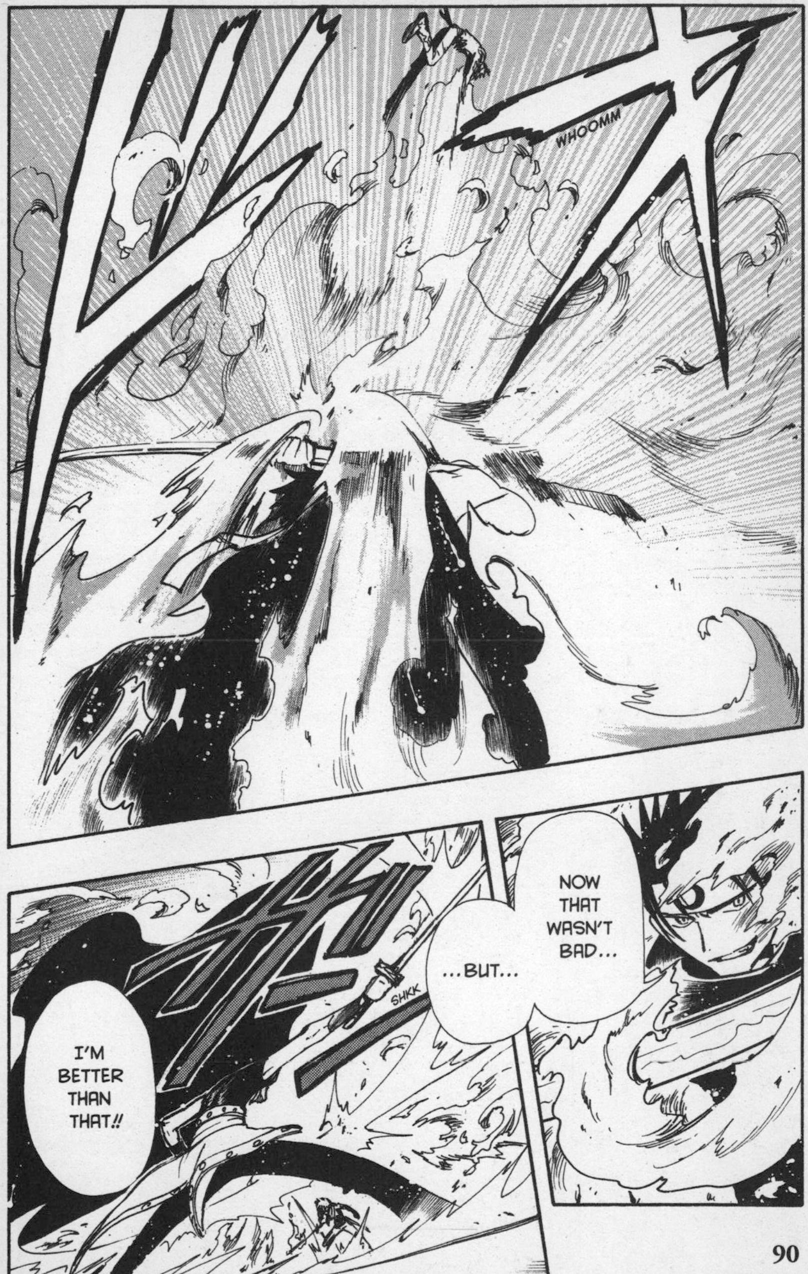
WHOOMM
NOW THAT WASN'T BAD...
...BUT...
SHKK
I'M BETTER THAN THAT!!

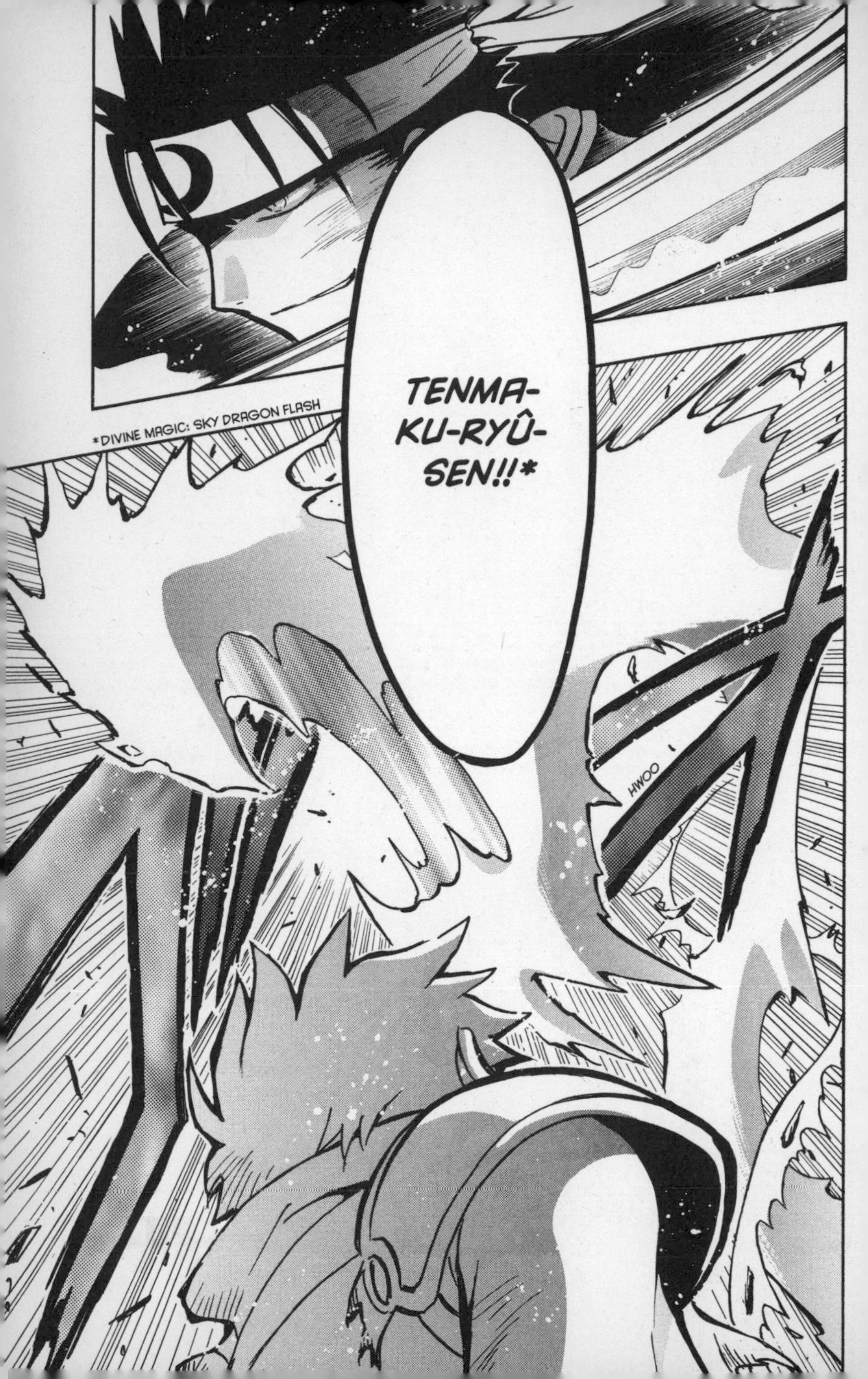
TENMA-KU-RYÛ-SEN!!*
*DIVINE MAGIC: SKY DRAGON FLASH
HWOO

ツバサ

RESERVoir CHRoNiCLE

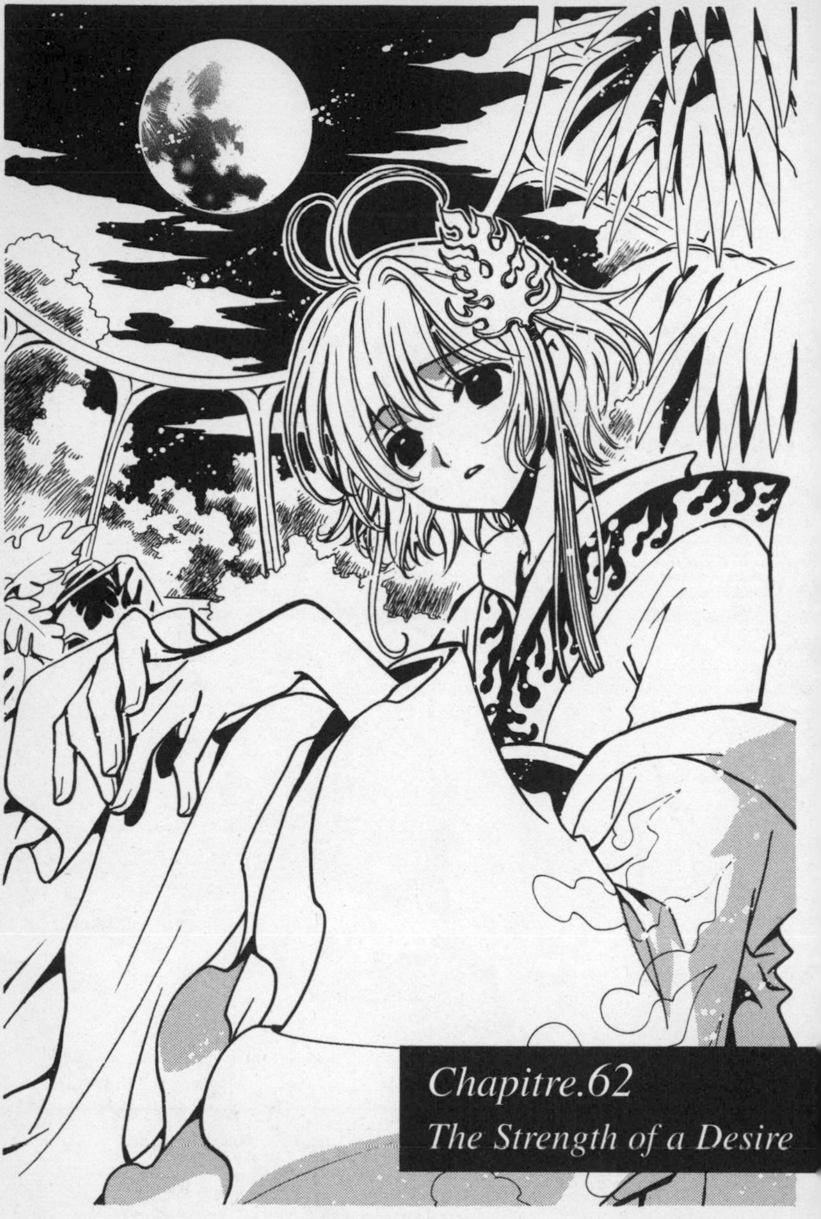
Chapitre.62
The Strength of a Desire

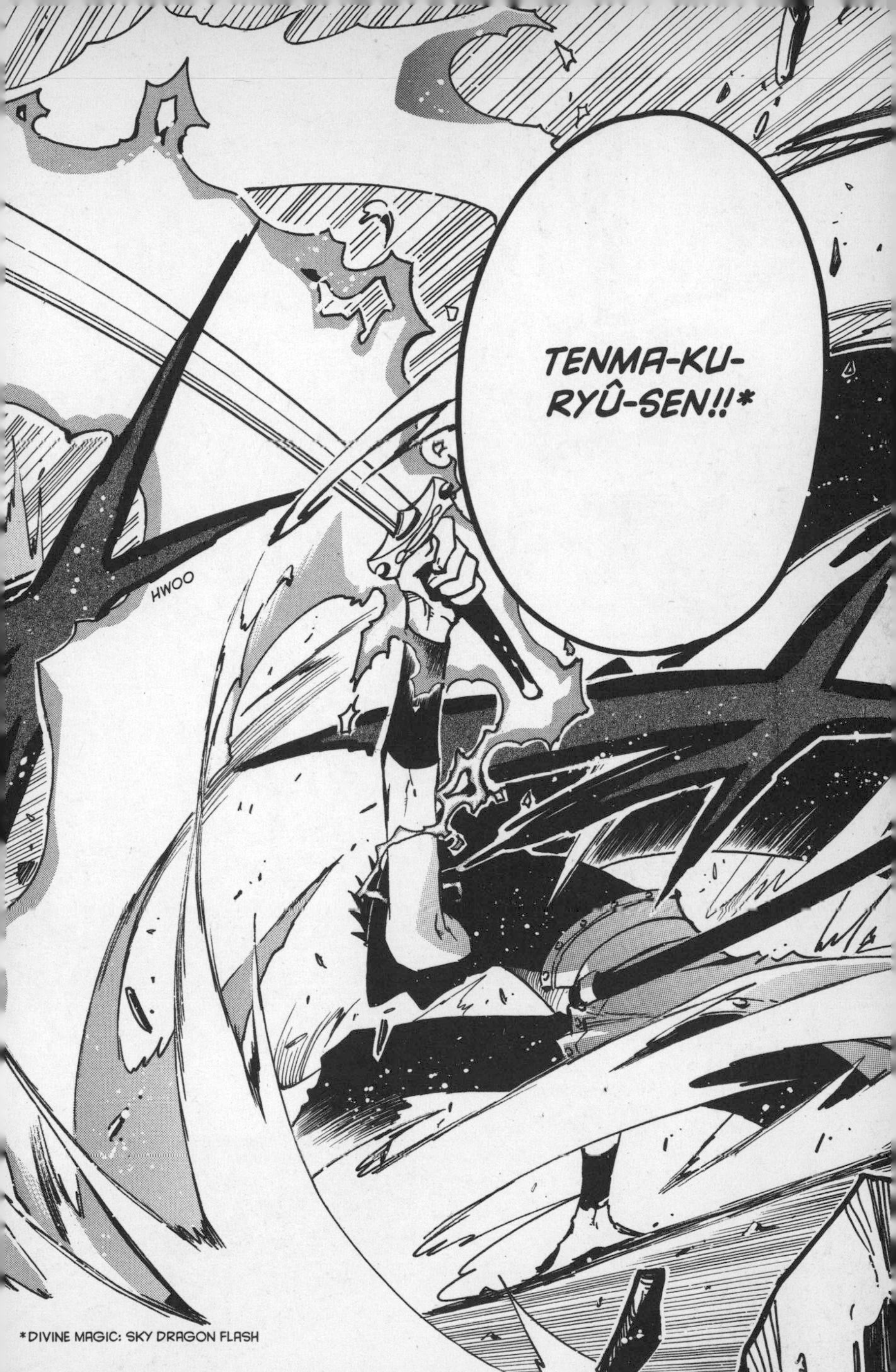
TENMA-KU-RYÛ-SEN!!*
HWOO

*DIVINE MAGIC: SKY DRAGON FLASH

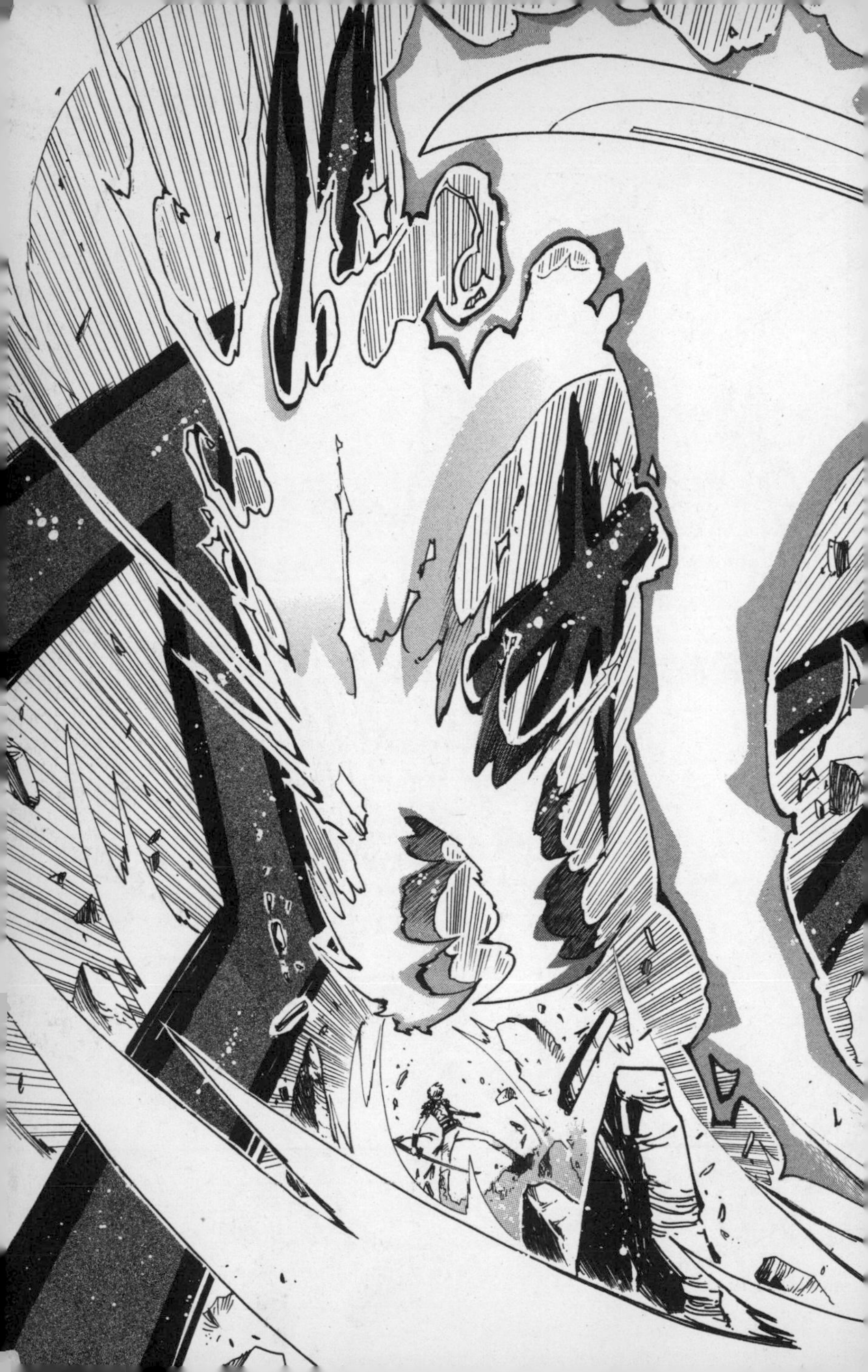

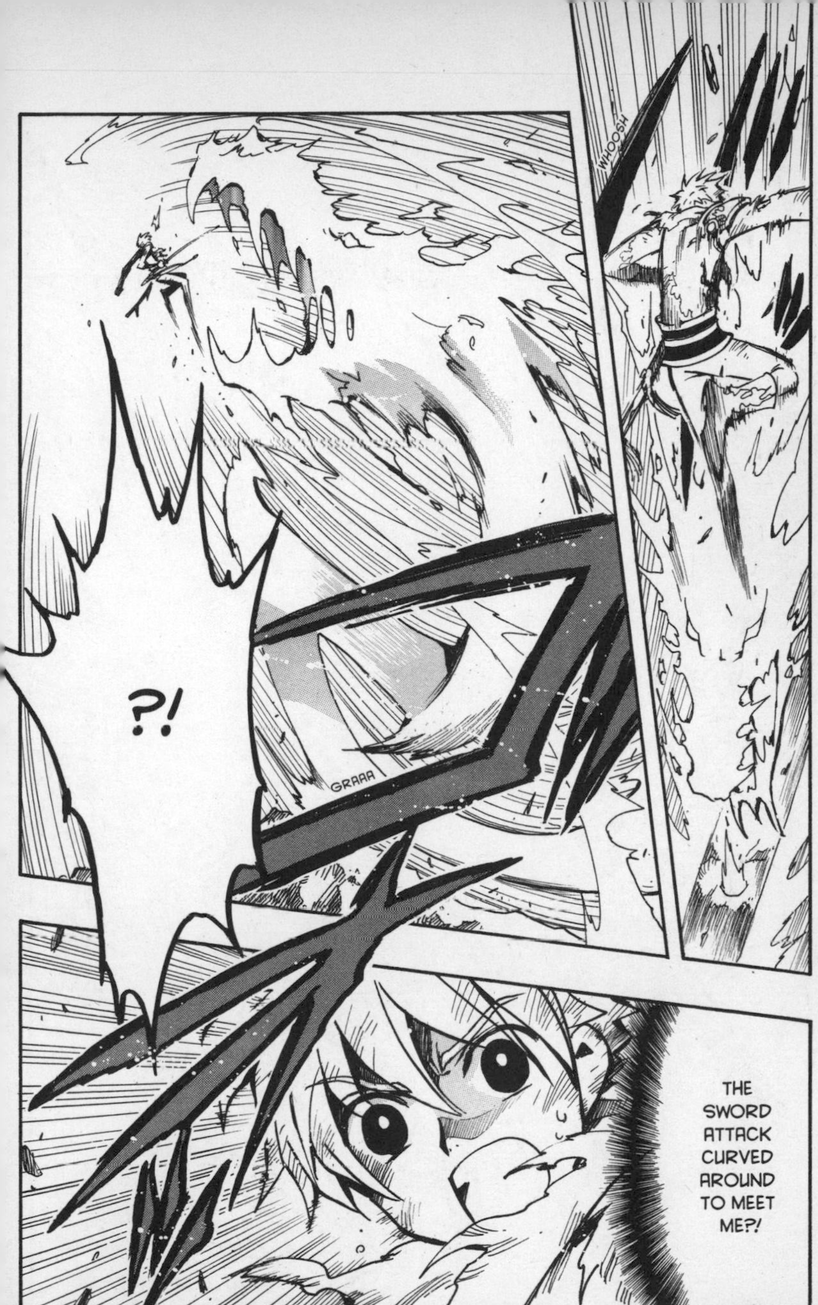
WHOOSH
GRAAA
?!
THE SWORD ATTACK CURVED AROUND TO MEET ME?!

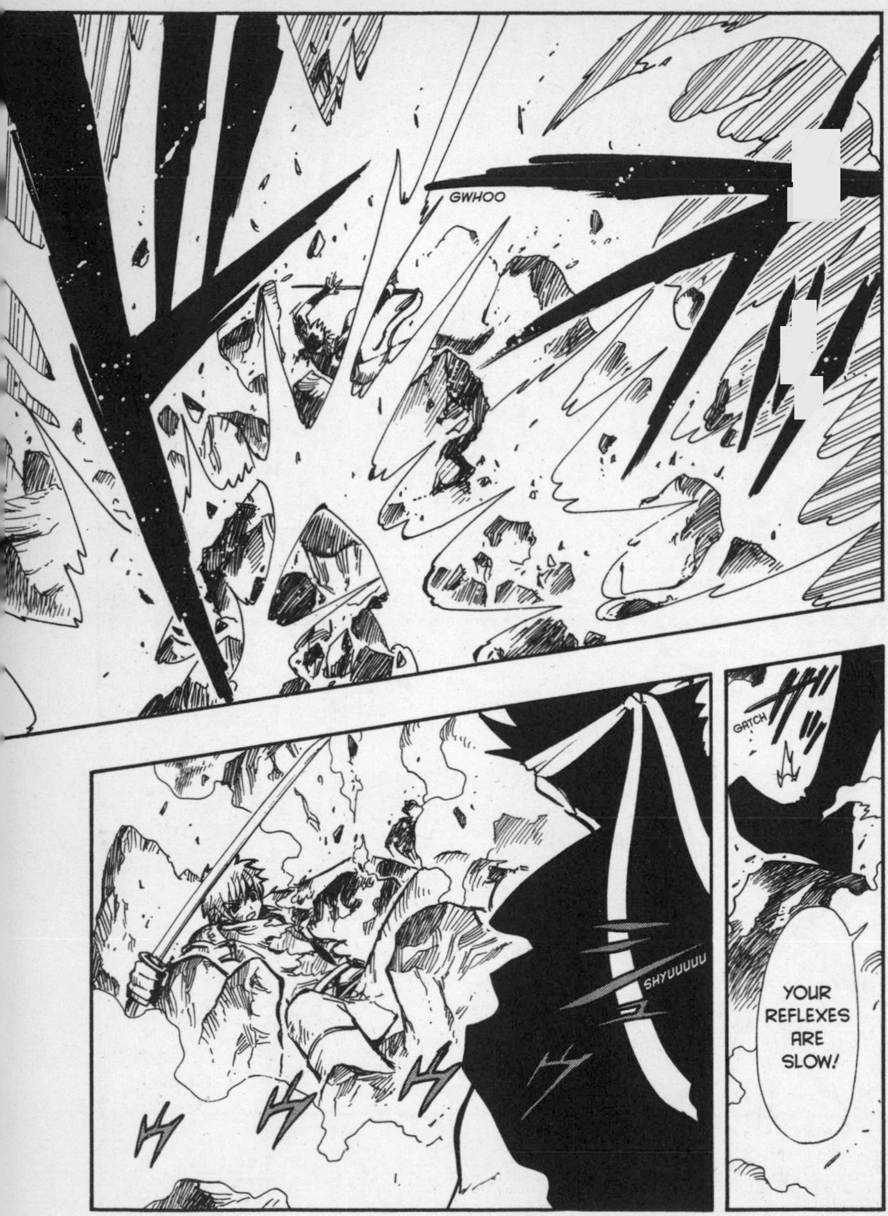
GWHOO
GATCH
YOUR REFLEXES ARE SLOW!
SHYUUUUU

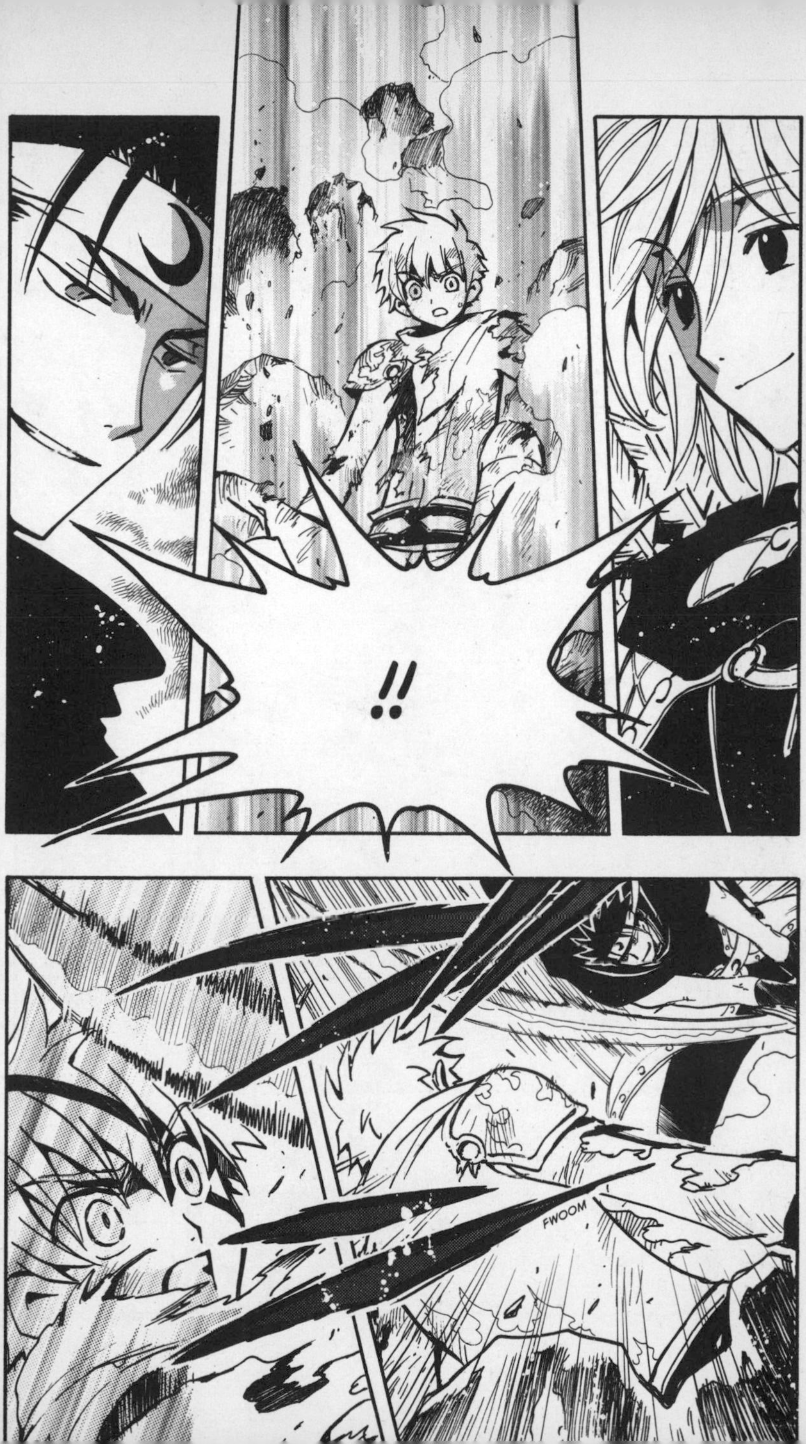
!!
FWOOM

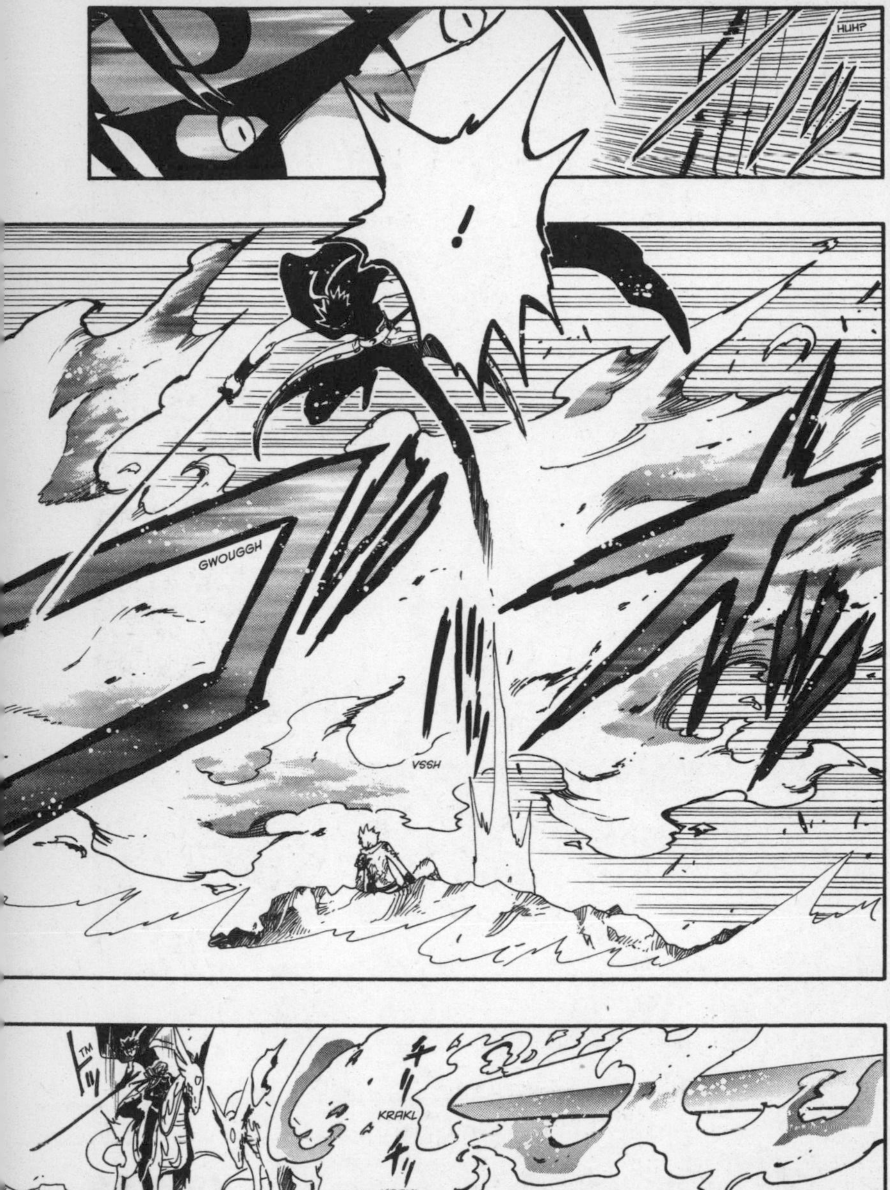
HUH?
!
GWOUGGH
VSSH
KRAKL
KRAKL

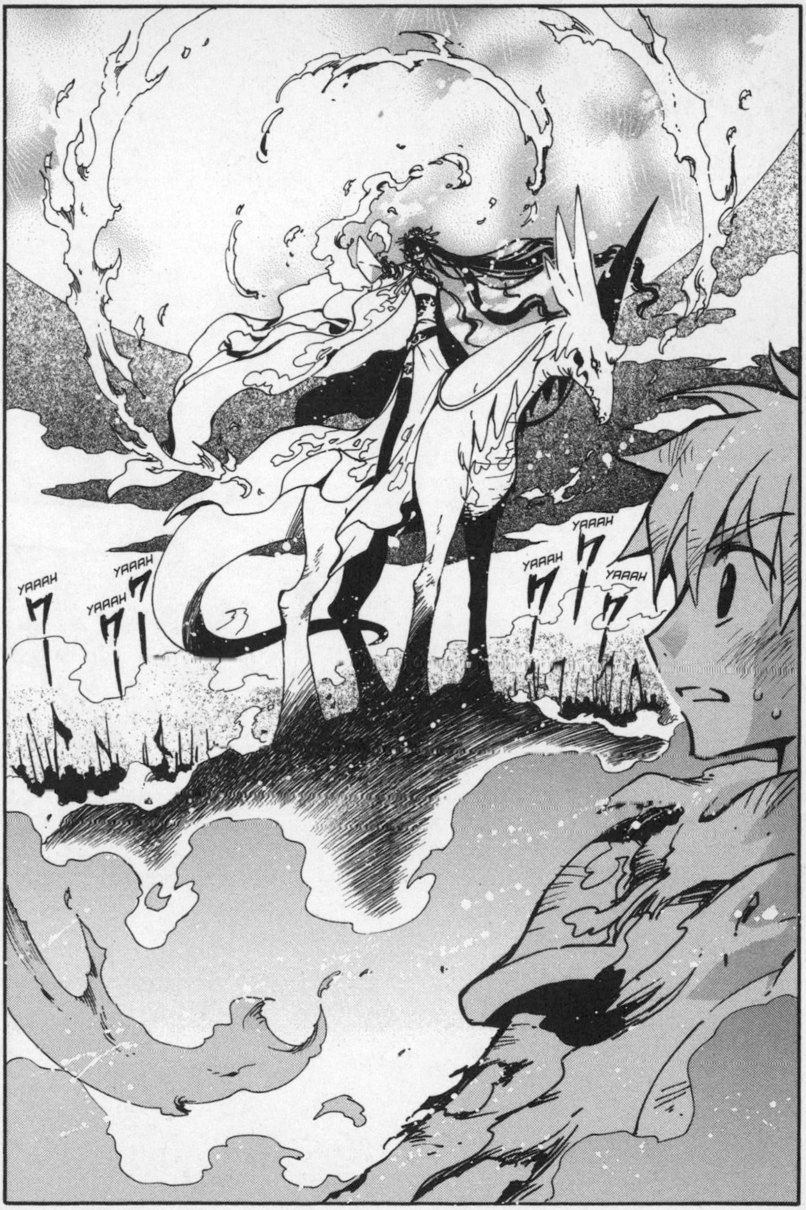
YAAAH
YAAAH
YAAAH
YAAAH
YAAAH
YAAAH

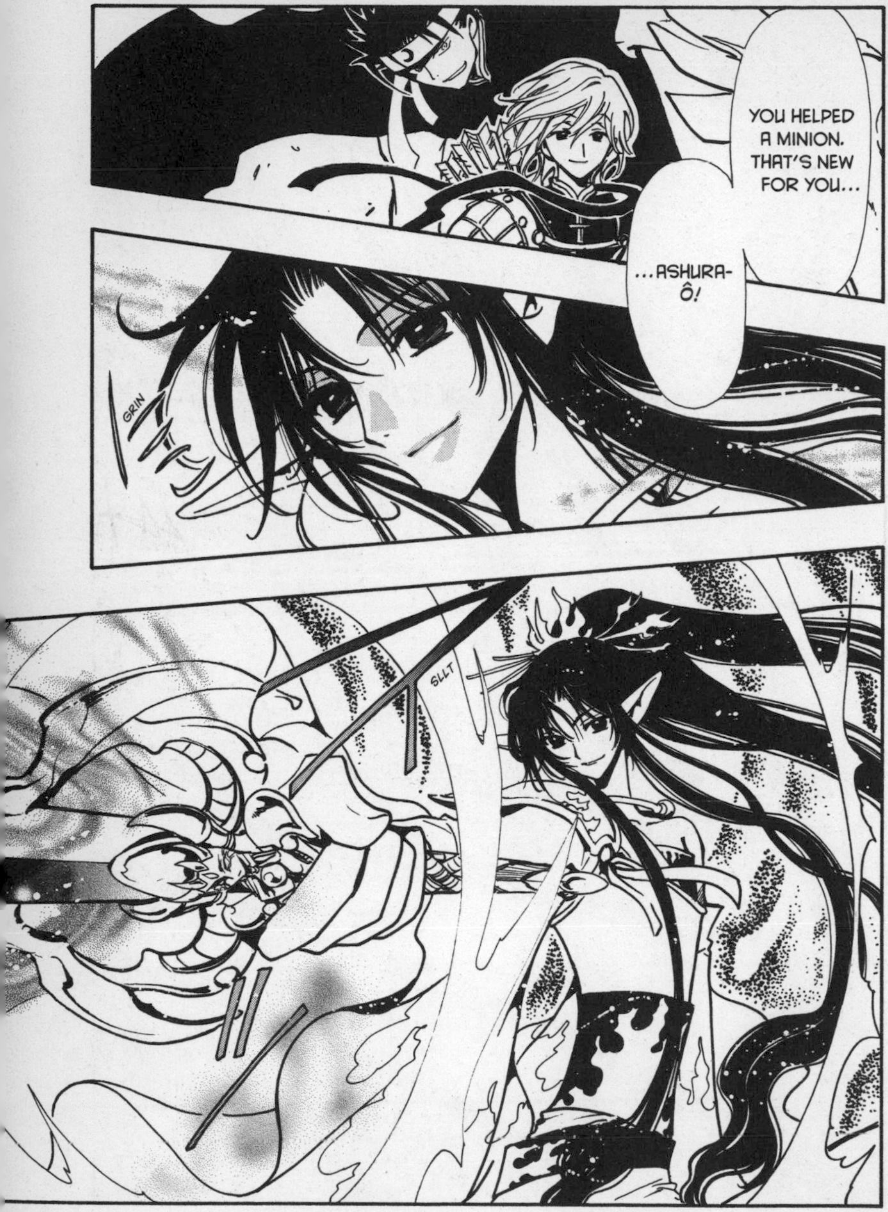
YOU HELPED A MINION. THAT'S NEW FOR YOU...
...ASHURA-Ô!
GRIN
SLLT

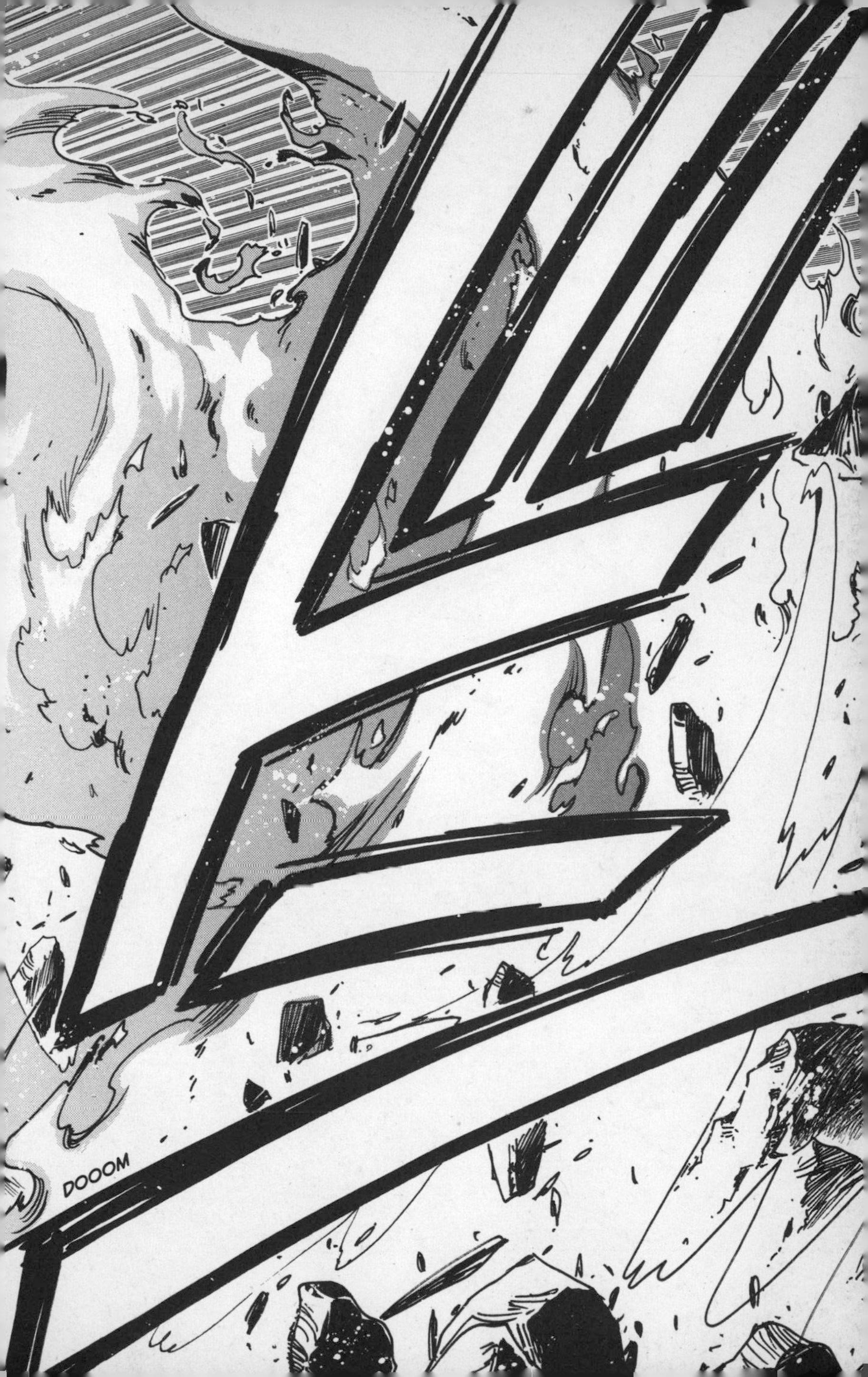
DOOOM

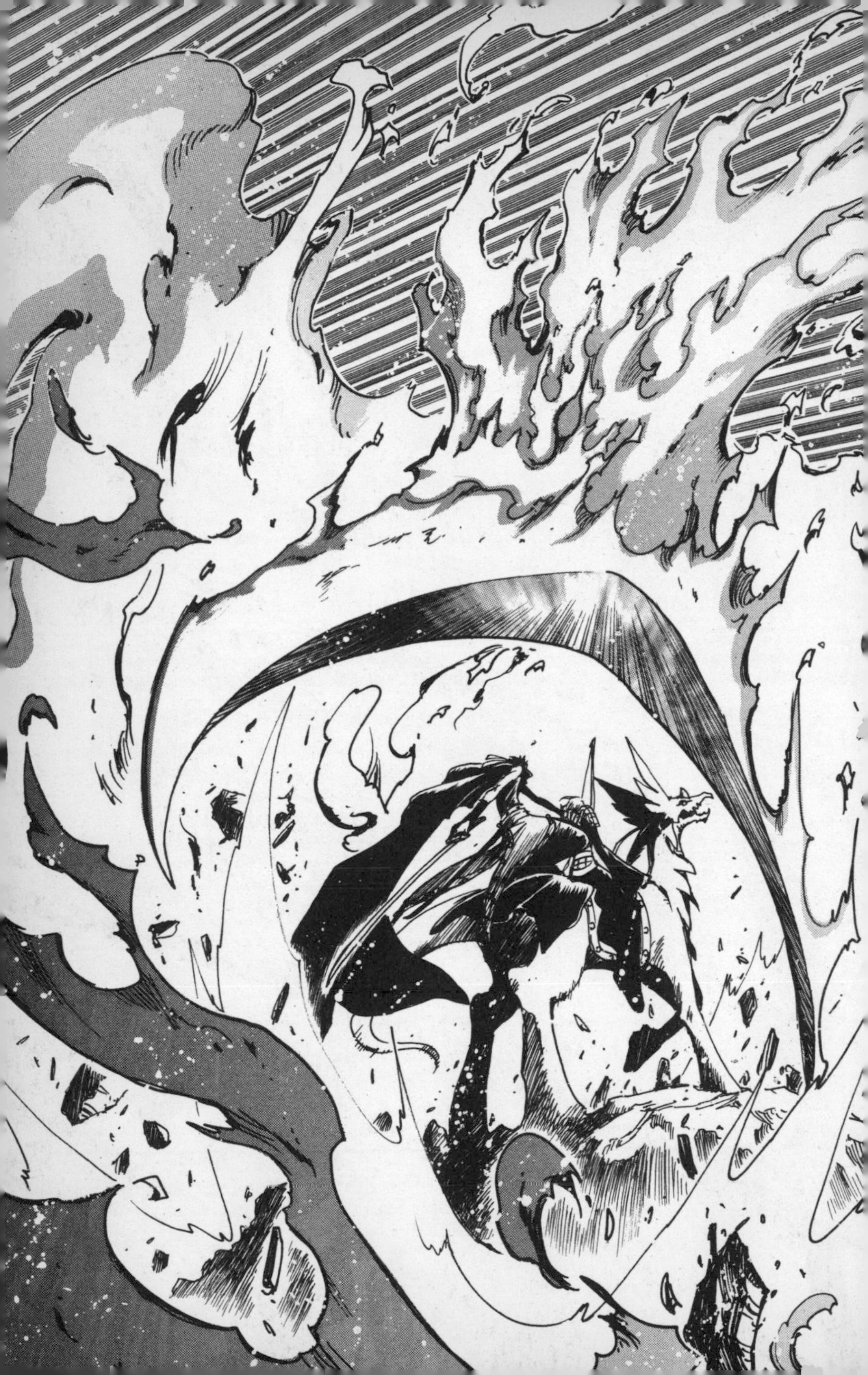

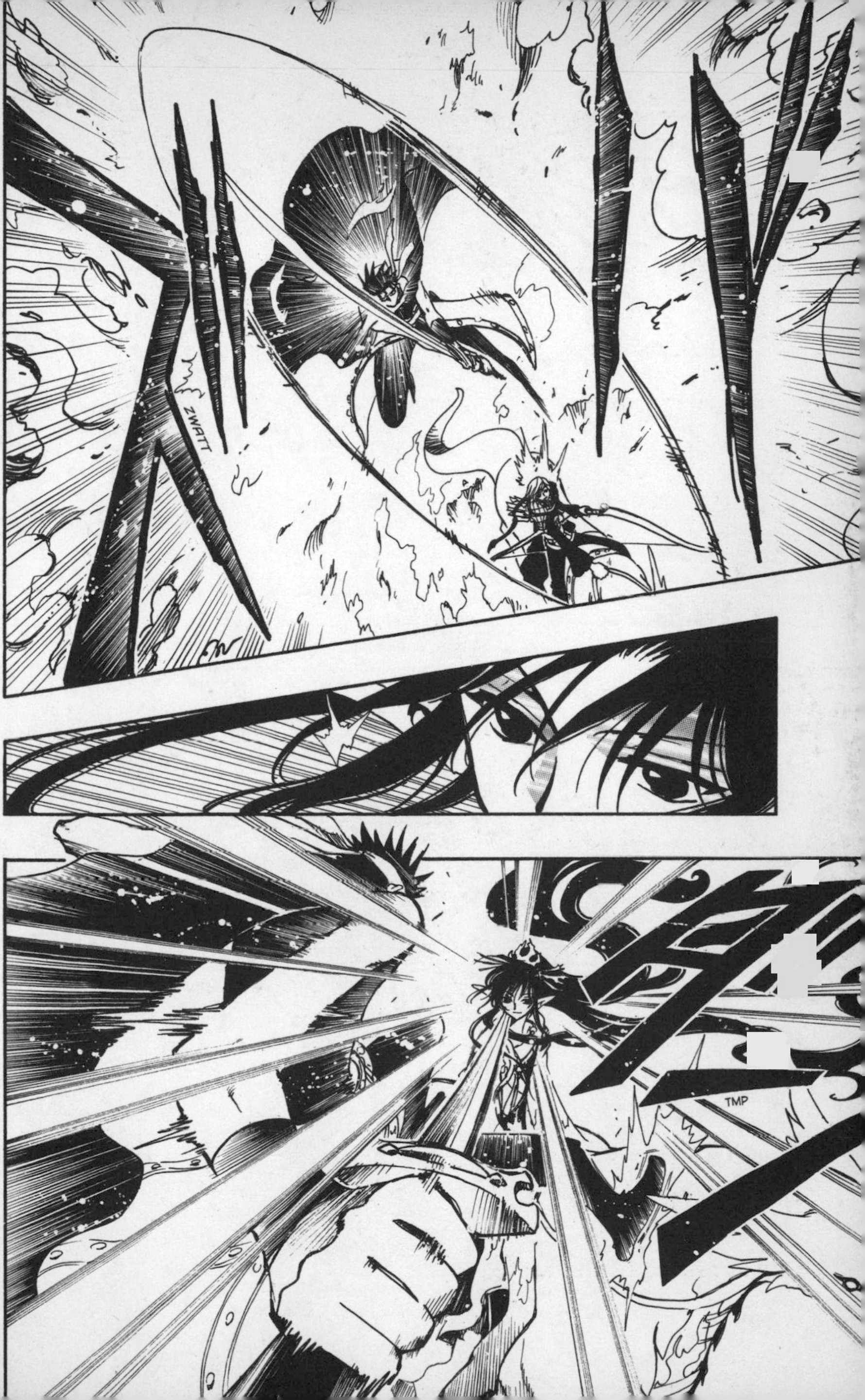
ZWATT
TMP

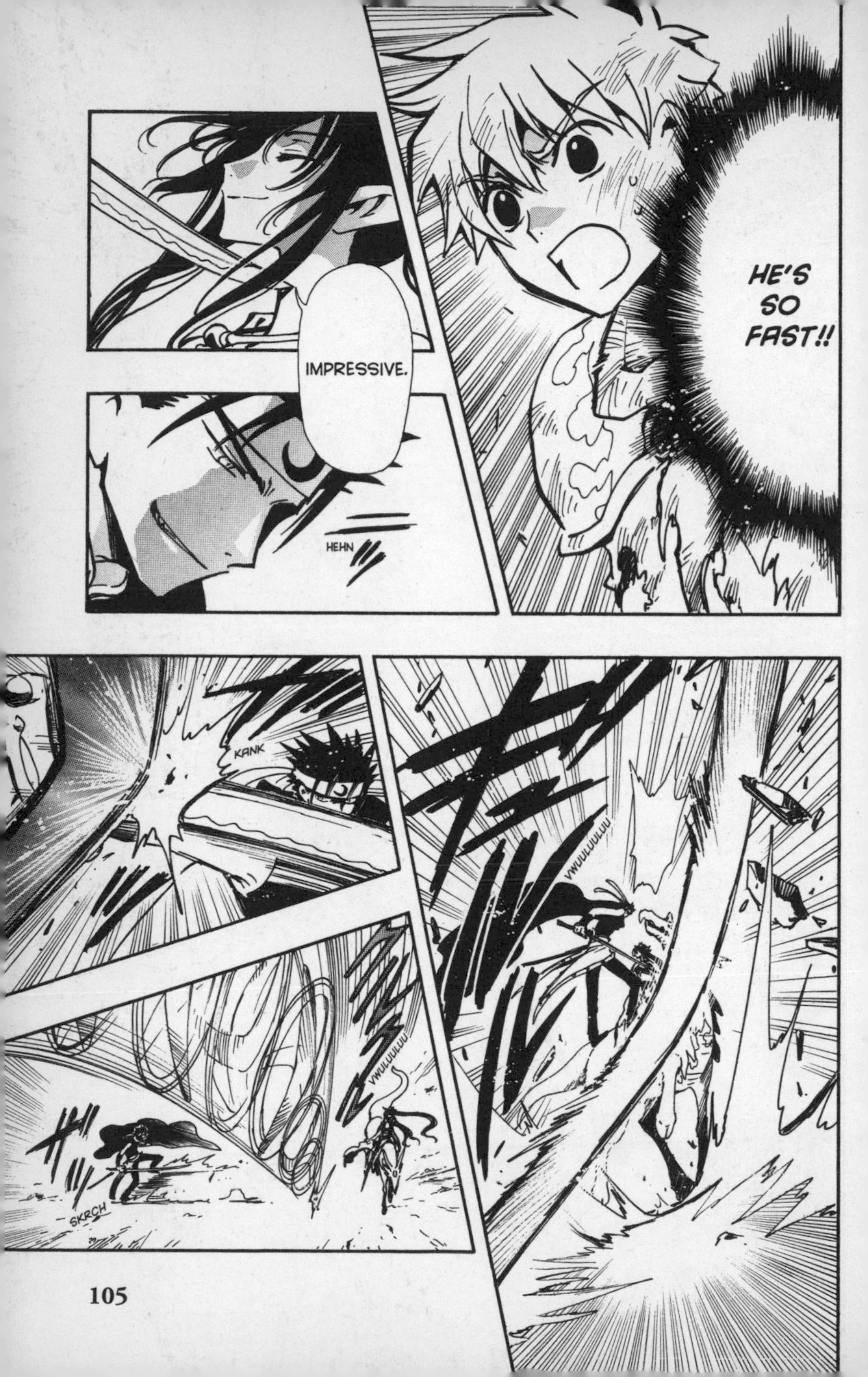
HE'S SO FAST!!
IMPRESSIVE.
HEHN
VWUULUULUU
KANK
VWULUULUU
SKRCH

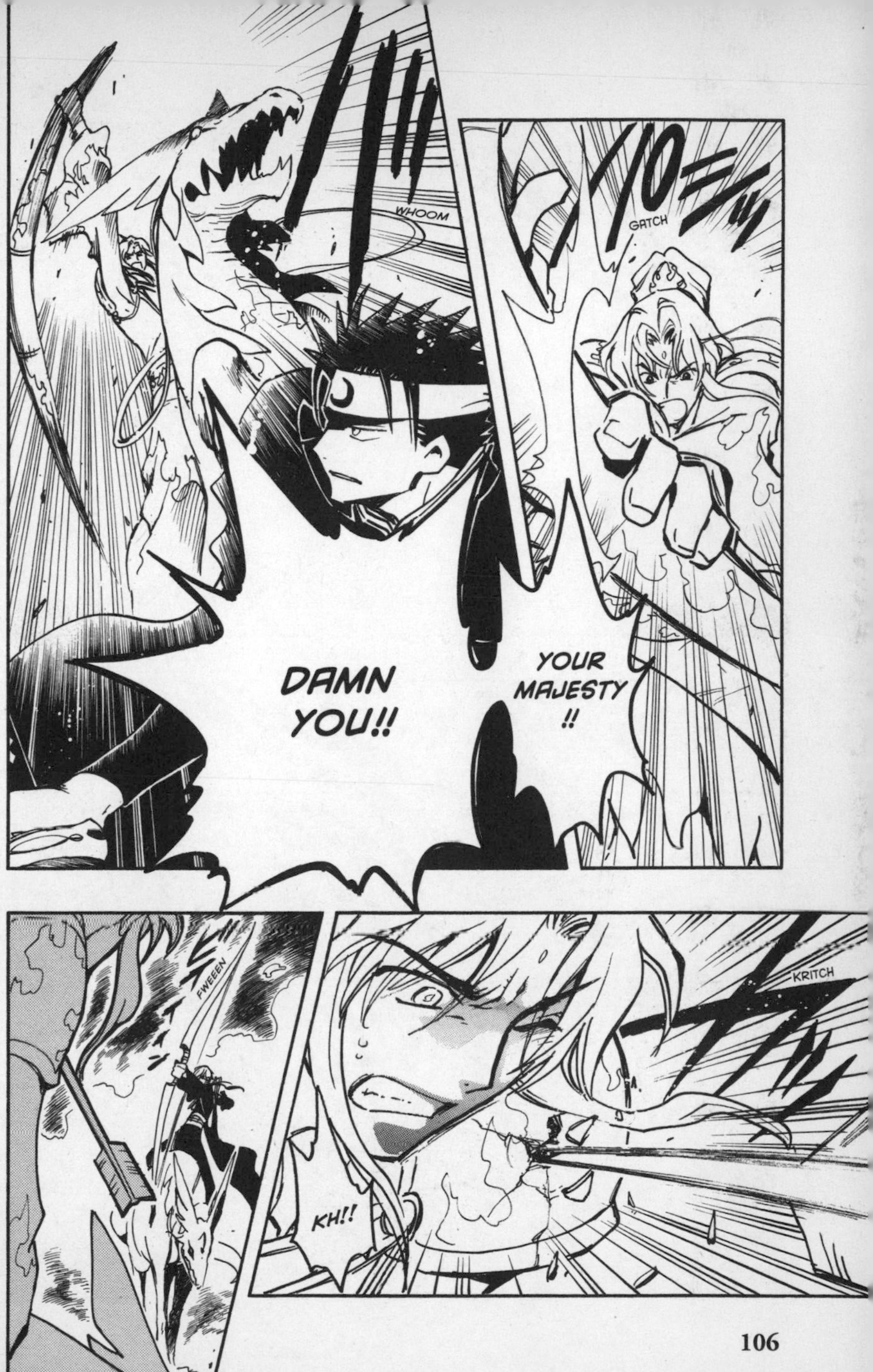
GRTCH
YOUR MAJESTY!!
WHOOM
DAMN YOU!!
KRITCH
KH!!
FWEEEN

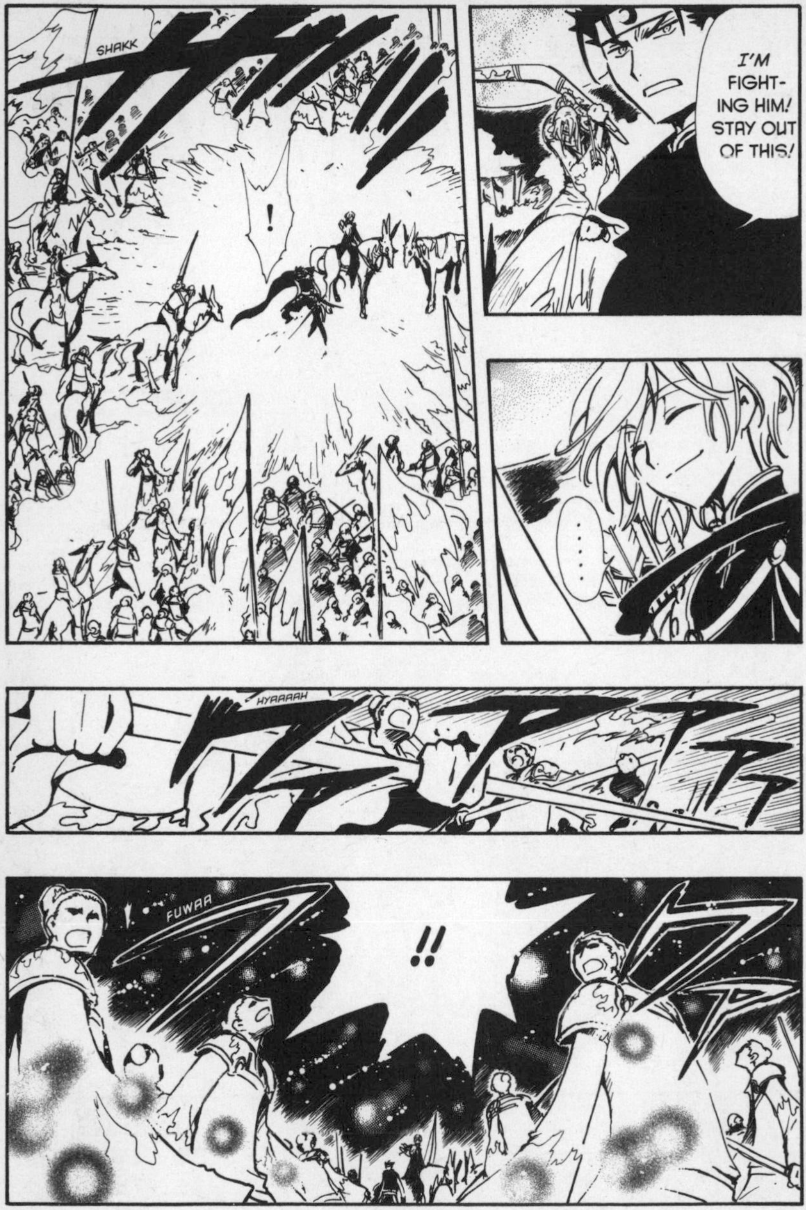
I'M FIGHT-ING HIM! STAY OUT OF THIS!
......
SHAKK
!
HYAAAAH
!!
FUWAA
!

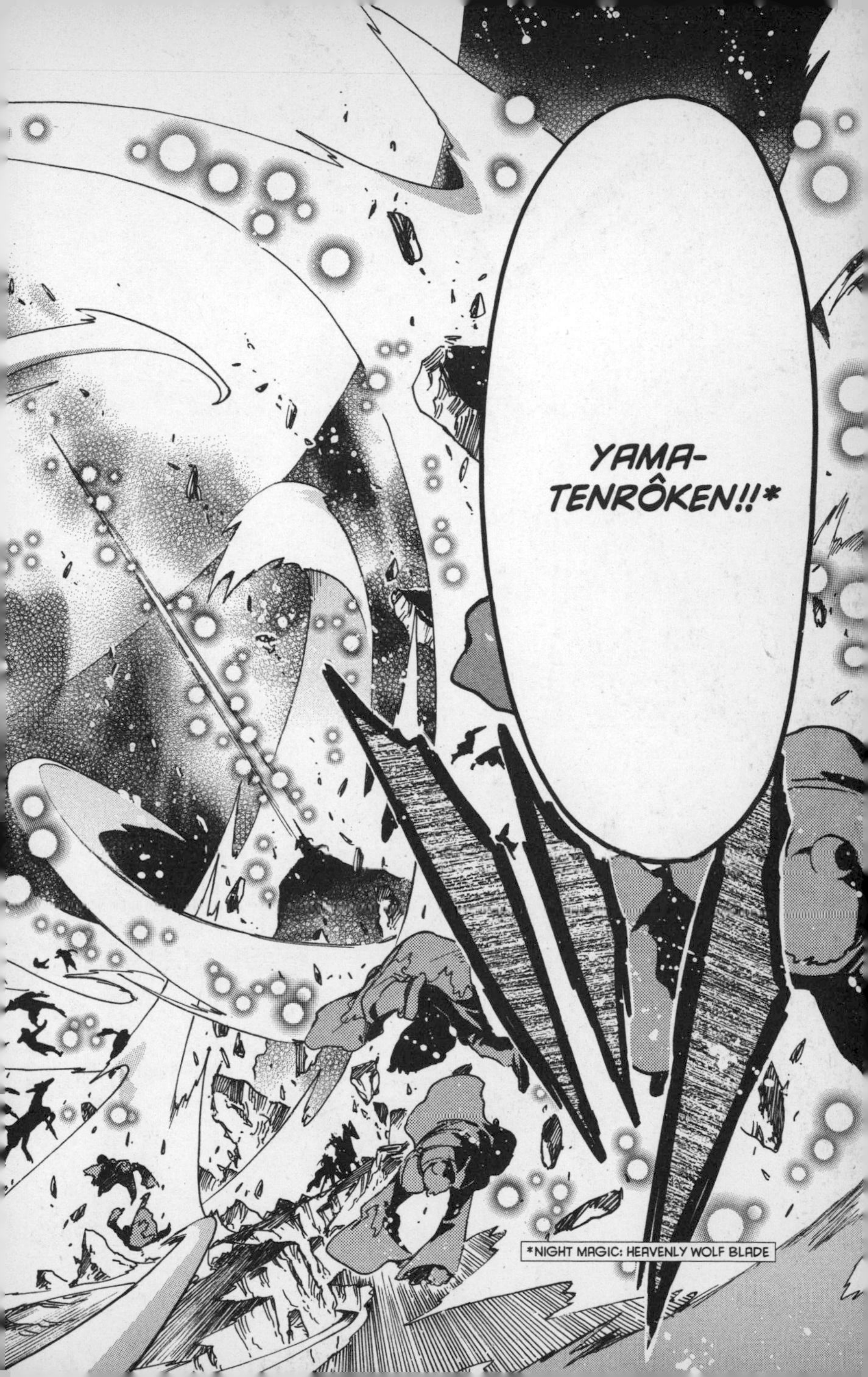
YAMA-TENRÔKEN!!*
*NIGHT MAGIC: HEAVENLY WOLF BLADE

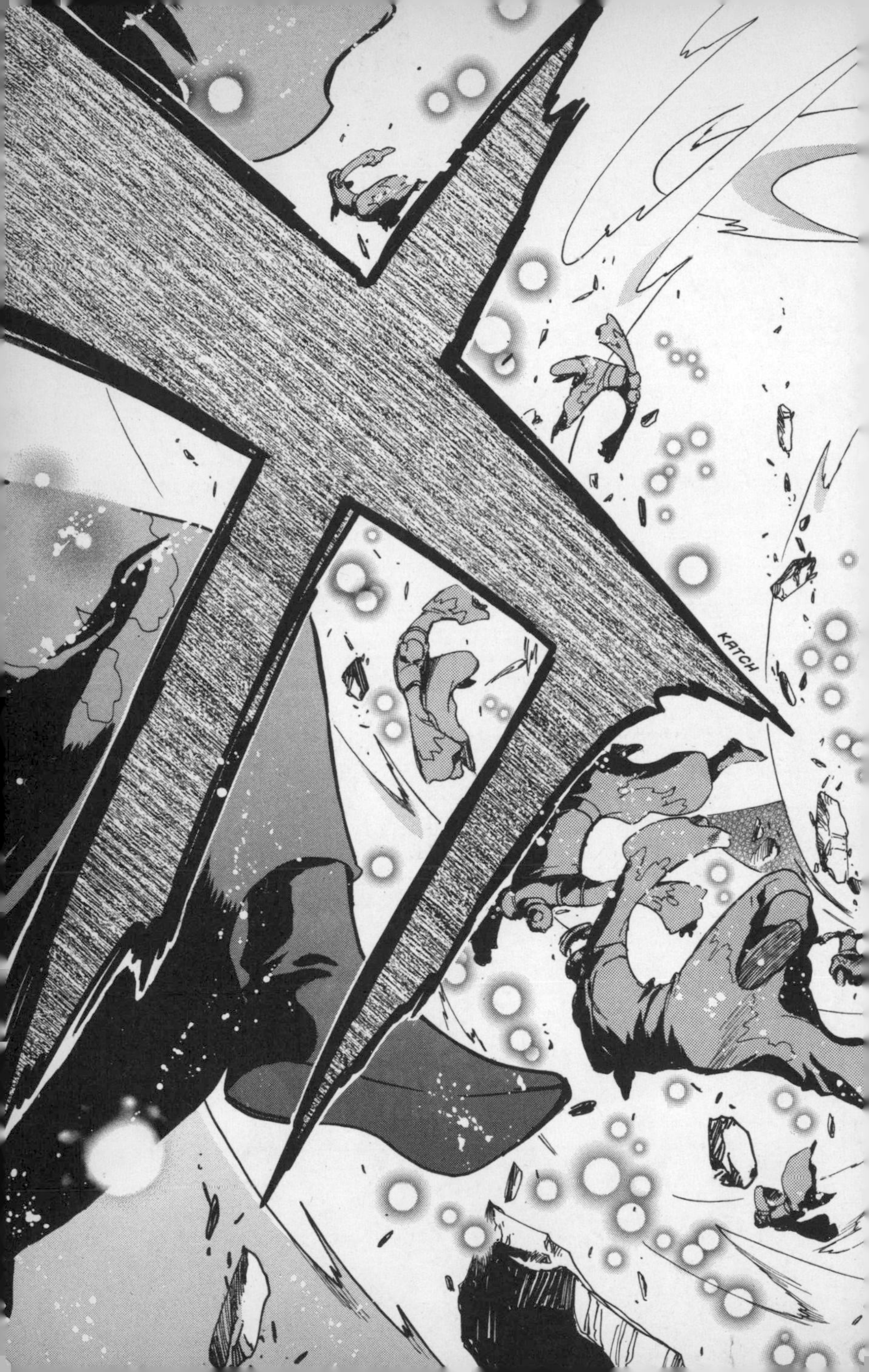
KATCH

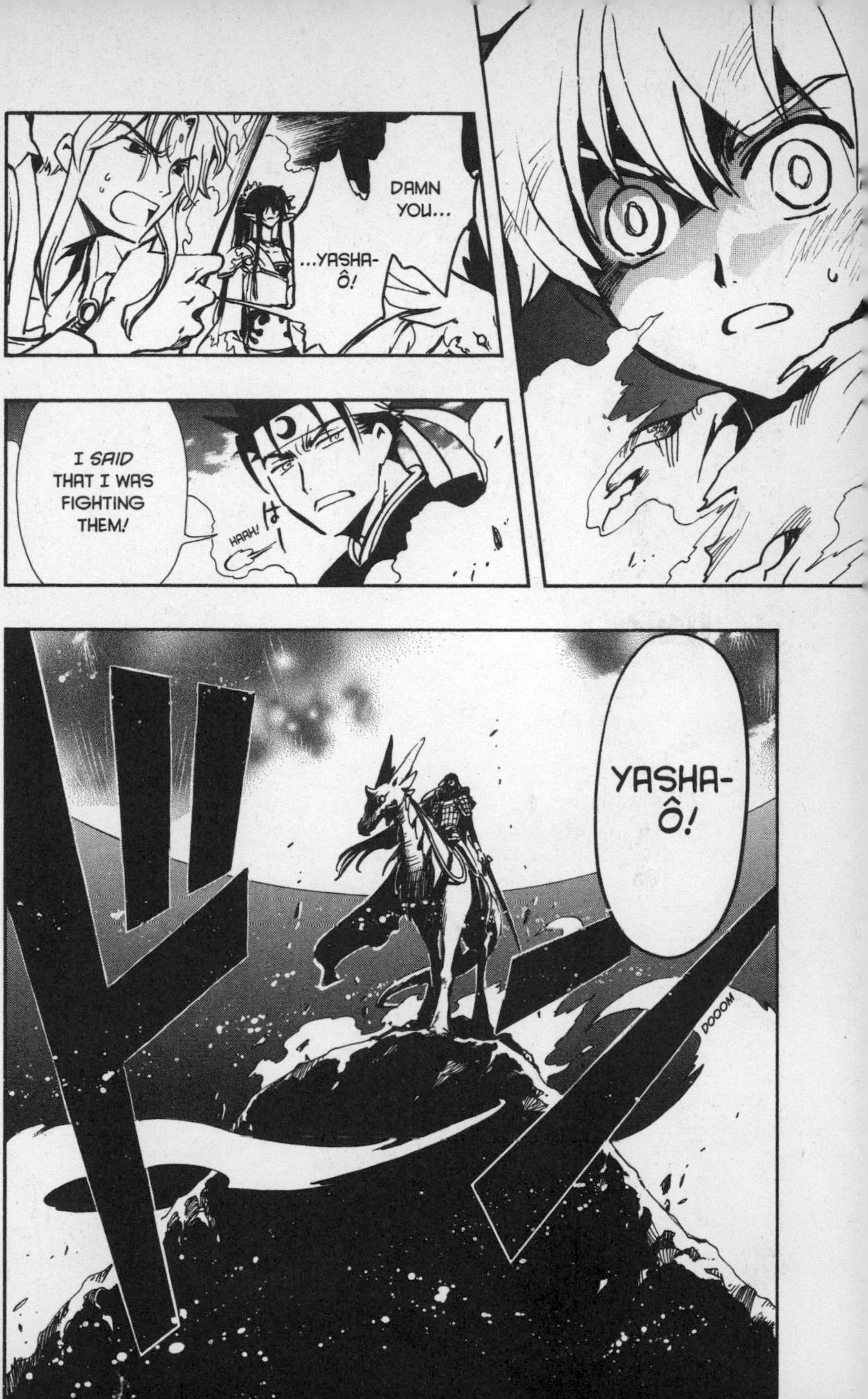
DAMN YOU...
...YASHA-Ô!
I SAID THAT I WAS FIGHTING THEM!
HAAH!
YASHA-Ô!
DOOOM

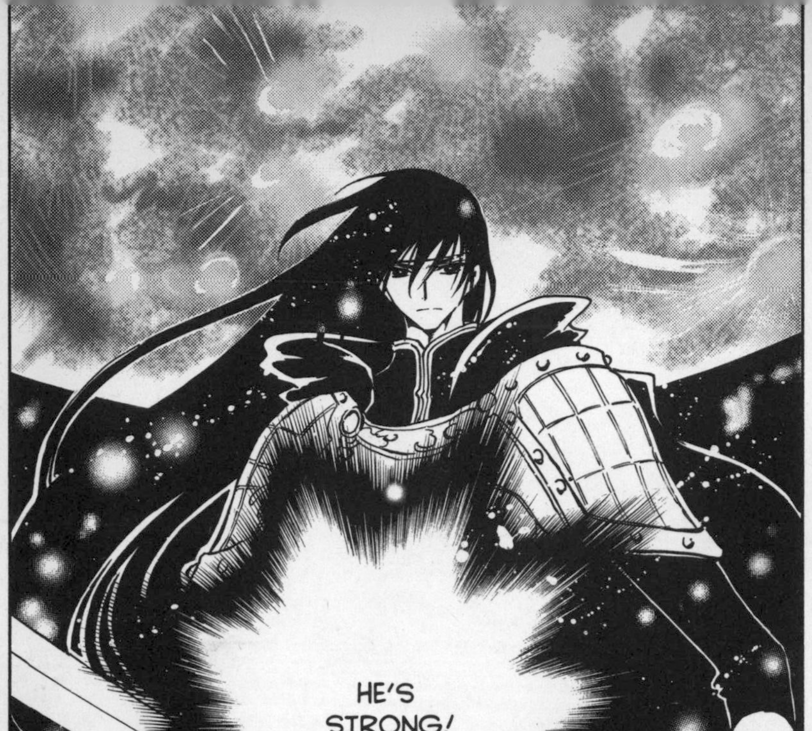
HE'S STRONG!

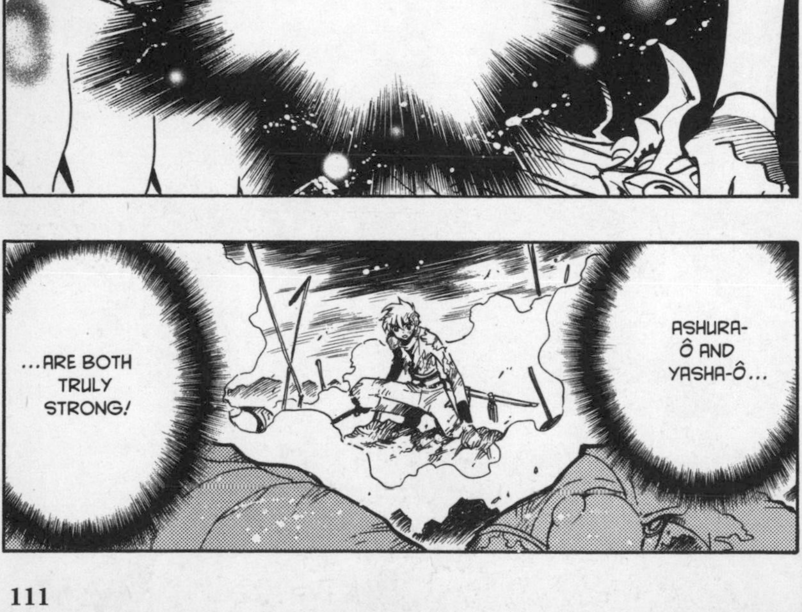
ASHURA-Ô AND YASHA-Ô...
...ARE BOTH TRULY STRONG!

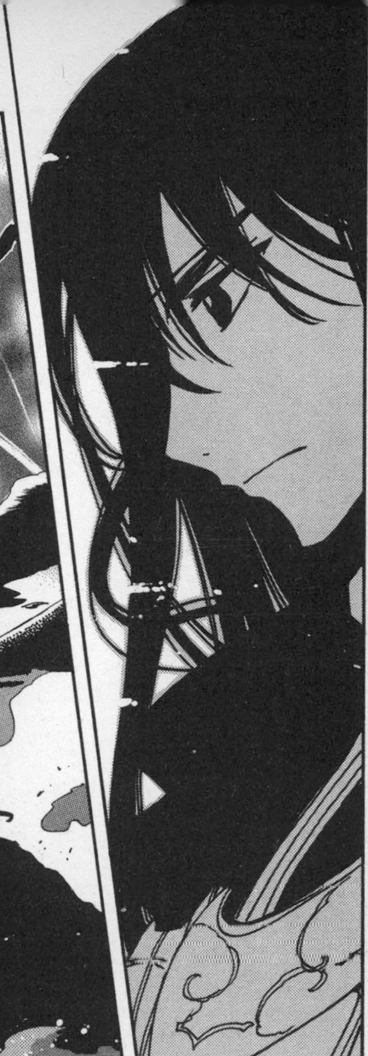

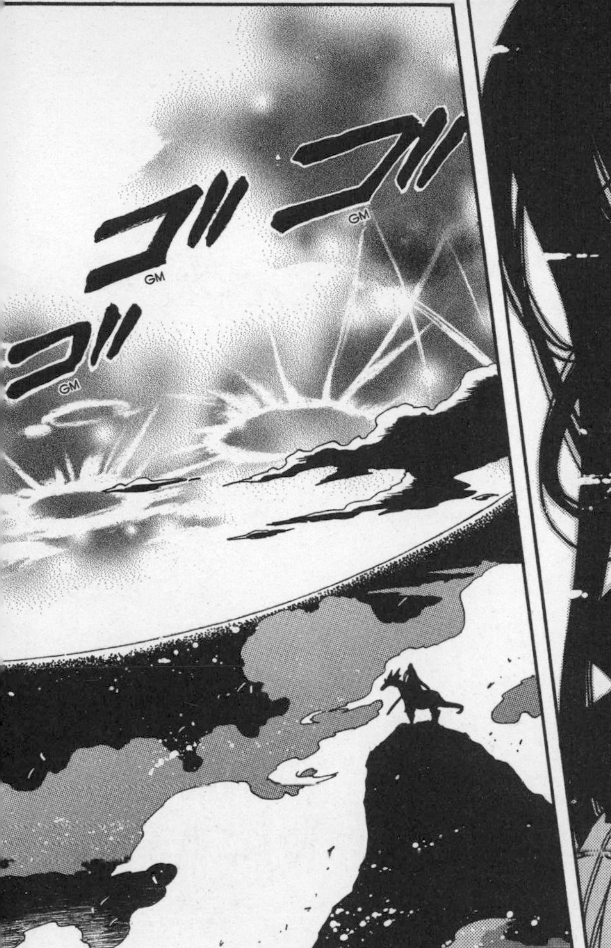
ゴ
GM
ゴ
GM
ゴ
GM

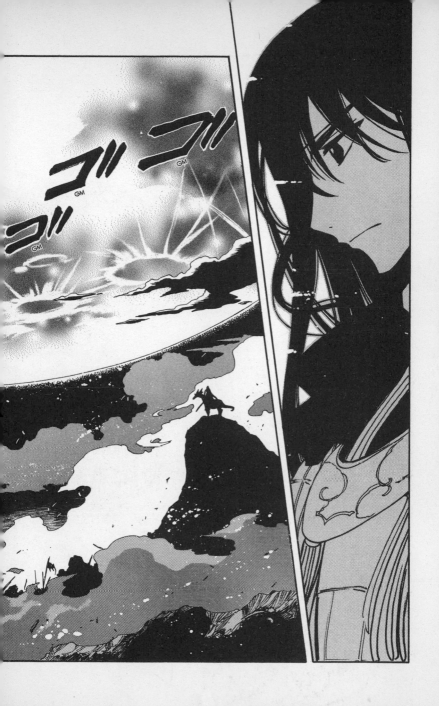

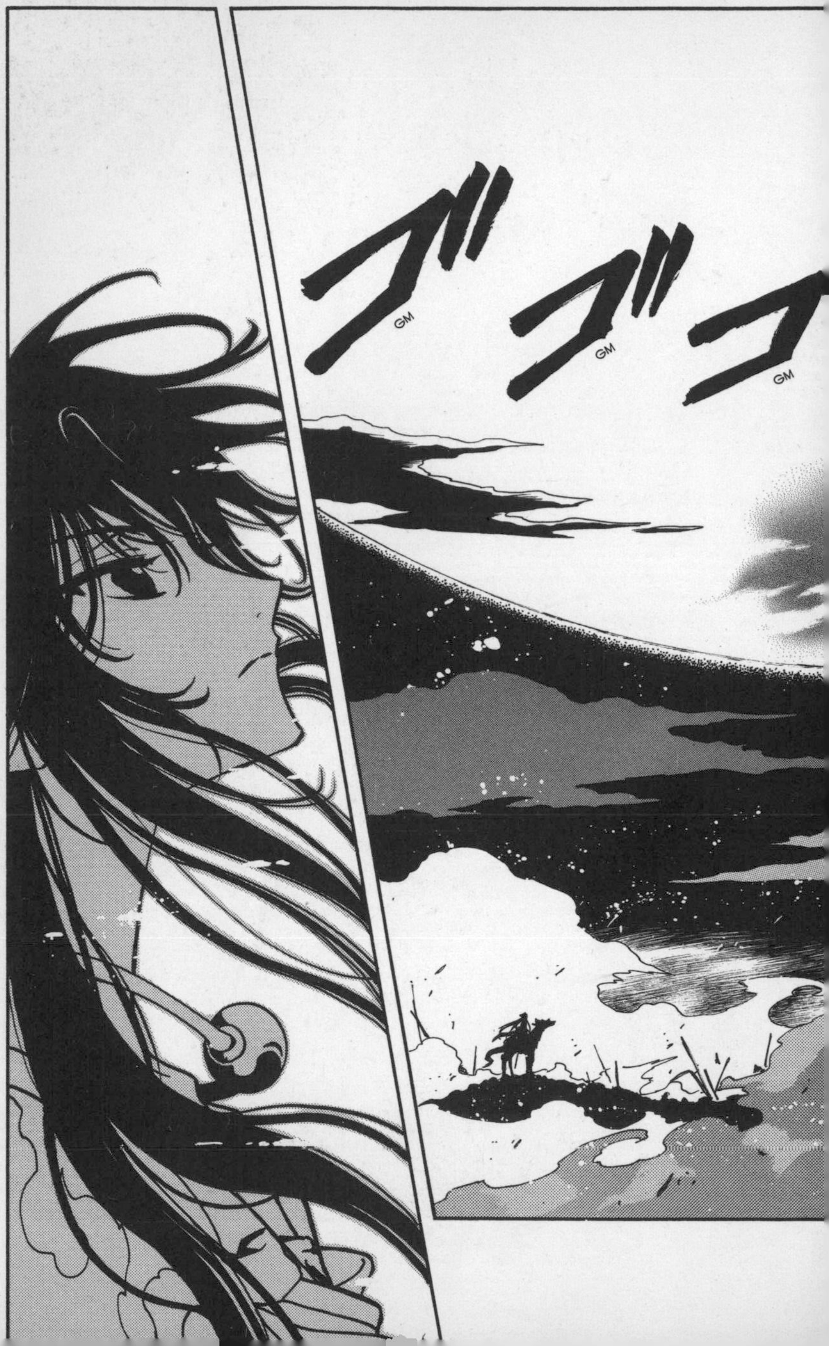
ゴ
GM
ゴ
GM
コ
GM

ツバサ

RESERVoir CHRoNiCLE

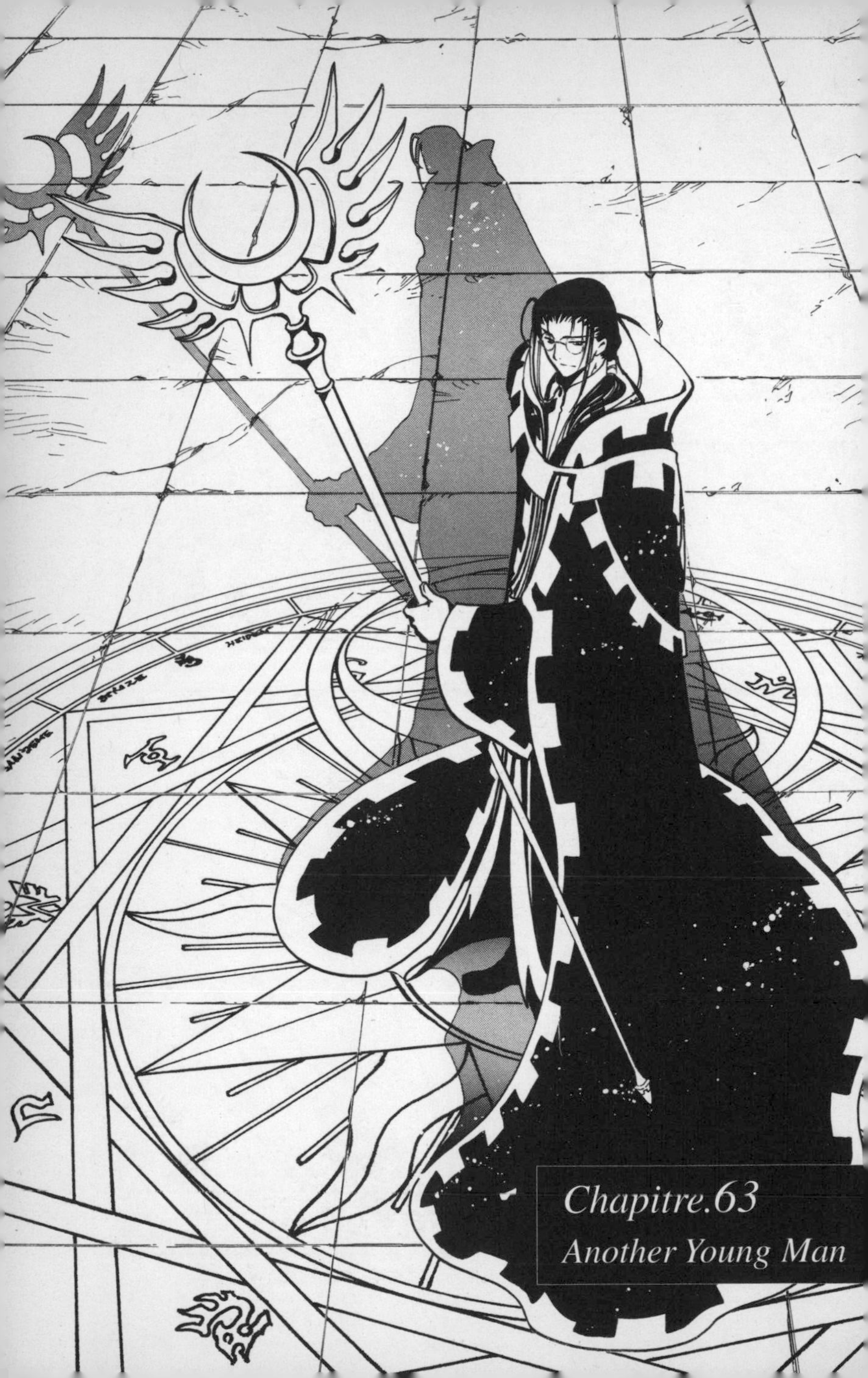
Chapitre.63
Another Young Man

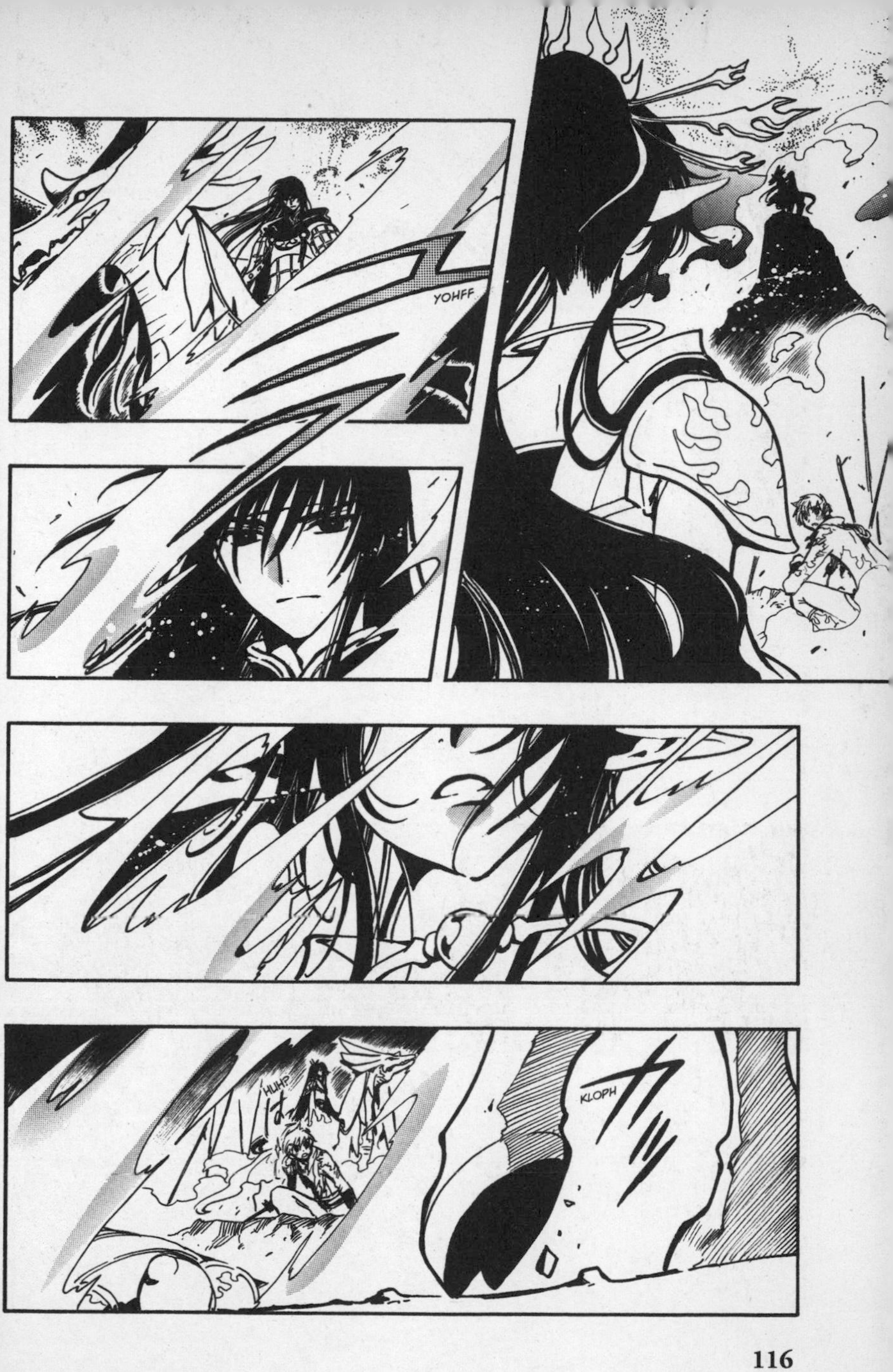
YOHFF
KLOPH
HUHP
は

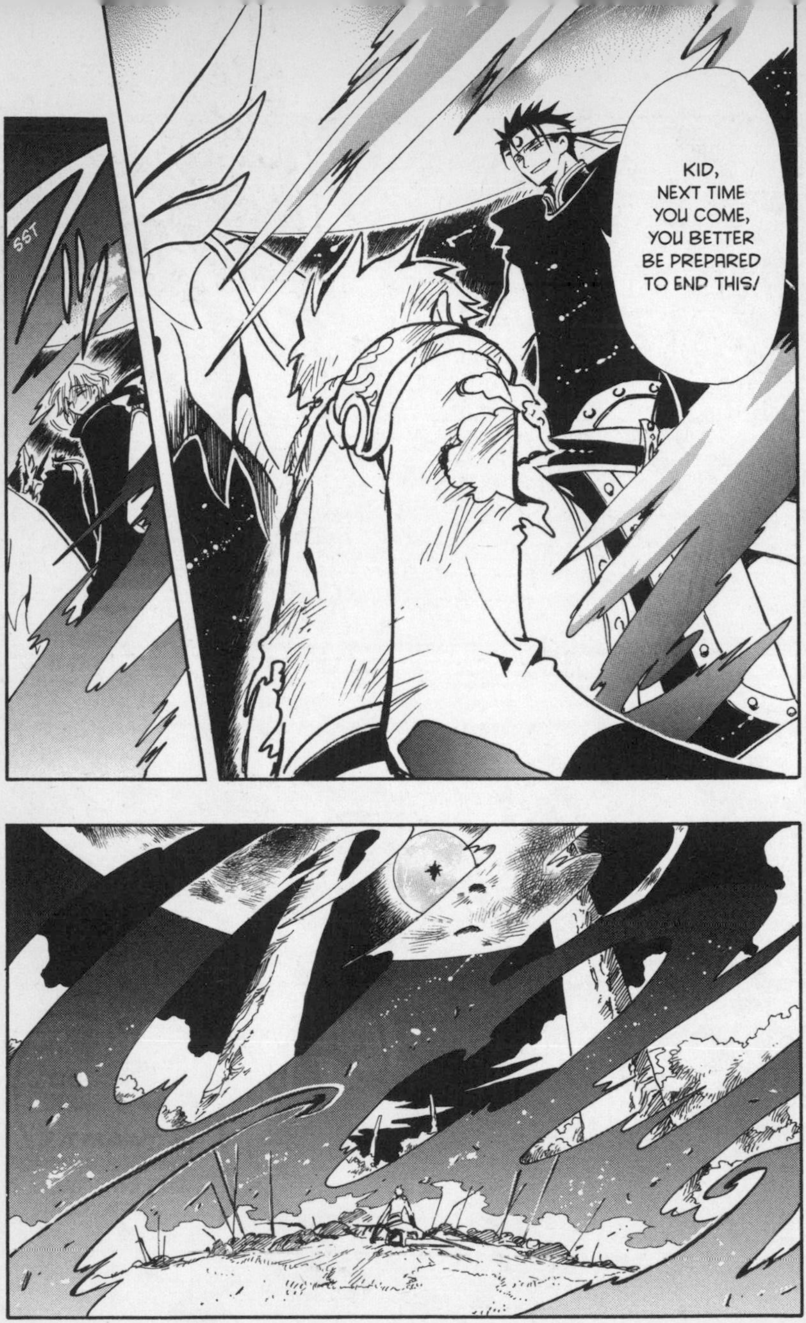
KID, NEXT TIME YOU COME, YOU BETTER BE PREPARED TO END THIS!
SST

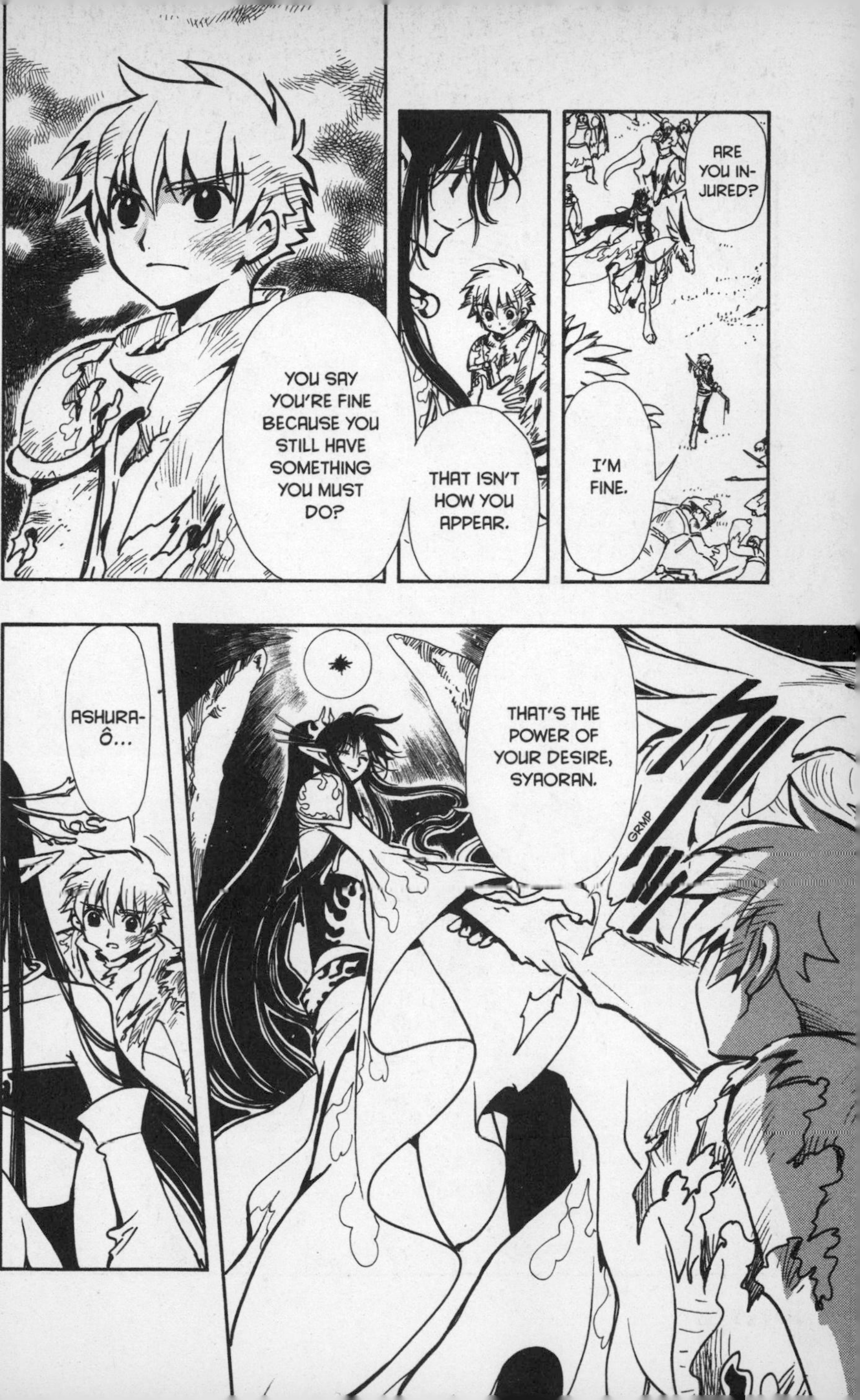
ARE YOU IN-JURED?
I'M FINE.
THAT ISN'T HOW YOU APPEAR.
YOU SAY YOU'RE FINE BECAUSE YOU STILL HAVE SOMETHING YOU MUST DO?
THAT'S THE POWER OF YOUR DESIRE, SYAORAN.
GRMP
ASHURA-Ô...

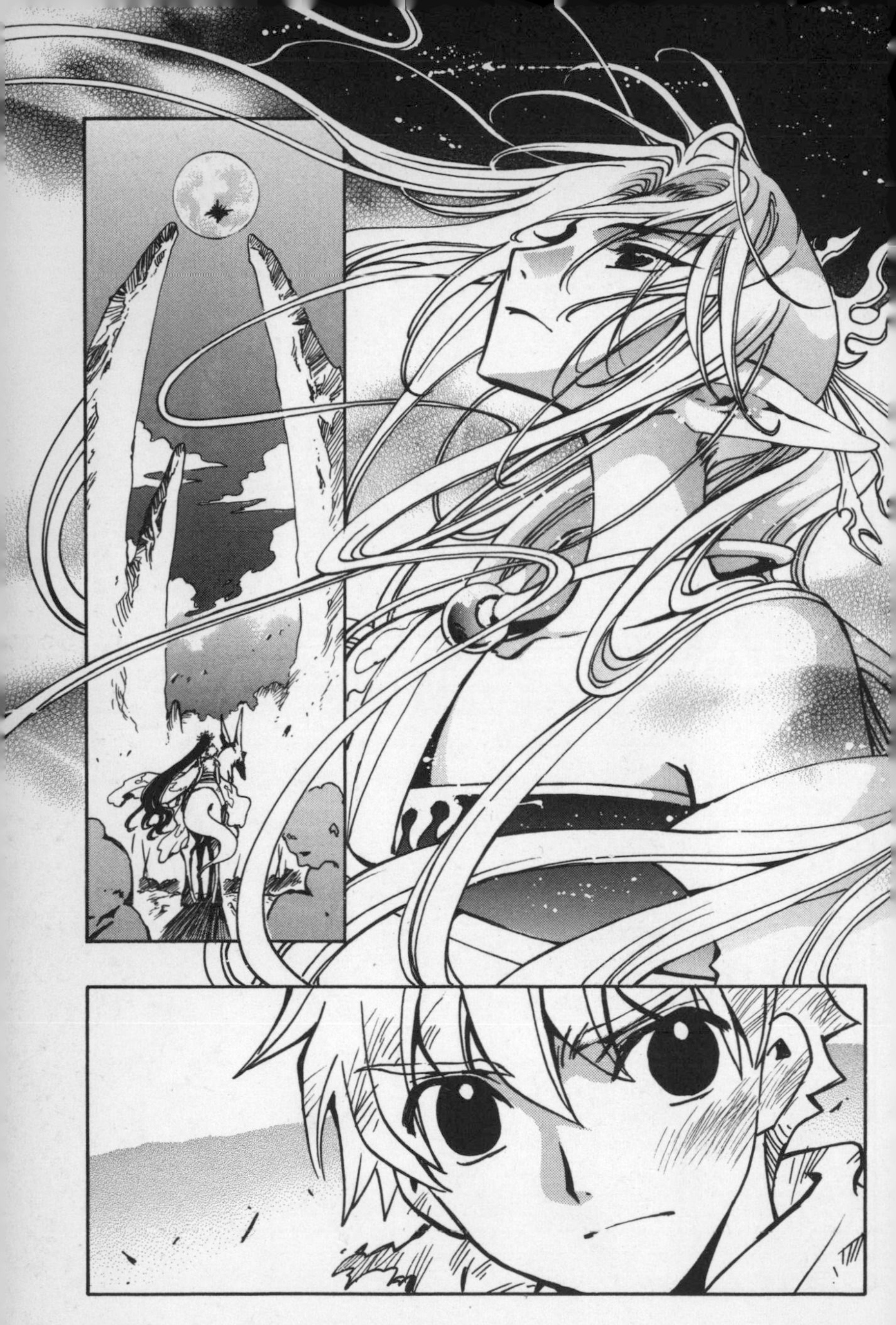

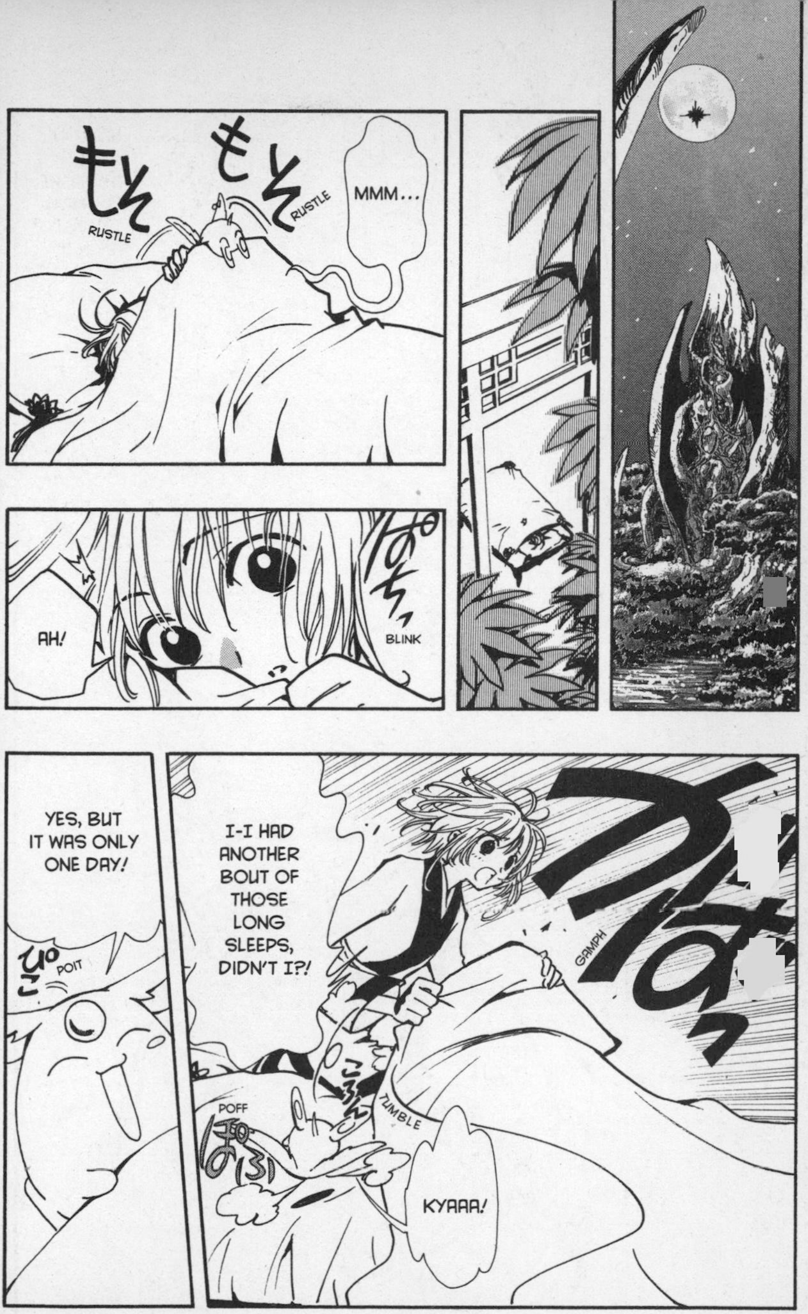
MMM...
もそ
RUSTLE
もそ
RUSTLE
BLINK
AH!
GAMPH
I-I HAD ANOTHER BOUT OF THOSE LONG SLEEPS, DIDN'T I?!
TUMBLE
POFF
KYAAA!
YES, BUT IT WAS ONLY ONE DAY!
POIT

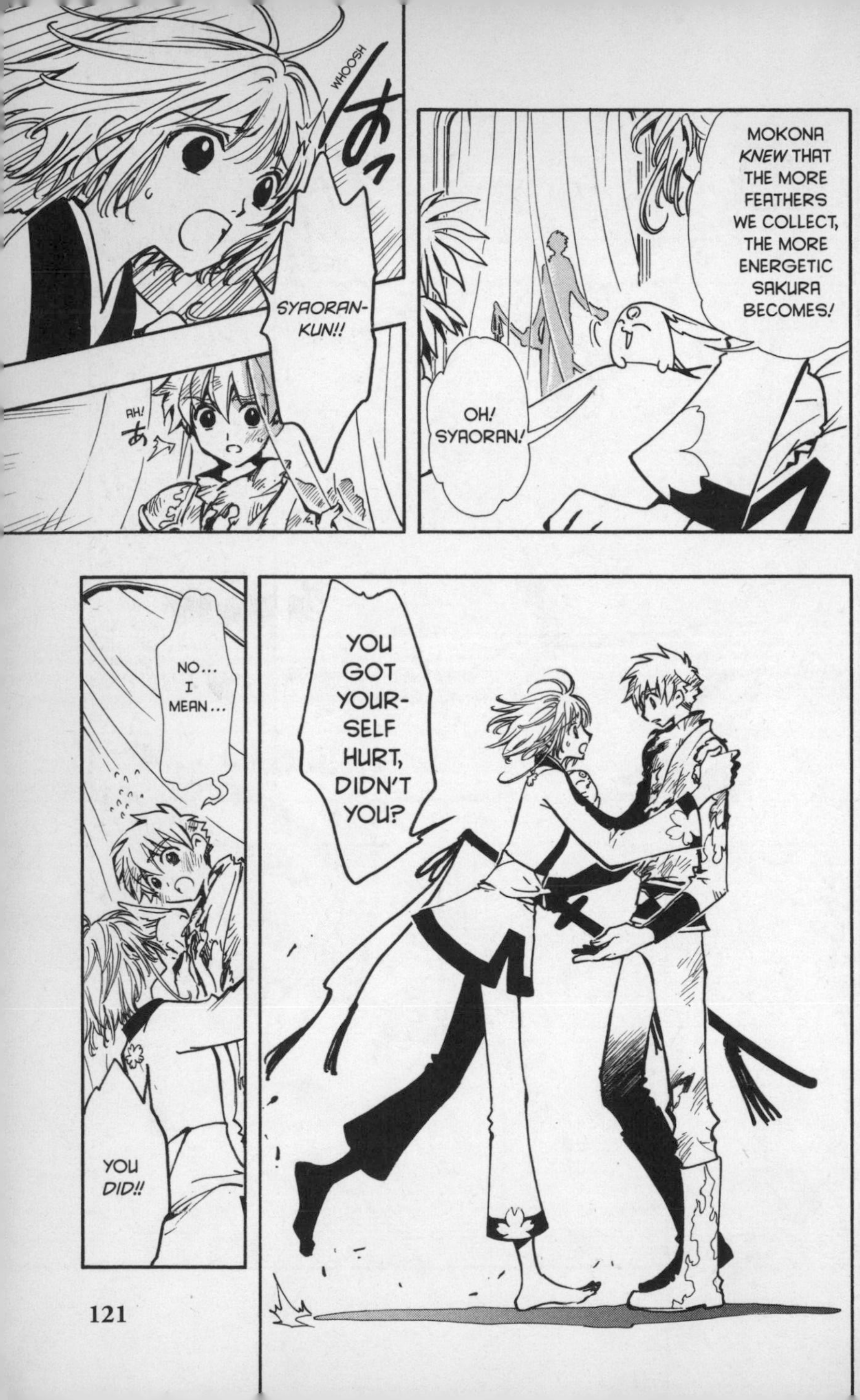

MOKONA *KNEW* THAT THE MORE FEATHERS WE COLLECT, THE MORE ENERGETIC SAKURA BECOMES!
OH! SYAORAN!
WHOOSH
おっ
SYAORAN-KUN!!
AH!
あ
YOU GOT YOUR-SELF HURT, DIDN'T YOU?
NO... I MEAN...
YOU DID!!

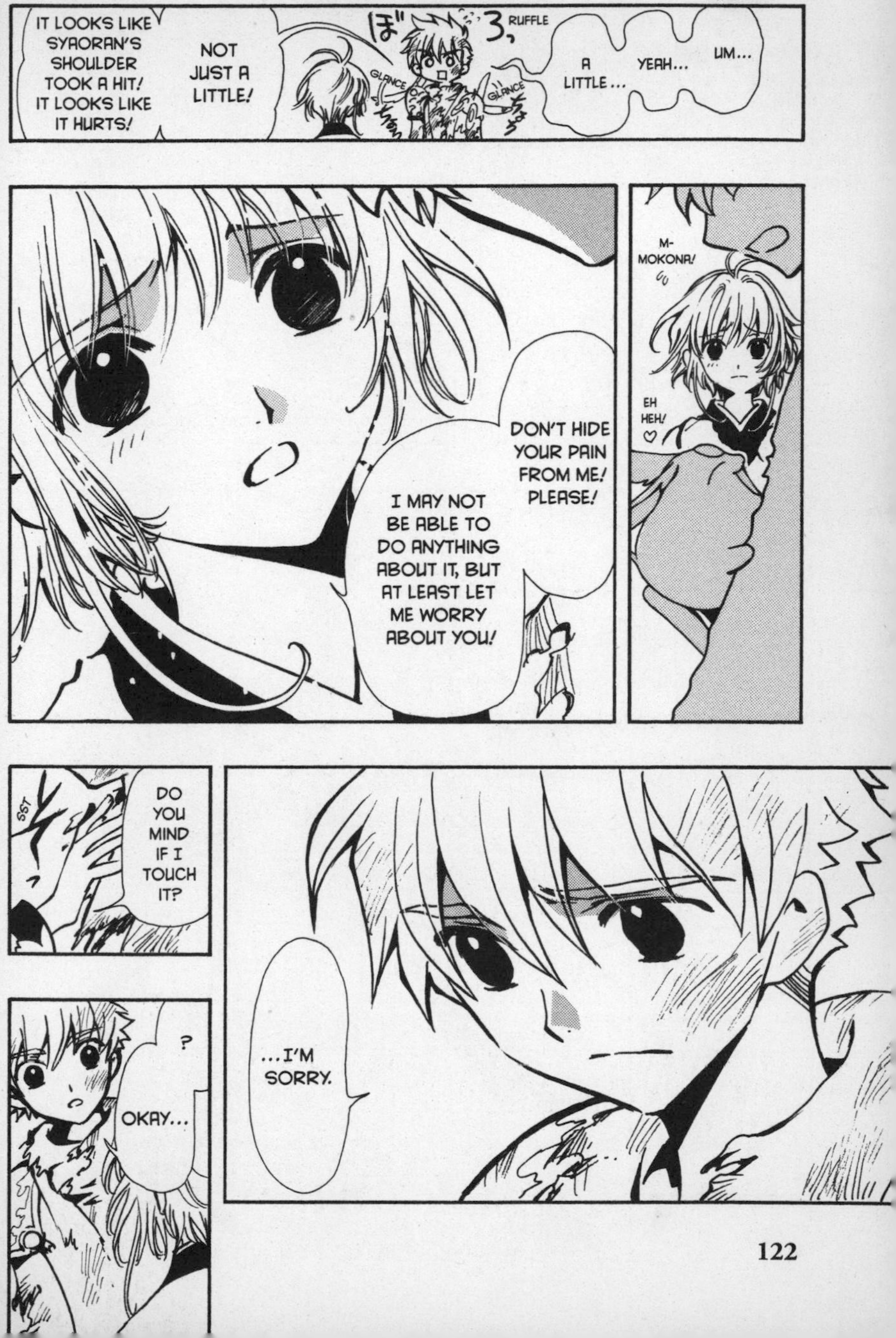
UM...
YEAH...
A LITTLE...
RUFFLE
GLANCE
GLANCE
NOT JUST A LITTLE!
IT LOOKS LIKE SYAORAN'S SHOULDER TOOK A HIT! IT LOOKS LIKE IT HURTS!
M-MOKONA!
EH HEH! ♡
DON'T HIDE YOUR PAIN FROM ME! PLEASE!
I MAY NOT BE ABLE TO DO ANYTHING ABOUT IT, BUT AT LEAST LET ME WORRY ABOUT YOU!
...I'M SORRY.
DO YOU MIND IF I TOUCH IT?
SST
?
OKAY...

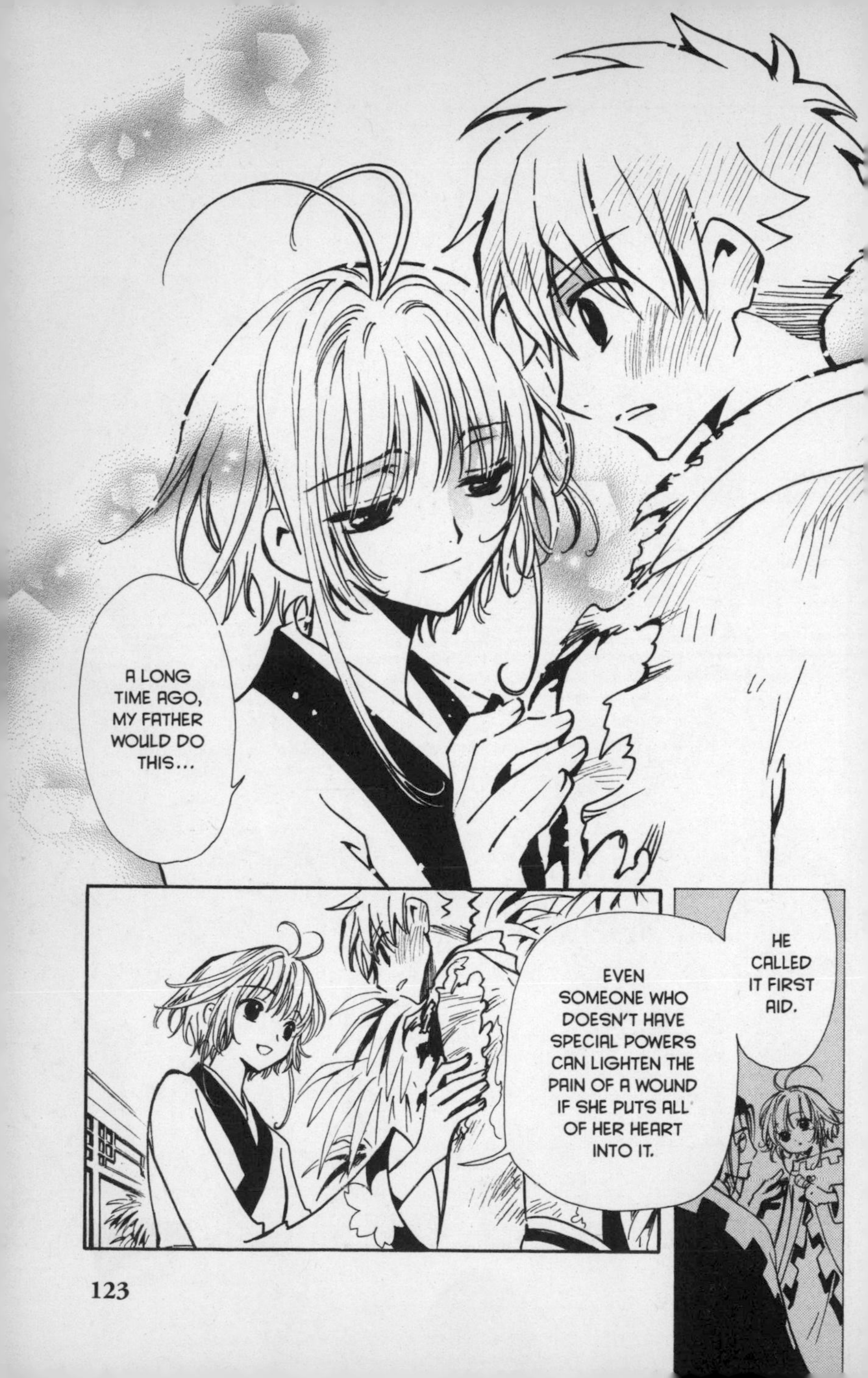
A LONG TIME AGO, MY FATHER WOULD DO THIS...
HE CALLED IT FIRST AID.
EVEN SOMEONE WHO DOESN'T HAVE SPECIAL POWERS CAN LIGHTEN THE PAIN OF A WOUND IF SHE PUTS ALL OF HER HEART INTO IT.

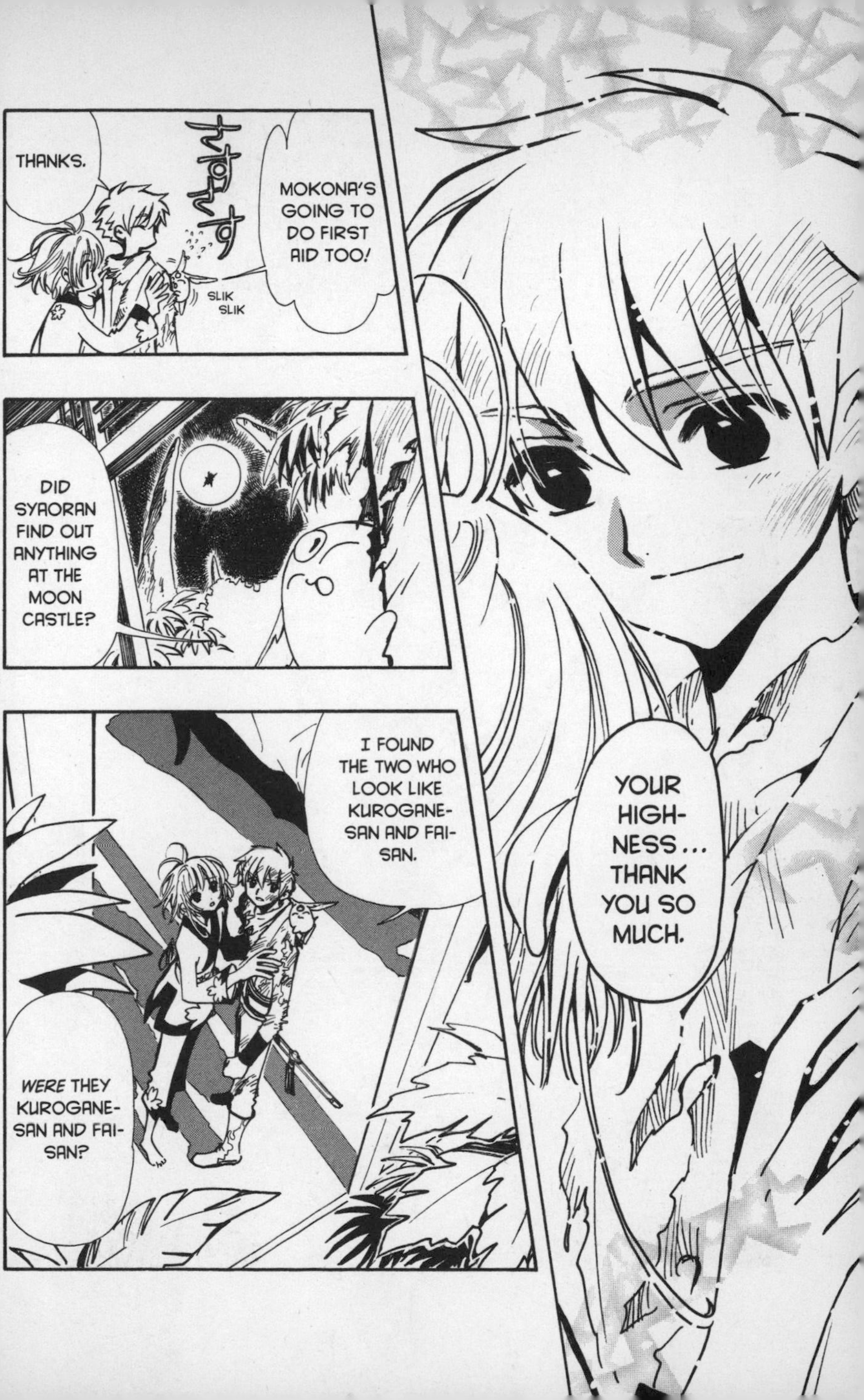
YOUR HIGHNESS... THANK YOU SO MUCH.
MOKONA'S GOING TO DO FIRST AID TOO!
SLIK SLIK
THANKS.
DID SYAORAN FIND OUT ANYTHING AT THE MOON CASTLE?
I FOUND THE TWO WHO LOOK LIKE KUROGANE-SAN AND FAI-SAN.
WERE THEY KUROGANE-SAN AND FAI-SAN?

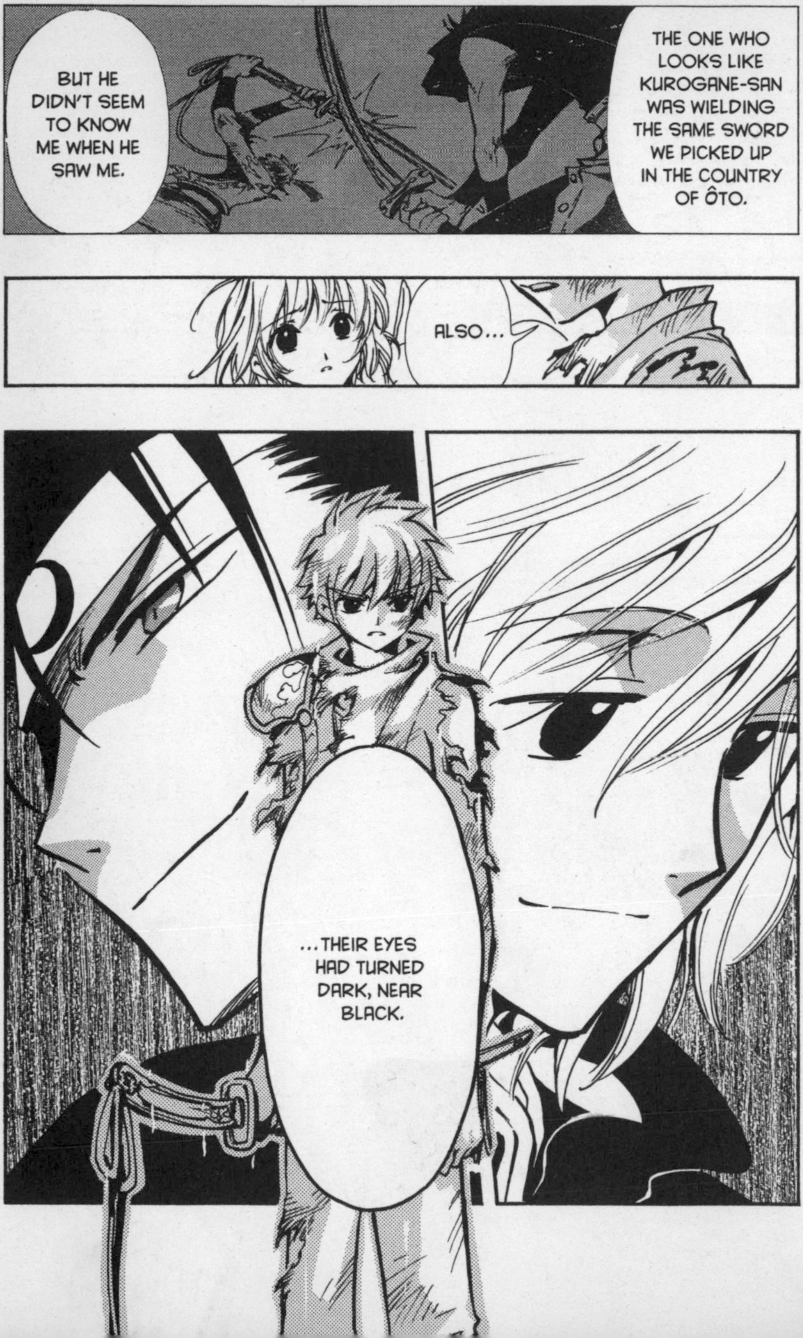
THE ONE WHO LOOKS LIKE KUROGANE-SAN WAS WIELDING THE SAME SWORD WE PICKED UP IN THE COUNTRY OF ÔTO.
BUT HE DIDN'T SEEM TO KNOW ME WHEN HE SAW ME.
ALSO...
...THEIR EYES HAD TURNED DARK, NEAR BLACK.

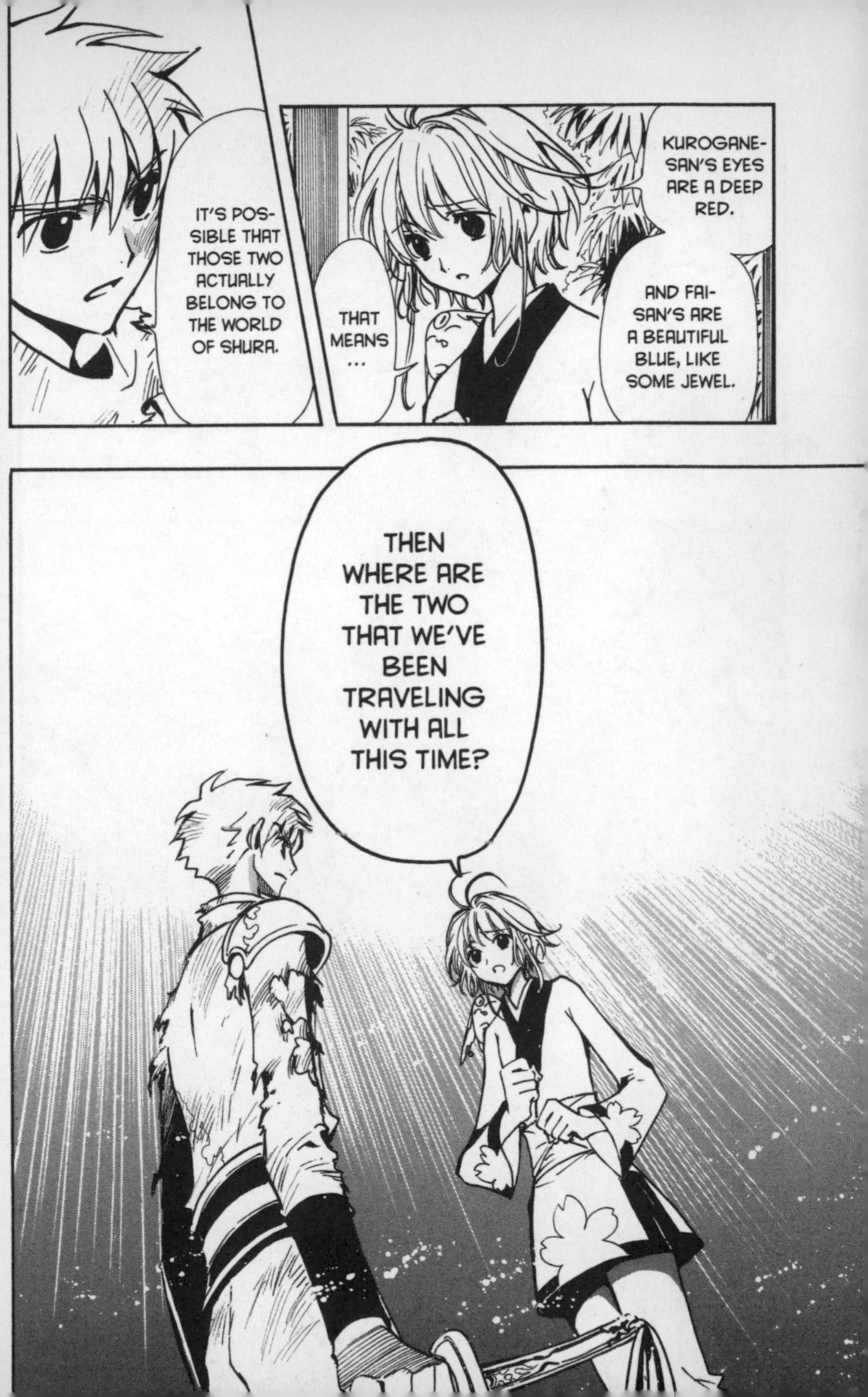
KUROGANE-SAN'S EYES ARE A DEEP RED.
AND FAI-SAN'S ARE A BEAUTIFUL BLUE, LIKE SOME JEWEL.
THAT MEANS ...
IT'S POSSIBLE THAT THOSE TWO ACTUALLY BELONG TO THE WORLD OF SHURA.
THEN WHERE ARE THE TWO THAT WE'VE BEEN TRAVELING WITH ALL THIS TIME?

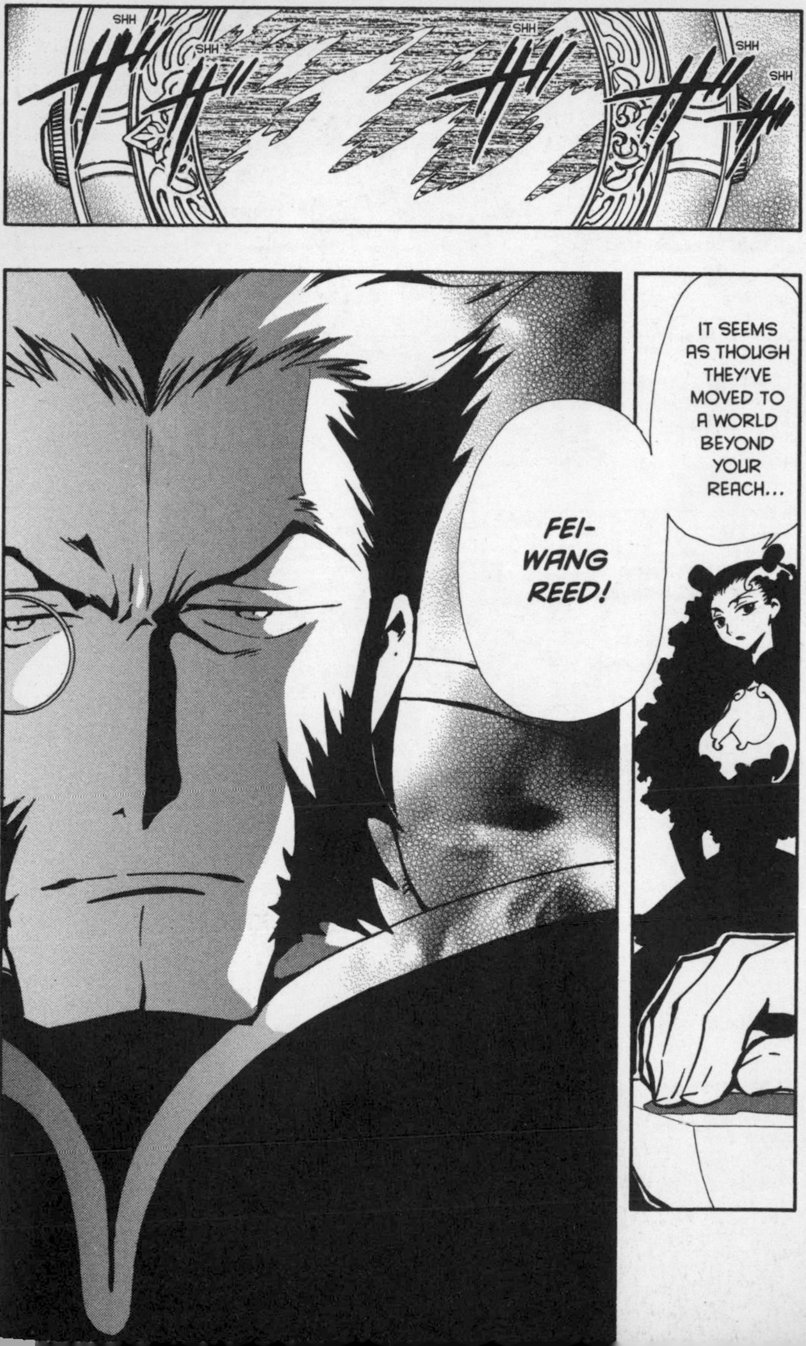
SHH
SHH
SHH
SHH
SHH
IT SEEMS AS THOUGH THEY'VE MOVED TO A WORLD BEYOND YOUR REACH...
FEI-WANG REED!

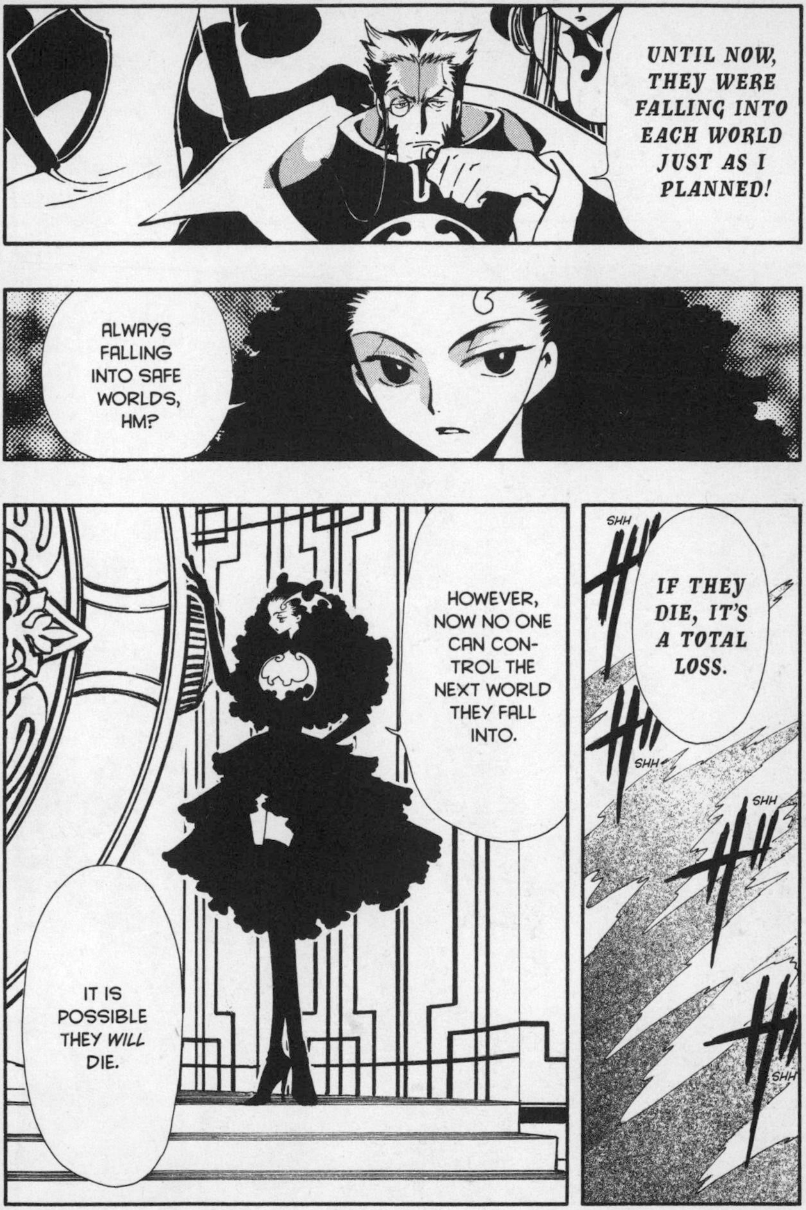
UNTIL NOW, THEY WERE FALLING INTO EACH WORLD JUST AS I PLANNED!
ALWAYS FALLING INTO SAFE WORLDS, HM?
SHH
IF THEY DIE, IT'S A TOTAL LOSS.
SHH
SHH
SHH
HOWEVER, NOW NO ONE CAN CONTROL THE NEXT WORLD THEY FALL INTO.
IT IS POSSIBLE THEY *WILL* DIE.

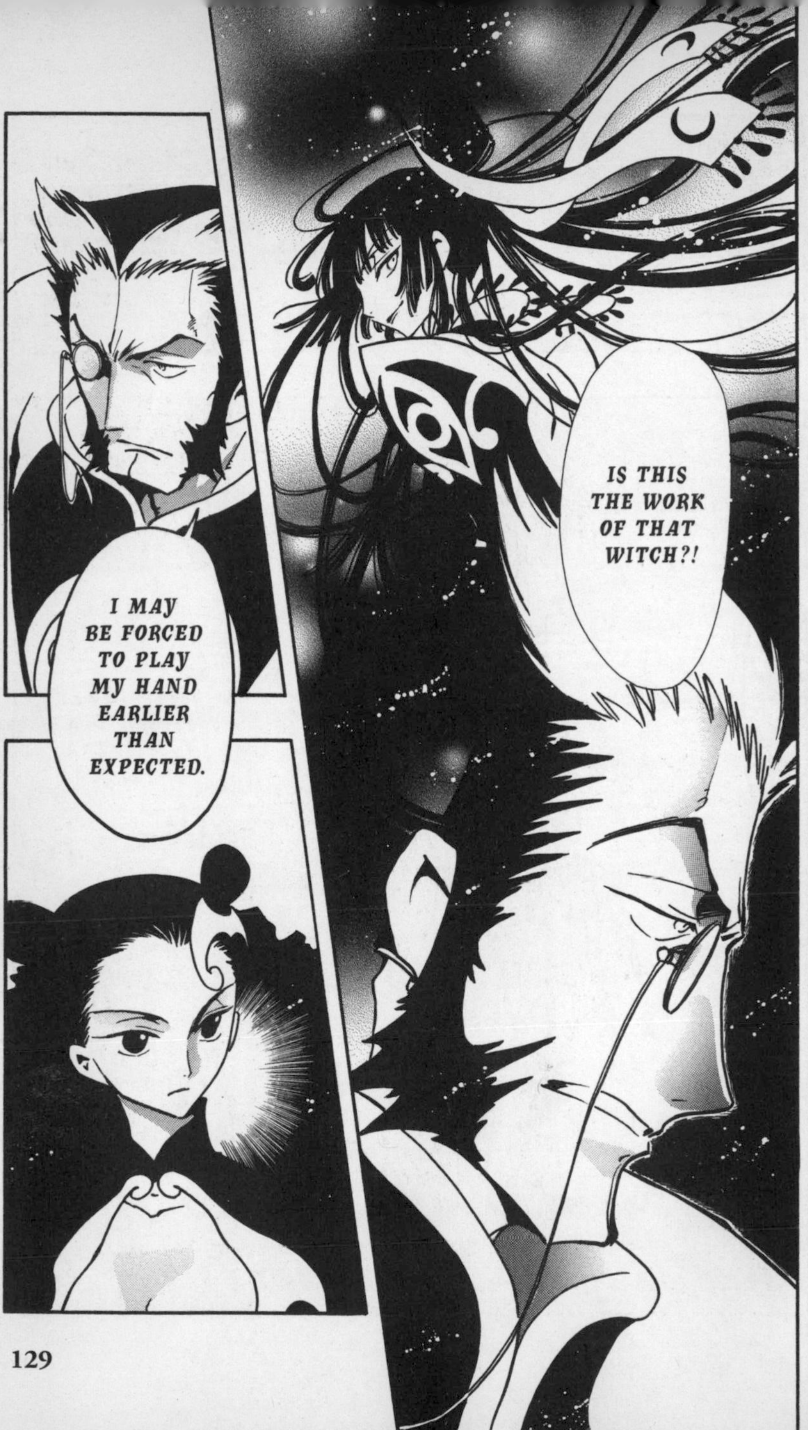
IS THIS THE WORK OF THAT WITCH?!
I MAY BE FORCED TO PLAY MY HAND EARLIER THAN EXPECTED.

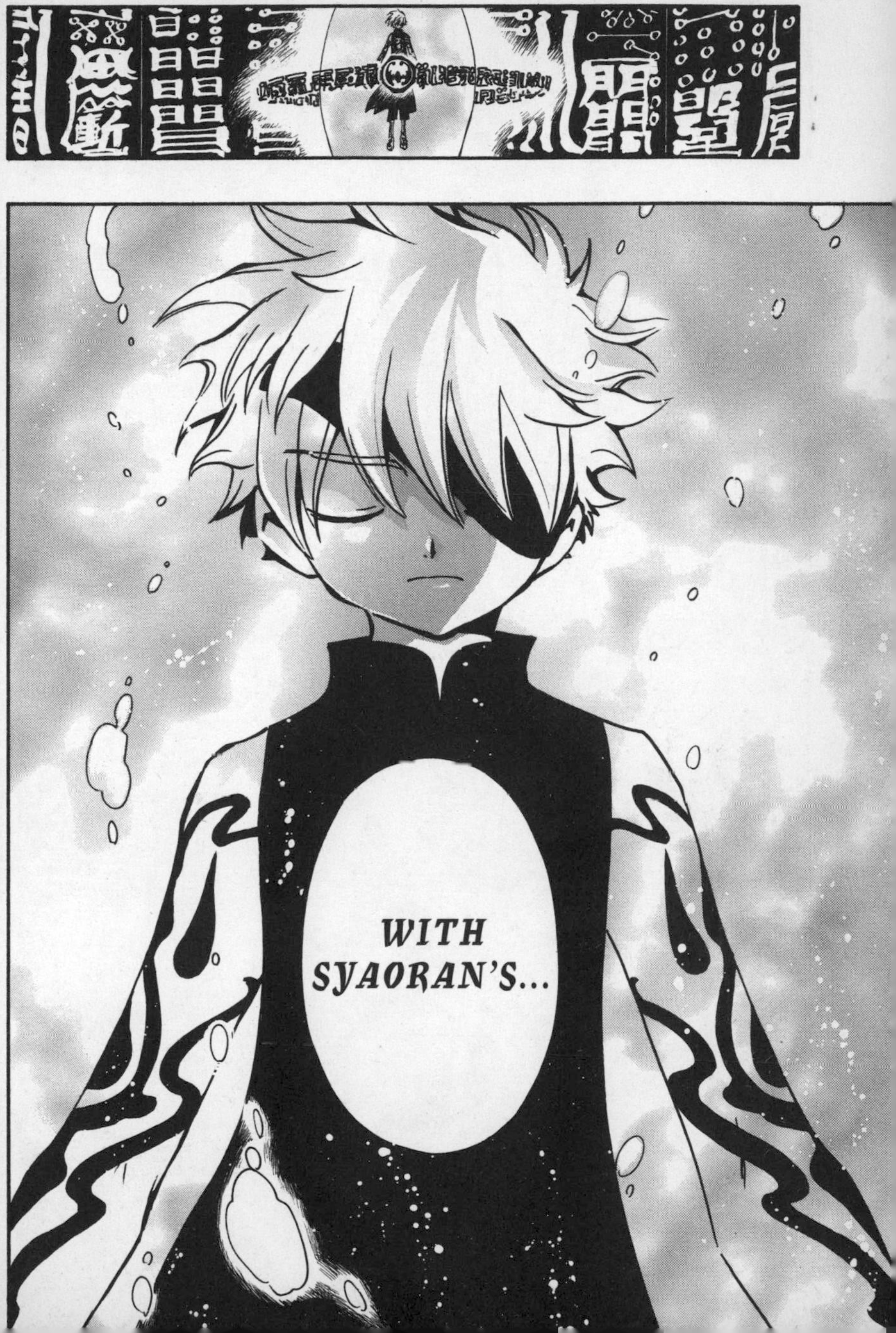
WITH SYAORAN'S...

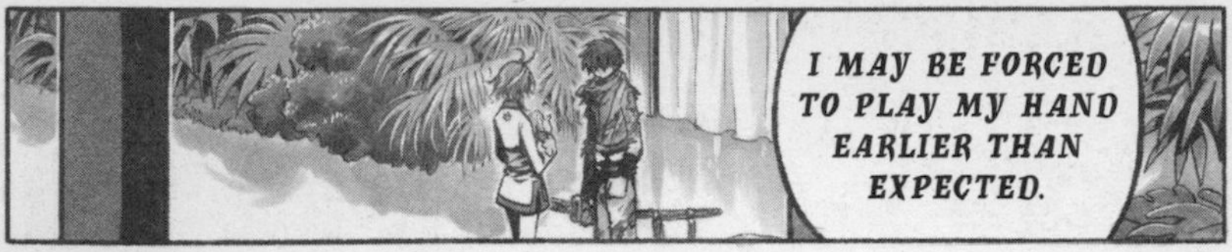
I MAY BE FORCED TO PLAY MY HAND EARLIER THAN EXPECTED.

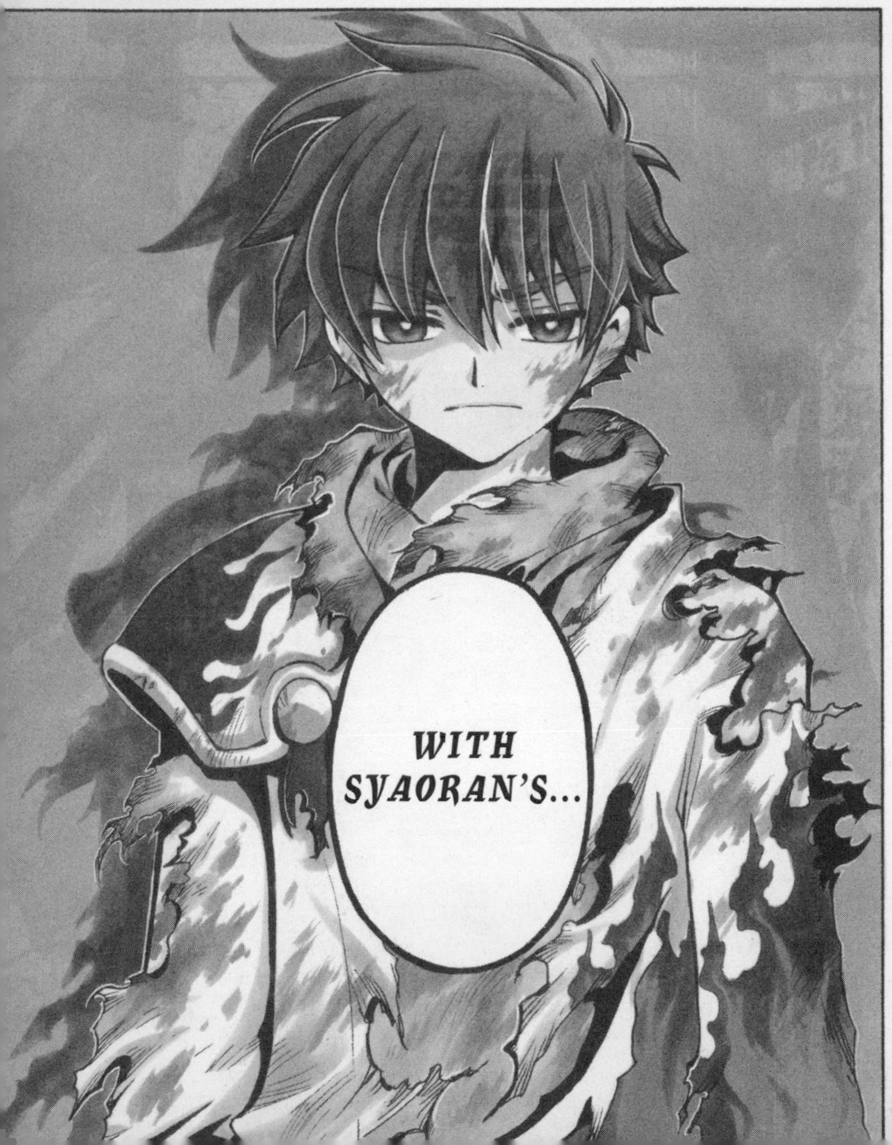
WITH SYAORAN'S...

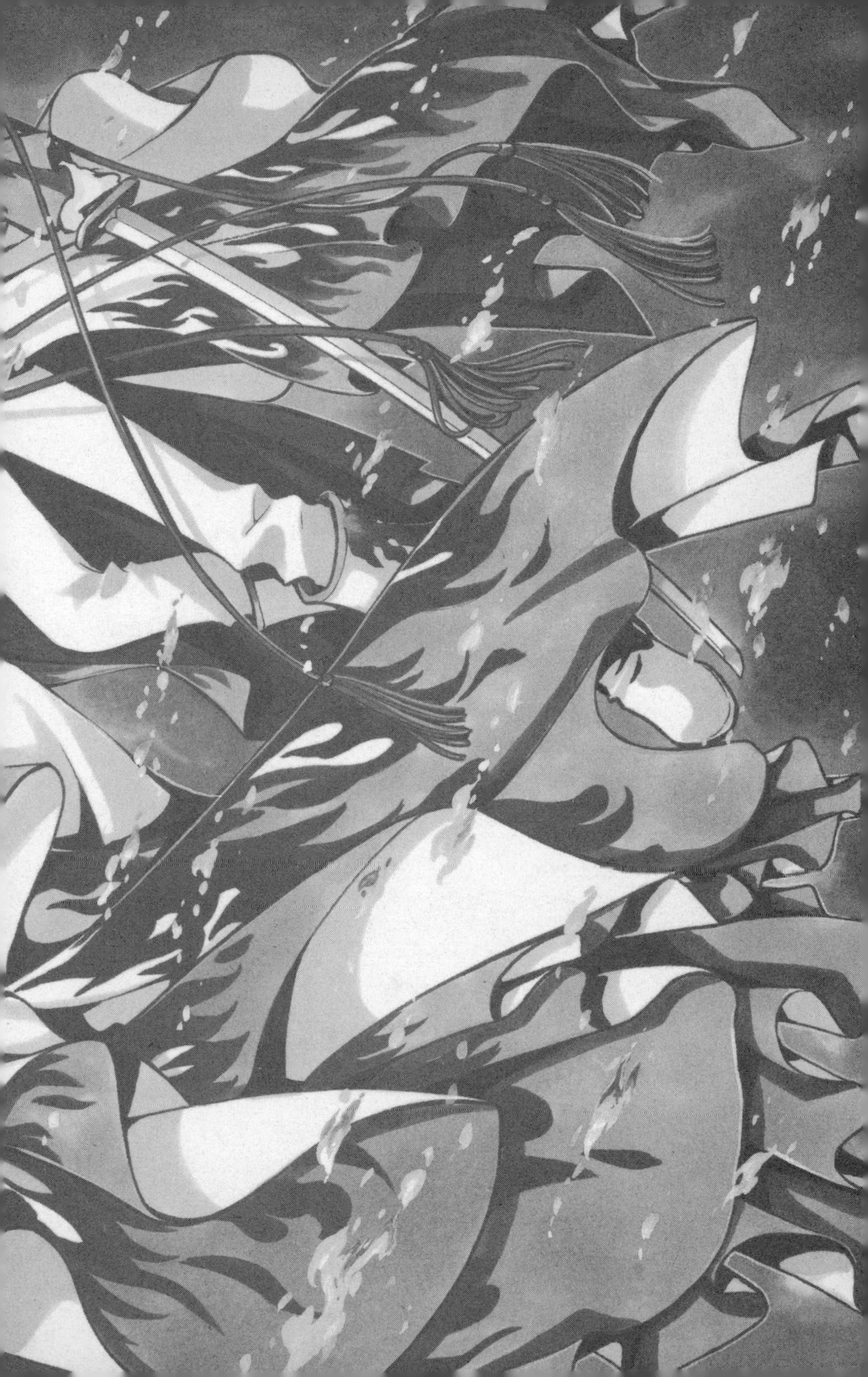

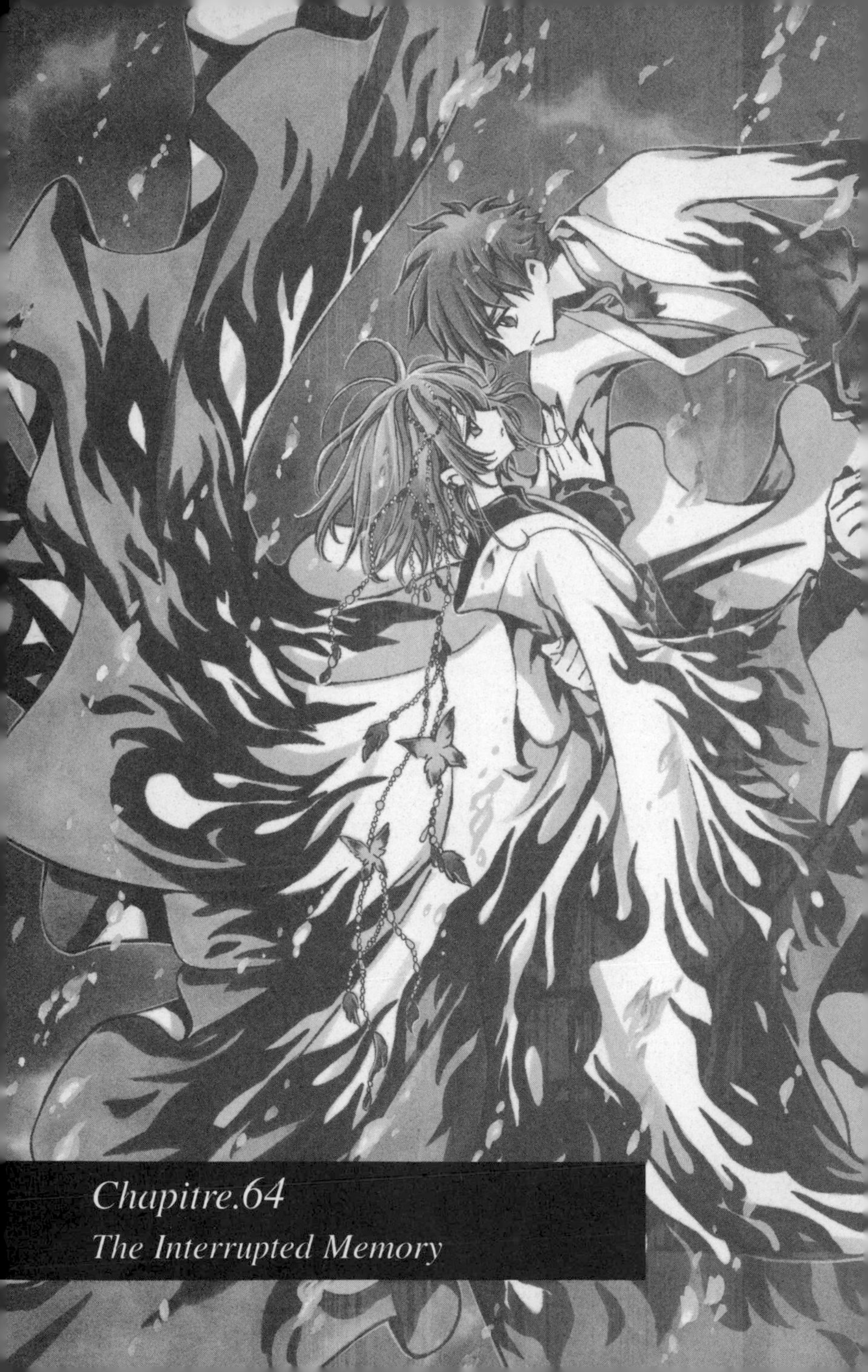

Chapitre.64

The Interrupted Memory

ツバサ
RESERVoir CHRoNiCLE

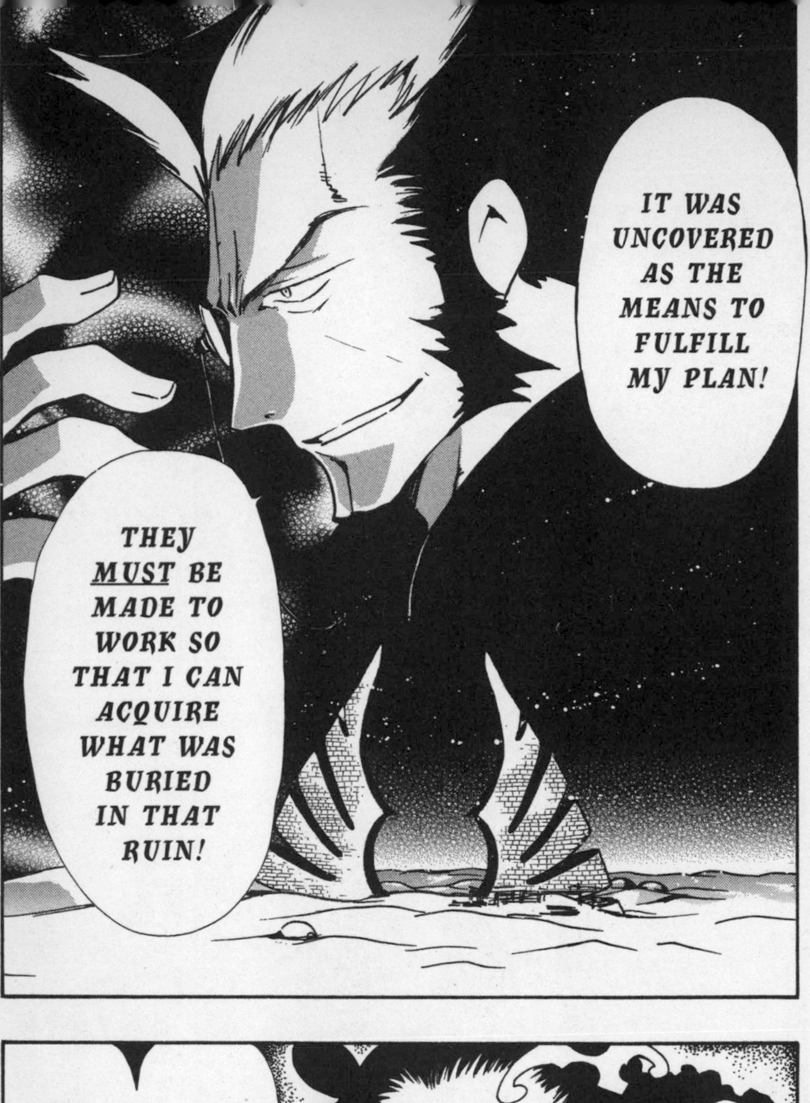
IT WAS UNCOVERED AS THE MEANS TO FULFILL MY PLAN!
THEY MUST BE MADE TO WORK SO THAT I CAN ACQUIRE WHAT WAS BURIED IN THAT RUIN!
.....
BUT... I DOUBT THAT THE WITCH WILL SIT STILL FOR THIS.
WILL YOU WIN? CAN YOU DEFEAT THE TIME-SPACE WITCH?

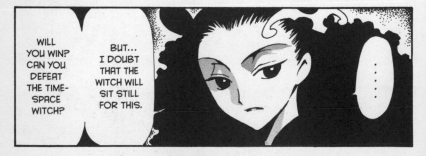

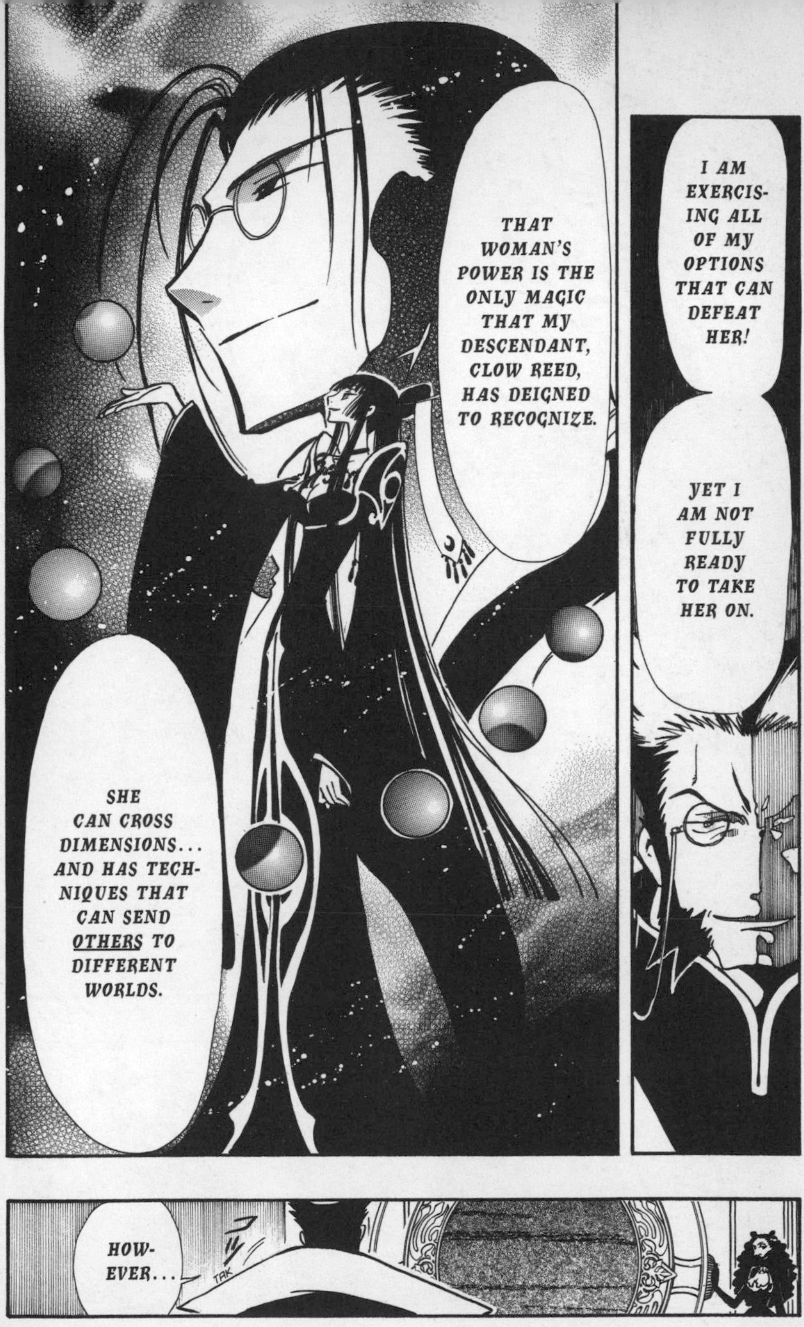
I AM EXERCISING ALL OF MY OPTIONS THAT CAN DEFEAT HER!
YET I AM NOT FULLY READY TO TAKE HER ON.
THAT WOMAN'S POWER IS THE ONLY MAGIC THAT MY DESCENDANT, CLOW REED, HAS DEIGNED TO RECOGNIZE.
SHE CAN CROSS DIMENSIONS... AND HAS TECHNIQUES THAT CAN SEND OTHERS TO DIFFERENT WORLDS.
HOWEVER...
TAK

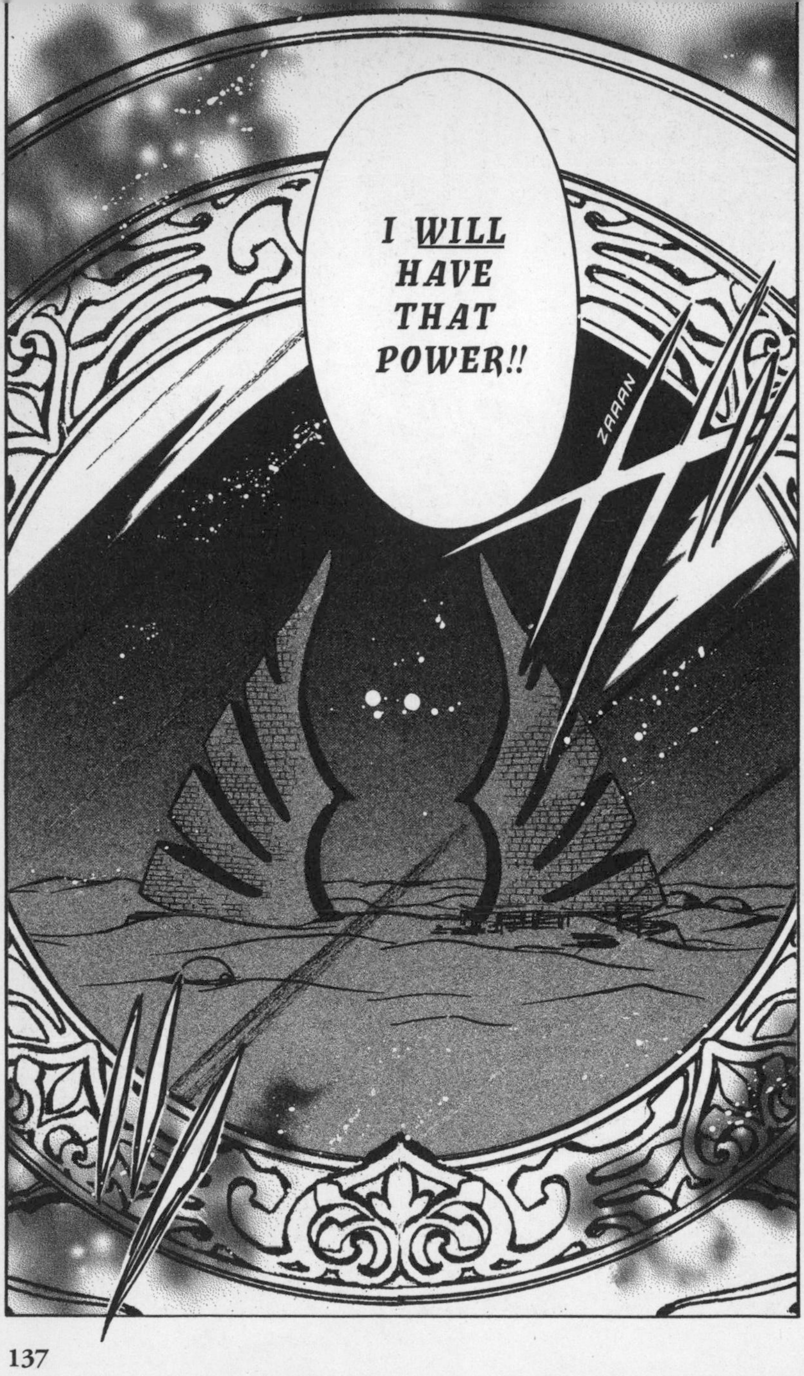
I WILL HAVE THAT POWER!!
ZARAAN

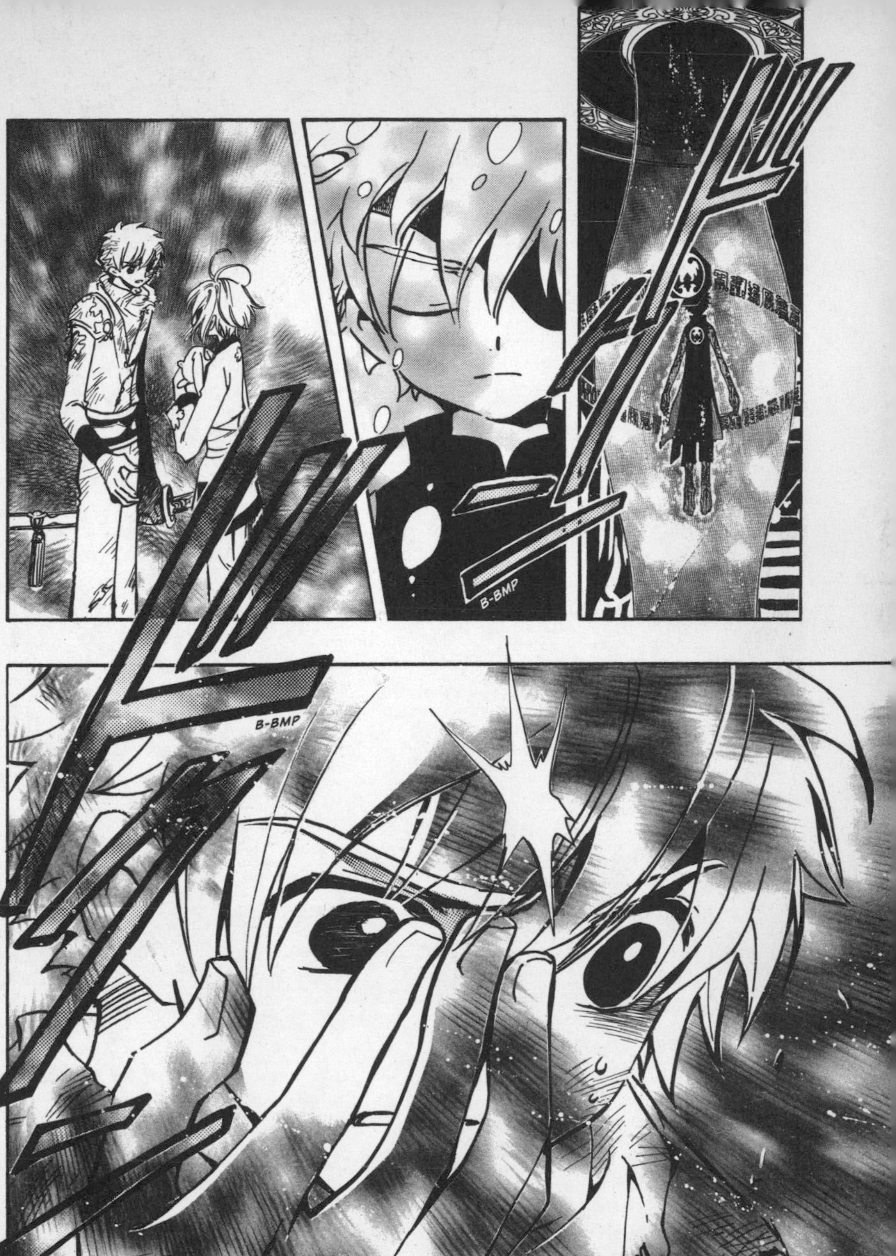
B-BMP
B-BMP

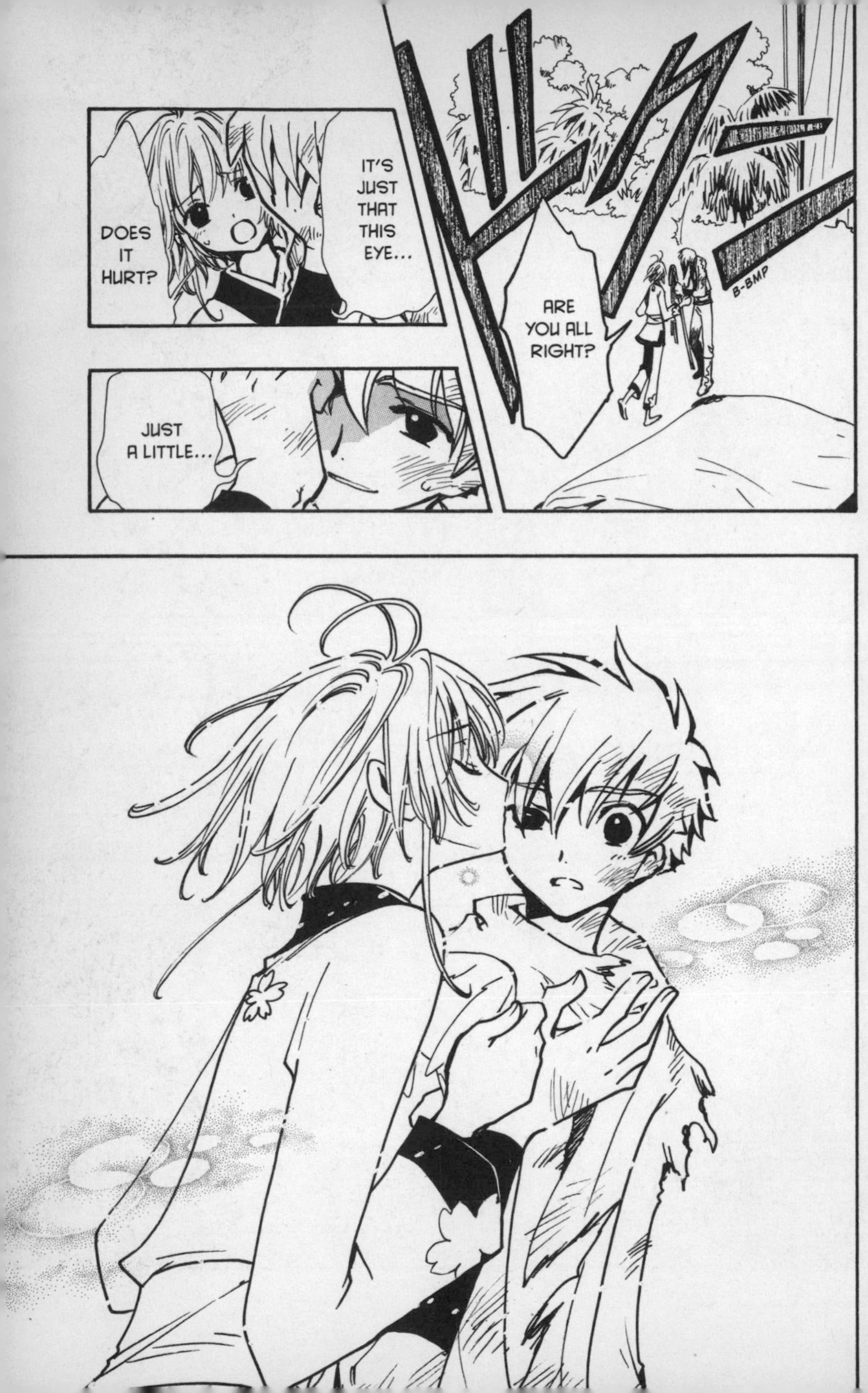
ARE YOU ALL RIGHT?
B-BMP
IT'S JUST THAT THIS EYE...
DOES IT HURT?
JUST A LITTLE...

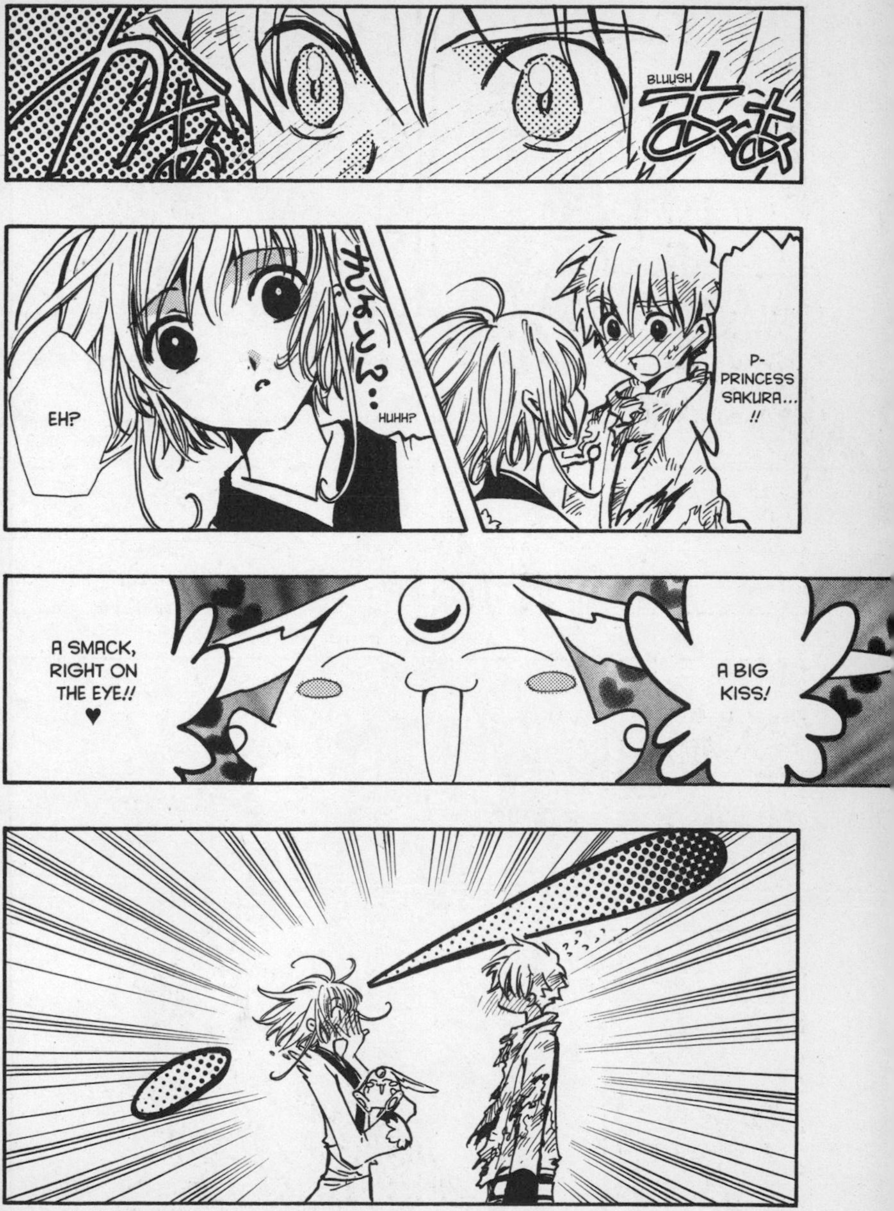
BLUUSH
P-PRINCESS SAKURA...!!
きょとん…
HUHH?
EH?
A BIG KISS!
A SMACK, RIGHT ON THE EYE!! ♥

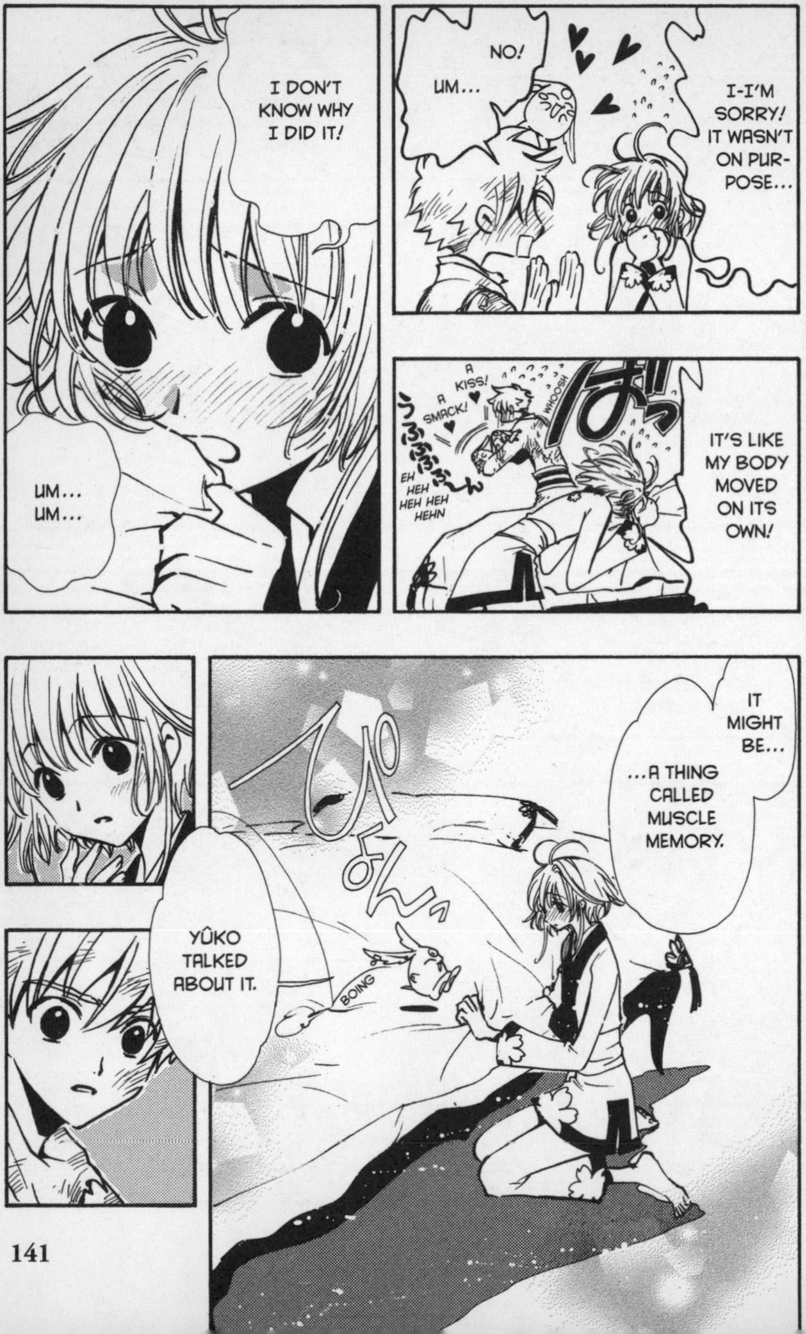
I-I'M SORRY! IT WASN'T ON PURPOSE...
NO!
UM...
IT'S LIKE MY BODY MOVED ON ITS OWN!
WHOOSH
A KISS!
A SMACK!
EH HEH HEH HEH HEHN
I DON'T KNOW WHY I DID IT!
UM... UM...
IT MIGHT BE...
...A THING CALLED MUSCLE MEMORY.
YÛKO TALKED ABOUT IT.
BOING

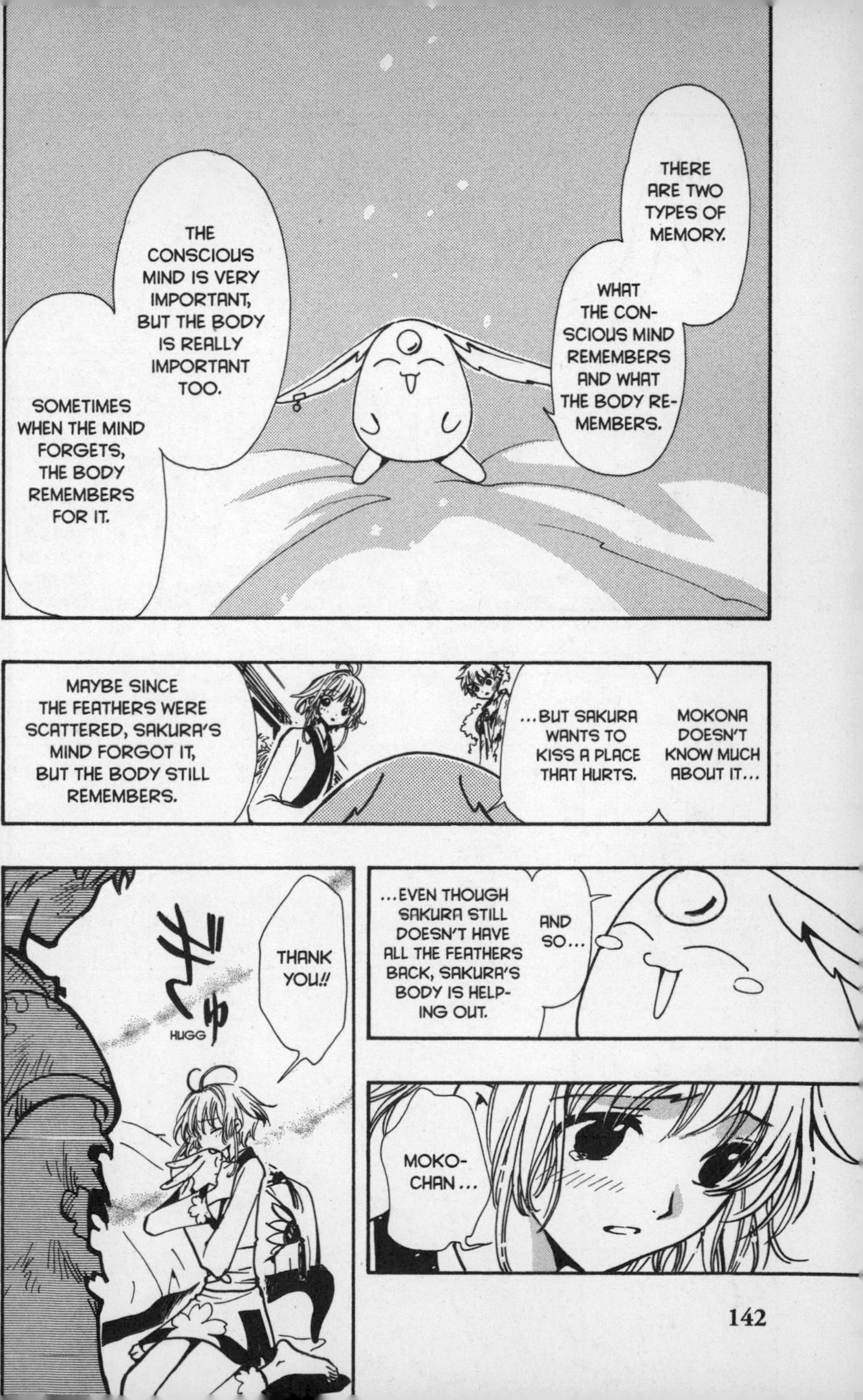
THERE ARE TWO TYPES OF MEMORY.
WHAT THE CONSCIOUS MIND REMEMBERS AND WHAT THE BODY REMEMBERS.
THE CONSCIOUS MIND IS VERY IMPORTANT, BUT THE BODY IS REALLY IMPORTANT TOO.
SOMETIMES WHEN THE MIND FORGETS, THE BODY REMEMBERS FOR IT.
MOKONA DOESN'T KNOW MUCH ABOUT IT...
...BUT SAKURA WANTS TO KISS A PLACE THAT HURTS.
MAYBE SINCE THE FEATHERS WERE SCATTERED, SAKURA'S MIND FORGOT IT, BUT THE BODY STILL REMEMBERS.
AND SO...
...EVEN THOUGH SAKURA STILL DOESN'T HAVE ALL THE FEATHERS BACK, SAKURA'S BODY IS HELPING OUT.
MOKO-CHAN...
HUGG
THANK YOU!!

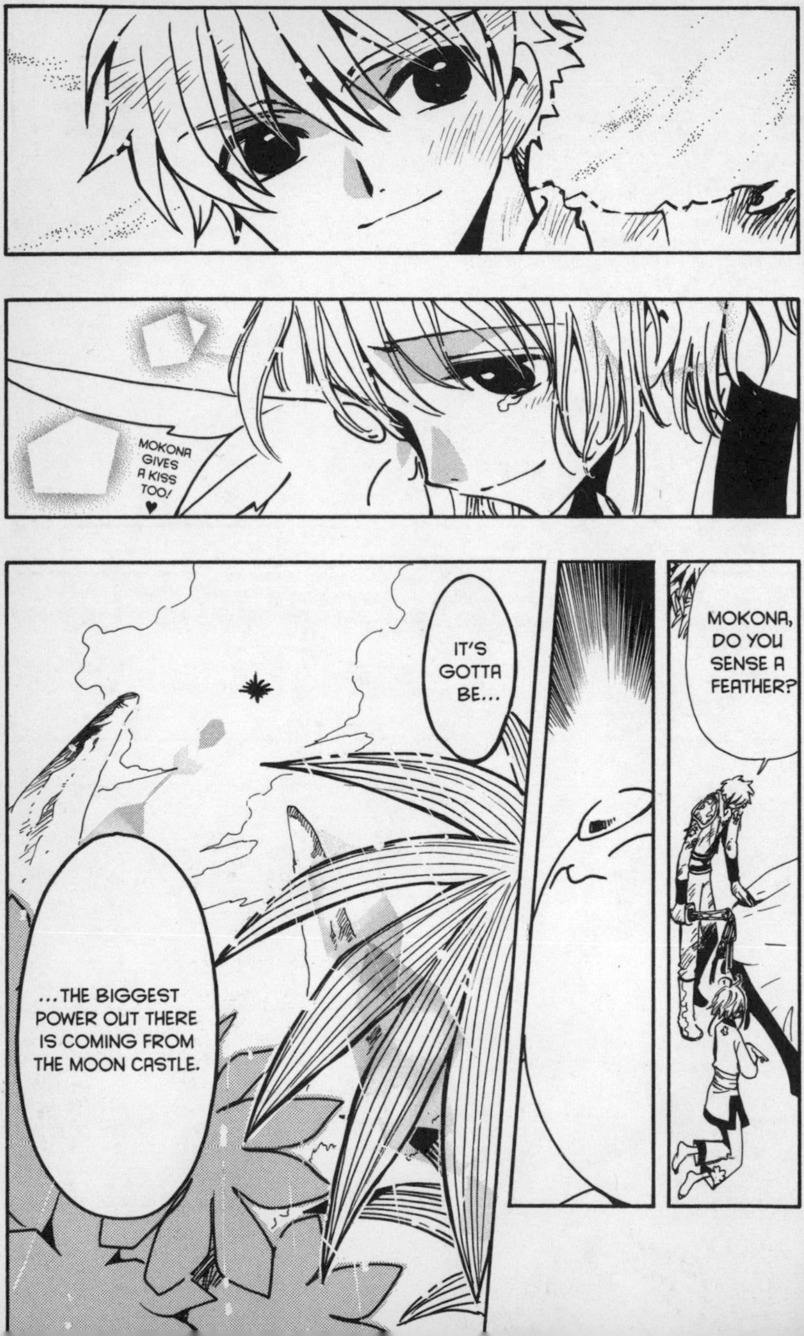
MOKONA GIVES A KISS TOO! ♥
MOKONA, DO YOU SENSE A FEATHER?
IT'S GOTTA BE...
...THE BIGGEST POWER OUT THERE IS COMING FROM THE MOON CASTLE.

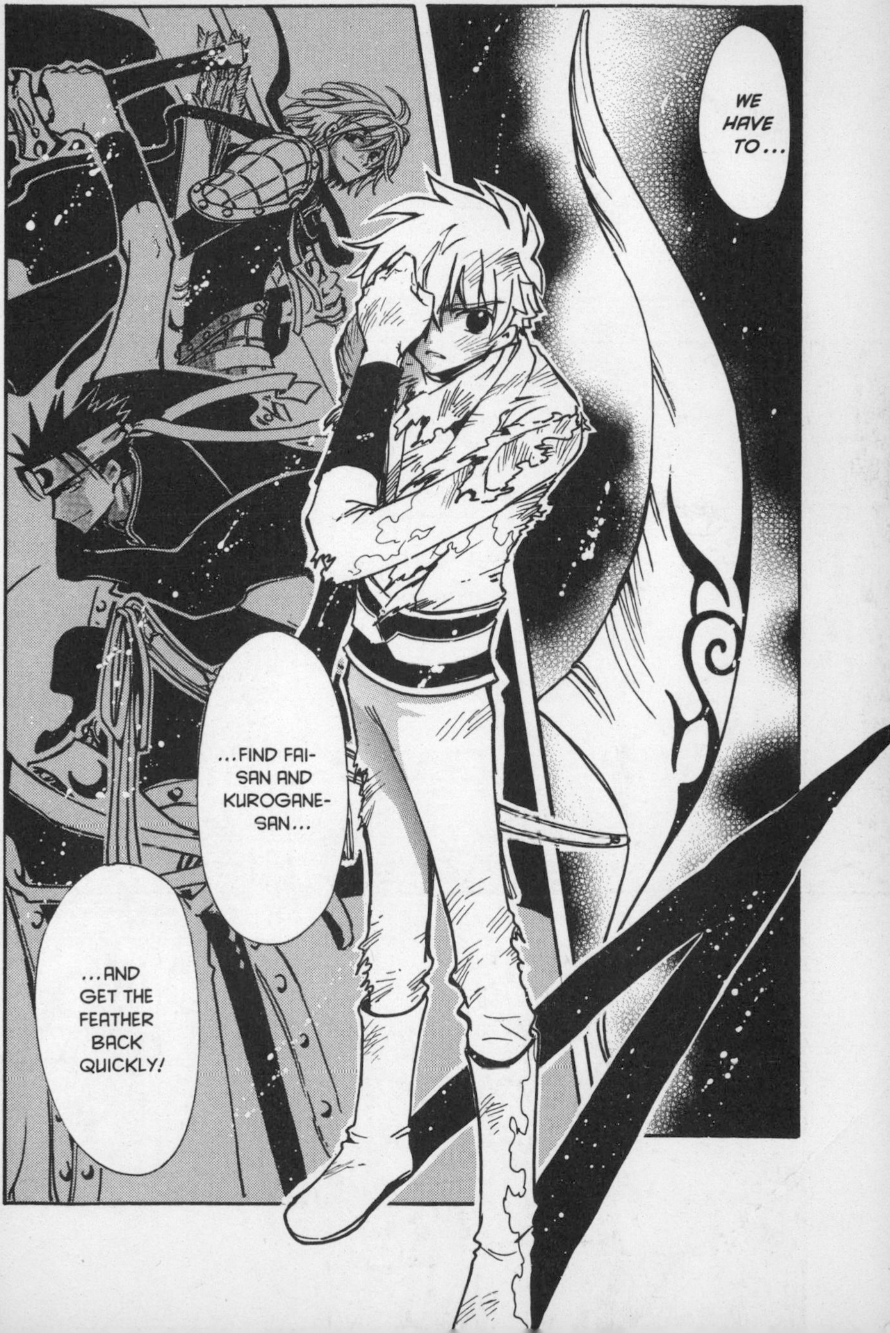
WE HAVE TO...
...FIND FAI-SAN AND KUROGANE-SAN...
...AND GET THE FEATHER BACK QUICKLY!

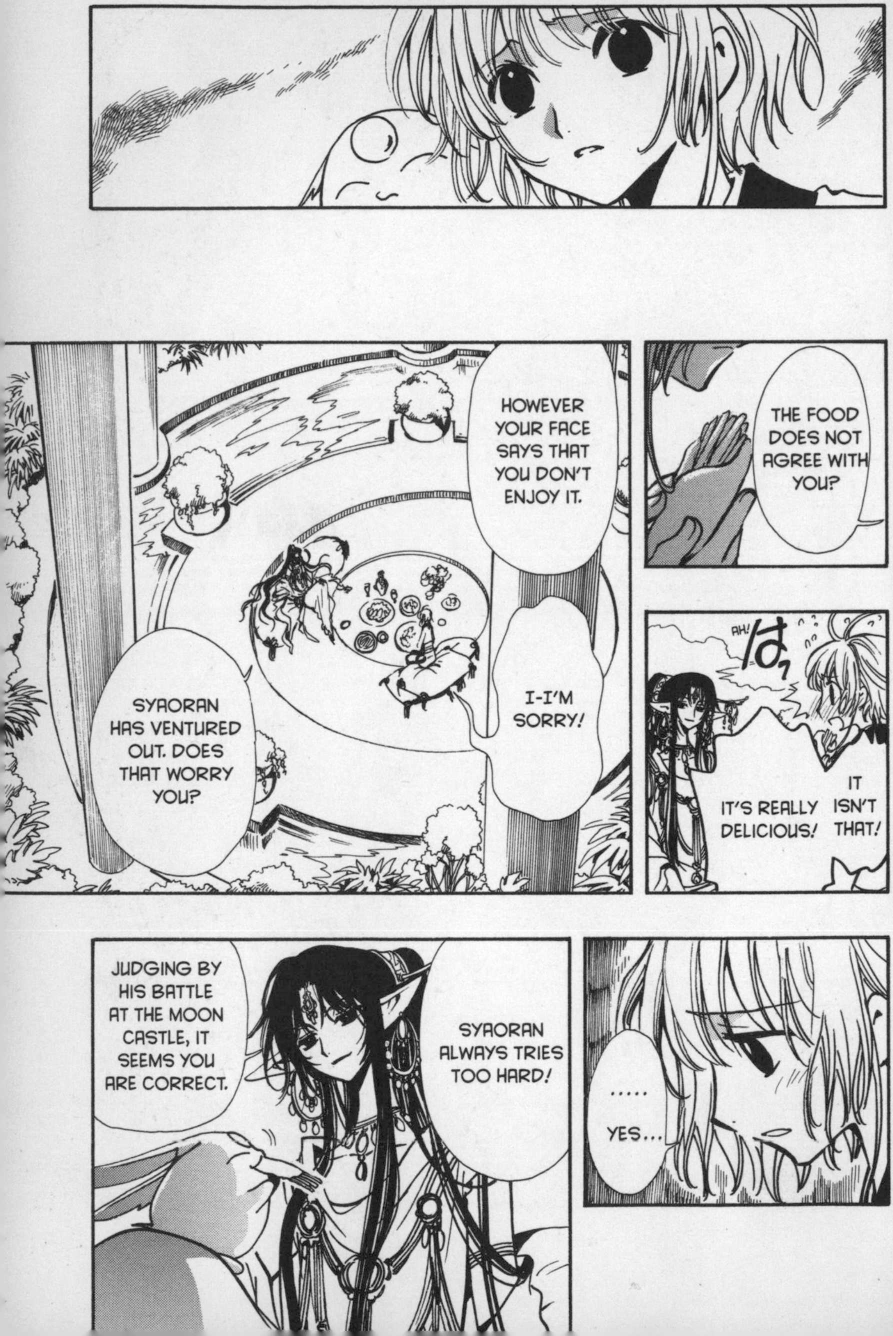
THE FOOD DOES NOT AGREE WITH YOU?
AH!
IT ISN'T THAT!
IT'S REALLY DELICIOUS!
HOWEVER YOUR FACE SAYS THAT YOU DON'T ENJOY IT.
I-I'M SORRY!
SYAORAN HAS VENTURED OUT. DOES THAT WORRY YOU?
.....
YES...
SYAORAN ALWAYS TRIES TOO HARD!
JUDGING BY HIS BATTLE AT THE MOON CASTLE, IT SEEMS YOU ARE CORRECT.

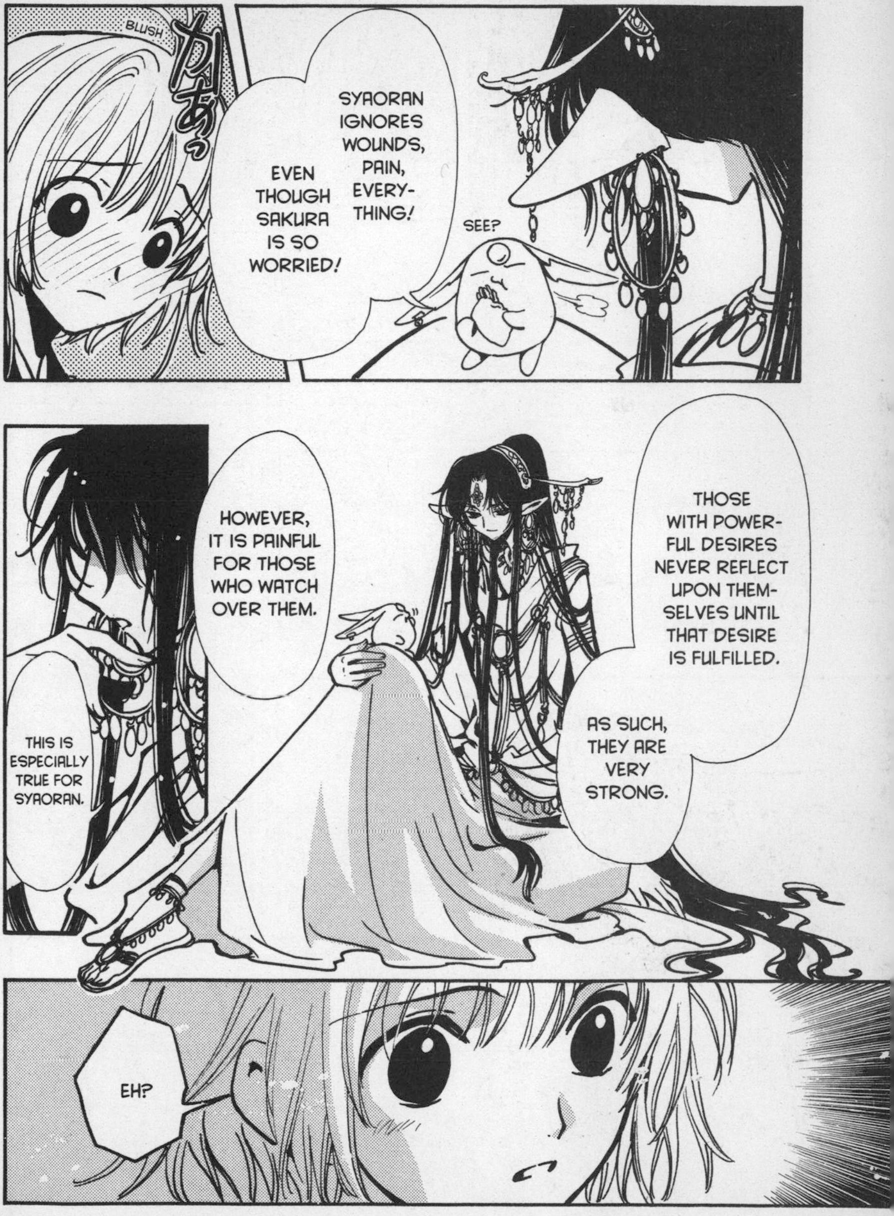
SYAORAN IGNORES WOUNDS, PAIN, EVERYTHING!
EVEN THOUGH SAKURA IS SO WORRIED!
SEE?
BLUSH
カァっ
THOSE WITH POWERFUL DESIRES NEVER REFLECT UPON THEMSELVES UNTIL THAT DESIRE IS FULFILLED.
AS SUCH, THEY ARE VERY STRONG.
HOWEVER, IT IS PAINFUL FOR THOSE WHO WATCH OVER THEM.
THIS IS ESPECIALLY TRUE FOR SYAORAN.
EH?

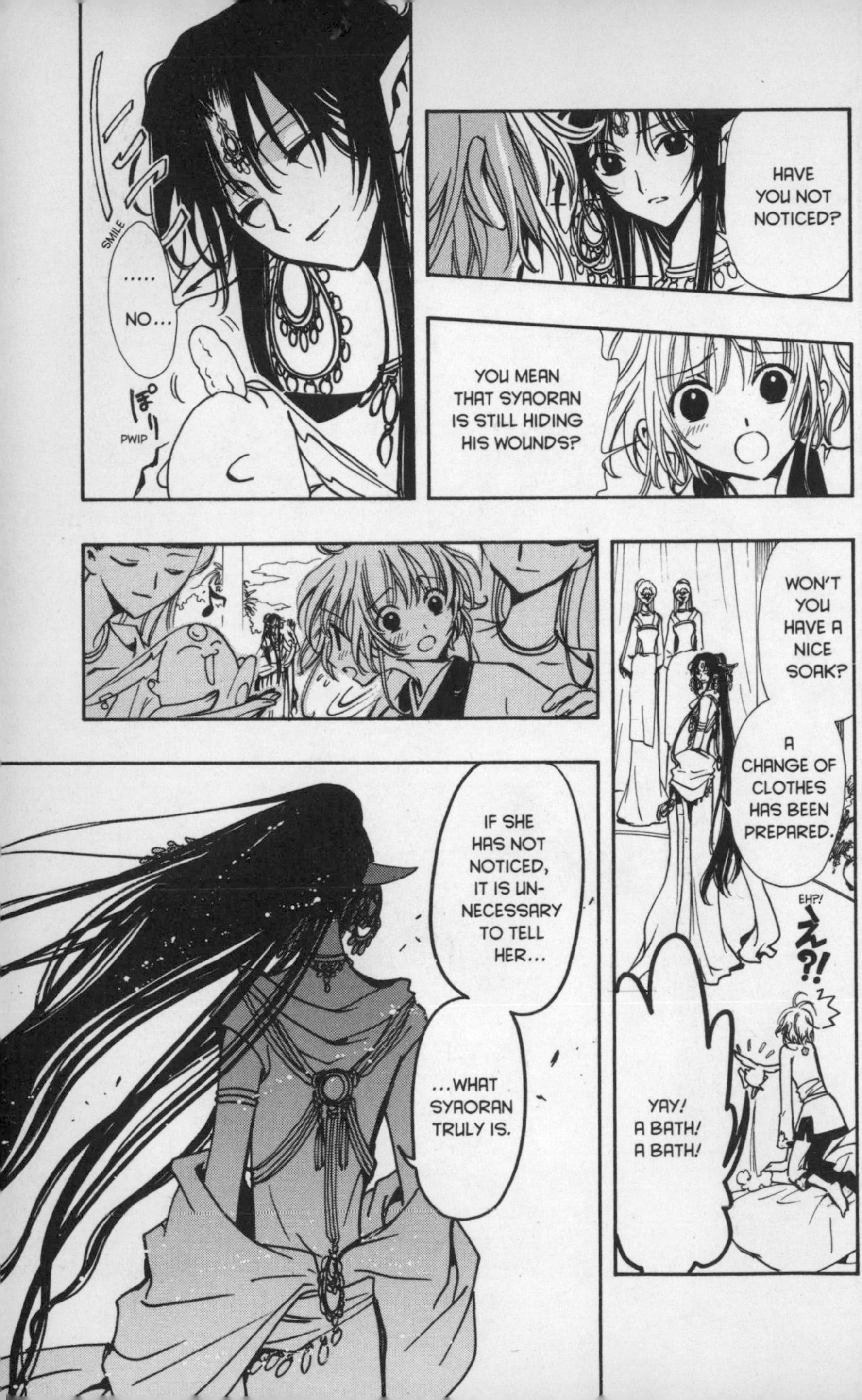
HAVE YOU NOT NOTICED?
YOU MEAN THAT SYAORAN IS STILL HIDING HIS WOUNDS?
SMILE
......
NO...
ぽり
PWIP
WON'T YOU HAVE A NICE SOAK?
A CHANGE OF CLOTHES HAS BEEN PREPARED.
EH?!
え?!
YAY! A BATH! A BATH!
IF SHE HAS NOT NOTICED, IT IS UN-NECESSARY TO TELL HER...
...WHAT SYAORAN TRULY IS.

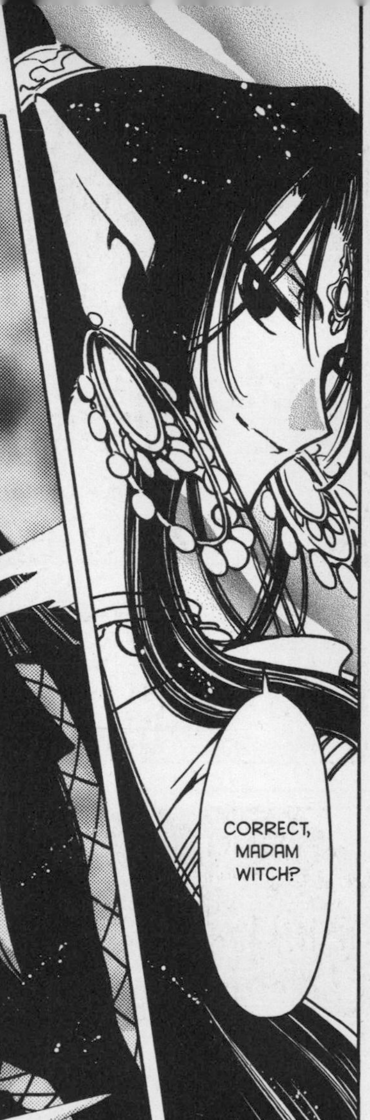
CORRECT, MADAM WITCH?

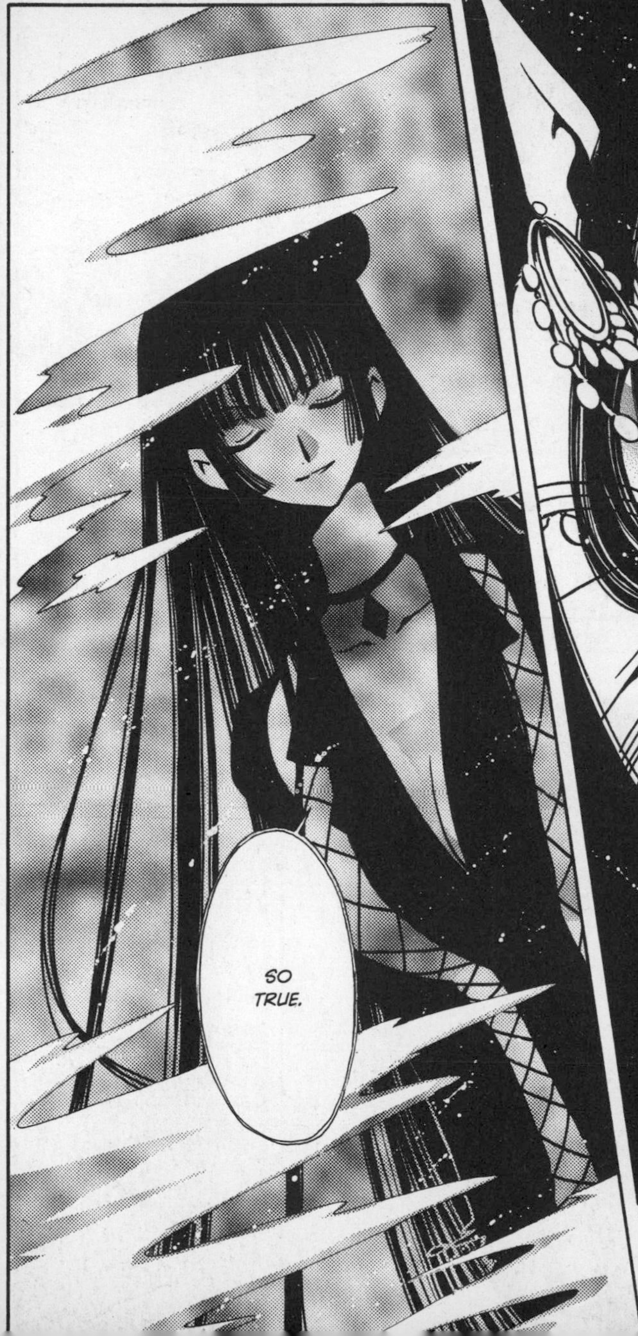
SO TRUE.

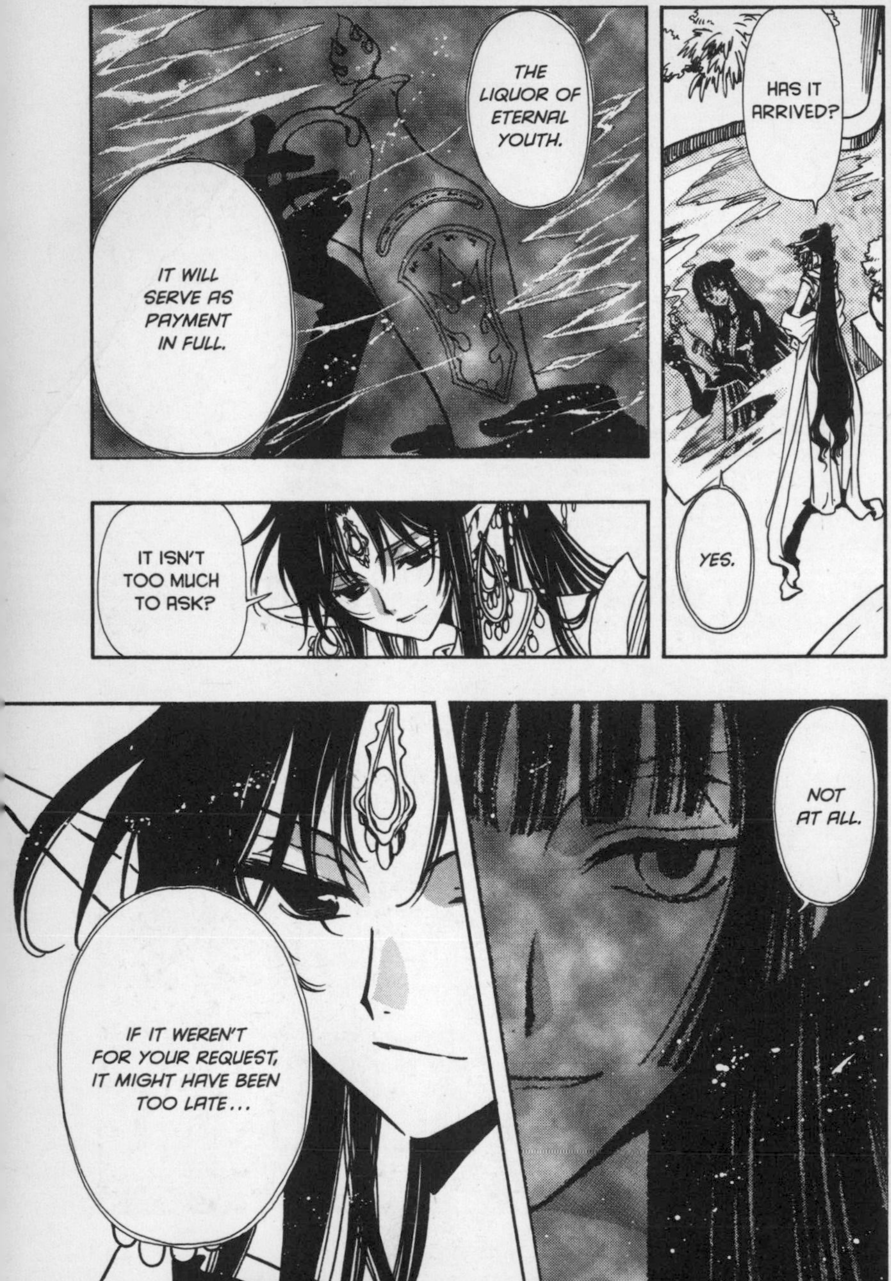
HAS IT ARRIVED?
YES.
THE LIQUOR OF ETERNAL YOUTH.
IT WILL SERVE AS PAYMENT IN FULL.
IT ISN'T TOO MUCH TO ASK?
NOT AT ALL.
IF IT WEREN'T FOR YOUR REQUEST, IT MIGHT HAVE BEEN TOO LATE...

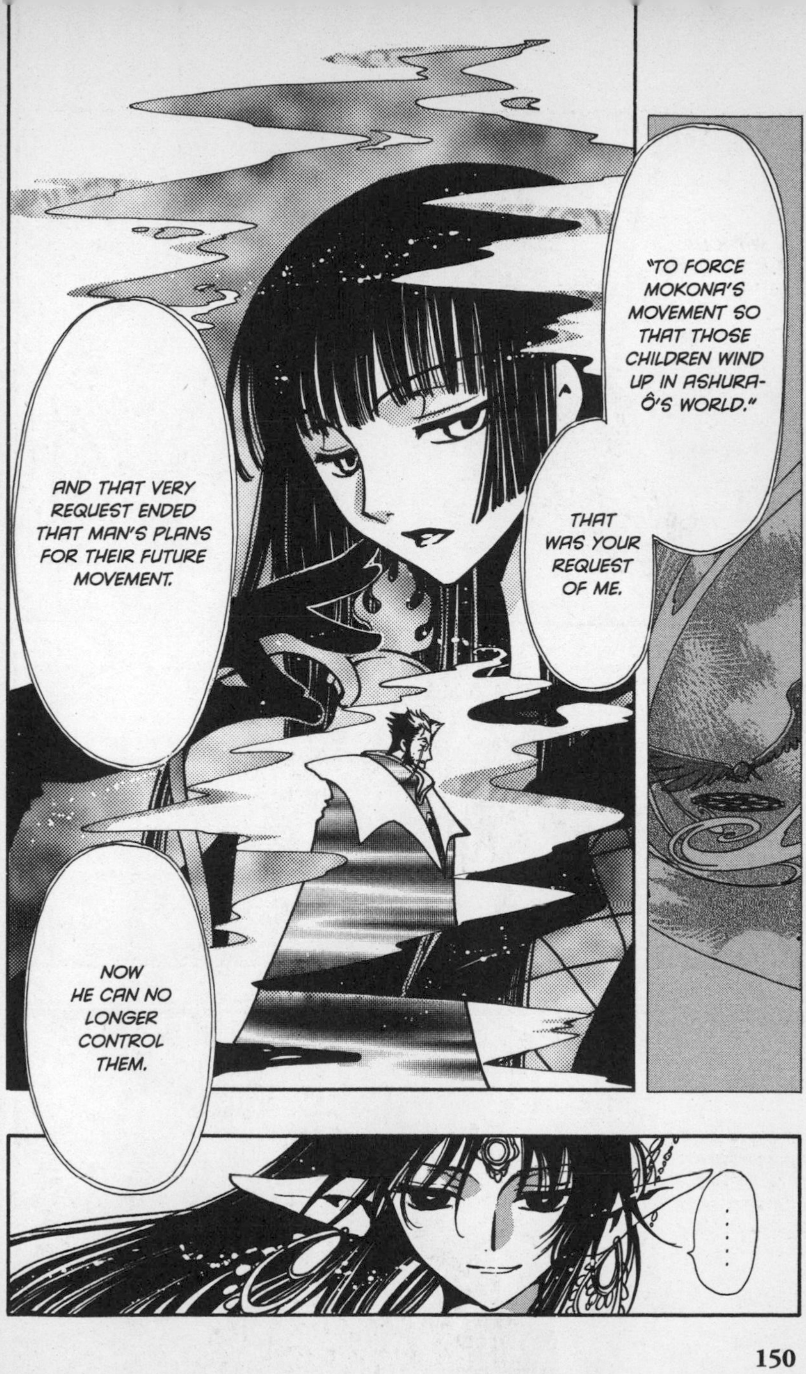
"TO FORCE MOKONA'S MOVEMENT SO THAT THOSE CHILDREN WIND UP IN ASHURA-Ô'S WORLD."
THAT WAS YOUR REQUEST OF ME.
AND THAT VERY REQUEST ENDED THAT MAN'S PLANS FOR THEIR FUTURE MOVEMENT.
NOW HE CAN NO LONGER CONTROL THEM.
.....

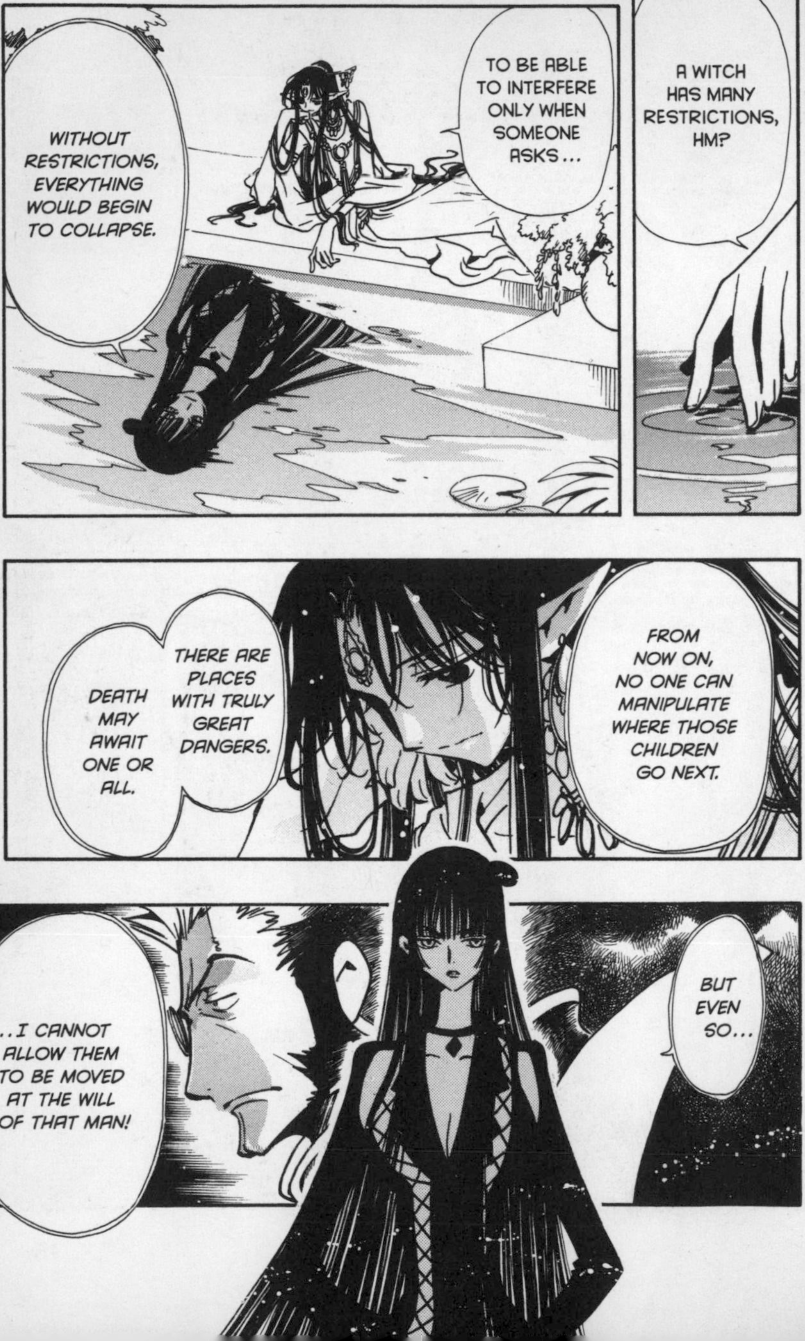
A WITCH HAS MANY RESTRICTIONS, HM?
TO BE ABLE TO INTERFERE ONLY WHEN SOMEONE ASKS…
WITHOUT RESTRICTIONS, EVERYTHING WOULD BEGIN TO COLLAPSE.
FROM NOW ON, NO ONE CAN MANIPULATE WHERE THOSE CHILDREN GO NEXT.
THERE ARE PLACES WITH TRULY GREAT DANGERS.
DEATH MAY AWAIT ONE OR ALL.
BUT EVEN SO…
…I CANNOT ALLOW THEM TO BE MOVED AT THE WILL OF THAT MAN!

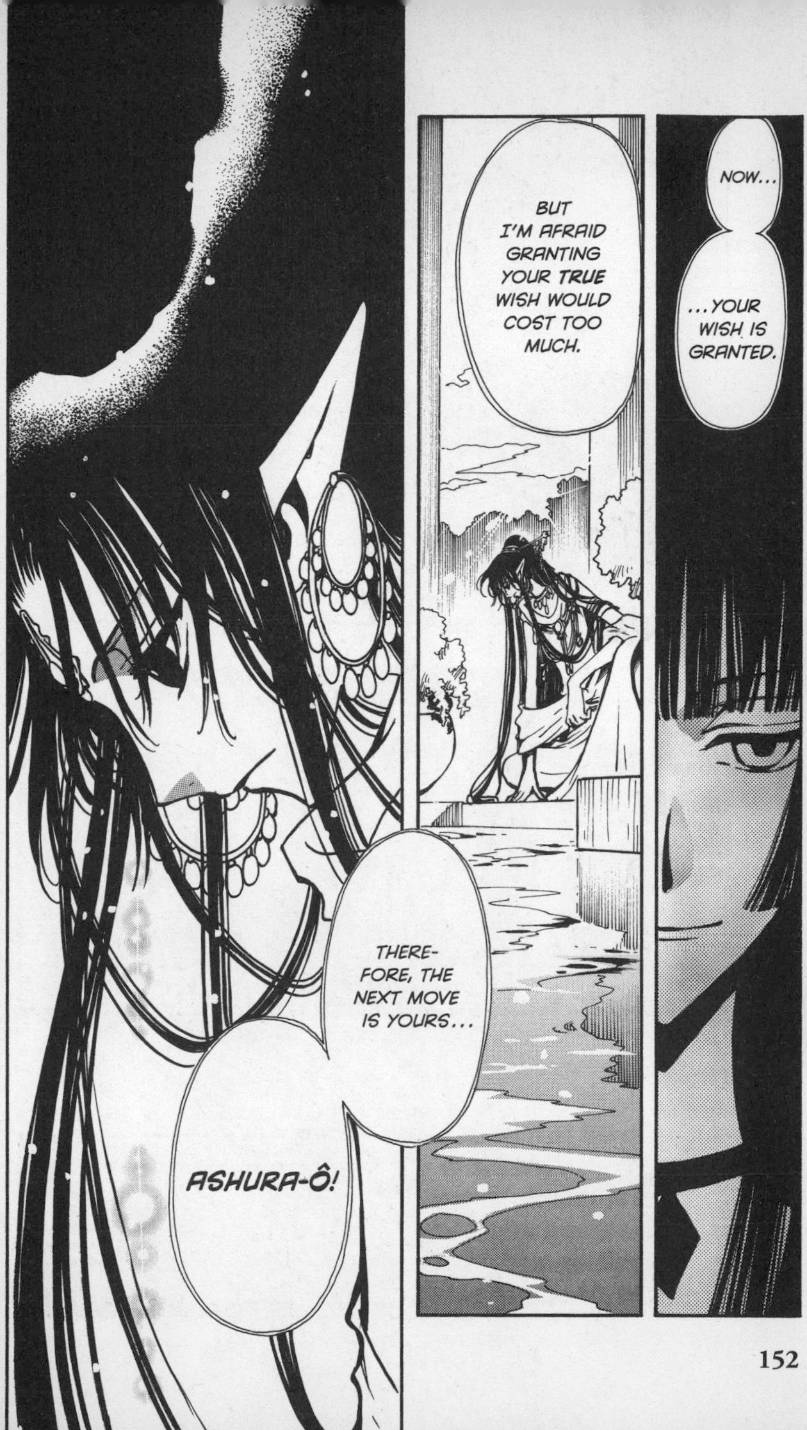
NOW...
...YOUR WISH IS GRANTED.
BUT I'M AFRAID GRANTING YOUR TRUE WISH WOULD COST TOO MUCH.
THERE-FORE, THE NEXT MOVE IS YOURS...
ASHURA-Ô!

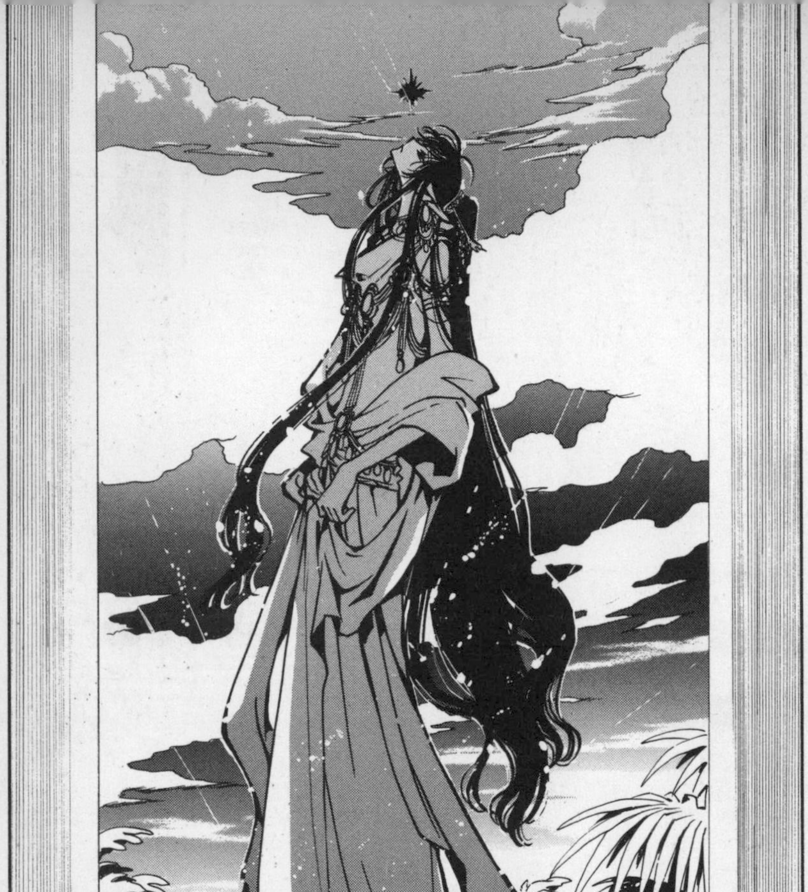

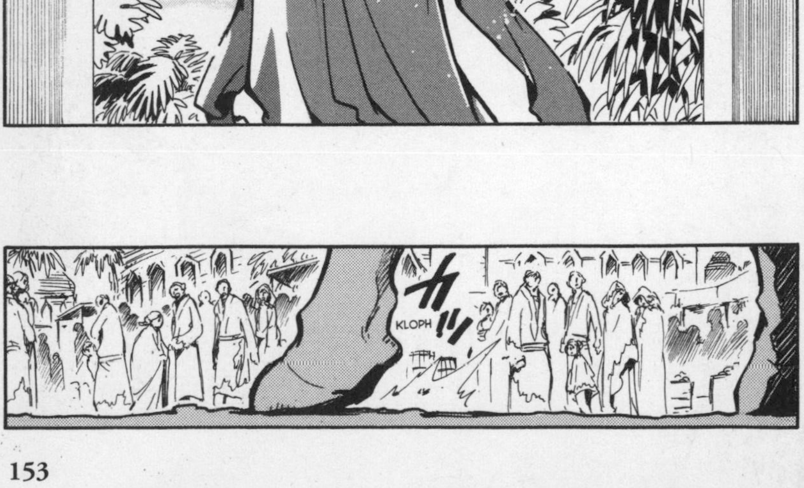
カッ!!
KLOPH

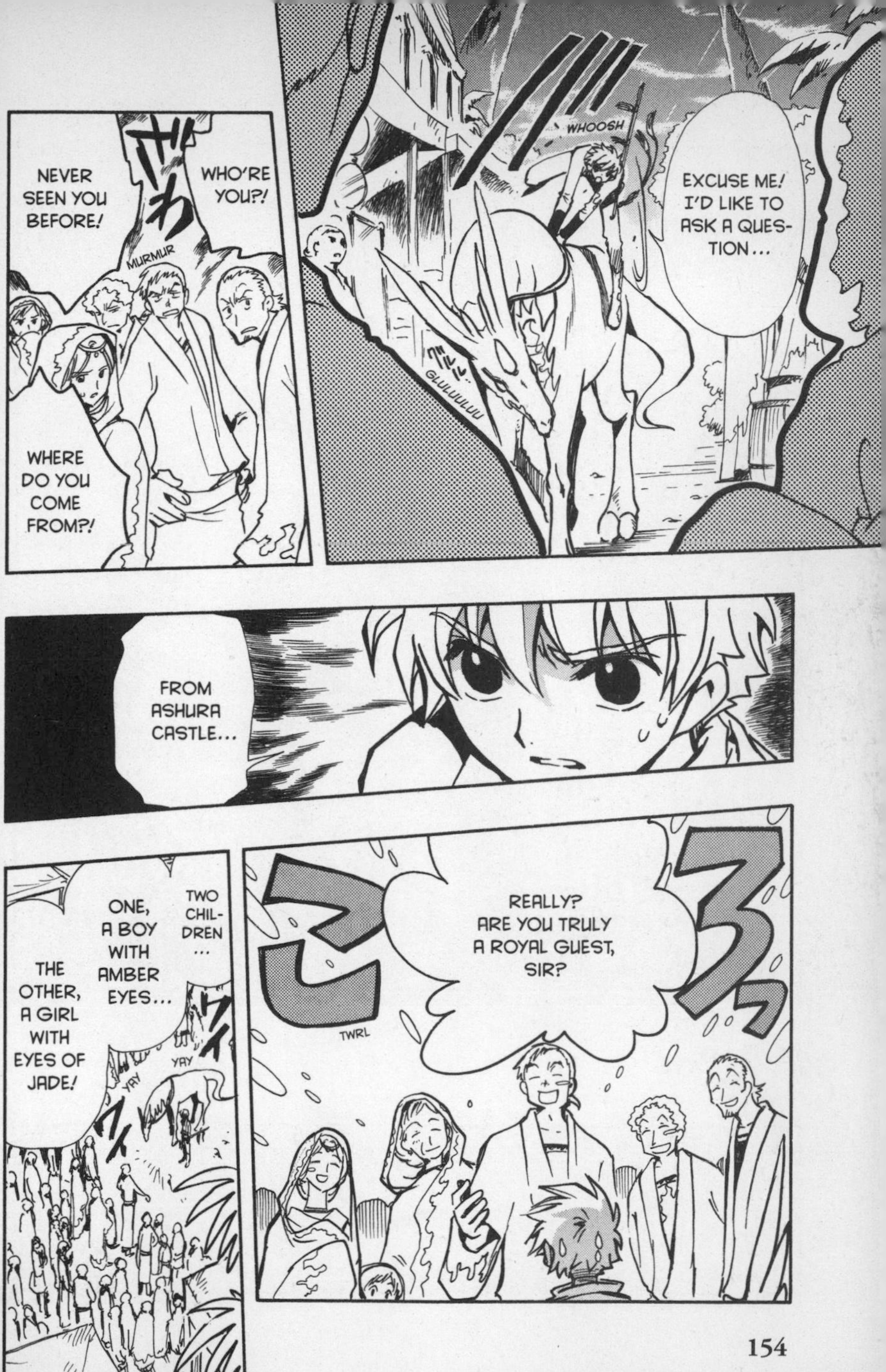
WHOOSH
EXCUSE ME! I'D LIKE TO ASK A QUESTION...
GLULULULU
WHO'RE YOU?!
NEVER SEEN YOU BEFORE!
MURMUR
WHERE DO YOU COME FROM?!
FROM ASHURA CASTLE...
REALLY? ARE YOU TRULY A ROYAL GUEST, SIR?
TWRL
TWO CHILDREN...
ONE, A BOY WITH AMBER EYES...
THE OTHER, A GIRL WITH EYES OF JADE!
YAY
YAY

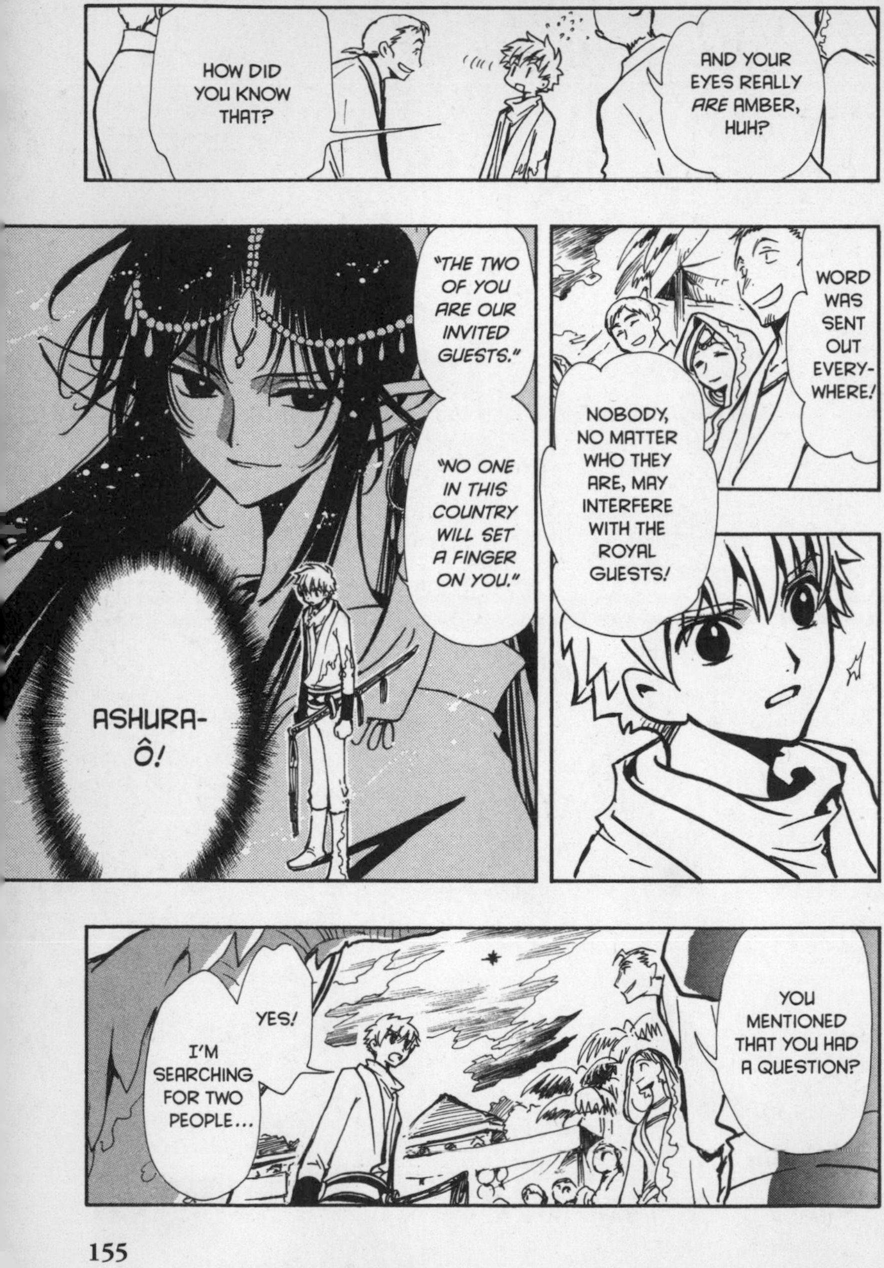
AND YOUR EYES REALLY *ARE* AMBER, HUH?
HOW DID YOU KNOW THAT?
WORD WAS SENT OUT EVERY-WHERE!
NOBODY, NO MATTER WHO THEY ARE, MAY INTERFERE WITH THE ROYAL GUESTS!
"THE TWO OF YOU ARE OUR INVITED GUESTS."
"NO ONE IN THIS COUNTRY WILL SET A FINGER ON YOU."
ASHURA-Ô!
YOU MENTIONED THAT YOU HAD A QUESTION?
YES!
I'M SEARCHING FOR TWO PEOPLE...

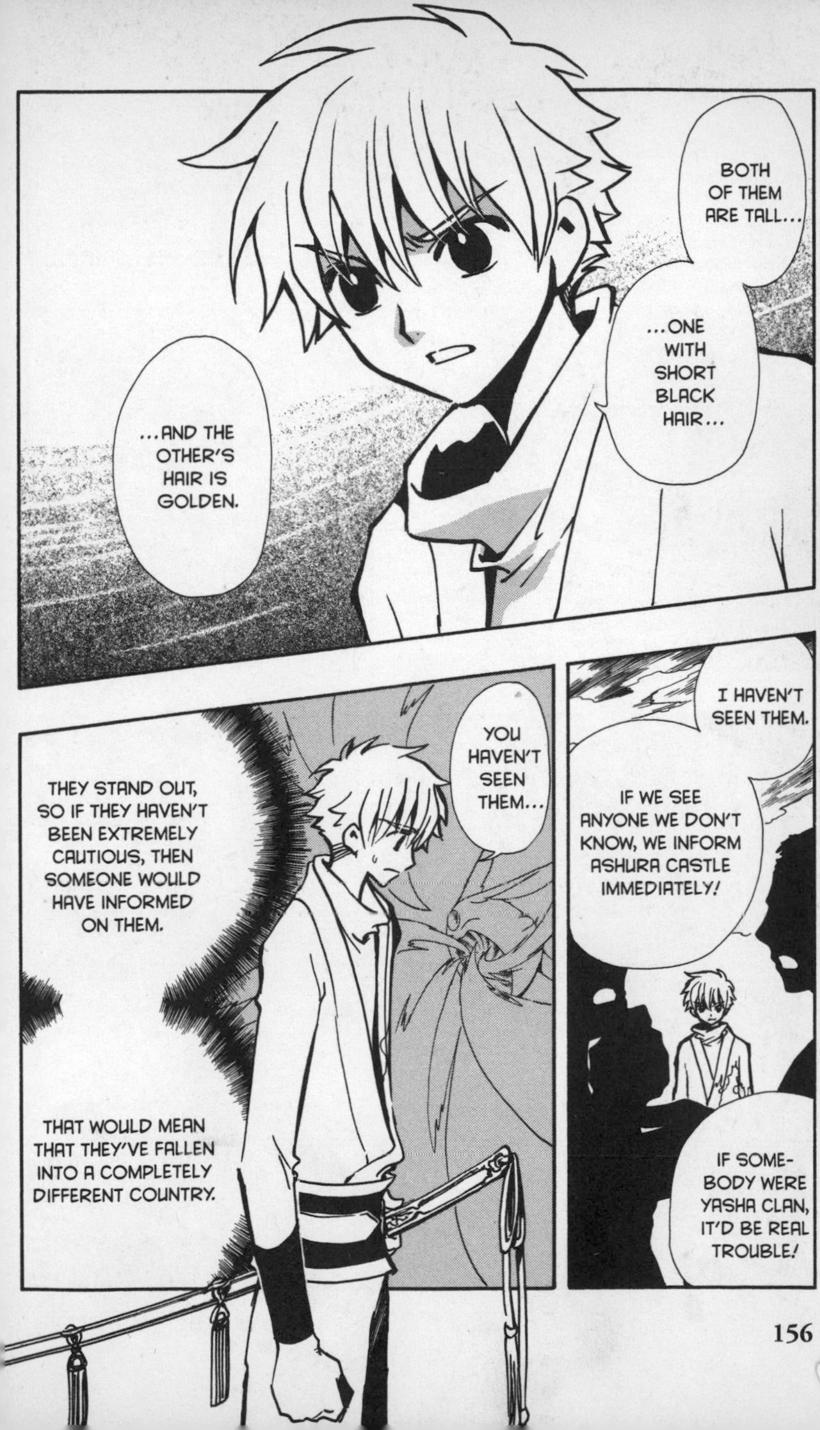
BOTH OF THEM ARE TALL...
...ONE WITH SHORT BLACK HAIR...
...AND THE OTHER'S HAIR IS GOLDEN.
I HAVEN'T SEEN THEM.
IF WE SEE ANYONE WE DON'T KNOW, WE INFORM ASHURA CASTLE IMMEDIATELY!
IF SOME-BODY WERE YASHA CLAN, IT'D BE REAL TROUBLE!
YOU HAVEN'T SEEN THEM...
THEY STAND OUT, SO IF THEY HAVEN'T BEEN EXTREMELY CAUTIOUS, THEN SOMEONE WOULD HAVE INFORMED ON THEM.
THAT WOULD MEAN THAT THEY'VE FALLEN INTO A COMPLETELY DIFFERENT COUNTRY.

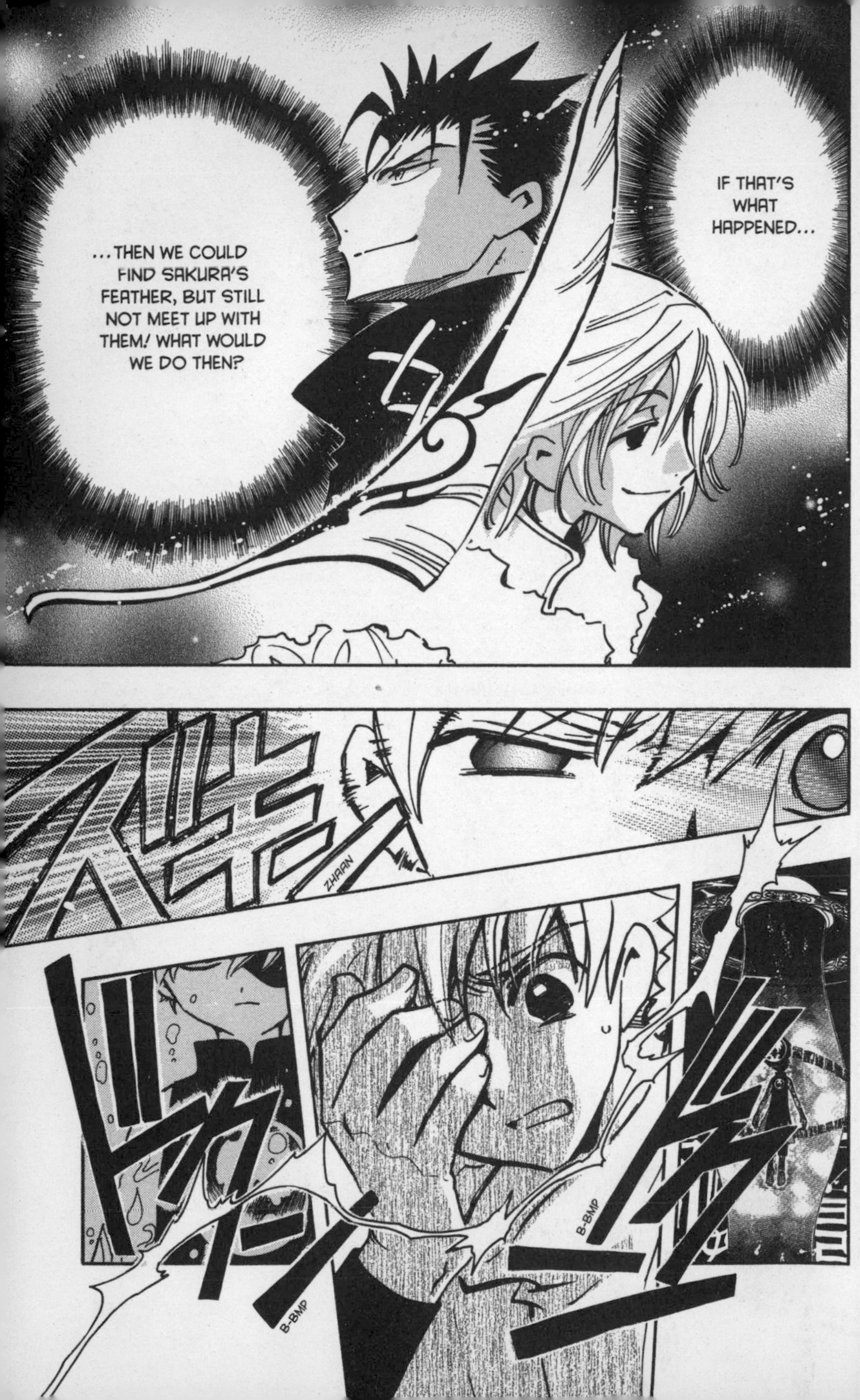
IF THAT'S WHAT HAPPENED...
...THEN WE COULD FIND SAKURA'S FEATHER, BUT STILL NOT MEET UP WITH THEM! WHAT WOULD WE DO THEN?
ZHAAN
B-BMP
B-BMP

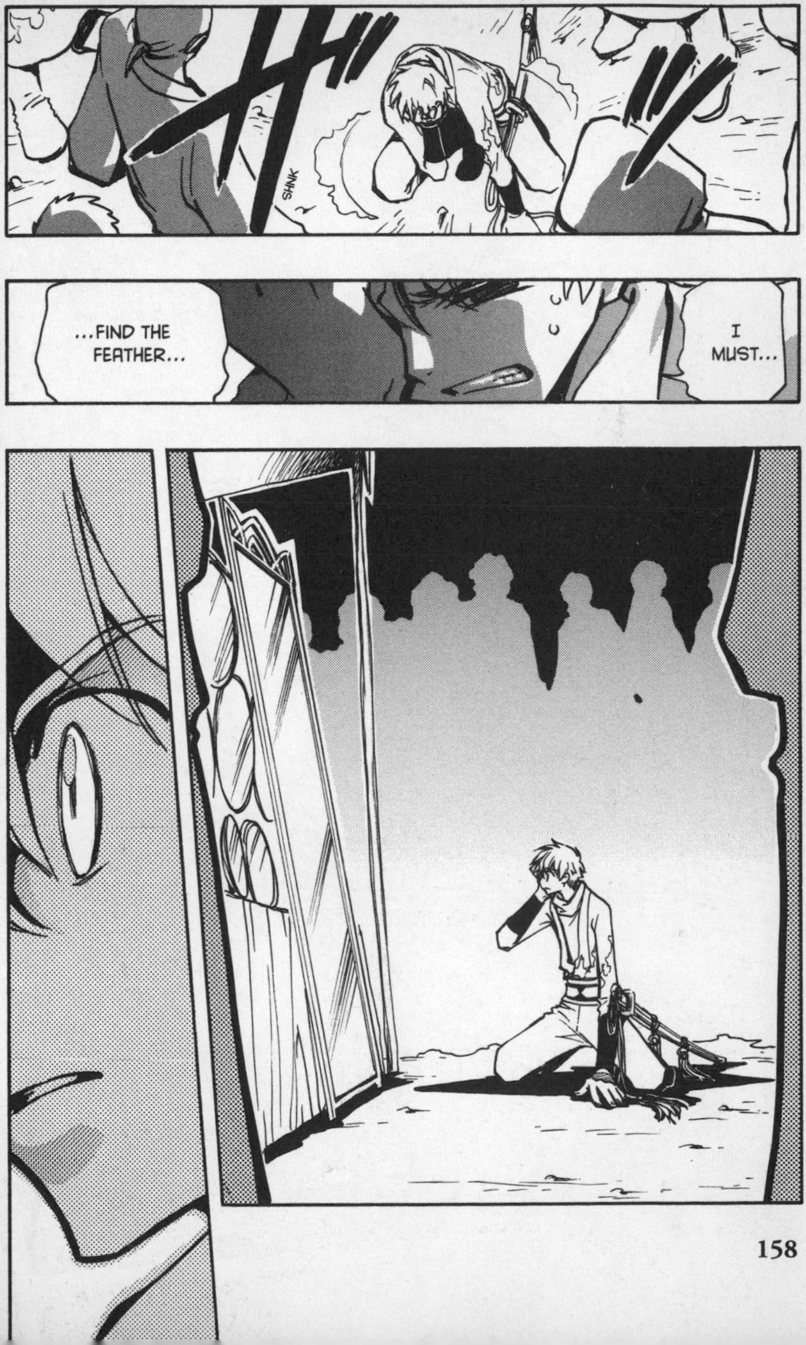
SHNK
I MUST...
...FIND THE FEATHER...

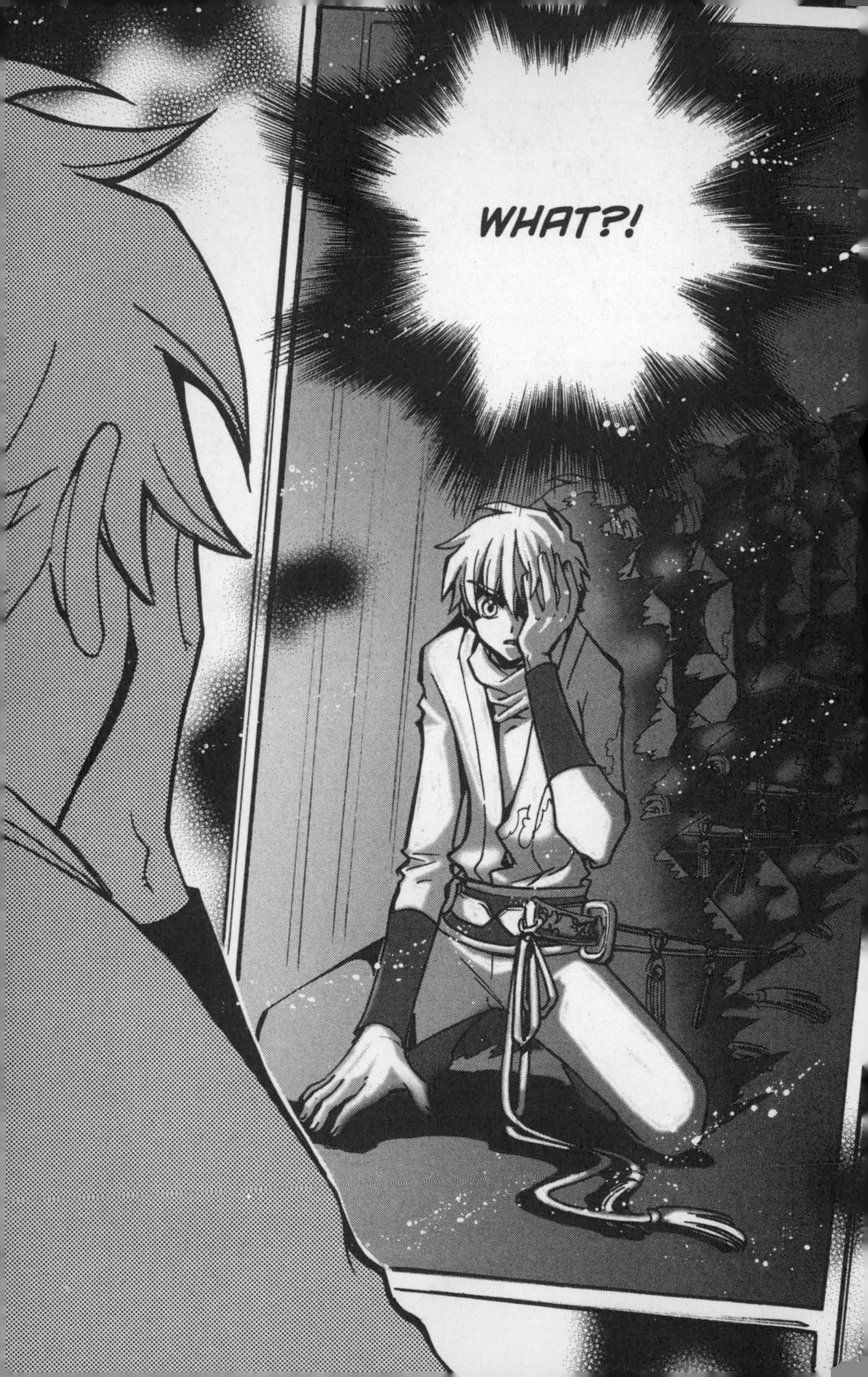
WHAT?!

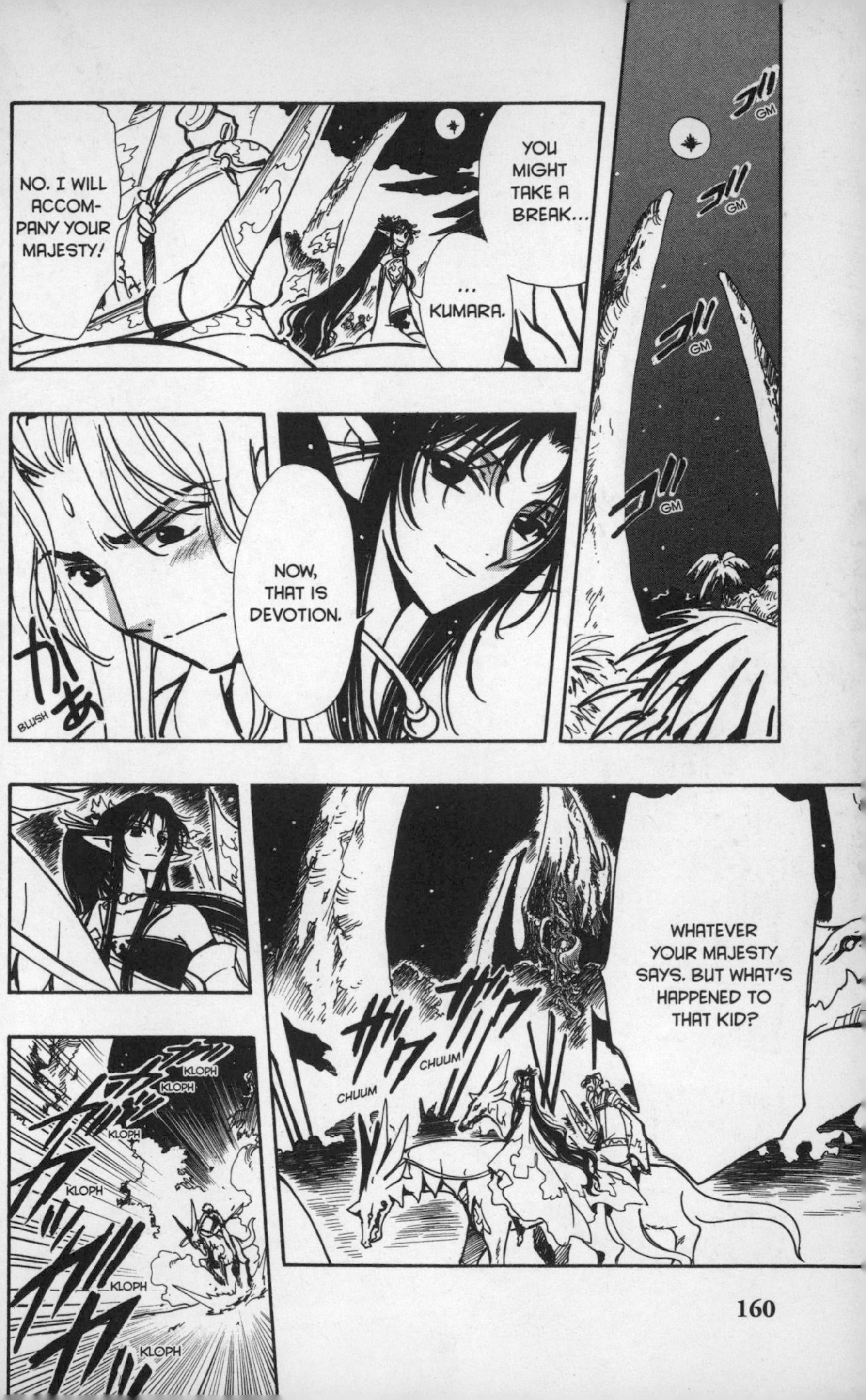
GM
GM
GM
GM
YOU MIGHT TAKE A BREAK...
... KUMARA.
NO. I WILL ACCOMPANY YOUR MAJESTY!
NOW, THAT IS DEVOTION.
BLUSH
WHATEVER YOUR MAJESTY SAYS. BUT WHAT'S HAPPENED TO THAT KID?
CHUUM
CHUUM
KLOPH
KLOPH
KLOPH
KLOPH
KLOPH
KLOPH

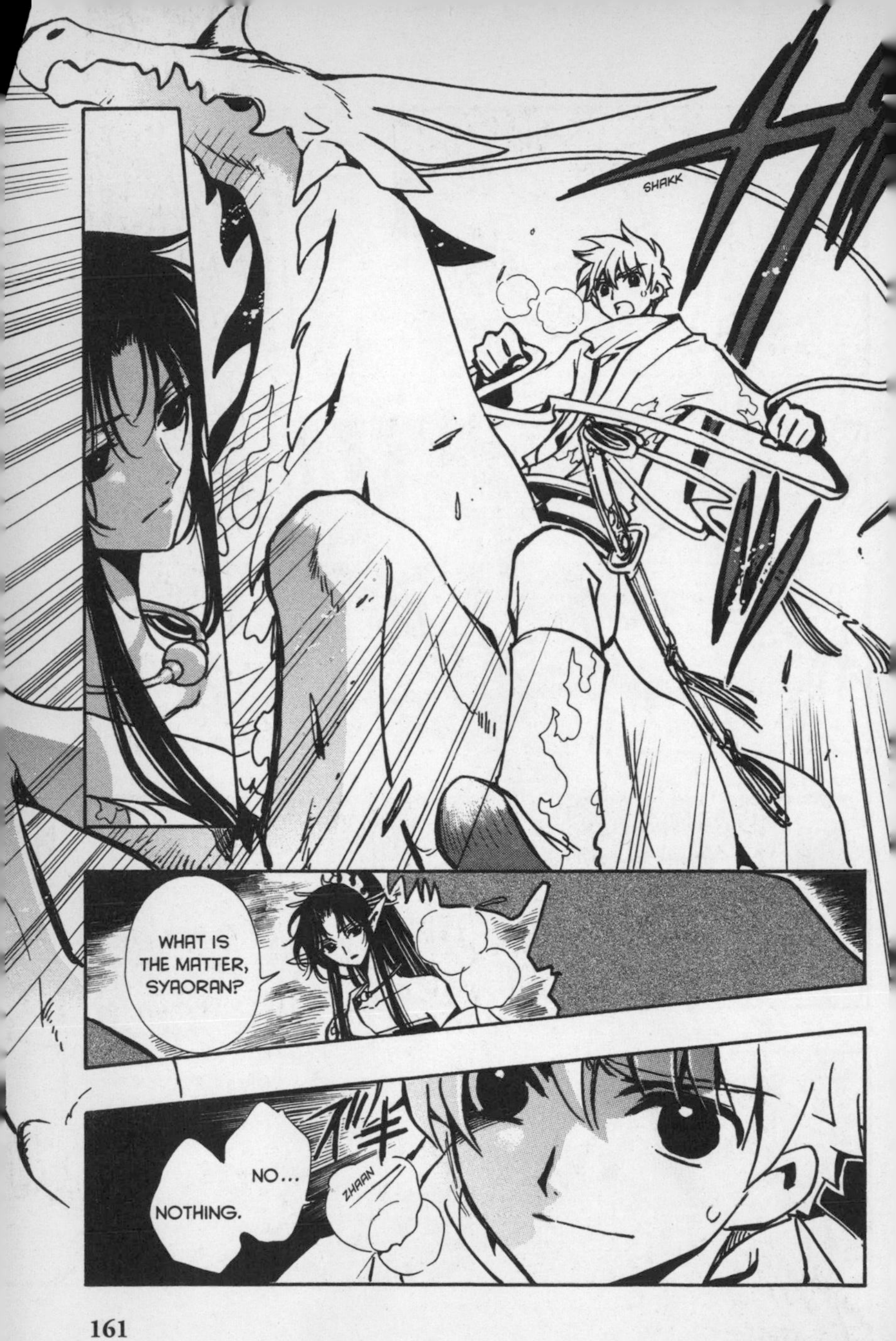
SHAKK
WHAT IS THE MATTER, SYAORAN?
NO...
NOTHING.
ZHAAN

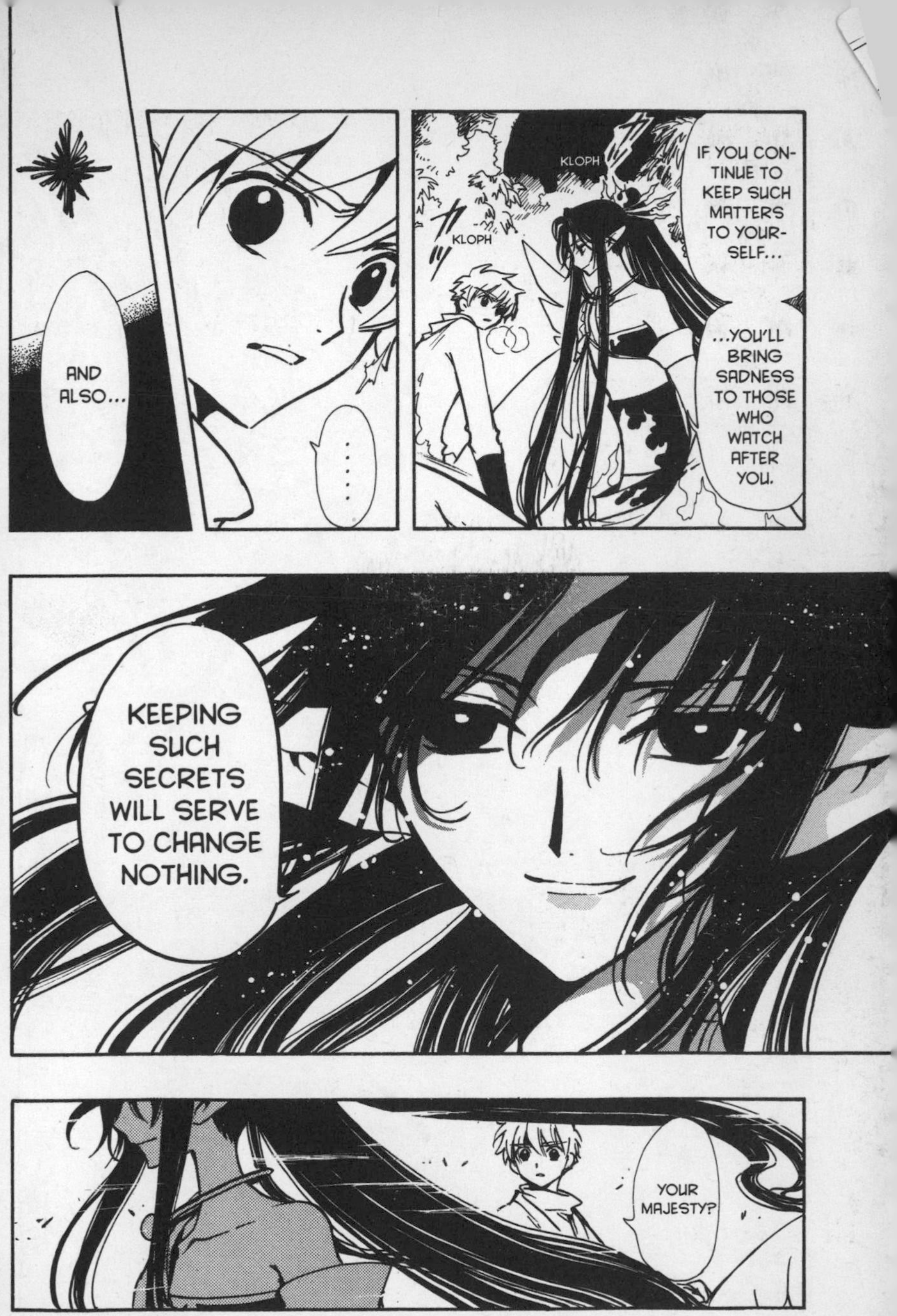
KLOPH
KLOPH
IF YOU CONTINUE TO KEEP SUCH MATTERS TO YOURSELF...
...YOU'LL BRING SADNESS TO THOSE WHO WATCH AFTER YOU.
......
AND ALSO...
KEEPING SUCH SECRETS WILL SERVE TO CHANGE NOTHING.
YOUR MAJESTY?

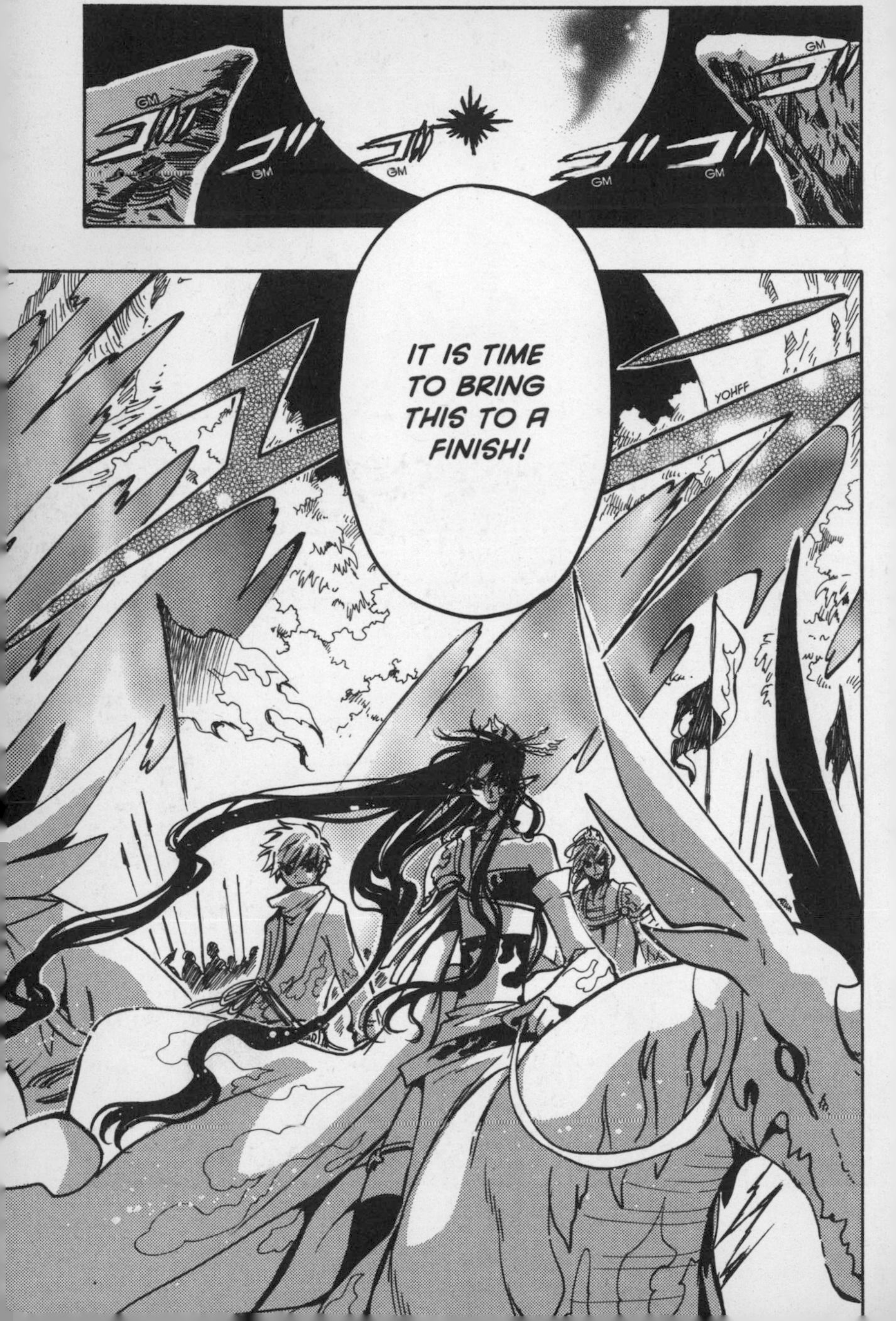
GM
GM
GM
GM
GM
GM
IT IS TIME TO BRING THIS TO A FINISH!
YOHFF

ツバサ

RESERVoir CHRoNiCLE

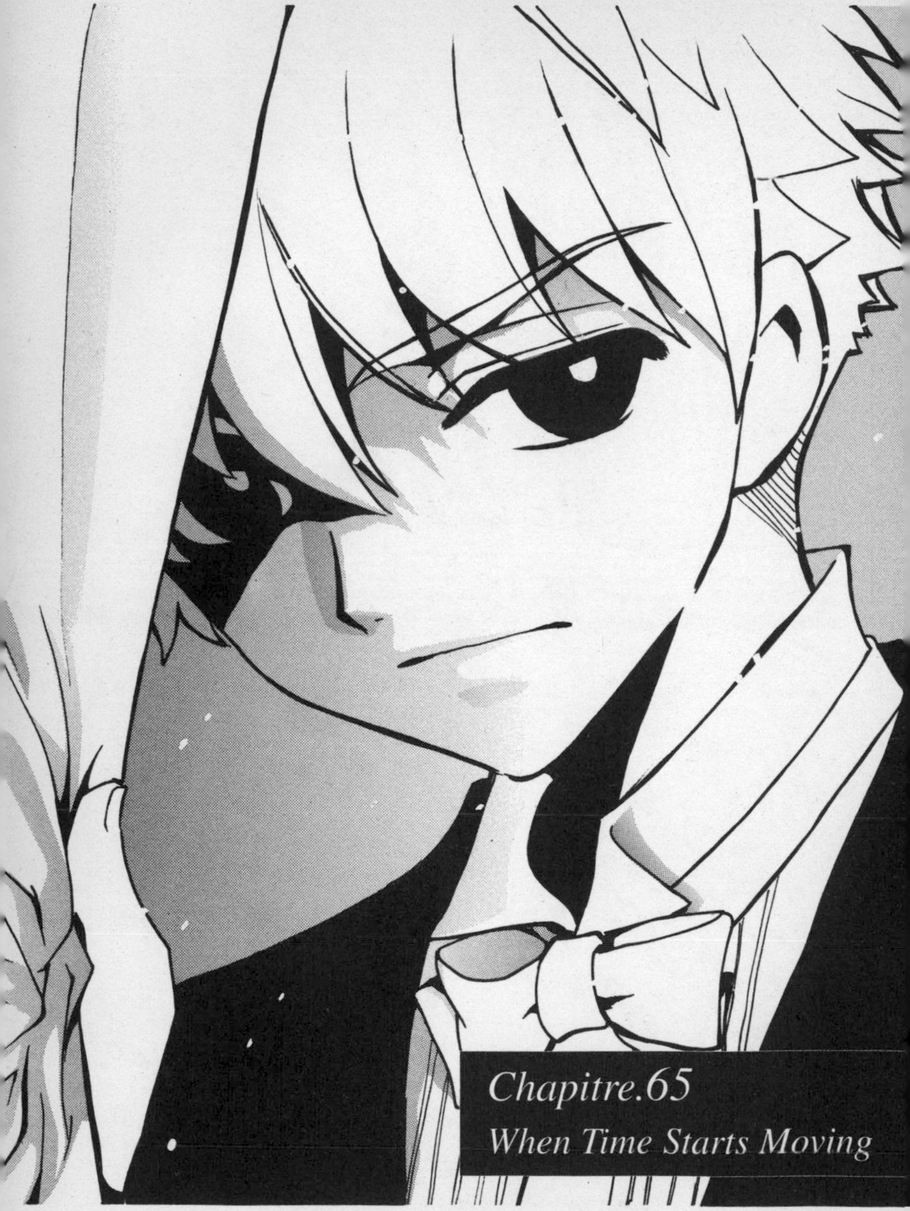
Chapitre.65
When Time Starts Moving

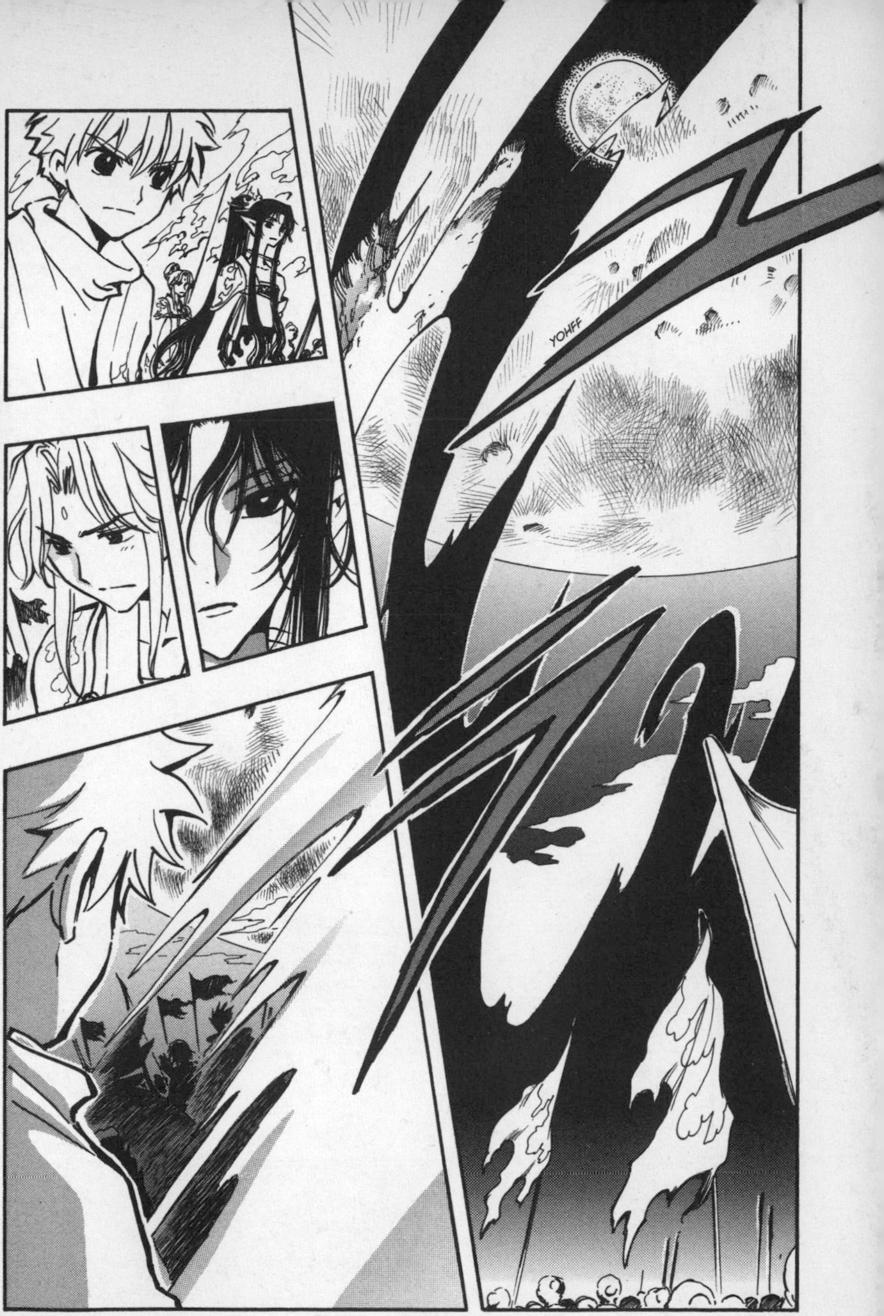
YOHFF

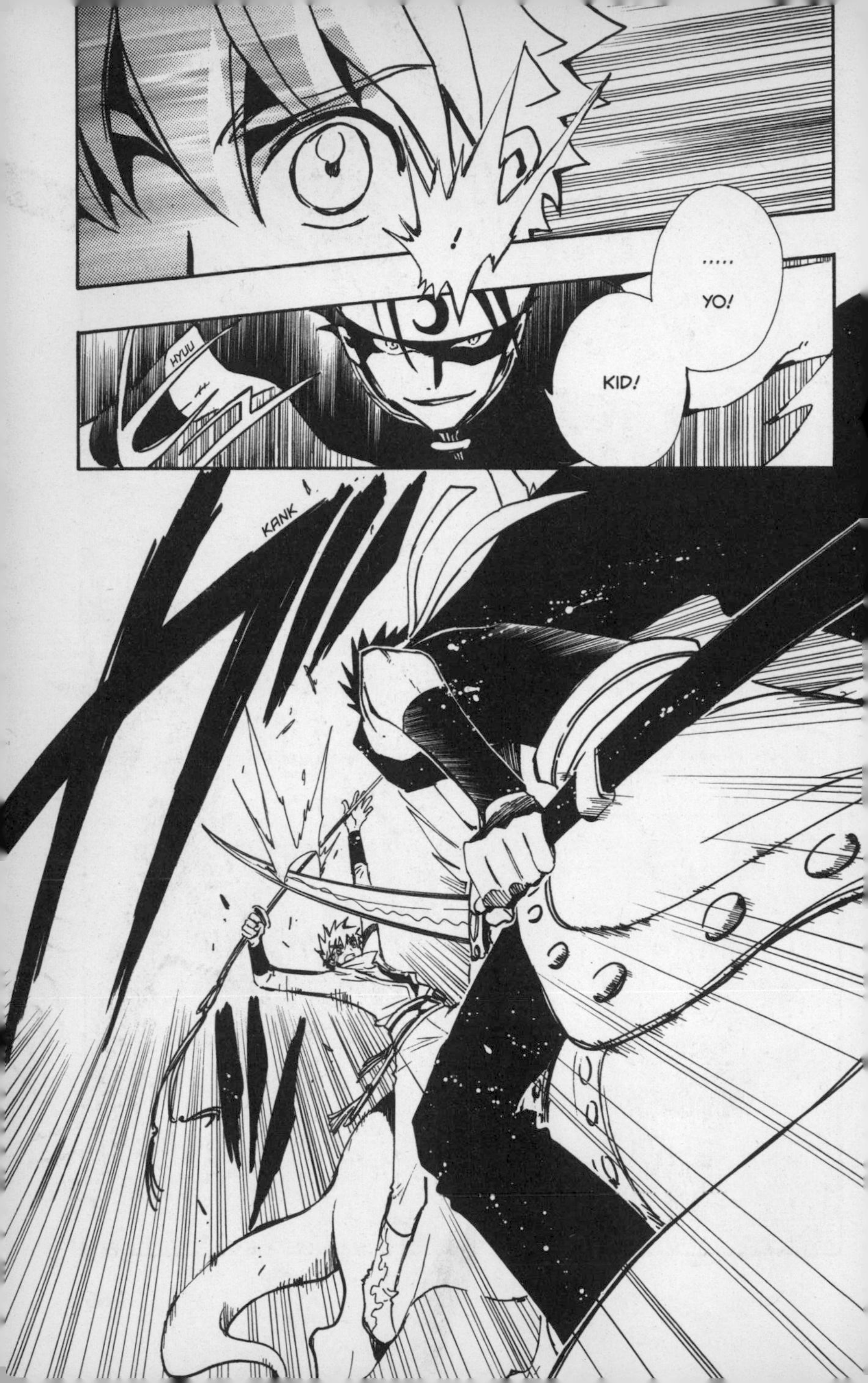
!
..... YO! KID!
HYUU
KANK

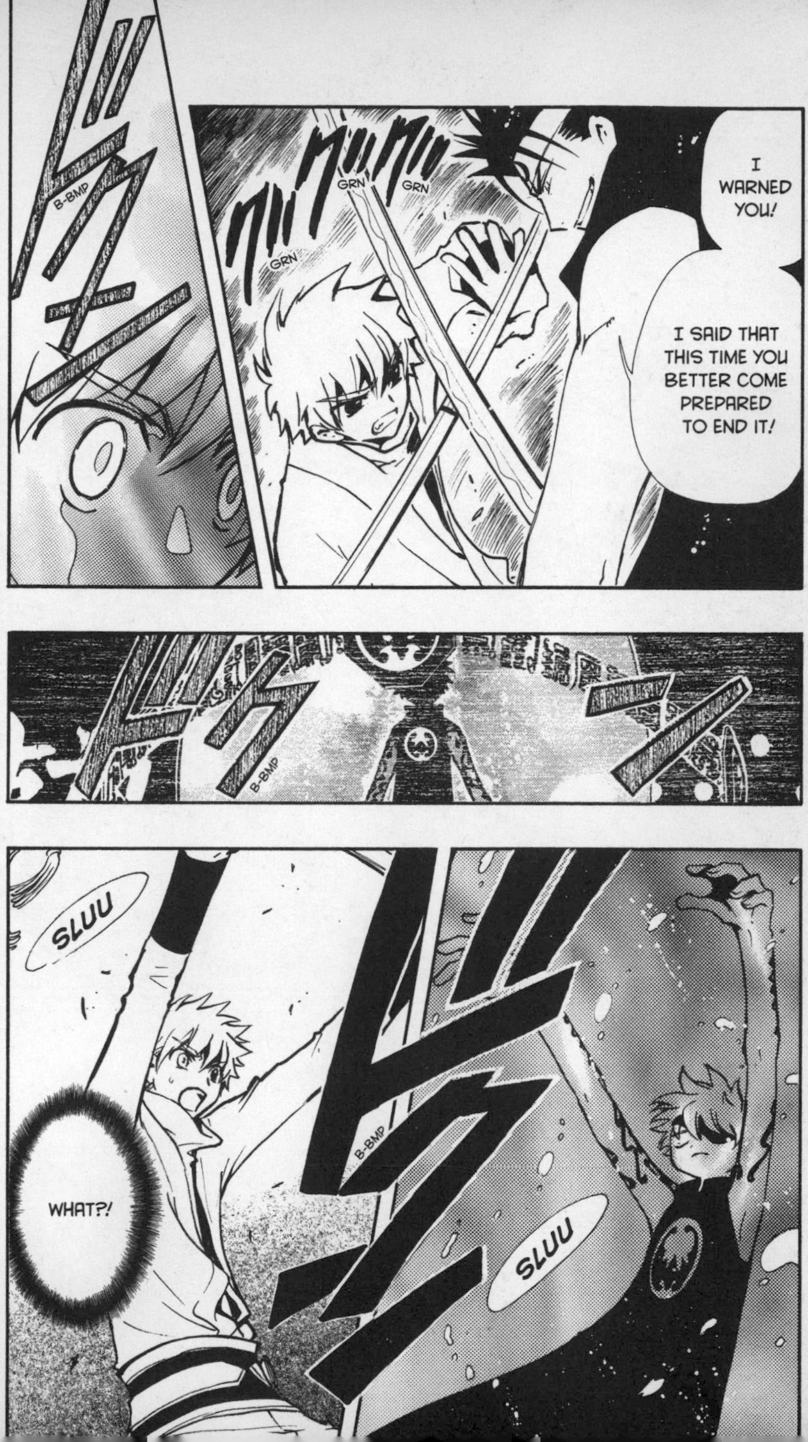
GRN
GRN
GRN
I WARNED YOU!
I SAID THAT THIS TIME YOU BETTER COME PREPARED TO END IT!
B-BMP
B-BMP
SLUU
B-BMP
SLUU
WHAT?!

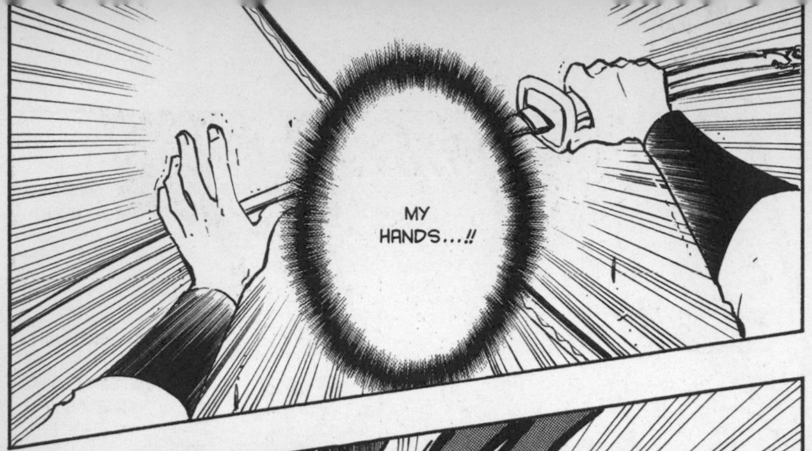
MY HANDS...!!
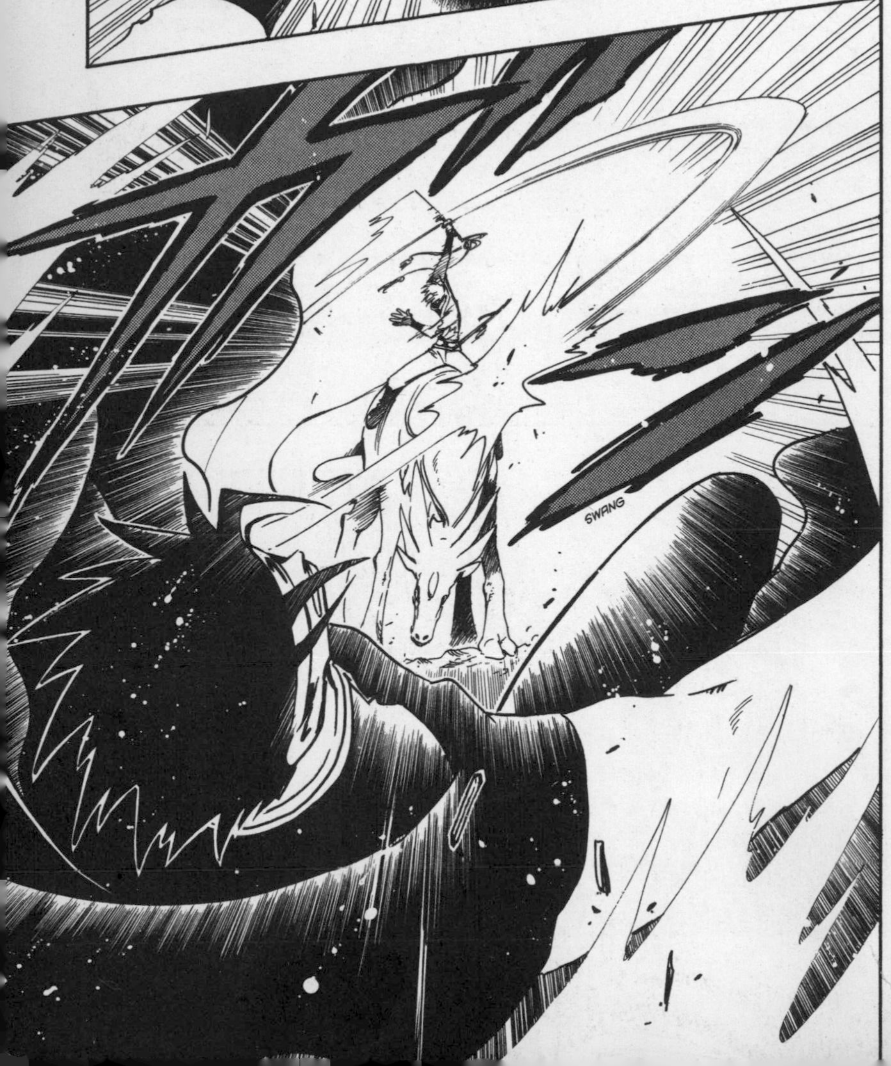
SWANG

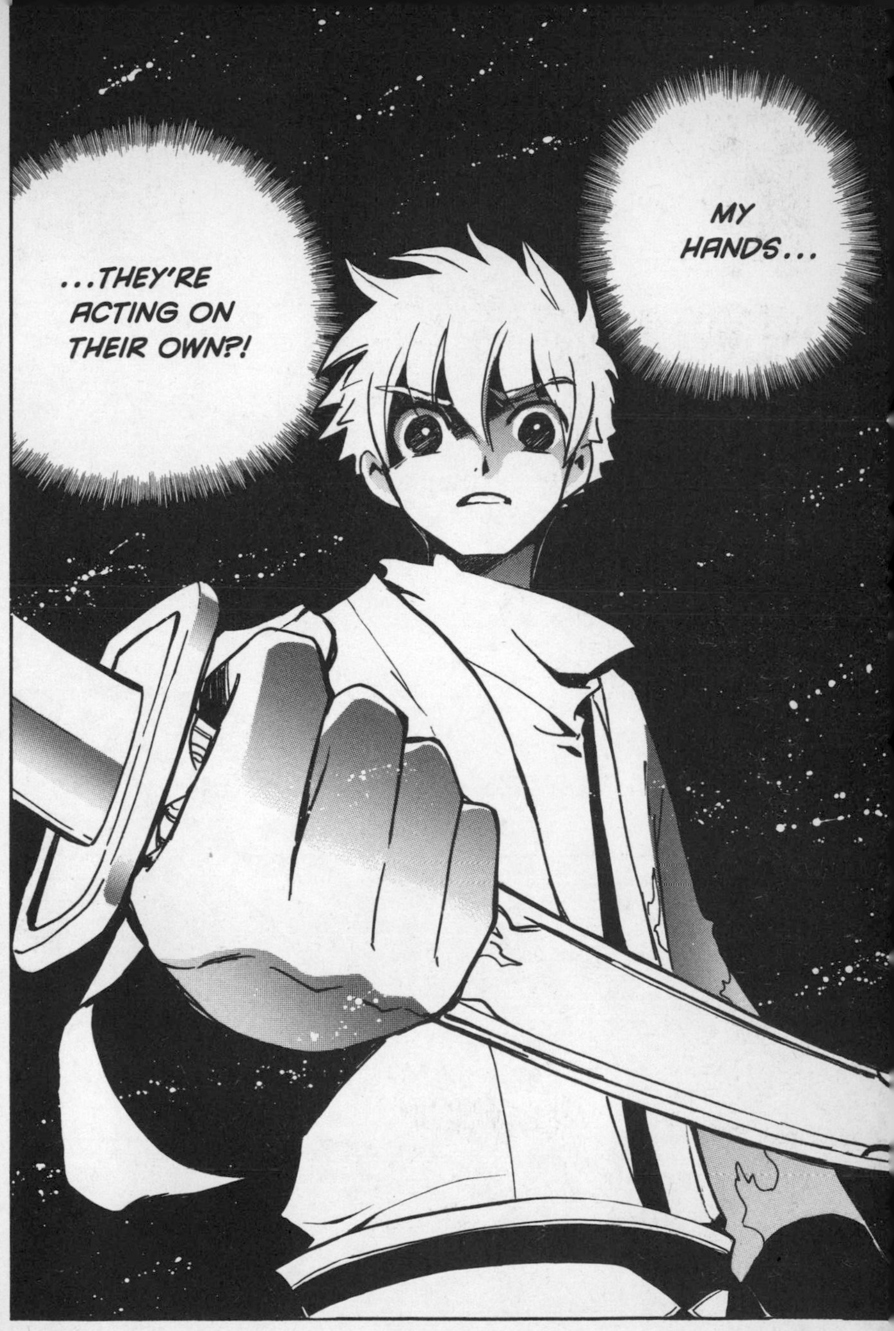
MY HANDS...
...THEY'RE ACTING ON THEIR OWN?!

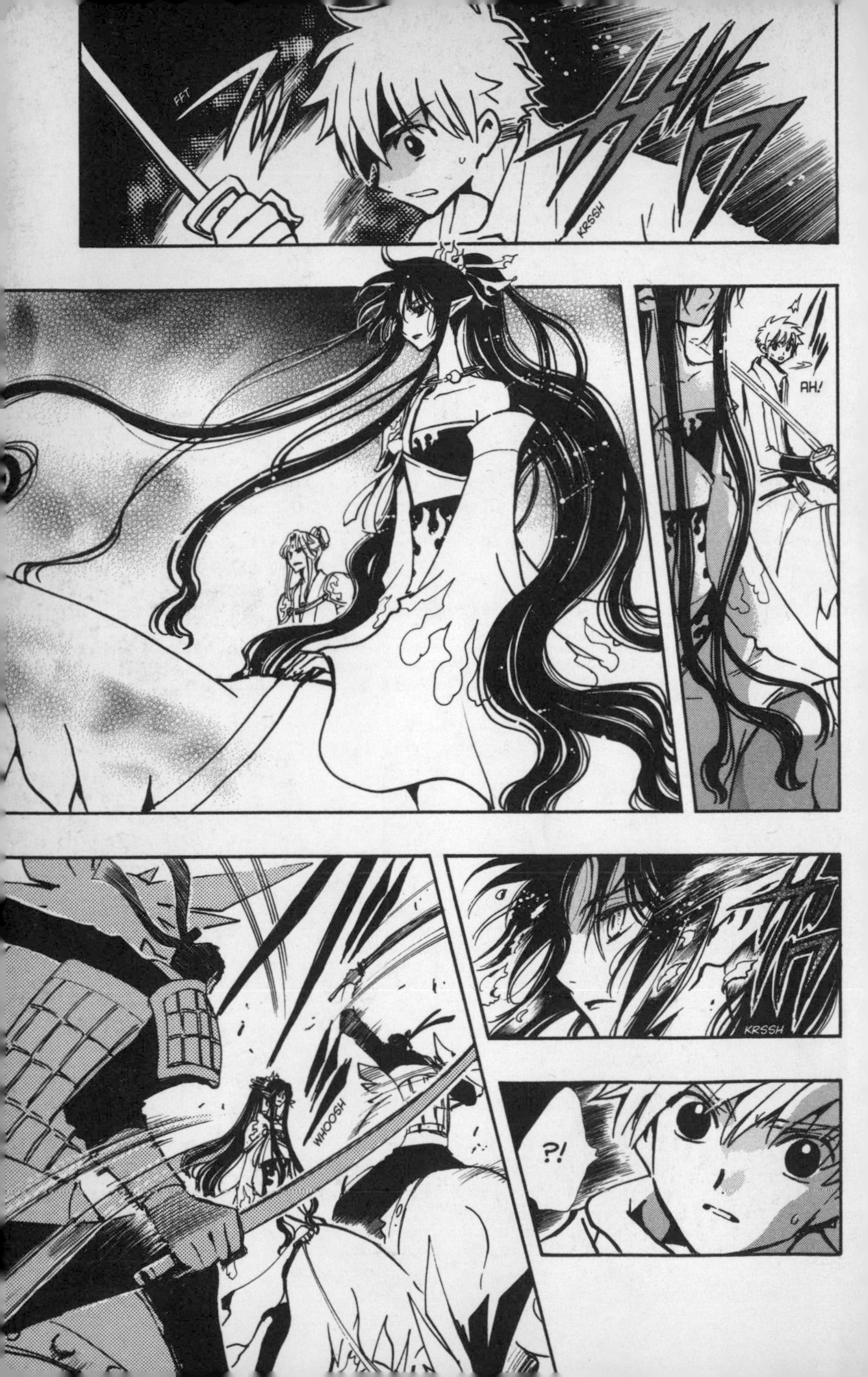
FFT
KRSSH
AH!
KRSSH
?!
WHOOSH

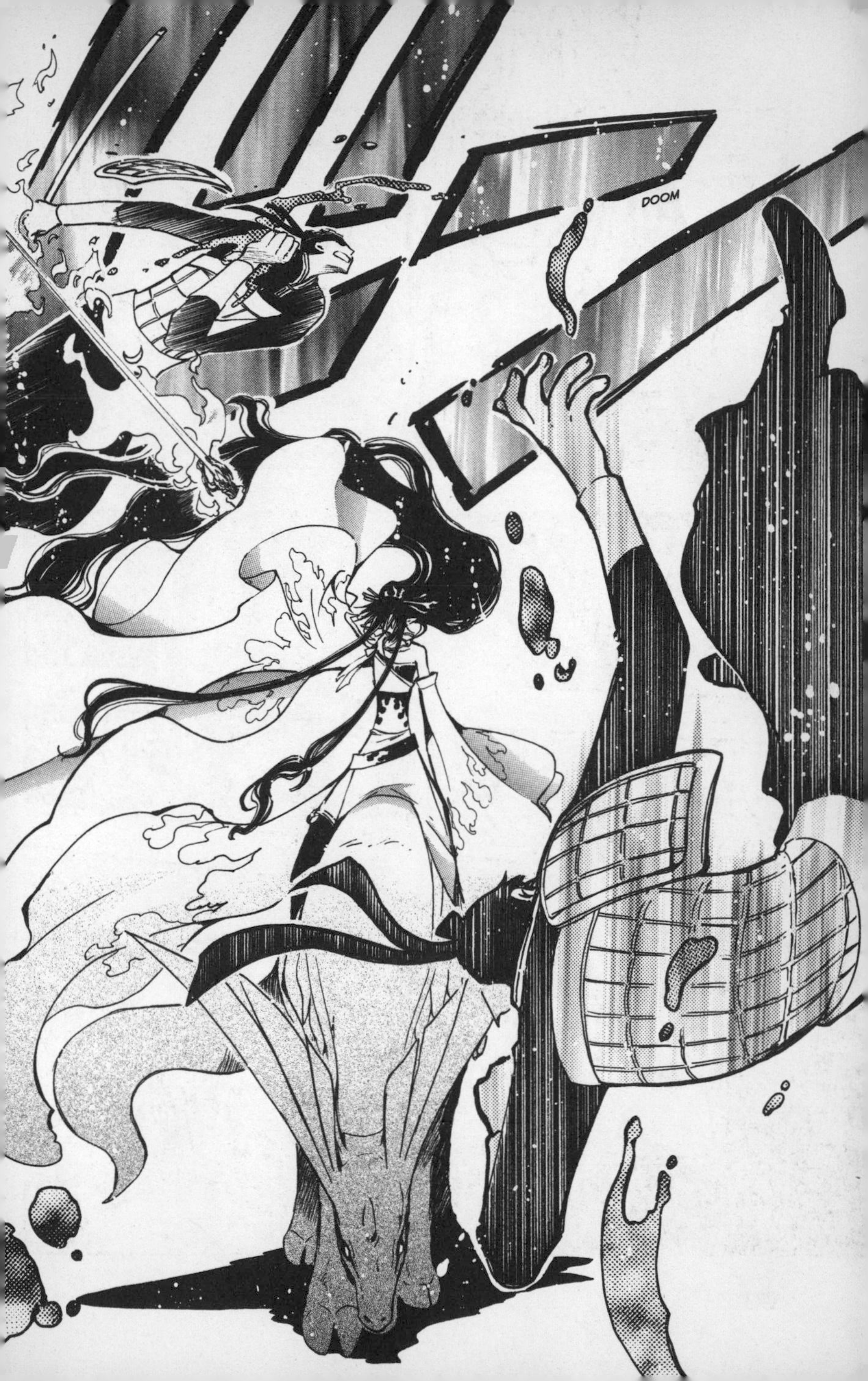
DOOM

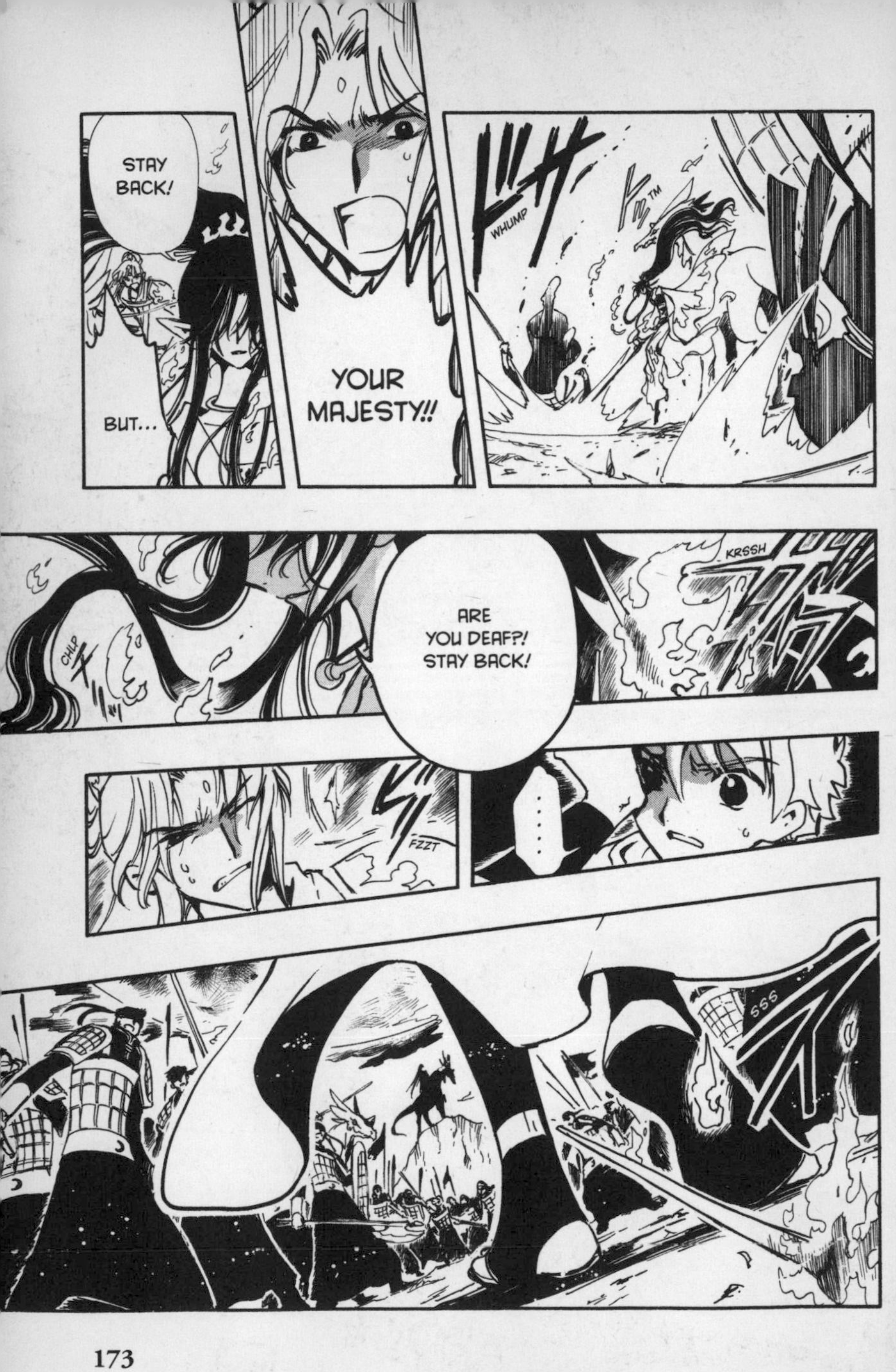
WHUMP
YOUR MAJESTY!!
STAY BACK!
BUT...
KRSSH
ARE YOU DEAF?! STAY BACK!
CHLP
.....
FZZT
SSS

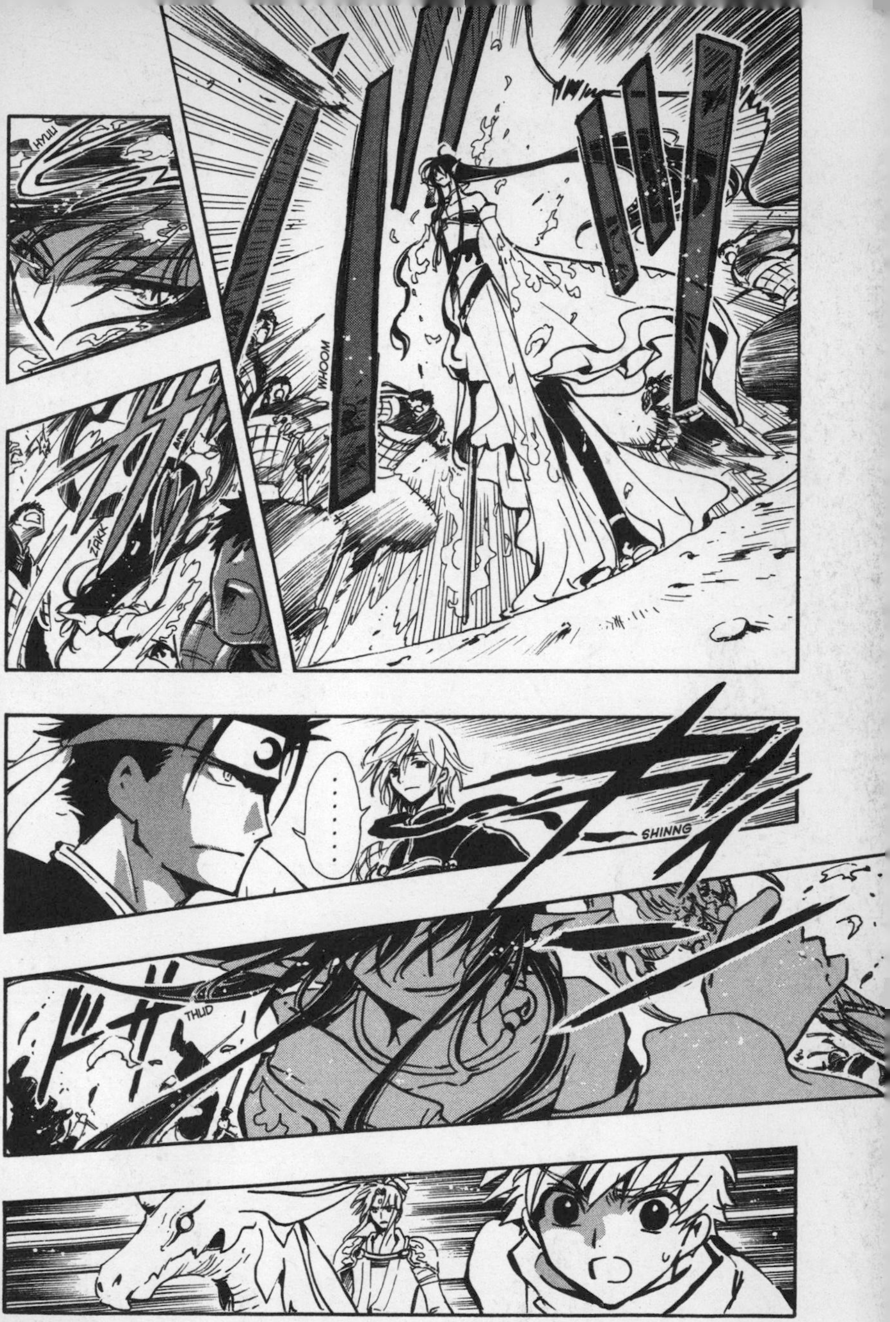
WHOOM
HYUU
ZAKK
......
SHINNG
THUD

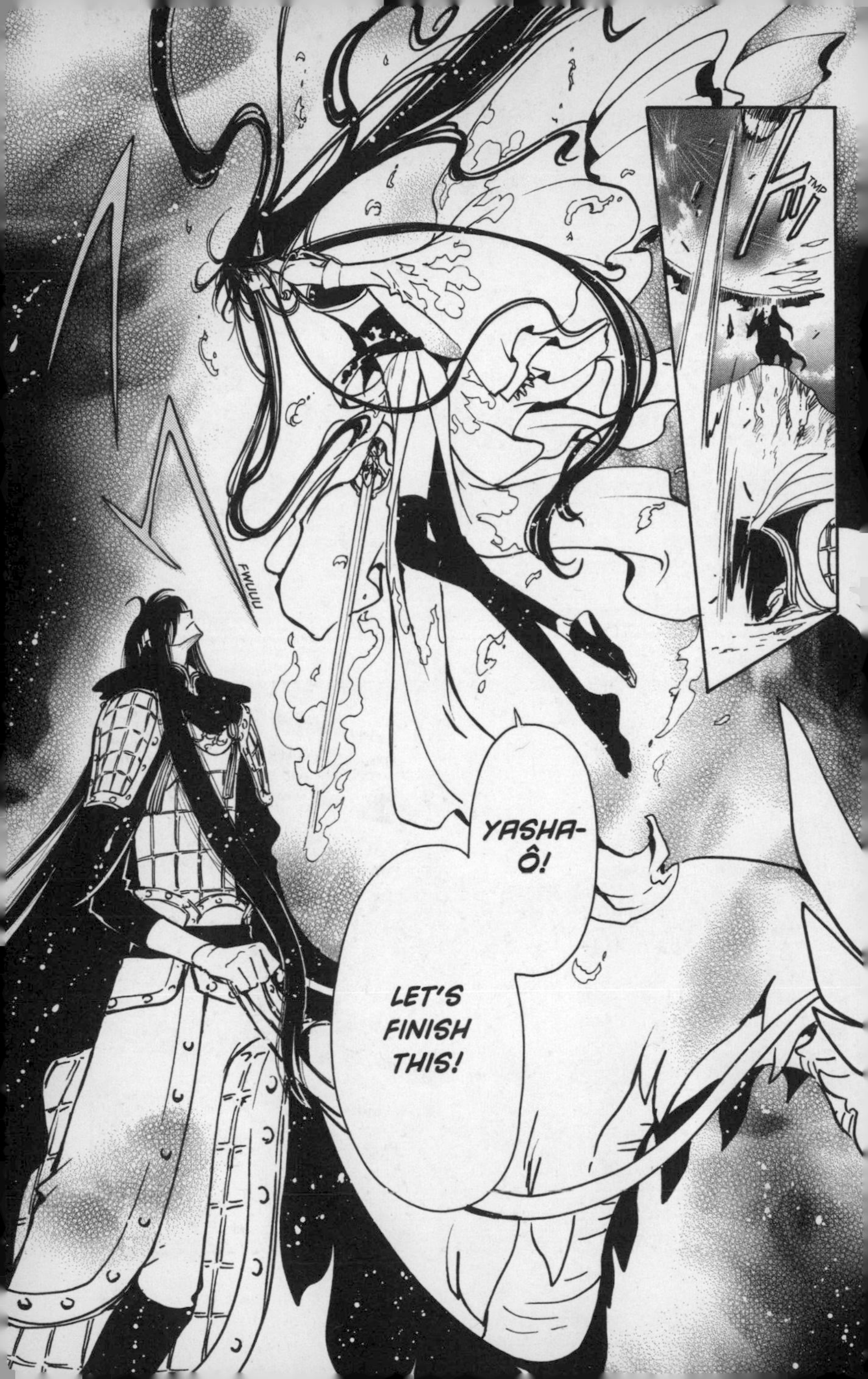
TMP
FWUUU
YASHA-Ô!
LET'S FINISH THIS!

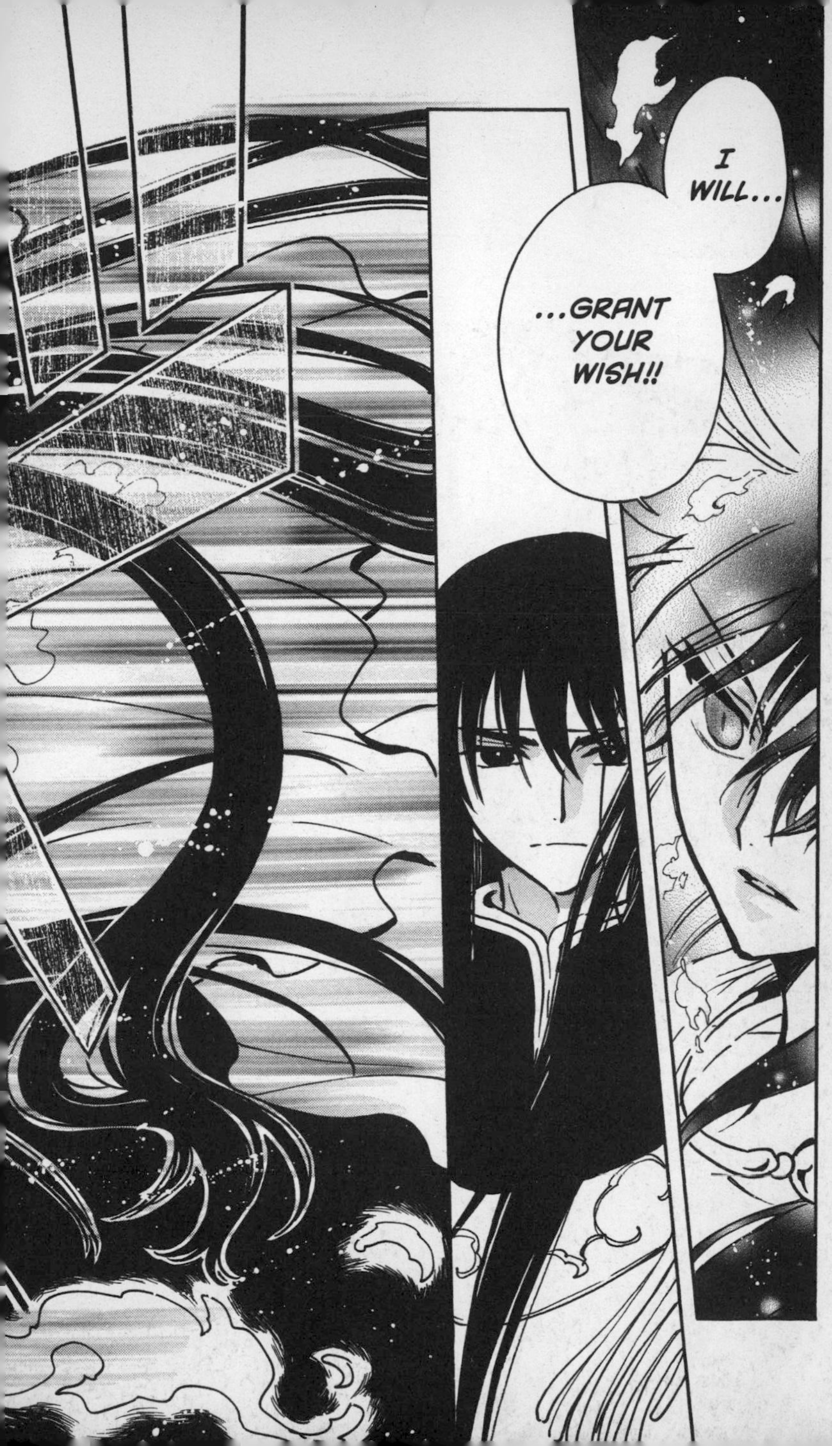
I WILL...
...GRANT YOUR WISH!!

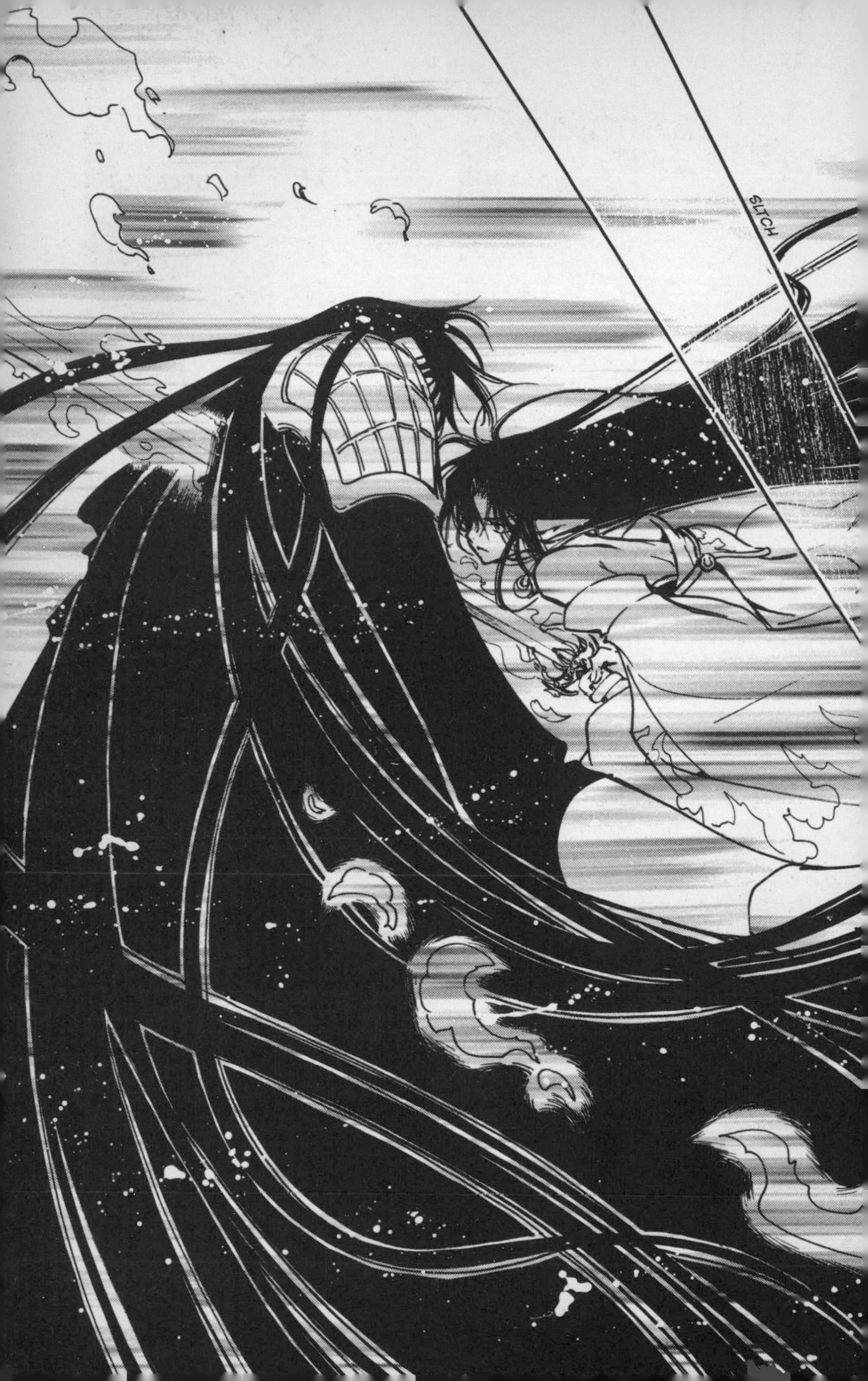
SLITCH

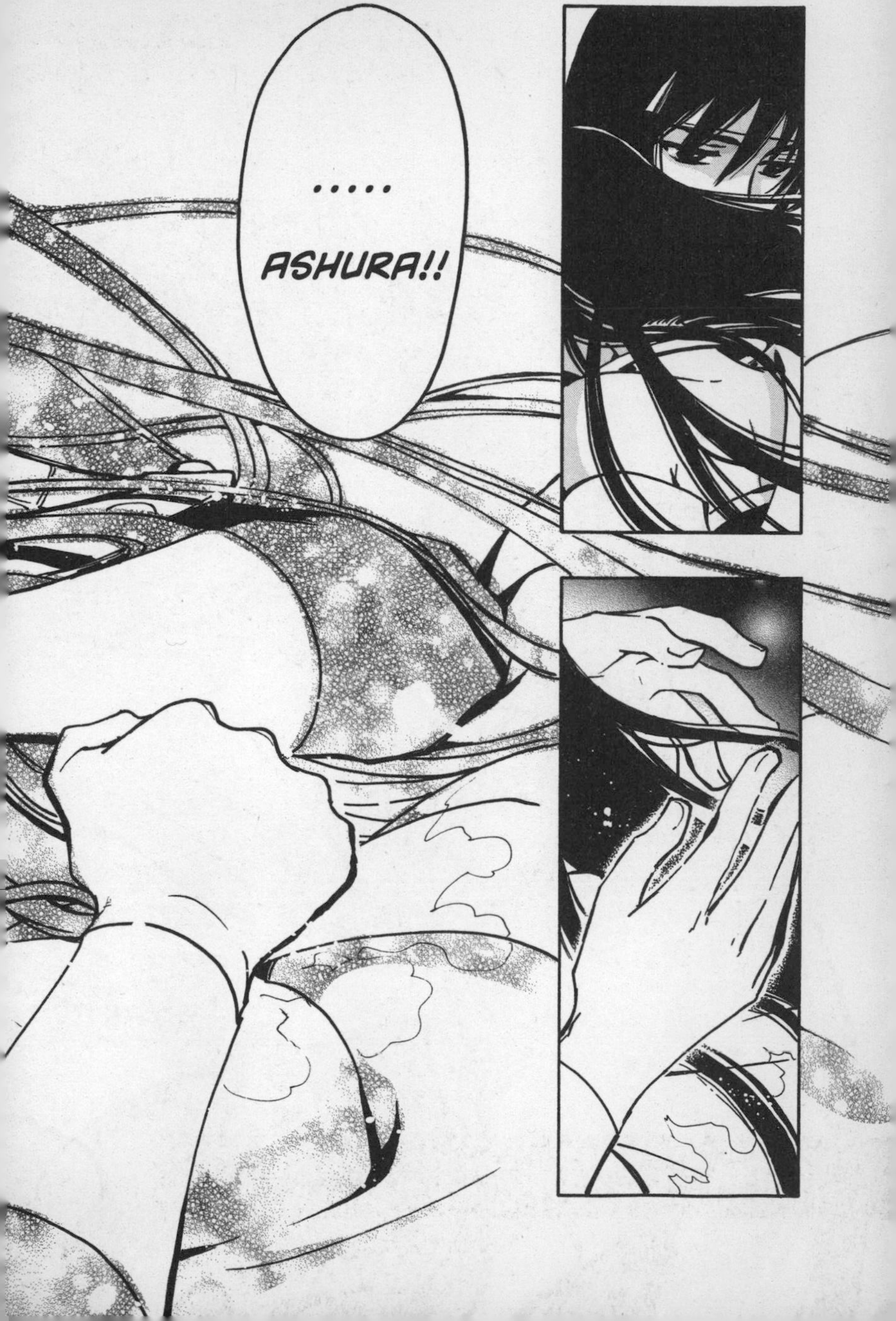
.....
ASHURA!!

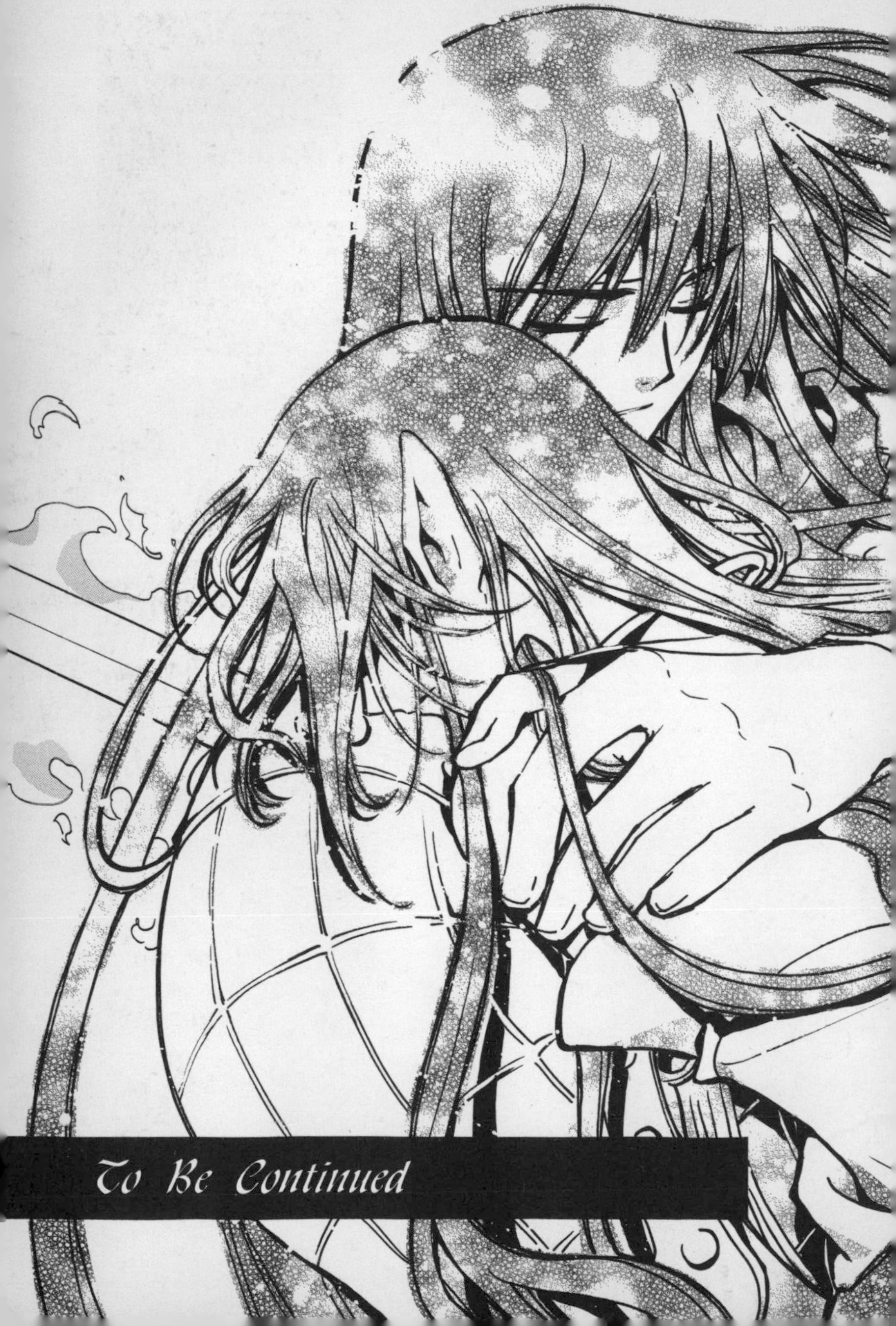
To Be Continued

About the Creators

CLAMP is a group of four women who have become the most popular manga artists in America—Ageha Ohkawa, Mokona, Satsuki Igarashi, and Tsubaki Nekoi. They started out as doujinshi (fan comics) creators, but their skill and craft brought them to the attention of publishers very quickly. Their first work from a major publisher was *RG Veda*, but their first mass success was with *Magic Knight Rayearth*. From there, they went on to write many series, including *Cardcaptor Sakura* and *Chobits*, two of the most popular manga in the United States. Like many Japanese manga artists, they prefer to avoid the spotlight, and little is known about them personally.

CLAMP is currently publishing three series in Japan: *Tsubasa* and *xxxHOLiC* with Kodansha and *Gohou Drug* with Kadokawa.

Translation Notes

Japanese is a tricky language for most Westerners, and translation is often more art than science. For your edification and reading pleasure, here are notes on some of the places where we could have gone in a different direction in our translation of the work, or where a Japanese cultural reference is used.

A Special Honorific for the Country of Shura

The Country of Shura is based on the world of RG Veda (which in turn is based on Hindu mythology), and they have a special honorific which is used in the Japanese version of Tsubasa.

-ô: Taken from the *kanji* for king, the -ô honorific is reserved for the high gods/heroes who are not only powerful, but also are rulers of their particular clans. The player character in the country of Ôto, Ryûô, was a character originated in RG Veda, and his name is made up of the *kanji* for dragon and king where the final ô sound is the same kind of honorific.

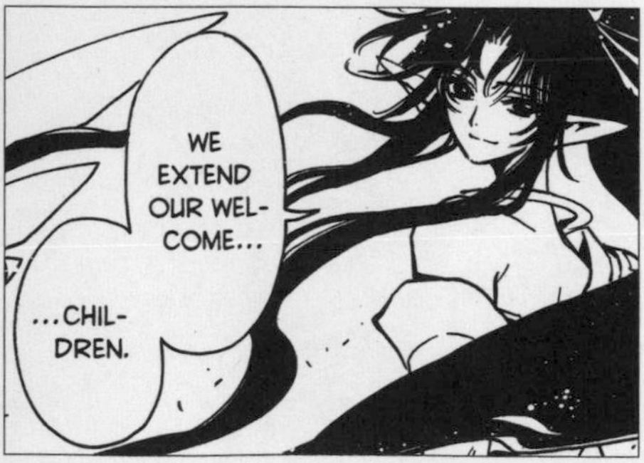
WE EXTEND OUR WEL-COME...
...CHIL-DREN.

Ashura's "Royal We"

It has long been the custom for kings to speak not only for themselves, but since they are (supposedly) a living embodiment of their country and people, they speak for everyone. Therefore, kings have been known to use the pronoun *we* when referring to themselves.

Ashura's Gender

The TokyoPop translation of RG Veda establishes Ashura as male. However, the dialogue of this book had no gendered pronouns or other indications of Ashura's sex. As with Mokona Modoki, we have striven to keep the character's gender as ambiguous as in the original. If you never noticed until you read this translation note, then we did our job correctly.

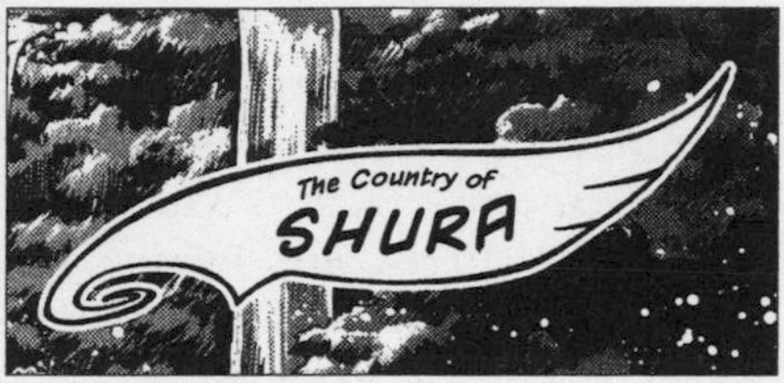

The Country of
SHURA

Page 42, The Country of Shura

Just so you know, the *kanji* for the country of Shura (a word meaning battle and carnage) are the same *kanji* used in the name of its god/king, Ashura-ô. Although Ashura-ô's sword is never mentioned in the text, the name of the sword is Shura, the same as the name of the country.

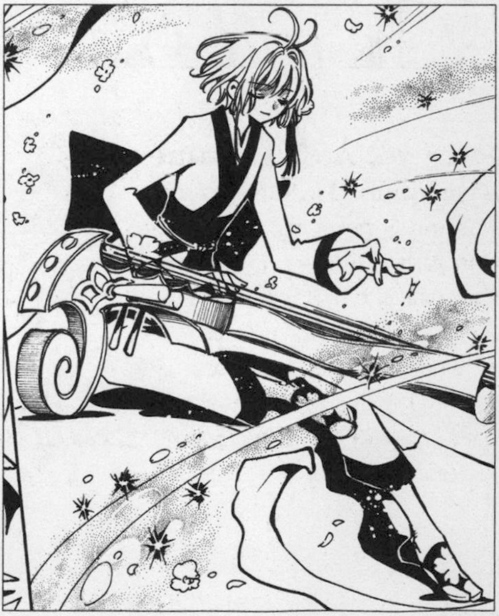

Page 50, Koto

The *koto* is considered one of the traditional musical instruments of Japan, although it is a Chinese import from around the seventh century A.D. It has thirteen strings arranged on movable bridges that are reset for each song, and it is played with the index finger, middle finger, and thumb.

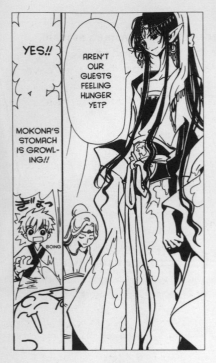

YES!!

AREN'T OUR GUESTS FEELING HUNGER YET?

MOKONA'S STOMACH IS GROWL-ING!!

BOING

Page 56, Mokona's Manners as a Guest

It is traditional for hosts to offer a guest everything in their power. The tradition for a guest is to refuse as much as possible and never admit to needing anything (because if guests need something it implies that the host has been neglecting them—and that is an insult). This display of manners is something Mokona either doesn't know or willfully ignores. But the reason Syaoran is so stressed about it is because Mokona is a part of Syaoran's group—if Mokona acts shamefully, Mokona's shame is Syaoran's shame as well. Fortunately Ashura isn't fazed by Mokona's lack of manners.

Page 78, Attack Names

As mentioned in the notes in volume 2, most anime, manga, and game fans are familiar with the attack names that the opponents shout at each other when making their attack. We know that it doesn't happen in real life, but it is a long-time entertainment convention.

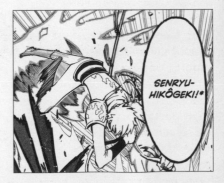

SENRYU-HIKÔGEKI!!*

183

Page 127, Fei-Wang Reed

The pronunciation guide next to the *kanji* characters of Fei-Wang Reed's name indicates that his name should be written with Chinese pronunciation. That makes sense since in Cardcaptor Sakura, Syaoran comes from Hong Kong, and his ancestor was also a sorcerer and a Reed, Clow Reed. What bloodline connection Fei-Wang Reed has with Syaoran is, as yet, still a mystery. The arbitrary decision comes when deciding to use the Cantonese Pin-yin spelling, Fei-Wong, or the Mandarin spelling, Fei-Wang. Though the Japanese pronunciation indicated is Fei-Wan, since a majority of China (and a majority

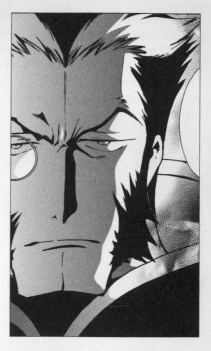

of Japanese students studying Chinese) speak Mandarin, we went with the Fei-Wang spelling.

The Pronunciation of Fai's Name

Around the same time that Tsubasa Volume 9 came out in Japan, another Tsubasa publication appeared: Tsubasa CHARACTere GuiDE. It summarizes the story, introduces the characters, points out crossover characters, and gives some background information such as production art, interviews, fan contributions, etc. Also included is a romanized (put into our alphabet) version of the characters' names. Considering the wide variety of arbitrary choices in making transliterations of names, two translators will almost never romanize a list of names the same way, and it was pleasing to see that only one continuing character's name was spelled Fye (as some fans spelled it before the Del Rey edition came out), but instead, the

way it is spelled in the CHARACTere GuiDE is Fay. Fay D. Flourite.

So if you've been pronouncing Fai's name as rhyming with the word "eye," then you've been pronouncing it properly. The Japanese pronunciation is pretty solid for this. Why spell it Fay? We can't say for sure, but if you use the Spanish pronunciation for "ay" it would have the same sound as the English word "eye," so that may be a clue to the answer.

Watch for Volume 10 of Tsubasa,
on sale now!

DETROIT PUBLIC LIBRARY

P9-DDM-449

TOMARE!

[STOP!]

You're going the wrong way!

Manga is a completely
different type of reading
experience.

To start at the *beginning*,
go to the *end*!

That's right! Authentic manga is read the traditional Japanese
way—from right to left. Exactly the *opposite* of how American
books are read. It's easy to follow: Just go to the other end of the
book, and read each page—and each panel—from right side to left
side, starting at the top right. Now you're experiencing manga as it
was meant to be.

FEB 08

CH